Reframing
Organizational
Culture

To Kent Moore
November 4, 1964—September 1, 1989

Reframing Organizational Culture

edited by

Peter J. Frost • Larry F. Moore • Meryl Reis Louis
Craig C. Lundberg • Joanne Martin

SAGE PUBLICATIONS
The International Professional Publishers
Newbury Park   London   New Delhi

For information address:

SAGE Publications, Inc.
2455 Teller Road
Newbury Park, California 93120

SAGE Publications Ltd.
6 Bonhill Street
London EC2A 4PU
United Kingdom

SAGE Publications India Pvt. Ltd.
M-32 Market
Greater Kailash I
New Delhi 110 048 India

Printed in the United States of America

Library of Congress Cataloging-in-Publication Data

Reframing organizational culture / [edited by] Peter J. Frost . . .
    [et al.].
        p. cm.
   Includes bibliographical references (p.   )
   ISBN 0-8039-3650-8(c). — ISBN 0-8039-3651-6 (p)
   1. Corporate culture — Congresses.   I. Frost, Peter J.
HD58.7.R435   1991
302.3'5—dc20   91-22013

FIRST PRINTING, 1991

Sage Production Editor: Astrid Virding

Contents

Preface

This book has been written and edited by us over the past 2 years. Some of it was written in Sydney, Australia, some in Boston, other parts were crafted in Ithaca, New York, in Palo Alto, California, in Vancouver, B.C. Parts of the draft were written in Beijing, China, and in Bali, Indonesia. As a group we met initially in Vancouver, B.C., on April 1, 1989 to decide on the shape and direction of the book. Ann West of Sage joined us for that meeting, as well as for our other joint session at picturesque Mountain Home Inn on Mt. Tamalpais outside San Francisco, in August 1990. Academics, it seems, are nomadic!

We benefited from the marvels of modern technology to coordinate the efforts of the five coeditors over the months of the project. We benefited also from the warmth, openness, trust, and energy each of us brought to the project. It sustained us in our discussions, ensured that conflicts were productive, and made the project one of much enjoyment for each of us.

We are much indebted to each of the authors whose work is published in this book. Some manuscripts were written specifically for *Reframing Organizational Culture,* others have been published elsewhere and are reproduced or edited with permission. They provide exemplars of culture research, expositions of ideas, critiques, and commentaries on organizational culture. They provide much of the substance of the book. Cultural perspectives developed and articulated by Joanne Martin and Debra E. Meyerson provide the framework for Part I of the book. The same perspectives also serve to organize the thinking and ideas that the five of us express in the concluding section of the book. Joanne Martin's contribution to the book is clearly very significant, and we are grateful for her insightful approaches to organizational culture. A more detailed exposition of her ideas on organizational culture can be found in *Harmony, Conflict and Ambiguity in Organizational Cultures.* We thank Meryl Louis for sharing with us her insights about fallacies in organizational research. We discuss these in Part II.

In Part I of this book, we examine three diffferent frames for thinking about and conceptualizing organizational culture. We use a number of empirical studies to illustrate these frames. In Part II of the book, we examine ways to think about researching organizational culture. We use an exemplar of research on culture (*Street Corner Society*), and a series of commentaries on the book by four different contemporary scholars and by its author, William F. Whyte, to make explicit for the reader many of the issues that must be faced when doing organizational research. We continue the conversation about researching organizational culture through the voices of a number of other experts who have wrestled with the complexities of cultural research in their work. We conclude Part II with a statement of our own views on the context and choices researchers face when conducting organizational research. In Part III, we attempt to ground or locate the presentation of the material in the book in the cognitive, emotional, and experiential frames of its creators. We do this by sharing with the reader our respective personal reflections on our careers thus far as scholars. We talk about our values, beliefs, emotions, and some of the experiences that have shaped who we are and how we do our research. We believe that doing this may help others gain a perspective on the human dimensions of the discourse we have orchestrated and participated in, to produce *Reframing Organizational Culture*. We close the book with an invitation to readers to go beyond us and create their own frames for studying culture.

We acknowledge the inspiration we have derived from our contacts with young scholars whose energy and idealism brings freshness to the field. One of our aims has been to create a book in which the conversations about theories and research on culture will stimulate their intellectual curiosity and future efforts. It is our hope that *Reframing Organizational Culture* will serve in useful ways to help them keep the study of organizational culture healthy and vigorous.

We express here our sincere thanks to Ann West, Acquisitions Editor at Sage. She was an integral part of this project from the beginning. She encouraged us, guided us, at times even chided us gently and with good effect, as we created and implemented the book. She caught the spirit of the book and with her knowledge, empathy, intellect, and support, made this a better product in countless ways.

Our sincere thanks to Sandra van Duyn, Joann Carmin, Elsie Young, and Aromie Noe for technical and secretarial support. They smoothed the path for us all along the way. Finally, we thank all those involved in the production process at Sage, especially Marie Louise Penchoen and Astrid Virding, who have put the finishing touches to the book so professionally.

Introduction

The thought manifests as the word
The word manifests as the deed
The deed develops into habit
And the habit hardens into character.
So watch the thought
And its ways with care
And let it spring from love
Born out of respect for all beings.

—DHARMA

In 1985, we published a book, *Organizational Culture,* that grew out of a conference on the topic held at the University of British Columbia, April 1-3, 1983. The book captured some of the excitement and enthusiasm about organizational culture that was evident in the field of organizational studies at that time. Although it had imperfections, some of which reflected the state of study of the topic at that time and some which were of our doing, it was read by a number of scholars in the field and at the time of writing this introduction is in its sixth printing. In 1989, we discussed with Ann West at Sage whether we should revise the book. Our sense of the topic of organizational culture was that it still had considerable potential as a focus for inquiry. The early and mid-1980s had been a time of faddishness about the topic, with consultants, academics, and managers reaching out to "organizational culture" as a link between the way people in organizations work and high company performance. By 1986 the peak of this fad seemed to have passed. Writers such as Smircich and Calas were describing culture as a concept that had been absorbed by those who *dominate* thinking about organization life—it had become thought of as a functionalist tool. But it was also a concept, they argued, that was *dead*—its vitality and promise stripped by the speed at which it had been uncritically adopted into the

1

lexicon of organizational science (Calas & Smircich, 1987). Others also pointed to the rapid shift in the first half of the decade from careful academic inquiry about organizational culture to a concern by academics for the functional, managerial applications of organizational culture (Barley et al., 1988). Yet others dismissed it as simply a fad with no enduring influence.

On the assumption that organizational culture was an important concept that needed long-term attention, a symposium was presented at the 1988 Academy of Management Conference in Anaheim, California. Titled "Rekindling the Flame: Researching the Meaning Still Embedded in the Culture Construct," it was chaired by Peter Frost, featured presentations by Debra Meyerson, Michael Owen Jones, Phil Mirvis, and Caren Siehl and a commentary by Patricia Riley. Two things about this symposium were interesting. First was the size of the attendance. The session was booked into a room that was designed for about 40 people. Given the perception among many in the Academy, including the presenters, that interest in culture had waned, this seemed more than adequate. In fact the actual attendance was almost double the capacity of the room. It was a standing-room-only crowd. A pleasant surprise to the panel! Organizational culture still appeared to have some attractiveness to scholars in the Academy of Management.

Second, and more important, the content of several presenters focused on empirical work on organizational culture, that is, either their own work or that of others that demonstrated quite clearly that good, careful research work was being done on the topic. It was particularly gratifying to learn that much of this work was being done by young scholars who were taking seriously the statements by researchers earlier in the decade about the importance and value of using a cultural lens to study organizations.

The conclusion of the panel at the end of the session, echoed by others in the audience, was that there was indeed life left in the study of organizational culture. The flame was still burning. What was needed to make a significant difference were sustained research efforts by many scholars, examining a variety of organizational issues, using culture as a frame for the work being done. This conclusion echoed one made by Harrison Trice in his critique of our book, *Organizational Culture,* in *Administrative Science Quarterly* (Trice, 1987). It meshed also with the sentiments of the five of us (Frost, Moore, Louis, Lundberg, and Martin) as we deliberated the usefulness of preparing a revised edition of *Organizational Culture.* We decided that it should not be revised, that it reflected something of what was being discussed as organizational culture at that time—"that was then and this is now," and anything we did together as a book-length project should have a fresh start as the decade was drawing to a close. The field had changed, we had changed, and it was time to rethink what organizational culture meant to us and perhaps to others.

On April 1st, 1989, exactly five years after the opening of the organizational culture conference at the University of British Columbia, we met in the Faculty of Commerce building at the same university to talk about organizational culture. Ann West, Acquisitions Editor of Sage, participated in the meeting. Over a period of two days, we deliberated on a number of issues relating to the topic and the purposes of any book we might write and edit. What resulted was the book that follows. We had several objectives in mind for this undertaking.

We wanted:

- To publish a book about organizational culture that would provide scholars interested in the topic—particularly young researchers interested in doing a dissertation or early post-doctoral research on organizational culture—with a discussion of both theory on organizational culture and empirical work that exemplified good research on the topic. Toward that end, we provide commentary throughout the book which provides a context for examining theory and research on organizational culture.

- To provide a framework that would allow the reader to examine any empirical piece on its own merits—as good research—but also to see it in a context of similarities and differences to other research on organizational culture. By 1989, we had each come to the conclusion that it was necessary and useful to see and understand organizational culture through several perspectives rather than a single one. We considered the framework of three cultural perspectives developed by Martin and Meyerson (1988) ideal for our purposes in this book, and this framework informs Part I as well as closing segments of the book. The description and illustration of these three perspectives, labeled integration, differentiation, and fragmentation, follows this introduction.

- To provide the reader, again with a particular eye to the interested beginning researcher, with a sense of the history of the field of organizational culture. We have done this by focusing on an early, well-known exemplar of cultural research. In the first section of Part II of the book, we reproduce a segment of the Appendix from *Street Corner Society* by William Foote Whyte (1955) in which Whyte describes the way he conducted this landmark study. To look at this piece through contemporary eyes, we asked four currently active culture researchers to prepare commentaries on Whyte's work. We conclude this exploration by asking William F. Whyte himself to respond to the four scholars and to take another look at *Street Corner Society* from his current perspective.

- To provide the reader with some treatment of ways one might *study* organizational culture. We chose to do this through an exploration of epistemology, rather than through a discussion of specific methods for studying the phenomenon. We asked four authors how they think about organizational culture when they study it. Three of these authors, Schein, Meyerson, and Rosen, are also contributors to Part I, so the reader may review their empirical efforts together with their reflections on research. The fourth author, Barbara Czarniawska-Joerges, provides a voice from the European tradition of scholarship on organizational culture. We invited Harrison M. Trice to comment on these four perspectives on doing organizational culture research and to provide his own perspective on this issue.

- To communicate to the reader that the study of organizational culture is an ongoing open process, that our frames of organizational culture in this book are not *the* frames, but simply serve as a heuristic to keep the process alive and vital. We believe very strongly that the process of discovery and invention in organizational studies is ongoing, an interaction of investigator and the subject of inquiry. (We differ among ourselves in terms of the degree to which we assume a distinction between investigator and subject.) Because of this belief, we have titled the book *Reframing Organizational Culture*. We intend this to signal that framing and reframing organizational culture is an ongoing kaleidoscopic process that will go on well beyond this book. It is a process that will be engaged in, perhaps by us, and hopefully by others who read the book and carry out research on the topic. We end the book with a challenge to the reader to go beyond what we have proposed as the meanings of organizational culture. To stimulate this thinking, we have included frames other than the primary ones of Martin and Meyerson. Furthermore, we invited a contribution from Linda Smircich and Marta Calas because we consider their voices on organizational culture to be important, provocative, and framebreaking. They did contribute with another attempt to break the frames. Perhaps the reader will find their voices, or perhaps not.

Finally we wanted to ground this project in its human dimension—to locate its editors as individuals whose values, emotions, biases, beliefs, and perceptions about the experiences of the research process have shaped what they write, select, and edit in their work. We believe this human dimension is present and influential in every enterprise. We certainly believe and feel that has been true for us. Our five personal statements are included in Part III. We each report and reflect on events in our research careers, discuss our current perspectives on organizational research, and ruminate on future directions in our work. We have brought our similarities and differences, our individual and collective experiences to bear on this book. We hope that by revealing something about ourselves and our individual voices we can help readers better understand the messages in *Reframing Organizational Culture*.

PART I

THINKING ABOUT
ORGANIZATIONAL CULTURE

Day & Night: © 1938 M.C. Esher Heirs/ Cordon Art-Baarn-Holland

Any number of the scientific concepts we accept today may be simply convenient schemata that impose order upon the experiences we have collected so far. They may have little or no relation to 'reality'. . . . A theory is thus neither true nor false; it simply works or it doesn't. Now it is true that many scientists (including myself) <u>believe</u> that their theories closely approximate or correspond to 'reality,' but this is an act of faith, for no 'proof' can be adduced for or against it. . . . The large number of modified or even discarded scientific theories should serve as a useful warning.

—GEORGE SCHWEITZER
(quoted in P. Freund, 1965, p. 281)

Introduction:
Ten Empirical Studies of Culture

In the 1980s there was a ground swell of enthusiasm for the study of organizational cultures. Some welcomed the topic of culture as a long overdue source of "fresh air," an antidote to sterile number crunching focused on easily measured variables. Others were attracted by the seductive promises of culture as a key to improved morale, loyalty, harmony, productivity, and—ultimately—profitability.

Since 1985, when we coedited our first volume on this subject, the proliferation of research on organizational culture has continued unabated. Given the abundance of research now available, it would seem reasonable to expect a theoretical consolidation of what has been learned from all this effort. This has not happened—for good reasons. Organizational culture researchers do not agree about what culture is or why it should be studied. They do not study the same phenomena. They do not approach the phenomena they do study from the same theoretical, epistemological, or methodological points of view. These fundamental disagreements have impeded the exchange of ideas and the ability to build upon others' empirical work. It has therefore been difficult to clarify what has been learned or how cultural studies contribute to other traditions of inquiry. No wonder, then, that research on organizational culture has sometimes been dismissed as a "dead end," as unrelated to mainstream theory, or as a fad that has failed to deliver on its promises (e.g., Barley, Meyer, & Gash, 1988; Calas & Smircich, 1987; Siehl & Martin, 1990).

7

What is needed is a theoretical framework that can capture the major similarities and differences among the various approaches to the study of organizational culture. Such a framework, if it is to be useful, must not threaten the integrity of these different approaches by creating pressures toward assimilation. Our goal is to understand why these fundamental disagreements exist, rather than to eradicate them in some unifying meta-theory. We have found the three-perspective framework, developed by Martin and Meyerson, to be helpful in this regard (Martin, in press; Martin & Meyerson, 1988; Meyerson & Martin, 1987).[1]

According to Martin and Meyerson's framework, three major perspectives have come to dominate research on organizational culture: integration, differentiation, and fragmentation. The *integration perspective* portrays culture predominantly in terms of consistency (across the various manifestations of a culture), organization-wide consensus about the appropriate interpretation of those manifestations, and clarity. From an integration perspective, cultural members agree about what they are to do and why it is worthwhile to do it. In this realm of clarity, there is no room for ambiguity.

In contrast, studies congruent with the *differentiation perspective* portray cultural manifestations as predominantly inconsistent with each other, (as for example when a formal policy is undermined by contradictory informal norms). According to these studies, to the extent that consensus emerges, it does so only within the boundaries of a subculture. At the organizational level of analysis, differentiated subcultures may co-exist in harmony, conflict, or indifference to each other. From a differentiation point of view, subcultures are islands of clarity; ambiguity is channeled outside their boundaries.

The *fragmentation perspective* views ambiguity as an inevitable and pervasive aspect of contemporary life. These studies, therefore, focus predominantly on the experience and expression of ambiguity within organizational cultures. Clear consistencies, like clear inconsistencies, are rare. According to this viewpoint, consensus and dissensus co-exist in a constantly fluctuating pattern influenced by changes, for example, in events, attention, salience, and cognitive overload. Any cultural manifestation can be, and is, interpreted in a myriad of ways. No clear organization-wide or subcultural consensus stabilizes when a culture is viewed from a fragmentation point of view.

Martin and Meyerson use these three cultural perspectives as descriptions of particular studies. A single study usually focuses on one of these perspectives, although a second or even a third perspective may be given

TABLE I.1. Defining Characteristics of the Three Perspectives on Organizational Culture

	Perspective		
Features	*Integration*	*Differentiation*	*Fragmentation*
Orientation to consensus	Organization-wide consensus	Subcultural consensus	Lack of consensus
Relation Among Manifestations	Consistency	Inconsistency	Not clearly consistent or inconsistent
Orientation to Ambiguity	Exclude it	Channel it outside subcultures	Acknowledge it

Source: Adapted from Table 1 in Martin and Meyerson (1988) and Figure 3 in Meyerson and Martin (1987).

minor attention. (For example, an integration study may acknowledge a subculture or an area of ambiguity, portraying these as deviations from a more pervasive and/or desirable integrated culture.) Although some individual researchers always write from a single perspective, other researchers change perspectives across studies, either because their theoretical preferences have changed and or because the characteristics of their data or their audience seem different.

These three perspectives, then, are not meant to pigeonhole individual researchers or even all the characteristics of a single piece of work. Rather, they offer a framework for deciphering what has—and has not—been learned from the proliferation of organizational culture research. Table I.1 summarizes the major elements of the three-perspective framework.

The remainder of Part I of this volume consists of ten empirical chapters. The first three chapters are representative of the integration perspective, the next four exemplify the differentiation viewpoint, and the final three are examples of the fragmentation perspective. We chose these chapters because they represent a broad spectrum of contemporary research on organizational culture and because, in our opinions, they are fine work.

The authors of these empirical chapters worked within tight space constraints. In order to reduce repetition across chapters, we asked each author to focus primarily on presenting his or her data, keeping theoretical and methodological material to a minimum. Without these restrictions, they might have offered an expanded treatment of theory and method and included, as a minor theme, data congruent with a second or even a third perspective. (References to more lengthy versions of these 10 studies, when available, are included.) Therefore, to the extent that such material is missing, the editors, not the authors, are to blame.

In the following sections, each of the three perspectives is explained in a bit more detail with abstracts of the relevant empirical chapters in each section. Finally, in Section ID, we argue, with Martin and Meyerson, that it is essential to use all three perspectives to develop a full understanding of any single cultural context and present a list of selected readings on each of the three perspectives.

IA
The Integration Perspective

According to Martin and Meyerson, the integration perspective assumes or asserts that a "strong" or "desirable" culture is characterized by consistency, organization-wide consensus, and clarity. Consistency refers to the pattern of relationships among the various cultural manifestations included in a cultural portrait; espoused values are consistent with formal practices, which are consistent with informal norms, stories, rituals, and so forth. This mutually reinforcing matrix of manifestations engenders organization-wide consensus. Cultural members share the same values and understandings, promoting a shared sense of loyalty, commitment, and—hopefully—productivity. This consensus breeds clarity; ambiguity is excluded from this approach to studying culture. These defining characteristics are predominant themes in the three empirical chapters that follow. In Chapter 1, Edgar H. Schein describes how entrepreneurs can create organizational cultures that reflect their own values, thereby achieving a sort of organizational immortality. This chapter summarizes three case studies. In the first, a founder imposed his assumptions and values on employees, constantly reinforcing these preferences by formal policies and personal example, and modifying them as circumstances dictated. Although this account stresses the development of organization-wide consensus, for example, by the recruitment of a management team with assumptions congruent with the founder's, deviations from this homogeneity are also noted. For example, some managers developed a sort of counter-culture and others failed to adopt the values and norms of the founder. These developments were seen as shortcomings and attributed to the founder's inability to send clear and consistent signals.

In the second case study, a founder supported his philosophy of management with consistent policies, norms, architecture, and interior design. The founder's beliefs were reinforced by hiring attitudinally homogeneous employees and attempting to create an organization-wide consensus. However, as the company grew, inconsistencies began to surface, creating dysfunctional conflicts, disorganization, and chaos. In this case study, an integrated culture showed signs of collapsing as the company grew.

In the third case study, an entrepreneur declined to leave a cultural legacy, preferring to sell his companies, as soon as they were firmly established, rather than become involved in the day-to-day management activities of a cultural creator. This chapter concludes that leaders can indeed create cultures cast in their own personal image, but that changing circumstances or personal preferences can also cause signs of differentiation or fragmentation to occur. Integration, then, is seen by these founders as a desirable, but not inevitable, outcome of the culture creation process.

This chapter is exceptional in that it is careful to include data congruent with all three theoretical perspectives. Nevertheless, this account fits predominantly within the integration perspective because evidence of subcultural differentiation and ambiguity is mentioned only as a secondary theme, a deviation from the integrated state these founders would prefer.

The second chapter in this section, by Peggy McDonald, describes the development of an integrated culture at The Los Angeles Olympic Organizing Committee. This is a highly emotional account, written by a participant-observer, of the fervent commitment experienced by members of a temporary organization. Although this study, like the preceding study of founders, emphasizes the role of the leader in the culture creation process, this account focuses primarily on the employees as they worked impossibly long hours, were moved to tears by organizational rituals, and spent their few hours of leisure time celebrating organizational achievements with other employees.

In this epitome of a "high participation" organization, cultural manifestations consistently reinforced each other. Nonfinancial, ideological reasons for joining such an organization (to be part of the "Olympic Spirit") were emphasized. To the extent that subcultures emerged in this context, (e.g., in the design group of which the author was a member), subcultural members were even more fanatically committed than the rest of the company. The few breaches in this monolithic whole (e.g., signs of stress or humor) served to release tension and enhance subsequent employee involvement. This chapter implicitly makes a seductive promise: consistency, organization-wide consensus, and clarity can combine to produce unusually high levels of loyalty, harmony, and commitment. In this account, an integrated culture is the key to productivity. Such promises of organizational effectiveness are characteristic of some (but not all) integration research.

The last integration chapter, by Stephen R. Barley, refrains from making explicit promises of organizational effectiveness. Instead, it analyzes the meanings of funeral directors' activities, offering a seamlessly integrated interpretation of seemingly disparate tasks. Closing the corpse's eyes, making the bed, opening the windows of the death room, and embalming the body are revealed to have a consistent theme: all are ways of making death seem lifelike. No emotionally disruptive hint of ambiguity or conflict is allowed to mar the funeral directors' choreographed presentation of a lifelike death.

In summary, studies written from an integration perspective define culture in terms of clear and consistent values, interpretations, and/or assumptions that are shared on an organization-wide basis. Therefore, to the extent that inconsistencies, conflict, ambiguities, or even subcultural differentiation appear in an integration study, they are seen as evidence of the absence of an "organizational culture" (see Chapter 17). Other studies, predominantly consistent with the Integration perspective, are listed at the conclusion of Part I.

1

The Role of the Founder in the
Creation of Organizational Culture

EDGAR H. SCHEIN

"The ghost of George Eastman still walks the halls."

—A senior Kodak manager

Organizations do not form accidentally or spontaneously. They are "created" because one or more individuals perceive that the coordinated and concerted action of a number of people can accomplish something that individual action cannot. Social movements or new religions begin with prophets, messiahs, or other kinds of charismatic leaders. Political groups are begun by leaders who articulate and sell new visions and new solutions to problems. Firms are created by entrepreneurs who have a vision of how the concerted effort of the right group of people can create a new product or service in the marketplace. The process of culture formation is, in each case, first a process of creating a small group.

In the typical business organization, this process will usually involve some version of the following steps:

1. A single person (founder) has an idea for a new enterprise.
2. The founder brings in one or more other people and creates a core group that shares a common vision with the founder. That is, they all believe that the idea is

AUTHOR'S NOTE: Adapted with permission from Chapter 9 of *Organizational Culture and Leadership,* by E. H. Schein, 1985. San Francisco, CA: Jossey-Bass.

a good one, is workable, is worth running some risks for, and is worth the investment of time, money, and energy that will be required.

3. The founding group begins to act in concert to create an organization by raising funds, obtaining patents, incorporating, locating space, and so on.

4. Others are brought into the organization as partners and employees, and a common history begins to be built. If the group remains fairly stable and has significant shared learning experiences, it will gradually develop assumptions about itself, its environment, and how to do things to survive and grow.

As those assumptions come to be taken for granted and drop out of awareness we have the makings of an organizational culture. The stability of those assumptions derives from the fact that together they provide group members with a way of giving meaning to their daily lives, setting guidelines and rules for how to behave, and, most important, reducing and containing the anxiety of dealing with an unpredictable and uncertain environment. Culture stabilizes and normalizes events and thus makes day-to-day functioning possible. Once a group has a shared set of assumptions, it will tend to cling to those assumptions. Hence culture is very difficult to change unless one changes the people in the group.

Founders usually have a major impact on how the group defines and solves its external problem of surviving and growing, and how it will internally organize itself and integrate its own efforts. Because they had the original idea, founders will typically have their own notion, based on their own cultural history and personality, of how to get the idea fulfilled. Founders not only have a high level of self-confidence and determination, but typically they also have strong assumptions about the nature of the world, the role that organizations play in that world, the nature of human nature and relationships, how truth is arrived at, and how to manage time and space (Schein, 1981, 1983, 1985a). Since they started the group, they tend to impose their assumptions on the group and to cling to them until such time as they become unworkable or the group fails and breaks up. As new members and leaders come into the group, the founder's assumptions and beliefs will gradually be modified, but they will always have the biggest impact on what will ultimately be the group's culture.

The Jones Food Company

Founder Jones was an immigrant whose parents had started a corner grocery store in a large urban area. His parents, particularly his mother, taught him some basic attitudes toward customers and helped him form the

vision that he could succeed in building a successful enterprise. He assumed from the beginning that if he did things right he would succeed and
could build a major organization that would bring him and his family a
fortune. Ultimately, he built a large chain of supermarkets, department
stores, and related businesses that became the dominant force in its market
area. Jones was the major ideological force in his company throughout its
history and continued to impose his assumptions on the company until his
death in his late seventies. Jones named the company after himself.

Jones assumed that his primary mission was to supply a high quality,
reliable product to customers in clean, attractive surroundings and that his
customers' needs were the primary consideration in all major decisions.
There are many stories about how Jones, as a young man operating the
corner grocery store with his wife, gave customers credit and thus displayed trust in them, always took products back if there was the slightest
complaint, and kept his store absolutely spotless to inspire customer
confidence in his products. Each of these attitudes later became a major
policy in his chain of stores and was taught and reinforced by close
personal supervision.

Jones believed that only personal example and close supervision would
ensure adequate performance by subordinates. He would show up at his
stores unexpectedly, inspect even minor details, and then "teach" the staff
what they should be doing by personal example, by stories of how other
stores were solving the problems identified, by articulating rules, and by
exhortation. He often lost his temper and berated subordinates who did not
follow the rules or principles he laid down.

Jones expected his store managers to be highly visible, to be very much
on top of their own jobs, and to supervise subordinates closely in the same
way he did. In later years these assumptions became a major theme in his
concept of "visible management," the assumption that a "good" manager
always had to be around to set a good example and to teach subordinates
the right way to do things.

Most of the founding group in this company consisted of the three
brothers of the founder, but one "lieutenant" who was not a family member
was recruited early and became, in addition to the founder, the main culture
creator and carrier. He shared the founder's basic assumptions about how
to run a business and set up formal systems to ensure that those assumptions
became the basis for operating realities. After Jones's death, this man
continued to articulate the theory of "visible management" and tried to set
a personal example of how to do it by continuing the same close supervision policies that Jones had used.

Jones assumed that one could only "win" in the marketplace by being highly innovative and technically on the forefront. He always encouraged his managers to try new approaches, brought in a variety of consultants who advocated new ways of dealing with human resource management, started selection and development programs through assessment centers long before other companies tried this approach, traveled to conventions and other businesses where new technological innovations were displayed, and generally was willing to experiment in order to improve the business. His view of truth and reality was that one had to find it wherever one could, and therefore, one had to be open to one's environment and never take it for granted that one had all the answers.

If things worked, Jones encouraged their adoption; if they did not, he ordered them to be dropped. Measuring results and solving problems were, for Jones, intensely personal matters, deriving from his theory of "visible management." In addition to using a variety of traditional business measures, he always made it a point to visit all of his stores personally and, if he saw things not to his liking, to correct them immediately and decisively even if that meant going around his own authority chain. He trusted only managers who operated by assumptions similar to his own and clearly had favorites to whom he delegated more authority.

Power remained very centralized in that everyone knew that Jones or his chief lieutenant could and would override decisions made by division or other unit managers without consultation and often in a very peremptory fashion. The ultimate source of power, the voting shares of stock, were owned entirely by Jones and his wife, so that after his death his wife was in total control of the company.

Jones was interested in developing good managers throughout the organization, but he never assumed that sharing ownership through granting stock options would contribute to that process. He paid his key managers very well but did not share ownership even with those who had been with the company from the beginning. His assumption was that ownership was strictly a family matter, to the point that he was not even willing to share stock with his chief lieutenant, close friend, and virtual co-builder of the company.

Jones introduced several members of his own family into the firm in key managerial positions and gave them favored treatment in the form of good developmental jobs that would test them early for ultimate management potential. As the firm diversified, family members were made heads of divisions, often with relatively little management experience. If a family member performed poorly, he would be bolstered by having a good manager introduced under him. If the operation then improved, the family member would likely be given the credit. If things continued badly, the family member would be moved out, but with various face-saving excuses.

Peer relationships among nonfamily members inevitably became highly politicized. They were officially defined as competitive, and Jones believed firmly in the value of interpersonal competition. Winners would be rewarded and losers discarded. However, because family members were in positions of power, managers had to know how to stay on the good side of those family members without losing the trust of their peers, on whom they were dependent.

Jones wanted open communication and high trust levels among all members of the organization, but his own assumptions about the role of the family and the correct way to manage were, to a large degree, in conflict with each other. Therefore, many of the members of the organization banded together in a kind of mutual protection society that developed a culture of its own. They were more loyal to each other than to the company and had a high rate of interaction with each other, which bred assumptions, values, and norms that became to some degree countercultural to the founder's.

Several points should be noted about the description given thus far. By definition, something can become part of the culture only if it works. Jones's assumptions about how things should be done were congruent with the kind of environment in which he operated, so he and the founding group received strong reinforcement for those assumptions. As the company grew and prospered, Jones felt more and more confirmation of his assumptions and thus became more and more confident that they were correct. Throughout his lifetime he steadfastly adhered to those assumptions and did everything in his power to get others to accept them.

At the same time, however, Jones had to share concepts and assumptions with a great many other people. So, as his company grew and learned from its own experience, his assumptions gradually had to be modified in some areas or he had to withdraw from those areas as an active manager. For example, in its diversification efforts, the company bought several production units that would enable it to integrate vertically in certain food and clothing areas where that was economically advantageous. But, because Jones learned that he knew relatively little about production, he brought in strong managers and gave them a great deal of autonomy. Some of those production divisions never acquired the culture of the main organization and the heads of those divisions never enjoyed the status and security that "insiders" had.

Jones had to learn somewhat painfully that he did not send as clear and consistent signals as he thought he did. He did not perceive his own conflicts and inconsistencies, and hence could not understand why some of this best young managers failed to respond to his competitive incentives and even left the company. He thought he was adequately motivating them and could not see that for some of them the political climate, the absence of stock options, and the arbitrary rewarding of family members made their own career progress too uncertain. Jones was perplexed and angry about much of this, blaming the young managers, while holding on to his own assumptions and conflicts.

Following his death, the company experienced a long period of turmoil because of the vacuum created by Jones's absence and the retirement of several other key culture carriers, but the basic philosophies of how to run stores were thoroughly embedded and remained. Various family members continued to run the company although none of them had the business skills that Jones had.

With the retirement of Jones's chief lieutenant, a period of instability set in, marked by the discovery that some of the managers who had been developed under Jones were not as strong and capable as had been assumed. None of Jones's children or their spouses was able to take over the business decisively, so an outside person was brought in to run the company. This person predictably failed because he could not adapt to the culture and to the family.

After several failures with outsider chief executive officers (CEOs) the family turned to a manager who had originally been with the company and had subsequently made a fortune outside the company in various real estate enterprises. This person was successful in revitalizing and stabilizing the company because of this understanding of the culture and the family dynamics. But these events suggest, as one would hypothesize, that the culture remained strong even after the death of the founder and new CEOs had to adapt to it if they were to be successful. It remains to be seen whether this person will attempt to change the culture if some of his own assumptions differ from Jones's, and how that process will play itself out.

The Action Company

The next example is the Action Company, a highly successful high technology manufacturing organization that has grown into a multi-billion dollar enterprise and is still under the management of its founder. Action's founder, Murphy, was a very dominant personality who had a clear theory of how things should be. He and four others founded the company because they believed they could build a product for which there would be a large market. They were able to convince investors because of their own credibility and the unanimity of their basic vision of the company's core mission. However, after some years they found that they did not share a vision of how to build an organization, and all except Murphy left the organization.

Murphy's assumptions about the nature of the world and how one discovers truth and solves problems were very strong and were reflected in his management style. He believed that good ideas could come from anyone, regardless of rank or background, but that neither he nor any other individual was smart enough to determine whether a given idea was correct. Murphy felt that open discussion in a group was the only way to test ideas and that one should not take action until an idea had survived the crucible of an active debate. One might have intuitions, but one should not act on them until they had been tested in the intellectual marketplace.

Murphy bolstered his assumption with a story that he told frequently to justify his pushing issues into groups. He said that he would often *not* make a decision because: "I'm not that smart; if I really knew what to do I would say so. But when I get into a group of smart people and listen to them discuss the idea, then I get smart very fast." Hence, Murphy set up a number of committees and groups and insisted that all ideas be discussed and debated before they were acted on. If he heard an idea examined from all angles, he thought he could judge how sound it was. Thus, Murphy set up groups as a kind of extension of his own intelligence and often used them to think out loud and get his own ideas straight in his head.

Murphy also believed that one could not get good implementation of ideas if people did not fully support them and that the best way to get support was to let people debate. He often told another story on himself: "But I also remember when I made a unilateral decision some years ago, started down the road and, when I looked over my shoulder, there was nobody there with me." Therefore, on any important decision, Murphy insisted on a wide debate, with many group meetings to test the idea and sell it down the organization and laterally. Only when it appeared that everyone wanted to do it and fully understood it would he "ratify" it.

Although Murphy's assumptions about decision making and implementation led to a very group-oriented organization, his theory about how to organize and manage work led to a strong individuation process, which reinforced his assumption that individuals are ultimately the source of creativity. His theory was that one must give clear and simple individual responsibility and then measure the person strictly on that area of responsibility. Groups could help to make decisions and obtain commitment, but they could not under any circumstances be held responsible or accountable.

Murphy believed completely in a proactive model of human nature and in people's capacity to master nature, a set of assumptions that appeared to be correlated closely with his engineering background. Hence, he always expected people to be on top of their jobs and was very critical of them, both in public and in private, if he felt that they were not completely in control. Recognizing that circumstances might change the outcome of even the best laid plans, Murphy expected his managers to renegotiate plans as soon as they observed a deviation. Thus, for example, if an annual budget had been set at a certain level and the responsible manager noticed after 6 months that he would overrun it or else miss the schedule, he was expected to get the situation under control, according to the original assumptions, or to come back to Murphy and senior management to renegotiate. It was absolutely unacceptable either not to know what was happening or to let it happen without informing senior management and renegotiating.

Murphy believed completely in open communications and the ability of people to reach reasonable decisions and make appropriate compromises if they openly confronted the problems and issues, figured out what they wanted to do, and were willing to argue for their solution and honor any commitments they made. He assumed that people have "constructive intent," a rational loyalty to organizational goals and shared commitments. Withholding information, playing power games, competitively trying to win out over another member of the organization on a personal level, blaming others for one's failures, undermining or sabotaging decisions one had agreed to, and going off on one's own without getting others' agreement all were defined as sins and brought public censure. But thinking for oneself and doing the smart thing were so highly valued that subordinates were expected to argue with their bosses if they thought what was being asked was "stupid" or, if the boss still insisted, were licensed to be insubordinate. Because the bosses lived in the same culture, they were, of course, less likely to issue peremptory orders and more likely to listen when their subordinates raised questions.

The architecture and office layout of Action reflected Murphy's assumptions about creativity and decision making. He insisted on open office landscaping; preferred cubicles for engineers instead of offices with doors; encouraged individualism in dress and behavior; and minimized the use of status symbols, such as private offices, special dining rooms for executives, and personal parking spaces. Instead, there were many conference rooms and attached kitchens to encourage people to interact comfortably.

This model of how to run an organization to maximize individual creativity and decision quality worked very successfully. The company experienced dramatic growth and had exceptionally high morale. However, as the company grew larger, people found that they had less time to negotiate with each other and did not know each other as well, making these processes more frustrating. Some of the paradoxes and inconsistencies among the various assumptions came to the surface. For example, to encourage individuals to think for themselves and do what they believed to be the best course of action, even if it meant insubordination, clearly ran counter to the dictum that one must honor one's commitments and support decisions that have been made. In practice the rule of honoring commitments was superseded by the rule of doing only what one believes is right.

When the company was small and everyone knew everyone else, there was always time to renegotiate, and basic consensus was high enough to ensure that, if time pressure forced people to make their own decisions and to be insubordinate, others would, after the fact, mostly agree with the decisions that had been made locally. In other words, initial decisions made at higher levels often did not "stick," but this did not bother anyone until the organization became larger and more complex. What was initially a highly adaptive system began to be regarded by more and more members of the organization as disorganization and chaos.

Murphy believed in the necessity of organization and hierarchy, but he did not trust the authority of position nearly as much as the authority of reason. Hence, managers were de facto granted authority only to the extent that they could sell their decisions, and, as indicated above, insubordination was not only tolerated but positively rewarded if it made sense and led to better outcomes. Managers often complained that they could not control any of the things they were responsible for; yet, at the same time, they believed in the system and shared Murphy's assumptions because of the kinds of people they were, the degree to which they had been socialized into the system, and, most importantly, the degree to which these assumptions had led to highly successful performance.

Murphy also believed that the intellectual testing of ideas, which he encouraged among individuals in group settings, could be profitably extended to organizational units if it was not clear what products or markets to go after. He was willing to create overlapping product/market units and let them compete with each other for success, not realizing, however, that such internal competition undermined openness of communication and made it more difficult for groups to negotiate decisions. Yet this way of doing things had enough success in the marketplace that Action managers came to believe in it as a way of operating in a rapidly shifting market environment. The company thrived on intelligent, assertive, individualistic people who were willing and able to argue for and sell their ideas.

The hiring practices of the company clearly reflected this bias. Each new hire had to undergo a large number of interviews and be convincing in each one of them to be viewed as a positive candidate. So, over the course of its first decade, the organization tended to hire and keep only those kinds of people who fitted the assumptions and were willing to live in the system even though it might at times be frustrating. The people who were comfortable in this environment and enjoyed the excitement of building a successful organization found themselves increasingly feeling like members of a family and were emotionally treated as such. Strong bonds of mutual support grew up at an interpersonal level, and Murphy functioned symbolically as a brilliant, demanding, but supportive father figure. These familial feelings were implicit but important, because they provided subordinates with a feeling of security that made it possible for them to challenge each other's ideas. When a proposed course of action did not make sense it might be severely challenged, and the person might even be accused of having "dumb" ideas, but he could not lose his membership in the family. Frustration and insecurity grew, however, as the size of the company made it more difficult to maintain the level of personal acquaintance that would make familial feelings possible.

Murphy represents an entrepreneur with a clear set of assumptions about how things should be, both at the level of how to relate externally to the environment and how to arrange things internally in the organization. His willingness to be open about his theory and his rewarding and punishing behavior in support of it led to both the selection of others who shared the theory and strong socialization practices that reinforced and perpetuated it. Consequently, the founder's assumptions are reflected in how the organization operates today. However, as noted above, Action also illustrates how a set of assumptions that works under one set of circumstances may become dysfunctional under other sets of circumstances. The growing frustration that resulted from trying to maintain such assumptions on a large scale in a more competitive environment has led to a number of efforts to reassess the organizational model and to figure out how to continue to be adaptive with the kind of culture that Action has developed.

Smithfield Enterprises

Smithfield built a chain of financial service organizations using sophisticated financial analysis techniques in an area of the country where insurance companies, mutual funds, and banks were only beginning to use such techniques. He was the conceptualizer and salesman, but once he had the idea for a new kind of service organization, he got others to invest in, build and manage it.

Smithfield believed that he should put only a very small amount of his own money into each enterprise because if he could not convince others to put up money, maybe there was something wrong with the idea. He made the initial assumption that he did not know enough about the market to gamble with his own money, and he reinforced this assumption publicly by telling a story about the one enterprise in which he failed. He had opened a retail store in a midwestern city to sell ocean fish because he loved it, assumed others felt as he did, trusted his own judgment about what the marketplace would want, and failed. Had he tried to get many others to invest in the enterprise, he would have learned that his own tastes were not necessarily a good predictor of what others would want.

Smithfield saw himself as a creative conceptualizer, not a manager, so he not only kept his financial investment minimal, but also did not get personally very involved with his enterprises. Once he put together the package, he found people he could trust to manage the new organization. These were usually people like himself who were fairly open in their approach to business and not too concerned with imposing their own assumptions about how things should be done.

One can infer that Smithfield's assumptions about concrete business goals, the best means to achieve them, how to measure results, and how to repair things when they were going wrong were essentially pragmatic. Whereas Jones had a strong need to be involved in everything, Smithfield seemed to lose interest once the new organization was on its feet and functioning. His theory seemed to be that one had to have a clear concept of the basic mission, test it by selling it to investors, bring in good people who understood what the mission was, and then leave them alone to implement and run the organization, using only financial criteria as ultimate performance measures.

If Smithfield had assumptions about how an organization should be run internally, he kept them to himself. The cultures that each of this enterprises developed therefore had more to do with the assumptions of the people he brought in to manage them, and, as it turned out, those varied a good deal.

And, if one analyzed Smithfield Enterprises as a total organization one would find little evidence of a "corporate culture" because there was no group that had a shared history and shared learning experiences.

This brief case illustrates that there is nothing automatic about founders imposing themselves on their organizations. It depends on their personal needs to externalize their various assumptions. For Smithfield the ultimate personal validation lay in having each of his enterprises become financially successful and in his ability to continue to form creative new ones. His creative needs were such that, after a decade or so of founding financial service organizations, he turned his attention to real estate ventures, then became a lobbyist on behalf of an environmental organization, and ultimately went into politics. Following a brief political career he went back into business, this time into mining enterprises, using the same philosophy that he had employed before.

Summary and Analysis

The above three cases illustrate how organizations begin to create cultures through the actions of their founders. Culture is learned and developed through a variety of explicit and implicit mechanisms, often based on explicit "teaching" by the founder or later leaders.

The things that solve a group's problems repeatedly and reduce anxiety will survive and become a part of the culture. But only solutions that are proposed or invented can become candidates for cultural elements. Cultures do not start from scratch. Founders and group members always have prior experience to start with. Powerful members will try to impose their assumptions as the proposed solutions to problems, and the group selects something to try before the process of learning can operate. The creation and embedding process, therefore, has to be viewed simultaneously as a learning and a teaching process. At every stage the role of the leader and the group must be understood if one is to make sense of how the culture evolves.

2

The Los Angeles Olympic Organizing Committee: Developing Organizational Culture in the Short Run

PEGGY McDONALD

The Los Angeles Olympic Organizing Committee was an unusual organization with an unusual task. Its purpose was to organize and operate the Games of the XXIIIrd Olympiad from July 28 to August 12, 1984, in Los Angeles, California. Shortly after that date the organization virtually ceased to exist.

The organizing effort began 1,051 days prior to the opening of the Games on March 26, 1979. Starting at that time with only a handful of employees, the organization grew immensely and rapidly, from 200 employees one year to 2,500 by early 1984. By the time the Games began, the Los Angeles Olympic Organizing Committee (LAOOC) had some 20,000 employees and 50,000 volunteers at its service.

One of the largest challenges the organizers faced was hiring and training this huge, short-term work force. It was understandably difficult to lure highly skilled and personable people from permanent jobs to join the Olympics effort. The glamour and excitement of working for an event with high visibility and historical implications could catch the attention of the target group of employees, but it took more to enlist and retain their services. Therefore, elaborate plans were laid to make each employee feel a personal stake in the Olympic movement, encouraging him or her to "Play a Part in History."

AUTHOR'S NOTE: Reprinted with permission from *Inside Organizations* by M. O. Jones, M. D. Moore, & R. C. Snyder (Eds.), 1988. Newbury Park, CA: Sage.

Formal orientation at the Olympic committee was done relatively well, given the brief time and the huge numbers of new recruits. A permanent organization has considerably more time to train and enculturate its new members than did the LAOOC. Given this situation, the staff's organizational learning came primarily from informal means, drawing heavily on the stories and behavior of co-workers. Myths and rituals sprang up surprisingly fast for such a young organization, although many were rooted in the history of the modern and ancient Olympic Games.

I experienced the orientation and training process of the LAOOC first-hand. I was hired April 1, 1984 at the height of the hiring upswing to work in the Design Department. It is difficult to separate my viewpoints from those of the organization or the department, but many notes and interviews initiated in my first contacts with the organization and continued until the Games have allowed me a measure of objectivity.

In much of what follows, I adopt an anthropological convention of speaking in the present, even though the Games have been played, the event is history, and I no longer work for the organization (which has been dismantled). I follow this convention both because I wrote this report before the Games occurred and because the present tense conveys more of the feeling of being "inside."

Orientation

At the initial orientation meeting, I was introduced to the LAOOC headquarters building in Marina del Rey, California. The building is a former helicopter factory and retains the high ceilings and wide-open floor plan of an industrial manufacturing site. The drab, sterile interior is fortunately relieved by the fabulous colors and shapes that are suspended from the ceiling in the form of banners and huge sculptural mobiles. The bullpen-like setting of many of the offices is brightened by the addition of large, colorful pillars and scaffolding that will be used to decorate the actual competition sites during the Games. These elements add a necessary interior decor to the physical space, while serving as a constant, vibrant reminder to the employees of their roles in the spectacle to come.

The process of entering the Olympic headquarters to see the workspace is not simple. Each visitor is subjected to approximately four waves of security, from simple oral identification to elaborate frisking and x-ray procedures. The exterior of the building is completely unmarked as belonging to the Los Angeles Olympic Organizing Committee. Rather, the uniformly dull building has only a large sign stating the street address. This makes insiders feel secure, but also serves as a constant reminder of the horror of the Munich Games, which were marred by political violence.

The formal orientation session introduced me to the format of LAOOC meetings. A large number of highly placed managers spoke to the group of 70, all speaking briefly and casually. They spoke of the organization's philosophy and purpose. Several key points that have been constantly reiterated are:

- The athlete comes first.
- Private sector financing will be used exclusively to avoid burdening the taxpayers. These are, then, the "Spartan" games.
- New building will be strictly limited.
- The committee structure will be highly decentralized, with many services contracted to private vendors and organizations.
- The community will gain long-term benefits from the committee's efforts.

Several of these goals are befitting of any short-term organization, whereas others are specific to this peculiar event. All have been evident in decisions made by the committee.

The orientation session continued with self-introductions of all those joining the staff. Besides name and duty, we were told to mention any previous Olympics we had attended (only a small proportion had done so). We were told for the first of many times that we were now playing a part in history. The scheduled "inspirational films" were deleted for time considerations. On the whole, the group left the small, bare room confused, overwhelmed with policies and procedures, and not particularly inspired or confident of the organization's ability to carry out its task.

All new staff members had their photos taken for a permanent identification badge, which was promised in two weeks. We did not yet sense the importance of the permanent blue badges, compared to the temporary red ones we wore. In an organization with a history as brief as the LAOOC's, even those with a week's seniority have a measurable difference in status, at least until the permanent identification badge arrives. For the unfortunate members of my entering group, our badges were delayed six weeks. This did little for our rapid adoption into the organization and did even less for our confidence in its ability to make things happen on time. Even among the holders of permanent blue badges, the numbers are sequentially ordered, so one can hear, "Wow! 131! What was it like back then?"

As a whole, the staff is extremely young, bright, and attractive. The manager of 42 can seem like an old timer. Although this may well be a function of the availability of workers and flexibility of careers among younger people, it does give the organization a different character. One can notice a lot of flirtation and socializing, and sex seems to be a frequent topic of conversation. The interest of the vast majority of the staff in athletics and other healthful, vigorous behavior is also a distinguishing feature.

Organizational Policy and Cultures

At orientation, new staff members are given a policies and procedures manual and are reminded of the most important rules. Only after we went to work in our departments did we begin to learn which ones really count and which are considered ridiculous. The most frequently discussed policies are the dress code, the need for numerous signatures on every transaction, the "Peter" test (named after Ueberroth), and parking restrictions.

The dress code stipulates that women should wear dresses and always must wear stockings and "proper undergarments." Men must wear neckties at all times and should not have beards. Many people take great offense at these restrictions, although to the knowledge of those I interviewed, no one has ever been fired for violating them. Many, though, have been warned or reprimanded. One woman, who was wearing long shorts one day in preparation for moving heavy boxes to the warehouse, was told by an older woman in a "gross polyester floral muu-muu" that she was attired inappropriately. For the two weeks' duration of the actual Olympic games, the entire staff will be working at the competition sites. The polyester uniforms that will be assigned are causing reactions ranging from apprehension to horror.

The pursuit of signatures on paper is the most obvious activity of staff members. Tight fiscal constraint is the motivation behind this, and the "Spartan" games philosophy prevails. Nevertheless, the staff appears to be quite action-oriented and is frustrated by the endless rounds of paperwork. Most staff members are acutely aware of the dwindling time (53 days as I write this report) and rail against the bureaucracy.

Coercion is used to force new staff members to become active participants in the international spirit of the Games. At the time of hire, each person, no matter how comparably important or insignificant her or his position appears, is randomly assigned a country. People are told that at any time Peter Ueberroth, the President of the Los Angeles Olympic Organizing Committee, could call someone into his office and ask the person to tell him everything about Somalia or Mozambique or whatever his or her assigned country is. The alleged purpose of this exercise is to have a ready source of current information should a delegation show up unexpectedly, but it clearly forces the new recruit to do homework and feel potentially pivotal to the organization. It also establishes an awareness of the chief executive in everyone's mind. I was told that, several months before I started, a delegation from Finland arrived. Peter called all four people in the organization who had been assigned Finland. Only one was prepared. The consequences were never clearly stated, but the impression given was that lack of preparation is grounds for immediate dismissal. When I received my assignment, I was relieved to see that I, too, had Finland. Presumably, someone was a Finnish expert by now.

Another sort of "Peter test" was announced at the orientation, striking fear into the hearts of most present, especially those many years removed from school and tests. All new staff members are required to take a test administered by the President himself. The material to be included includes "everything" about the history of the Olympic Games, current international and local news, and infinite details about the LAOOC. Horror stories abound about unexpectedly being required to name the countries in Africa, the city council members in Los Angeles, and the sports commissioners for 23 events at the 1984 Games. Those being tested are given 24 hours' warning. The test is as treacherous as promised, but studying for it does help quickly acquaint the newcomer to the organization and its environment. No one has ever been fired for not performing well on the "Peter test," but it is widely reported that Peter came down to personally congratulate the only person ever to have received a perfect score.

The fourth frequently discussed policy is the newly instituted parking permit system. The huge increase in staff has finally filled the extremely large outdoor parking lot. Additional parking was arranged at a sponsor's headquarters some 20 minutes away (though advertised as 10 minutes). Each department head was assigned enough parking permits for approximately two-thirds of her or his staff. Others must park in the distant lot and be shuttled to and from the LAOOC headquarters according to a fixed and inconvenient schedule. Department heads divided the passes in a variety of ways—randomly, by favoritism, by seniority, or by rank within the department. The discussion about who has passes, who doesn't, and how to beat the system is an absorbing subject of hallway conversations.

Other organizational policies, some tacit, govern a great deal of the mood at the LAOOC. One of the first stories I heard was about the person who was fired for not walking fast enough. With so much to do in such a short period of time, the staff is frenzied, and people sprinting down the hallways are a frequent sight. By contrast, those moving calmly can appear sluggish. Through this recurrent story, the organization seems to be applauding expeditiousness and, perhaps inadvertently, hyperactivity.

The staff is encouraged to eat "on campus" at the "Cafe du Coubertin," named for Baron Pierre de Coubertin, founder of the modern Olympic Games. It has standard cafeteria fare, varied by the day and thoroughly unexciting. The staff, though, is offered a $2.00 per day subsidy to eat at the Cafe, which makes for a cheap, or sometimes free, lunch. Keeping the staff in the same location for lunch presumably reduces downtime caused by lengthy drives or too many errands. It does increase camaraderie among staff, with common food to complain about. Additionally, the Cafe is used as a site for information dispersal. It sports a "Days to Go" calendar; a route map of the Torch Relay's progress, which is updated daily; and a screening room, which shows inspirational Olympic newsreels at lunch. Uniforms for the Games are modeled at lunch, and sports demonstrations occur weekly. It is impossible to eat regularly in the cafeteria without becoming genuinely excited about the Olympic Games and, by transference, the LAOOC.

The only three sources of revenue for the 1984 Games are television rights, ticket sales, and sponsors' fees. Of these, sponsors have the highest profile. The current jokes about "Official Toilet Paper of the 1984 Olympics" are even more frequent within the committee, where sponsors seem to run rampant. As staff members, we are required to use the official Brother typewriters, IBM computers, Xerox copy machines, and even official printers and pin manufacturers. We receive free M & M's, Snickers candy bars, and Perrier water. Free Coca-Cola and coffee machines line the halls. It can get unnerving. I noticed a delivery man with a handcart full of boxes wearing his t-shirt inside out. I joked with him about it, and he replied that the loading dock required all delivery people to turn their company shirts inside out if they were not from a sponsoring firm. Investigating this, I found that a sponsor had complained to Peter Ueberroth, saying, "How much did Joe's Printing pay to be a sponsor?" Official sponsors paid an average of $11 million dollars for the right to be Official.

The colorful look of the Games is called "festive federalism." A conscious effort was made to select a color scheme for use in buildings, uniforms, pageantry, and all printed material that will not reflect political

themes. The predominant magentas, aquas, vermilions, purples, and peri-
winkle blues of the palette are not found in any country's flag. They fill
the building and the publications and soon will fill the street and venues
of competition. Although most employees were expecting red, white, and
blue as the colors, the festive federal look of colorful bars, stars, and
confetti has caught on and is evident even in crudely made employee
notices for parties. Indeed, one large staff party not officially related to the
LAOOC called itself "Venuization Sensation" (for the process of sending
employees permanently out to the competition venues for the duration of
the Games) and required all people attending to wear a minimum of three
festive federal colors. In attendance at the party was Sam the Eagle, the
Disney-created official mascot of the 1984 Games. Party-goers, out of the
work environment, took special pains to continue the mood and look of the
Olympics. The organizational culture has become powerful quickly.

Also in an effort to use the staff to spread Olympic awareness throughout
the community, the LAOOC has a company store. The store has a variety
of Olympic paraphernalia available at terrific discounts. Many sponsors
such as Converse shoes, Vuarnet sunglasses, and Sony consumer electron-
ics have made their products available to Olympics staff and volunteers at
dealer cost. Although these bigger-ticket items are reserved for staff only,
employees are encouraged to purchase the Olympic trinkets to give away.
The major item in this category is Olympic pins, which have spawned an
intense trading process that accompanies every Olympics. For the 1984
Olympics, approximately 400 approved pins have been developed, and
many staff members have become serious collectors. Pin trading can
become quite vicious, with incidents of hoarding and swindling. The *Los
Angeles Times* actually devoted a lengthy article to "pin fever."

There is a strictly enforced security policy that prohibits cameras in the
building. Many staff members have expressed a desire to photograph the
sprawling and colorful offices for their own mementos, but have been
unable to do so. The first photograph of the interior I was able to show
anyone was in an article in *Time* magazine. Similarly, the offices are
constantly full of television cameras shooting documentary footage, interviews, and reports. It seems ironic to disallow camera use by staff, and
complaints are frequent.

As the end of the organization's tenure draws near, and with it the staff's
jobs, one of the most common topics of conversation is future plans. People
are understandably distressed. Severance pay is being offered to employees
of six months' duration or more, but that does not ease the tension. When
Peter Ueberroth announced that he would be accepting the job of Commis-

sioner of Baseball after the Games, the administration hoped it would be an inspiration to employees looking for ways to combine their Olympics responsibilities with previous job experience. Instead, animosity developed to the point that the administration instituted a job placement service. The service collected resumes from all who were interested, and convinced a number of sponsors to hold currently available jobs open until after the Olympics so staff members could fill them. Predictably, the only jobs currently being offered by the Job Opportunity Office are for data processors, secretaries, and security guards, leaving the vast majority of employees, who were told they were the "cream of the crop," on their own.

Departmental Culture and Interaction

In joining a large organization like the LAOOC, the anchor and key socializing unit seems to be the department. With so many new employees constantly coming on board, few people can keep track of many names beyond their own department. I joined the Design Department, and without the overt activities planned by the administration to stimulate organizational unity and common purpose, I would have become completely loyal to the Design Department alone.

Projects move along at a brisk pace at the Olympic committee, but deadlines seem to move faster. The Design Department, as a service provider, is at the tail end of the project production process, and therefore suffers from the delays of others to an acute degree. The department consists of 11 people, who are completely responsible for maintaining a consistent visual image in all printed material for the Olympic Games. There is no doubt that people are overworked, but so are the majority of the Olympic staff. The department interacts with virtually every department in the organization, sometimes on an adversarial level, dealing with design, budgets, deadlines, purchasing, and constant changes and delays. The people in design are on the whole more creative and potentially more volatile than other department staffs. Conflicts are inevitable, and all parties are constantly reminding each other that we are all on the same side—that is, a spectacular event is the bottom line.

The most common method of dealing with the overwhelmingly tense and stressful environment is through humor. The whole department laughs a lot at stories, situations, and silly practical jokes that reflect the organization. While showing reams of files to client departments, you will run across a huge plastic cockroach or a particularly trashy *Singles Register* porno magazine. The momentary shock and embarrassment are relieved by the hysterical laughter of co-workers watching your expression. When Olympic staff rings looking much like high school rings were offered, the plastic ring-sizer for fingers ended up being circulated through interoffice mail with an official-looking memo asking the recipient to measure another appendage and report immediately to Thelma in Health Services. For people balancing an average of 30 immediately pending projects per day, this level of humor is a catharsis.

The design staff tends to sit together at lunch causing a scene with loud laughter, and reveling in its position as the only group engaging in raucous behavior. Every small department within the LAOOC must have a sense that it is the sole possessor of reason, commitments, and integrity. The Design Department is no exception. It is also the sole possessor of a camera within the building, a Polaroid, presumably for design documentation but used more frequently for ridiculous staff portraits (for instance, with push pins seemingly stuck into foreheads) or photos imitating our boss, the Design Director.

As in many organizations, complaining about the boss is a frequent pastime. The Design Director has a distinct voice that is eminently imitable. At least once an hour, someone will loudly imitate a "Huh?". The current Design Director is the third in that position since the LAOOC was formed. To its credit, the committee hired him after he had written a lengthy, scathing, but very accurate expose in a major national design magazine of the failings of the LAOOC in handling the look of the Games correctly. The former Design Director had quit in frustration after complaining that by submitting design work to top management for review, "major design decisions are being made by two lawyers and a color-blind travel agent!" (Jones, Moore, & Snyder, 1988, p. 8). It is reportedly true that Peter Ueberroth is color-blind and, as the former president of a travel agency, has no professional design expertise. With the new Design Director, the policy was changed to keep artistic and creative decisions within the department trained to deal with them.

The vaunted precision of the Design Department is a problem when dealing with other departments. While publicly defending the Olympics and the LAOOC at every turn, the design staff does seem to derive a quiet pleasure in seeing the incompetence of other departments. When a "trial-run" shooting tournament was held a month ago, the news that someone had forgotten to bring the ammunition, forcing competitors and spectators to wait around for several hours, was met by ill-concealed glee from those in the Design Department who had dealt with the shooting department's neglect of deadlines. Similarly, the recent failure of the ticketing machines at the grand opening of ticketing centers was met with "I told you so's" from design staff.

The department functions efficiently from an organizational standpoint, because all staff members will work together diligently most of the time. Certain rituals of language and action keep everyone working on an even keel. Just when tensions are running highest, someone will slide in a wheeled typing chair across the department, imitating a luge in the Winter Olympics. Alternatively, someone will loudly say, "No budget? No problem," reacting to our most common dilemma. On mornings when the fever pitch begins immediately after people walk in the door, someone will inevitably say at 9:00 a.m., "Is it lunch yet?" And lastly, when a particularly nasty project is assigned, a coordinator will sarcastically intone, "Make my day."

Organizational Efforts to Create a Culture

The Los Angeles Olympic Organizing Committee has no problem finding appropriate ways to inspire the staff. Celebrities and the media pay a great deal of attention to the dealings of the committee, and every staff member can share the feeling of being in the center of attention. It is certainly an unusual job that presents its employees the opportunity to read about their staff meetings as front-page news.

The symbols exist. The problem is in communicating them to the staff in a manner that involves everyone and generates a shared purpose. The most effective means the LAOOC has used is without a doubt the "staff meeting," which includes every employee and volunteer. Every two to three weeks, loudspeakers are turned up throughout the building to announce an important guest who will address the staff. The result is sometimes pandemonium, as when it was announced the morning after the California presidential primary that Jesse Jackson would be addressing the staff in five minutes behind the building. Evacuation officers were used to get the crowd calmly out the back doors. Other recent speakers have included Howard Cosell and Tom Bradley. Most of these meetings are casual, but the largest, most formal gatherings are real production masterpieces.

My first experience in a large staff meeting was a hastily prepared effort to let the staff know the latest news on the Olympic boycott by the Soviets. Many people heard radio reports on their way to work, and the news spread like wildfire throughout the staff. Many people's projects were directly affected by the pullout. A memo went around in the morning telling staff not to discuss the incident by phone. At noon, the executive vice president called everyone to the central bullpen area, where the entire staff stood around people's desks watching a small stage. The executive vice president read aloud the exact wording of the Soviet news release and expressed a great deal of hope that they would reconsider. He then quickly changed the subject to the morning's launch of the torch relay and gave an inspiring talk about teamwork and the increased importance of the work we were all doing. The staff stumbled back to their desks, tentatively hopeful.

I attended an orientation meeting at the USC McDonald's Swim Stadium for all people who would be staffing the pool and the USC Olympic Village during the Games. There were approximately 5,000 people in attendance. Fifteen different people gave two-minute speeches, standing on the pool deck surrounded by the flags of every competing nation. Their talks were informative, but the crowd really came alive when they were treated to a demonstration by the world champion synchronized swimming team. The performance was so glorious that the participants suddenly realized what their Olympic role meant. As I looked around, many people were crying, clapping, and screaming for more. It was a stirring sight.

The Jesse Jackson staff meeting was not exciting for political reasons. Most of the staff are probably staunch Republicans, but their enthusiasm was generated by his "star" status. As the staff waited in the hot sun for his helicopter to land on the roof, they eyed the stage set up next to the cafeteria. Many comments were heard like, "He's probably going to announce the luncheon special." "No, he's going to tell us to eat before 11:30 or after 1:00 to avoid the rush." The poised television cameras added to the excitement.

When the Reverend Jackson arrived, the crowd went wild. It was not an ordinary staff meeting. Peter Ueberroth talked about Jackson's role in negotiating with the Russians. Jackson spoke at length about the symbolic role the Olympics play in world peace and harmony. He spoke of the importance of athletics in increasing the self-esteem of minorities. He was given a torch from the torch relay by the granddaughter of the legendary Jesse Owens. He ran in place with it, smiling for the television cameras. The crowd shrieked. They happily stampeded back into the building. Although Jesse Jackson had nothing to do with any of the staff's projects, the affirmation of the purpose and importance of our task was well-timed.

The most inspirational and largest staff meeting by far was orchestrated to coincide with the anniversary of the date the Games were awarded to

Los Angeles. The boosterism behind the meeting was transparent, but the meeting was terribly effective by doing exactly what it set out to do—make the staff feel part of the organization, and a part of history.

The staff was herded into the normally forbidding and drab warehouse. It had been transformed. Banners, bunting, and festive federal columns disguised the walls. A huge stage with a grand piano and movie screen had been constructed at one end and the entire room was filled with white wooden chairs. As each staff member entered, he or she was handed a specially designed, festive federal commemorative mug half full of champagne. Heroic music was playing that turned out to be the first presentation of the music that will be used for opening and closing ceremonies. The Director of Human Resources led us in a toast to the anniversary and to the fact that this was the first time alcohol had ever been served at a staff function.

A fellow staff member sang several songs she had written, accompanied on the piano by a man dressed like a combination of Michael Jackson and Liberace. The crowd groaned at the signs of a homespun talent show, but the woman's songs were surprisingly funny, singing about the L.A. "Oh Oh" C., being "venuized" and making nasty innuendoes about top management personalities. We saw the brand new orientation film that is a tear-jerker, heard from former Olympic medal winners, and were introduced to a lovely old woman who had been an organizer of the 1932 Los Angeles Olympics and is now volunteering five days a week for the current Games. The staff could see the commitment that the Olympics would inspire and gave the woman a five-minute standing ovation. Many were crying by this time. The executive vice president spoke in very human terms about the Games and the staff's role and told funny stories about the LAOOC's beginnings.

Finally, a vice president who had been on the road for several days with the torch relay as it ran through small towns throughout the East and Midwest shared a few of his favorite moments. As he told about the runner going over a winding road in the hills of West Virginia and encountering a man standing alone on the top of a hill with a trumpet playing "America the Beautiful" as the torch passed, there was not a dry eye in the house. The speaker himself broke down, overcome by emotion, and could not continue for several minutes. The staff filed out to the strains of ceremonial music, clutching their commemorative mugs and pins reading "Team '84" that were handed to them at the exit.

Conclusion

The fleeting nature of the Los Angeles Olympic Organizing Committee compressed the time available for the natural development of an organizational culture. The management made the conscious decision that it would use all available historical and ceremonial resources to provide its employees with a common sense of identity as rapidly as possible. This intense environment proved to be a fertile field for symbolic interaction and expressive behavior.

The focus appeared to be on inspiring individuals to strive for a common goal, rather than encouraging group interaction for the same purpose. This was sensible, because beyond the Games there would be no need for these people to interact, and long-range behavior modification was unnecessary. As long as each individual was motivated to perform at her or his peak for the duration of the Games, and retained pleasant memories of having "played a part in history," the human resources role of the Olympics was successful.

The LAOOC is not necessarily a model of how to organize and generate traditions, loyalty, and dedication. But it is certainly an example of the creation of organizational culture in the short run—of how beliefs, stories, jokes, rituals, and ceremonies arose out of an unusual combination of circumstances, both orchestrated and spontaneous.

3

Semiotics and the Study of Occupational and Organizational Culture

STEPHEN R. BARLEY

Organizational theorists often claim that culture is best understood as a set of assumptions or an interpretive framework that undergirds daily life in an organization or occupation. However, despite such theoretical pronouncements, few organizational researchers have actually bothered to study the deep structure of a work setting. Instead, most have focused on symbolic phenomena that lie on the surface of everyday life: stories, myths, logos, heroes, and assorted other verbal or physical artifacts. For this reason, cultural research typically belabors the obvious while failing to reveal the core of the interpretive system that lends a culture its coherence.

One explanation for this state of affairs may be that researchers trained primarily in psychology and sociology simply lack the theoretical and empirical tools that would enable them to study a culture's interpretive core. Structural anthropology and the field of semiotics offer one such set of tools.[1] The purpose of this chapter is to demonstrate how ethnosemantic and semiotic analysis can be used to identify and analyze the *sine qua non* of any cultural system: redundancies of interpretation and practice. The research itself charts a portion of the culture of an occupation that eventually touches the lives of many Americans, the occupation of funeral directing.

AUTHOR'S NOTE: This chapter was originally published in 1983 under the same title in *Administrative Science Quarterly, 23*, 393-413. Excerpts from pages 399-410 of that volume are reprinted here with permission from *Administrative Science Quarterly*.

An Approach to Collecting Semiotic Data

The study extended over a three-month period, during which I observed and conducted multiple interviews in a community-oriented funeral home in a metropolitan neighborhood of an eastern-seaboard city. The funeral home was operated by two brothers who were both funeral directors and who had inherited their business from their father, the home's founder. They employed two apprentices and approximately ten part-time pallbearers. The home drew most of its clientele from the surrounding community, which was populated by individuals of Catholic faith and Irish, Italian, Polish, and Lithuanian descent. Consequently, the business was weighted toward traditional Catholic funerals and exemplified a form of organization that Pine (1975) called the "professional service model" of funeral directing and Habenstein (1962) termed "the local funeral home." Since my purpose was to discover how a funeral director understands funeral work, I chose to limit my work to one home and to make semantic codes rather than funeral work or funeral homes per se the focus of analysis.

The initial task was to uncover the basic units of semiotic analysis: signs that have relevance for funeral directors.[2] However, because the theory presumes that anything can function as a sign, I faced the problem of discovering which signs are germane to the funeral director's understanding of his work.[3] Moreover, because I sought signs with the ultimate objective of delineating the structure of codes, it was imperative to devise a research strategy to identify groups of signs that the informants considered relevant and related. The solution to this methodological problem was initially to employ a broad ethnographic approach that progressively came to pivot on the use of ethnosemantic techniques to create semantic taxonomies and trees.[4] The data collection progressed through three analytically distinct, but actually overlapping, phases.

During the earliest weeks of the research, I familiarized myself with the funeral home and funeral work by combining observation in the funeral home with interviews of the funeral directors. Because I was primarily concerned with the funeral director's interpretations of objects, events, and actions, I considered observation to be subservient to the interviews and, therefore, drew on observation primarily to generate topics for discussion. All interviews were taped and transcribed within 36 hours of the interview to ensure that elicited interpretations were preserved accurately and available for planning subsequent interviews. As the body of interview data accumulated, lengthy interviews became the central tactic of data collection, and observation became less and less important.

The first interviews were broad-ranging, loosely structured discussions that covered such general topics as the director's career, the history of the family's business, the nature of the home's clientele, the layout and decor of the home, and overviews of various funeral tasks such as preparing a body or making a removal. The interview strategy was to introduce a topic and then to encourage the director to speak for as long as possible by requesting elaboration of points the informant might make in the course of the interview. To move the informants toward monologues about their work, I assumed a nondirective style of interrogation and employed techniques of client-centered therapy: paraphrase, reflection, summary, and minimal encouragements to speak. By allowing the flow of the early interviews to be directed by the informant, I strove to minimize the effect of my own conceptions on the structuring of the talk in order to capture the funeral director's own interpretations as they organized his accounts of funeral work.

After the first several weeks of interviews, the transcripts were analyzed to discover domains of objects, events, and action into which the funeral directors seemed to segment the flow of their work. Spradley (1979) offered the following definition of a domain: "Any symbolic category which includes other categories . . . all members of which will share at least one feature of meaning" (p. 100). The "one feature of meaning" is generally guaranteed by the cover term that labels the domain. Among the 56 domains identified for further investigation were the following: "types of funeral home furnishings," "phases of a funeral," "types of removals," "stages of restoration," and "kinds of clients." At that point in time, most of the domains were only partially elaborated. For example, I knew that funeral directors spoke of "hospital removals," but I did not know that "home removals" and "nursing home removals" existed and that these contrast with hospital removals within the domain, "types of removals." Consequently, during the second phase of the research, I used the analysis of previous transcripts to formulate interview schedules to elicit the categories and subcategories that composed each domain. Thus, interviews became more structured, and as the domains were elaborated, my interview strategy began to include ethnosemantic questioning techniques formally known as "question frames" (e.g., "What kinds of W's are there?" "Is X a type of equipment essential for a wake?" "Is Y a phase of the funeral?" "Is Z part of restoration?"). Question frames elicit data from which semantic trees or taxonomies for each of the domains can be constructed. (See Kay, 1969, for a brief, but superb, discussion of semantic trees and taxonomies.)

Using Glaser and Strauss's (1967) notion of saturation, I considered a domain to be elaborated when, after several interviews, I could no longer elicit any new elements that a funeral director would include in that domain. The items composing a domain were then written on 3×5 cards to form Q-sort decks. The Q-sorts were used for two purposes. By giving an informant the cards for a specific semantic domain along with instructions to sort the cards into "piles that make sense," the structure of the taxonomy or tree was verified or, if necessary, modified. Secondly, by asking the informant to explain his rationale for the groups so formed, dimensions were elicited along which the informant compared and contrasted items in the domain, thereby yielding what ethnosemanticists term an attribute analysis. Once a domain is mapped in terms of a structural and attribute analysis, the researcher not only possesses a phenomenologically related collection of signs (e.g., items in the domain), but also the informant's interpretations of the items, which become the data base for analyzing the semiotic processes that structure the items into a system of signs or a denotative code.[5]

As the domains multiply and become saturated, commonalities among particular domains emerge. In my experience, the commonalities first appeared as stock interpretations that informants used to justify, subsume, and order the activities, objects, and events that compose diverse domains. For example, typical interpretations that the funeral directors used to justify their activities included the following: "convenience versus inconvenience," "putting people at ease," and the "naturalness or unnaturalness" of certain presentational ploys. These reflexive, subsuming, and recurring interpretations are the basic data from which connotative codes were mapped during the third and final phase of the research. These interpretations resemble themes that suggest that widely divergent domains are somehow quite similar in the funeral director's view of the world.

When mapping the structure of a connotative code, the researcher must ascertain whether a common pattern of signification leads the informant to interpret each item in a particular domain similarly. One technique for such a mapping is to create new question frames that use the themes as invariants (e.g., "Is X a way to put people at ease?") and other frames that treat the themes as variables ("What are all the ways you try to X?"). A second technique to verify the overarching interpretations given to a domain involves focusing on each individual object, act, or event that composes each domain. Based on an understanding of the attributes of each item, I proposed to the informant another item or behavior that appeared to possess attributes opposite to the item of concern and then noted how this changed the informant's interpretations. Because each item was tested to ensure that it elicited the same thematic interpretation, discussions of the signs composing a given domain were staggered across time to monitor the consistency of the accounts collected.

When two or more separate domains evoke the same connotations, the researcher has evidence to justify the hypothesis that the domains represent diverse denotative codes that are created by similar signifying processes. The remainder of this chapter will elaborate how such structural similarity gives rise to parallelisms of meaning across quite diverse arenas of action and thereby produces the consistency necessary for attributing an occupational or organizational perspective.

The Semiotics of Funeral Work

For the funeral director, the typical case consists of a series of events: taking the call, removing the body, making arrangements with the family, embalming and preparing the body, holding a wake, holding a funeral, and, finally, interment. There are a number of analytically distinct types of complications that can disrupt the smooth flow of such events. For the purpose of this discussion, however, we need only consider those complications that are understood to arise out of mourners' expressive behaviors and are deemed "uncontrollable" in that they are not open to the funeral director's direct intervention. From the funeral director's point of view, acutely expressive behavior can interrupt the pacing of funeral events, upset the "dignity" of the scene, and thereby hamper his work. Expressive behaviors are unresponsive to planning, scripting, or routinization, and their probability cannot be predicted with accuracy. Nevertheless, funeral directors do attempt to divert such disruptions by influencing participants' perceptions in ways that they think might render the emotional tone of the funeral scenes more manageable. Because his role is not the role of priest or counselor, the funeral director seeks to moderate stress by making funeral scenes appear more "natural" or "normal."

When funeral directors speak of "naturalness" as a quality to be attained in a particular funeral scene, they refer to the desirability of arranging cues or creating a set of signs to mitigate perceptions of death that they believe might disturb participants. Falling death rates, the shift toward holding wakes in funeral parlors rather than in private homes, and hospitalization of the terminally ill have distanced Americans from death during the 20th century. Moreover, we rarely have occasion to attend a funeral until late in life. Consequently, funeral scenes are unfamiliar, and the sight of the deceased's body can trigger unpredictable behavior. The funeral director seeks to create the appearance of normality or naturalness whenever the living are in the presence of the dead. This intention underlies strategies that organize the execution of many different activities; for example, preparation of the body, removal of the deceased from a home, and choice of the funeral home's decor.

Code of Posed Features

Perhaps the most significant occasion when the body is present in the midst of the living occurs when the corpse is "laid out" for a wake. To make the "viewing" more palatable, the funeral director or an apprentice "prepares the remains." Preparation refers to two broad categories of procedures designed to simulate a lifelike appearance: (1) embalming, replacing the corpse's blood with a preservative fluid; and (2) restoration, which includes posing the corpse's features, applying cosmetics, clothing the corpse, and positioning it in the casket. The latter activities involve creating a set of signs to communicate to funeral participants the image of a restfully sleeping person. Hence, we may speak of a code of posed features, a cosmetic code, a clothing code, and a code of positions. However, here I will consider only the first of the codes because my intent is to illustrate the similarity of codes across, rather than within, domains of action.

After cleansing the body, the funeral director "poses" the deceased's features by closing the eyes and mouth. Because the corpse's face will be viewed most closely at the wake, posing should do more than simply hide a death stare or counteract rigor mortis' opening of the mouth; it should also simulate the visage of a sleeping person. Consequently, funeral directors distinguish among methods for posing the corpse's features on the basis of the quality of the signs they produce. For example, there are two ways to close a corpse's eyes, the "abutting" and "overlap" methods. When using the overlap method, the funeral director lays the upper eyelid over the lower eyelid, whereas with the abutting method he joins the eyelids at their edges. Although the overlap method requires less time and skill, funeral directors prefer the abutting method for open viewings because it more closely approximates the visual configuration achieved when living persons close their eyes.

In everyday life we have all had occasion to wonder if someone is asleep. To make such a judgment, we look for indices that we take as signs of sleep: Are the person's eyes closed? Is breathing occurring? Is the person reclining? Are there other contextual cues, such as a pillow, that suggest intent to sleep? Moreover, we might distinguish between light, peaceful sleep and heavy, fitful sleep by noticing how heavily the person is breathing and whether the person's mouth is open or closed. If the person is reclining and breathing lightly with mouth and eyes shut, we will probably infer that the individual is sleeping peacefully. Notice, however, that any one of these indices is insufficient to justify the inference. There are numerous instances when individuals recline, breathe lightly, close their mouths, or shut their eyes without sleeping. Rather, it is the juxtaposition (metonymy) of all these signs under the proposition of a sleeping person that allows any one of them to carry the meaning of peaceful sleep.[6]

In posing a corpse's features the funeral director seeks to recreate metaphorically the system of metonymical signs that we take as indices of peaceful sleep. The code is metaphorical because the signs are created on the face of a corpse which, in its unposed state, might be signified by a stare, an open mouth, and the absence of breathing. The code of posed features is diagrammed as a structural schematic in Figure 3.1. As the diagram suggests, the code of posed features is built on a basic opposition between two semantic domains: living, sleeping persons and dead persons (represented by the two major blocks of the diagram). Hence, in the everyday world (as in Figure 3.1), an unposed corpse and a sleeping person are marked by antithetical attributes (open vs. closed mouth, light breathing vs. no breathing, etc.). Yet the purpose of posing is to suggest that corpses and sleeping people have attributes in common. Thus posing creates a metaphor by arranging for the corpse to be associated with cues (expressions) normally associated with peaceful sleep (content). Therefore, in terms of the diagram, the corpse in its posed state presumably shifts semantic domains to become aligned with its opposite.

The code also functions by metonymy. Not only are the posed features juxtaposed to one another so that each reinforces the other's message, but they are also intended to override those attributions of sleeping persons that the funeral director cannot simulate (e.g., breathing, rapid eye movement). The first metonymical structure is similar to melodic contiguity and is schematically portrayed in Figure 3.1 as a vertical stack of expressions (abutting method, mouth closed, reclining), each of which is presumably linked to the content "peaceful sleep." The second metonymical structure, a quality for quantity metaphor similar to using "crown" to signify "king," appears in the diagram in that the metonymical stack of expressions associated with the "posed corpse" is "shorter" than the stack associated with the "living, sleeping person."

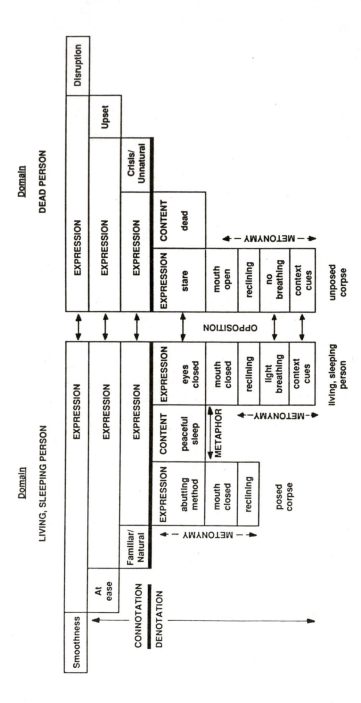

Figure 3.1. Diagram of Code of Posed Features

Thus at the first level of signification (the denotative level or the lower portion of the diagram), the code of posed features is a metonymical array of metaphorical signs for another metonymical array of indices used in everyday life. The code shifts the corpse from one semantic domain to another and, therefore, suggests that opposites are similar. The code's rule might be stated as: Manipulate a corpse's facial features to simulate metaphorically the metonymical system of expressions used as typical indices of sleep.

The denotations are intended to produce a flawless funeral. The funeral director intends not only that funeral participants read the metonymical metaphors as signifying peaceful sleep, but also that these signs will suggest, in turn, a "familiarity" or "naturalness" that will put the participants "at ease." From the funeral director's point of view, participants who are at ease are less likely to disrupt a smoothly flowing funeral. This series of interpretations that the funeral director associates with the posing of features is diagrammed as the connotative code in Figure 3.1. Note that at each successive level the connotations are directly antithetical to interpretations the funeral director presumes would be elicited by a corpse whose features had not been posed (the connotative code of each semantic domain is opposed). Only by such an oppositional structure does the code of posed features make sense. Signs have no meaning unless they are contrasted with other signs in a system.[7]

Code of Furnishings

Given that the espoused goal of restoration is to present a viewable corpse, one might expect that the posing and positioning of the corpse, the use of cosmetics, and the choice of clothing would build toward a common end. Therefore, the underlying codes might be expected to signify similarly. However, the funeral director's desire to build impressions of familiarity and naturalness extend beyond the domain of preparations. Recognizing that the funeral home is alien for the average individual, the funeral director chooses a decor and plans the architecture of the home to play down perceptions of the unfamiliar and to dissociate the home from the church environment. In fact, the funeral home is said to be an "extension of the person's home" and the strategy of design is explained as follows:

> Your basic idea is to give them some place comfortable and pleasing to the eye to come to . . . (you hope that) they can enjoy being here for a period of time

because of the decor, forgetting about what they're here for. At least it gives them something to look at. (Barley, 1983a, p. 397)

Each chapel in the home is furnished with comfortable stuffed chairs and couches similar to those found in the living rooms of private homes. Although the design of the furniture is not ultramodern, neither are the pieces Victorian. The furniture is upholstered in light colors and the carpets of the rooms match the upholstery. Positioned among the chairs and couches are end tables, with table lamps, and coffee tables. The furniture is grouped in small clusters that create conversational niches. The paintings on the walls of the chapels depict spring and summer landscapes. In fact, the only overly religious symbols are the crucifix that hangs above the casket and the spiritual stand, both of which are used in Catholic funerals. Each chapel opens into a larger, similarly furnished smoking room where smokers can congregate. The smoking room provides ample space for participants to gather, with the corpse out of sight.

Figure 3.2 maps the code of furnishings. The structural analogies between the furnishing code and the code of posed features are readily apparent from the diagram. The code builds on a presumed familiarity with the appearance of typical living rooms and churches. Obviously, the funeral director's conception of what his clients take to be the typical furnishings of a church and a living room are bound by tacit assumptions about the religion and social class of his clientele. As before, the code has both metaphoric and metonymical properties. The metaphor implies that a funeral parlor has more in common with a typical home than it does with a church, even though, like the latter, it is a setting for the rituals of death. Like a living room, and unlike a church, a funeral parlor offers the opportunity to sit comfortably and converse with other participants, as well as the option of avoiding religious reminders. Moreover, the individual signs reinforce each other, as well as the metaphor, by the juxtaposition in space. The spatial configuration of the furnishings is intended to obfuscate the necessary trappings of a funeral home that the funeral director cannot eliminate. When sitting in carefully arranged clusters of chairs or when frequenting the smoking room, one can avoid confronting the corpse.

The denotative codes of furnishings is built on the following rule: Choose a decor to devise an array of indices commonly associated with living rooms and combine this metonymical array with an appropriate color scheme to imply metaphorically that funeral chapels and living rooms have something in common. The first level of signification is intended to connote a sense of familiarity that is opposed to the ritualistic

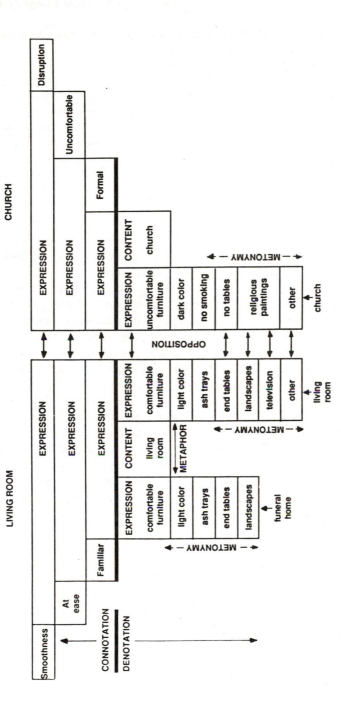

Figure 3.2. Diagram of Furnishing Code

49

formality of a church-like setting. The funeral director presumes that participants are, therefore, led by the decor to feel more relaxed and, hence, are less likely to behave in ways that might disrupt the smooth flow of the funeral.

The connotative significations of the furnishing code are identical to those the funeral director attributes to the code of posed features. Apparently the two denotative codes evidence the same connotative system, since the expressions and contents of the signs are coupled by similar conventions. Just as two words can be denotative synonyms, so two codes can be connotatively synonymous.

Codes of Removals

The code of posed features and the code of furnishing are both systems of signs intended to influence the perceptions and behaviors of bereaved persons actually visiting the funeral home. The funeral home is not the only setting, however, where funeral participants or outsiders can come into contact with the corpse or observe the funeral director and his staff performing the more unpleasant aspects of funeral work. Such a situation may occur when removing the body from the place of death.

On the basis of the context of the death, the funeral director distinguishes between three major types of removals: hospital removals, nursing home removals, and home removals. Hospital removals present little difficulty for a funeral home's staff because hospitals are prepared to handle deaths expediently and most maintain morgue facilities that enable the funeral director or his staff to remove the body at their own discretion and under circumstances in which their activity is unlikely to be observed by people unaccustomed to death. Nursing home and private home removals are more difficult, however, not only because they require immediate attention or because their architecture and lack of refrigeration facilities are likely to complicate the funeral staff's activities, but because there is a good chance that uninitiated onlookers will be on the scene. These complications are most likely in the case of a home removal.

Individuals who die at home by way of a sudden heart attack or accident usually are first attended by an ambulance squad who typically transport the body to a hospital for an autopsy, after which the funeral director makes the removal from the hospital. Hence, most home removals occur when an individual dies in bed during sleep or after being confined to bed by an illness. Upon discovering the body, the family typically notifies relatives and friends so that by the time the funeral staff arrives on the scene a number of people may have gathered. In making a home removal, the funeral director's primary objective is to get the body from the house as quickly as possible, without attracting undue attention to the work, and to limit the survivor's awareness of what has happened.

Upon arriving at the scene, the funeral director finds out where the body is located and then persuades one member of the family or a friend to gather the rest of the onlookers in a room away from the scene of death. Typically the funeral director suggests they adjourn to the kitchen for a cup of coffee. Having positioned the onlookers away from the scene, the funeral staff moves whatever furniture is necessary to provide open access for the litter, but the path is also cleared to assure that no unwanted noise might be caused by bumping the stretcher into pieces of furniture. Noises are avoided to guard against, among other things, the perception that the staff has dropped the body.

In addition to removing the body, the staff makes adjustments to the room. Closed shades or curtains are opened to allow sunlight into the room, and windows are opened during the removal to allow fresh air to remove any odors. The bedding is stripped from the bed and folded—except when the corpse has stained the sheets, in which case the funeral staff removes them along with the body. Sometimes the bed is actually remade without the sheets and the room is tidied.

The strategic rearrangement of the room is based on a code that is intended to reconstruct what the room may have looked like before it became a death room and to suggest that a removal did not occur. The code presumes that clean, unoccupied bedrooms are characterized by a metonymical array of signs: open shades, fresh air, order, made beds, and sunlight. On the other hand, sick rooms are known by an array of opposite attributes (see Figure 3.3). By reconstructing this system of metonymical signs, the funeral staff attempts to create an icon, a metaphor, that compares the death room to a clean, unoccupied room. At least for the funeral director, rooms of the latter type are understood to be more normal than death rooms. Hence, the removal code operates by the very same mechanisms as do the codes the funeral director employs in the funeral home. Thus the structure of the code as it is schematically portrayed in Figure 3.3 is identical to the structure of the two codes discussed earlier. The fewer the reminders of death and the removal, the more smoothly the removal may proceed.

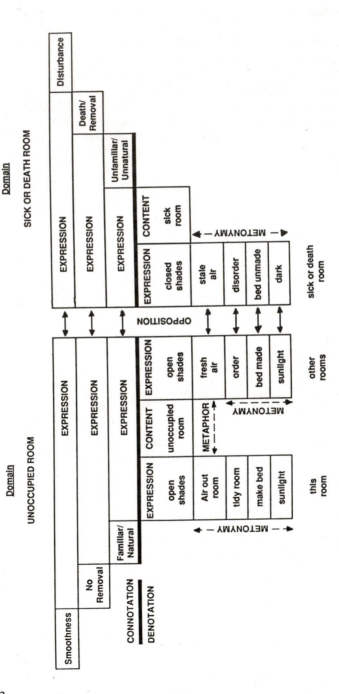

Figure 3.3. Diagram of Removal Code

52

Conclusion

One sometimes senses that organizational theorists lay too heavy an emphasis on overtly symbolic phenomena as indicators of cultural processes. Clearly, logos, stories, colorful terms, and arcane rituals are symbolic in nature, and it is reasonable to identify and study them. From the semiotic perspective, however, terms, tales, and totems are but lit candles hovering above both the icing and cake of culture. A semiotics of culture urges the realization that anything can be an expressive sign capable of signification. Once we recognize the pervasiveness of signification, we are no longer constrained to look for cultural phenomena in the overtly symbolic and can focus on how members of an organization or occupation interpret a wide range of phenomena including chairs, air, and sunlight— entities so mundane as to appear irrelevant to the well-intentioned but culturally ignorant researcher.

Notes

1. Semiotics is an eclectic and amorphous field that traces its roots to the teachings of Ferdinand de Saussure (1966), the father of modern structural linguistics and to the pragmatic philosophy of Charles Peirce (1958). As such its practitioners included linguists, literary critics, anthropologists, and a small number of interpretive sociologists. Defined as the study of signs or systems of signs (codes), semiotics concerns the principles by which signification occurs. Signification refers to both the processes by which events, words, behaviors, and objects carry meaning for members of a given community and the content they carry.

2. In semiotics, a sign is understood to be the relationship between or the union of a *sign-vehicle* (an expression or form such as a word, sound, or colored light) and the *signified,* the content or message conveyed by the sign-vehicle. The link between expression and content is arbitrary in the sense that it is a convention of the group to which the sign's users belong. A system of signs constitutes a code. A code can be decomposed into four elements: (a) a set of expressions, (b) a set of contents, (c) rules for coupling expressions to contents, and (d) a set of alternative responses contingent on the combination (Eco, 1976, pp. 36-47). The last element is crucial for the study of cultures since its inclusion transforms the definition of a code from that of a set of signs into a general model for social action: behavior becomes a function of interpretations of a situation.

3. Since funeral directing is an occupation populated by males (Pine, 1975), the masculine form of the third person pronoun will be used throughout the discussion to underscore the occupation's demography.

4. Ethnosemantics, as developed by the early cognitive anthropologists, consists of a set of eliciting techniques designed first to bring to the surface the relevant lexemes in a given semantic domain of the language of the people under study, and then to map the semantic attributes of each lexeme. Cognitive anthropologists hold that the resulting semantic structures correspond to the cultural rules members use to categorize facets of their physical or social world. Anthropologists have used ethnosemantic techniques to portray the rules governing the use of

color categories (Conklin, 1955), disease terms (Frake, 1961), and especially kinship terms (Goodenough, 1956; Lounsbury, 1956, 1969). The interested reader should consult Frake (1964), Metzger and Williams (1963), Tyler (1969) and especially Spradley (1979) for a detailed explanation of classic ethnosemantic techniques.

5. A denotative code refers to the "literal" meaning of a sign or the sign's most proximal interpretation. Denotations are what dictionaries typically offer. A "connotative code" refers to a sign's "excess" meaning: a connotation is what a sign implies for the members of some community. Thus, if I say that my friend is a "Republican" you will know that he is a member of a specific political party, the term's denotation. However, you are also likely to derive from my statement a number of interpretations or inferences about my friend's social beliefs. Hence, the term "Republican" connotes as well as denotes.

6. Signs signify by metonymy when expressions are related to contents by contiguity or juxtaposition. The classic definition of *metonymy* in rhetoric is: a quality or aspect standing for the entity of which it is an attribute. Hence, by metonymy we use "crown" to signify "king." Signs whose expressions are naturally associated with their contents (as smoke stands for fire) also signify by metonymy. *Metaphor* is signification by similarity or analogy. When a crown is used to signify a brand of margarine, it is used metaphorically to suggest that both objects share regal qualities. The crucial difference between metonymy and metaphor as semiotic processes can be summarized by the following rule of thumb: Metonymical signification occurs when expression and content are both part of the same domain or context; metaphorical significations mixes domains or contexts.

7. Opposition is a critical concept in semiotics. The mechanism of opposition suggests that we know what something means, in part, by knowing what it does not mean. For example, the word "up" has no meaning without the opposed concept of "down."

IB
The Differentiation Perspective

An integration study's claims of organization-wide unity are not fully attentive to alternative points of view. In contrast, according to Martin and Meyerson, a differentiation study views organizational cultures as a mosaic of inconsistencies. Meanings are sometimes shared, yes, but primarily within subcultural boundaries. Within these boundaries, all is clear. Ambiguities appear only in the interstices between subcultures.

The four chapters in this section exemplify the differentiation perspective. In Chapter 4, John Van Maanen looks with skepticism beneath the apparently benign and beguiling surface of the "Happiest Place on Earth." According to this account, several groups of Disneyland employees saw themselves as distinct: bilingual tour guides, ride operators whose work required special skills (such as jungle boat narration or driving an expensive vehicle), operators of rides requiring less skill, lowly sweepers, and those relegated to serving coke and peanuts. Each of these subcultures was further differentiated, as gender, class, and organizational status were reflected in complex patterns of interaction. Maintaining these subcultural boundaries required work. For example, the operators of the yellow submarines devised inventive ways to escape the attention of their all-too-vigilant supervisors and created wet "accidents" to punish rude customers.

Management attempted to control these deviant forms of employee behavior, for example through classroom orientations to "Disneyland Corporate Culture." These control attempts were often met with disdain; clearly they were not completely successful. Claims of harmony and the appearance of homogeneity (everyone smiling, dressed in clean costumes, and uniformly polite) masked a plethora of inconsistencies and group antagonisms. Under the surface, this was a culture marked by differences. Yet, in spite of this complexity, from the perspective of any one subculture, things appeared clear. Ambiguity and confusion seldom surfaced in this world of clearly understood subcultural differences.

In Chapter 5, Michael Rosen explores subcultural differences among participants at a ritual. The management of Spiro and Associates, an advertising agency, sponsored an annual breakfast. Speakers touted the achievements of the company, rewarded high performing employees, and attempted to create a feeling of shared bonhomie. This study looks beneath this surface to examine how management's attempt to create a single, shared experience and a single, shared interpretation of recent organizational events (such as a pay freeze) masked conflicts of interest between management and employees. In addition, cultural manifestations, such as dress codes, revealed how class, gender, and hierarchical status differentiated agency employees into a nested set of subcultures, each with its own distinctive pattern of reaction. This study unpeels layers of inconsistencies within a single ritual event, revealing a clear and apparently unbreachable gulf between the rhetoric and interests of management and the skeptical, detached reactions of groups of employees. In this world of difference, the lines of conflict were clearly drawn.

Chapter 6, the third differentiation study, was written by Ed Young. This study, like much differentiation research, focuses on relatively disempowered employees who are clustered at the lower levels of organizational hierarchies. In this case, two groups of machinists who produced different commodities (work wear and bags) had quite different orientations toward the management of the firm. Members of the "work wear" group formed an "enhancing" subculture, eager to please management, perform well, and earn more money—even if it meant working overtime. In contrast, the "bags" group was a counter-culture, alienated from management, reluctant to work overtime, interested primarily in their leisure activities, and wary of rhetoric that denied the danger of potential layoffs.

Members of the two subcultures invested considerable emotional energy in maintaining the cleavage between their groups (e.g., by having separate collections to buy the roses they all wore on St. George's Day). Such intergroup differences, however, were minor when compared to the class-associated gap between labor and management at this firm. In this study, as at Spiro's agency, the study of difference entailed an awareness of class-based conflicts of interest.

The final exemplar of differentiation research is by Jean M. Bartunek and Michael K. Moch. This chapter details the ways various subcultures at a bakery reacted to change agents hired to conduct a "quality of working life" intervention. The joint labor-management committee established to oversee the project cooperated with the change agents. In contrast, top management at the bakery was sometimes antagonistic, attempting on occasion to take control of the project. Local plant management was also antagonistic, attempting to maintain managerial prerogatives. Line employees attempted to use the intervention as a means of obtaining amenities or countering past grievances. Machinists (a highly skilled and privileged group of blue-collar employees) consistently resisted the intervention, in part because they saw themselves as competing with line employees who stood to benefit from the program.

Interestingly, much of the machinists' ire was directed, not toward the management of the bakery, but toward relatively disempowered blue-collar employees, particularly women. A sensitivity to issues of class, gender, and race is a characteristic shared by many (but not all) differentiation studies. In this kind of research, demographic inequalities in the society surrounding the organization are reflected in subcultural differences within an organization's boundaries. What is unique about a given organization's culture, then, is the particular mix of subcultural differences that emerges within a particular organizational context.

Further examples of research predominantly congruent with the differentiation perspective are listed at the conclusion of Part I.

4

The Smile Factory:
Work at Disneyland

JOHN Van MAANEN

Part of Walt Disney Enterprises includes the theme park Disneyland. In its pioneering form in Anaheim, California, this amusement center has been a consistent money maker since the gates were first opened in 1955. Apart from its sociological charm, it has, of late, become something of an exemplar for culture vultures and has been held up for public acclaim in several best-selling publications as one of America's top companies, most notably by Peters and Waterman (1982). To outsiders, the cheerful demeanor of its employees, the seemingly inexhaustible repeat business it generates from its customers, the immaculate condition of park grounds, and, more generally, the intricate physical and social order of the business itself appear wondrous.

Disneyland as the self-proclaimed "Happiest Place on Earth" certainly occupies an enviable position in the amusement and entertainment worlds as well as the commercial world in general. Its product, it seems, is emotion—"laughter and well-being." Insiders are not bashful about promoting the product. Bill Ross, a Disneyland executive, summarizes the

AUTHOR'S NOTE: This paper has been cobbled together using three-penny nails of other writings. Parts come from a paper presented to the American Anthropological Association Annual Meetings in Washington D.C. on November 16, 1989 called "Whistle While You Work." Other parts come from Van Maanen and Kunda (1989). In coming to this version, I've had a good deal of help from my friends Steve Barley, Nicloe Biggart, Michael Owen Jones, Rosanna Hertz, Gideon Kunda, Joanne Martin, Maria Lydia Spinelli, Bob Sutton, and Bob Thomas.

corporate position nicely by noting that "although we focus our attention on profit and loss, day-in and day-out we can not lose sight of the fact that this is a feeling business and we make our profits from that."[1]

The "feeling business" does not operate, however, by management decree alone. Whatever services Disneyland executives believe they are providing to the 60 to 70 thousand visitors per day that flow through the park during its peak summer season, employees at the bottom of the organization are the ones who most provide them. The work-a-day practices that employees adopt to amplify or dampen customer spirits are therefore a core concern of this feeling business. The happiness trade is an interactional one. It rests partly on the symbolic resources put into place by history and park design but it also rests on an animated workforce that is more or less eager to greet the guests, pack the trams, push the buttons, deliver the food, dump the garbage, clean the streets, and, in general, marshal the will to meet and perhaps exceed customer expectations. False moves, rude words, careless disregard, detected insincerity, or a sleepy and bored presence can all undermine the enterprise and ruin a sale. The smile factory has its rules.

It's a Small World

The writing that follows[2] represents Disneyland as a workplace. It is organized roughly as an old-fashioned realist ethnography that tells of a culture in native categories (Van Maanen, 1988). The culture of interest is the Disneyland culture but it is not necessarily the same one invented, authorized, codified, or otherwise approved by park management. Thus the culture I portray here is more of an occupational than a strictly organizational one (Van Maanen & Barley, 1985).

This rendition is of course abbreviated and selective. I focus primarily on such matters as the stock appearance (vanilla), status order (rigid), and social life (full), and swiftly learned codes of conduct (formal and informal) that are associated with Disneyland ride operators. These employees comprise the largest category of hourly workers on the payroll. During the summer months, they number close to four thousand and run the 60-odd rides and attractions in the park.

They are also a well-screened bunch. There is—among insiders and outsiders alike—a rather fixed view about the social attributes carried by the standard-make Disneyland ride operator. Single, white males and females in their early twenties, without facial blemish, of above average height and below average weight, with straight teeth, conservative groom-ing standards, and a chin-up, shoulder-back posture radiating the sort of good health suggestive of a recent history in sports are typical of these social identifiers. There are representative minorities on the payroll but because ethnic displays are sternly discouraged by management, minority employees are rather close copies of the standard model Disneylander, albeit in different colors.

This Disneyland look is often a source of some amusement to employees who delight in pointing out that even the patron saint, Walt himself, could not be hired today without shaving off his trademark pencil-thin mustache. But, to get a job in Disneyland and keep it means conforming to a rather exacting set of appearance rules. These rules are put forth in a handbook on the Disney image in which readers learn, for example, that facial hair or long hair is banned for men as are aviator glasses and earrings and that women must not tease their hair, wear fancy jewelry, or apply more than a modest dab of makeup. Both men and women are to look neat and prim, keep their uniforms fresh, polish their shoes, and maintain an upbeat countenance and light dignity to complement their appearance—no low spirits or cornball raffishness at Disneyland.

The legendary "people skills" of park employees, so often mentioned in Disneyland publicity and training materials, do not amount to very much according to ride operators. Most tasks require little interaction with customers and are physically designed to practically insure that is the case. The contact that does occur typically is fleeting and swift, a matter usually of only a few seconds. In the rare event sustained interaction with customers might be required, employees are taught to deflect potential exchanges to area supervisors or security. A Training Manual offers the proper proce-dure: "On misunderstandings, guests should be told to call City Hall . . . In everything from damaged cameras to physical injuries, don't discuss anything with guests . . . there will always be one of us nearby." Employees learn quickly that security is hidden but everywhere. On Main Street, security cops are Keystone Kops; in Frontierland, they are Town Mar-shalls; on Tom Sawyer's Island, they are Cavalry Officers, and so on.

Occasionally, what employees call "line talk" or "crowd control" is required of them to explain delays, answer direct questions, or provide directions that go beyond the endless stream of recorded messages coming from virtually every nook and cranny of the park. Because such tasks are so simple, consisting of little more than keeping the crowd informed and moving, it is perhaps obvious why management considers the sharp ap-pearance and wide smile of employees so vital to park operations. There is little more they could ask of ride operators whose main interactive tasks with visitors consist of being, in their own terms, "information booths," "line signs," "pretty props," "shepherds," and "talking statues."

A few employees do go out of their way to initiate contact with Disneyland customers but, as a rule, most do not and consider those who do to be a bit odd. In general, one need do little more than exercise common courtesy while looking reasonably alert and pleasant. Interactive skills that are advanced by the job have less to do with making customers feel warm and welcome than they do with keeping each other amused and happy. This is, of course, a more complex matter.

Employees bring to the job personal badges of status that are of more than passing interest to peers. In rough order, these include: good looks, college affiliation, career aspirations, past achievements, age (directly related to status up to about age 23 or 24 and inversely related thereafter), and assorted other idiosyncratic matters. Nested closely alongside these imported status badges are organizational ones that are also of concern and value to employees.

Where one works in the park carries much social weight. Postings are consequential because the ride and area a person is assigned provide rewards and benefits beyond those of wages. In-the-park stature for ride operators turns partly on whether or not unique skills are required. Disneyland neatly complements labor market theorizing on this dimension because employees with the most differentiated skills find themselves at the top of the internal status ladder, thus making their loyalties to the organization more predictable.

Ride operators, as a large but distinctly middle-class group of hourly employees on the floor of the organization, compete for status not only with each other but also with other employee groupings whose members are hired for the season from the same applicant pool. A loose approximation of the rank ordering among these groups can be constructed as follows:

1. The upper-class prestigious Disneyland Ambassadors and Tour Guides (bilingual young women in charge of ushering—some say rushing—little bands of tourists through the park);
2. Ride operators performing coveting "skilled work" such as live narrations or tricky transportation tasks like those who symbolically control customer access to the park and drive, the costly entry vehicles such as the antique trains, horse-drawn carriages, and Monorail);
3. All other ride operators;
4. The proletarian Sweepers (keepers of the concrete grounds);

5. The sub-prole or peasant status Food and Concession workers (whose park sobriquets reflect their lowly social worth—"pancake ladies," "peanut pushers," "coke blokes," "suds divers," and the seemingly irreplaceable "soda jerks").

Pay differentials are slight among these employee groups. The collective status adheres, as it does internally for ride operators, to assignment or functional distinctions. As the rank order suggests, most employee status goes to those who work jobs that require higher degrees of special skill, relative freedom from constant and direct supervision, and provide the opportunity to organize and direct customer desires and behavior rather than to merely respond to them as spontaneously expressed.

The basis for sorting individuals into these various broad bands of job categories is often unknown to employees—a sort of deep, dark secret of the casting directors in personnel. When prospective employees are interviewed, they interview for "a job at Disneyland," not a specific one. Personnel decides what particular job they will eventually occupy. Personal contacts are considered by employees as crucial in this job-assignment process as they are in the hiring decision. Some employees, especially those who wind up in the lower ranking jobs, are quite disappointed with their assignments as is the case when, for example, a would-be Adventureland guide is posted to a New Orleans Square restaurant as a pot scrubber. Although many of the outside acquaintances of our pot scrubber may know only that he works at Disneyland, rest assured, insiders will know immediately where he works and judge him accordingly.

Uniforms are crucial in this regard for they provide instant communication about the social merits or demerits of the wearer within the little world of Disneyland workers. Uniforms also correspond to a wider status ranking that casts a significant shadow on employees of all types. Male ride operators on the Autopia wear, for example, untailored jump-suits similar to pit mechanics and consequently generate about as much respect from peers as the grease-stained outfits worn by pump jockeys generate from real motorists in gas stations. The ill-fitting and homogeneous "whites" worn by Sweepers signify lowly institutional work tinged, perhaps, with a reminder of hospital orderlies rather than street cleanup crews. On the other hand, for males, the crisp, officer-like Monorail operator stands alongside the swashbuckling Pirate of the Caribbean, the casual cowpoke of Big Thunder Mountain, or the smartly vested Riverboat pilot as carriers of valued symbols in and outside the park. Employees lust for these higher status positions and the rights to small advantages such uniforms provide.

A lively internal labor market exists wherein there is much scheming for the more prestigious assignments.

For women, a similar market exists although the perceived "sexiness" of uniforms, rather than social rank, seems to play a larger role. To wit, the rather heated antagonisms that developed years ago when the ride "It's a Small World" first opened and began outfitting the ride operators with what were felt to be the shortest skirts and most revealing blouses in the park. Tour Guides, who traditionally headed the fashion vanguard at Disneyland in their above-the-knee kilts, knee socks, tailored vests, black English hats, and smart riding crops were apparently appalled at being upstaged by their social inferiors and lobbied actively (and, judging by the results, successfully) to lower the skirts, raise the necklines, and generally remake their Small World rivals.

Important, also, to ride operators are the break schedules followed on the various rides. The more the better. Work teams develop inventive ways to increase the number of "time-outs" they take during the work day. Most rides are organized on a rotational basis (e.g., the operator moving from a break, to queue monitor, to turnstile overseer, to unit loader, to traffic controller, to driver, and, again, to a break). The number of break men or women on a rotation (or ride) varies by the number of employees on duty and by the number of units on line. Supervisors, foremen, and operators also vary as to what they regard as appropriate break standards (and, more importantly, as to the value of the many situational factors that can enter the calculation of break rituals—crowd size, condition of ride, accidents, breakdowns, heat, operator absences, special occasions, and so forth). Self-monitoring teams with sleepy supervisors and lax (or savvy) foremen can sometimes manage a shift comprised of 15 minutes on and 45 minutes off each hour. They are envied by others and rides that have such a potential are eyed hungrily by others who feel trapped by their more rigid (and observed) circumstances.

Movement across jobs is not encouraged by park management but some does occur (mostly within an area and job category). Employees claim that a sort of "once a sweeper, always a sweeper" rule obtains but all know of at least a few exceptions to prove the rule. The exceptions offer some (not much) hope for those working at the social margins of the park and perhaps keep them on the job longer than might otherwise be expected. Dishwashers can dream of becoming Pirates, and with persistence and a little help from their friends, such dreams just might come true next season (or the next).

These examples are precious, perhaps, but they are also important. There is an intricate pecking order among very similar categories of employees.

Attributes of reward and status tend to cluster, and there is intense concern about the cluster to which one belongs (or would like to belong). To a degree, form follows function in Disneyland because the jobs requiring the most abilities and offering the most interest also offer the most status and social reward. Interaction patterns reflect and sustain this order. Few Ambassadors or Tour Guides, for instance, will stoop to speak at length with Sweepers who speak mostly among themselves or to Food workers. Ride operators, between the poles, line up in ways referred to above with only ride proximity (i.e., sharing a break area) representing a potentially significant intervening variable in the interaction calculation.

These patterns are of more than slight concern because Disneyland, especially in the summer, can be compared quite usefully to a college mixer where across-sex pairing is of great concern (Schwartz & Lever, 1976). More to the point, what Waller (1937) so accurately called the "rating and dating complex" is in full bloom among park employees. The various modern forms of mating games are valued pastimes among Disneyland employees and are often played with corporate status markers in mind. Thus, when Yvone, the reigning Alice in Wonderland, moved in one summer with Ted, a lowly Sweeper, heads were scratched in puzzlement even though most knew that Yvone was, in her other life, a local junior college student and Ted was in premed at USC. The more general point is that romance flourishes in the park and, at least, if folklore is our guide, marriages made in Disneyland are not uncommon.

Even when not devoted strictly to pairing-off objectives, employee pastimes usually involve other employees. Disneyland's softball and volleyball leagues, its official picnics, canoe races, employee nights at the park, beach parties, and so on provide a busy little social scene for those interested. Areas and rides, too, offer social excitement and bonuses such as when kegs of beer are rolled out at an off-site party after work crews break turnstile records ("We put 33,147 on the mountain today"). During the summer, some night crews routinely party in the early morning while day shift crews party at night. Sleep is not a commodity greatly valued by many employees caught up in a valued social whirl.

The so-called youth culture is indeed celebrated in and out of the park. Many employees, for example, live together in the large and cheap (by Los Angeles standards) apartment complexes that surround Disneyland. Employees sometimes refer to these sprawling, pastel, and slightly seedy structures as "the projects" or "worker housing." Yet, the spirited attractiveness of the collective, low-rent lifestyle for those living it is easily grasped by a few landlords in the area who flatly refuse to rent to Disneyland employees during the summer as a matter of principle and, maybe, sorry experience because these short-term rentals serve as amusement parks for off-duty Disneylanders who, as they say, "know how to party."

A fusion of work and play is notable, however, even when play seems to be the order of the occasion. Certainly no Disneyland get-together would be complete without ride operators launching into their special spiel practiced (or heard continuously on tape) at work:

> Welcome aboard the African Queen folks. My name is John and I'll be your guide and skipper for our trip down these rivers of adventure. As we pull away from the loading dock, turn around and take a last look at the people standing there, it may be the last time you ever see them . . . Please keep your hands inside the boat as we go past these hungry alligators, they're always looking for a hand out . . . And now we return to civilization and the greatest danger of all, the California freeways.

The figurative parallel of this party is, of course, the atmosphere of a most collegial college. It has a literal parallel as well.

Paid employment at Disneyland begins with the much renowned University of Disneyland whose faculty runs a day-long orientation program (Traditions I) as part of a 40-hour apprenticeship program, most of which takes place on the rides. In the classroom, however, newly hired ride operators are given a very thorough introduction to matters of managerial concern and are tested on their absorption of famous Disneyland fact, lore, and procedure. Employee demeanor is governed, for example, by three rules:

> First, we practice the friendly smile.
> Second, we use only friendly and courteous phrases.
> Third, we are not stuffy—the only Misters in Disneyland are Mr. Toad and Mr. Smee.

Employees learn too that the Disneyland culture is officially defined. The employee handbook put it in this format:

> Dis-ney Cor-po-rate Cul-ture (diz'ne kor'pr'it kul'cher) *n* 1. Of or pertaining to the Disney organization, as a: the philosophy underlying all business decisions; b: the commitment of top leadership and management to that philosophy; c: the actions taken by individual cast members that reinforce the image.

Language is also a central feature of university life and new employees are schooled in its proper use. Customers at Disneyland are, for instance, never referred to as such, they are "guests." There are no rides at Disneyland, only "attractions." Disneyland itself is a "Park," not an amusement center, and it is divided into "back-stage," "on-stage," and "staging" regions. Law enforcement personnel hired by the park are not policemen, but "security hosts." Employees do not wear uniforms but check out fresh "costumes" each working day from "wardrobe." And, of course, there are no accidents at Disneyland, only "incidents."

So successful is such training that Smith and Eisenberg (1987) report that not a single Disneyland employee uttered the taboo and dread words "uniform," "customer," or "amusement park" during the 35 half-hour interviews they conducted as part of a study on organizational communication. The *Los Angeles Times* (July 28, 1988) also gives evidence on this matter, quoting a tour guide's reaction to the employee's annual canoe races. "It's a good release," she says, "it helps you see the other cast members (park employees) go through the same thing you do." Whether or not employees keep to such disciplined talk with one another is, of course, a moot point because the corporate manual is concerned only with how employees talk to customers or outsiders.

The university curriculum also anticipates probable questions ride operators may someday face from customers and they are taught the approved public response. A sample:

Question (posed by trainer):   What do you tell a guest who requests a rain check?
Answer (in three parts):   We don't offer rain checks at Disneyland because (1) the main attractions are all indoors; (2) we would go broke if we offered passes; and (3) sunny days would be too crowded if we gave passes.

Shrewd trainees readily note that such an answer blissfully disregards the fact that waiting areas of Disneyland are mostly outdoors and that there are no subways in the park to carry guests from land to land. Nor do they miss the economic assumption concerning the apparent frequency of Southern California rains. They discuss such matters together, of course, but rarely raise them in the training classroom. In most respects, these are recruits who easily take the role of good student.

Classes are organized and designed by professional Disneyland trainers who also instruct a well-screened group of representative hourly employees straight from park operations on the approved newcomer training methods and materials. New-hires seldom see professional trainers in class but are brought on board by enthusiastic peers who concentrate on those aspects of park procedure thought highly general matters to be learned by all employees. Particular skill training (and "reality shock") is reserved for the second wave of socialization occurring on the rides themselves as operators are taught, for example, how and when to send a mock bobsled caroming down the track or, more delicately, the proper ways to stuff an obese adult customer into the midst of children riding the Monkey car on the Casey Jones Circus Train or, most problematically, what exactly to tell an irate customer standing in the rain who, in no uncertain terms, wants his or her money back and wants it back now.

During orientation, considerable concern is placed on particular values the Disney organization considers central to its operations. These values range from the "customer is king" verities to the more or less unique kind, of which "everyone is a child at heart when at Disneyland" is a decent example. This latter piety is one few employees fail to recognize as also attaching to everyone's mind as well after a few months of work experience. Elaborate checklists of appearance standards are learned and gone over in the classroom and great efforts are spent trying to bring employee emotional responses in line with such standards. Employees are told repeatedly that if they are happy and cheerful at work, so, too, will the guests at play. Inspirational films, hearty pep talks, family imagery, and exemplars of corporate performance are all representative of the strong symbolic stuff of these training rites.

Another example, perhaps extreme, concerns the symbolic role of the canonized founder in the corporate mythology. When Walt Disney was alive, newcomers and veterans alike were told how much he enjoyed coming to the park and just how exacting he was about the conditions he observed. For employees, the cautionary whoop, "Walt's in the park," could often bring forth additional energy and care for one's part in the production. Upon his death, trainers at the University were said to be telling recruits to mind their manners because, "Walt's in the park all the time now."

Yet, like employees everywhere, there is a limit to which such overt company propaganda can be effective. Students and trainers both seem to agree on where the line is drawn for there is much satirical banter, mischievous winking, and playful exaggeration in the classroom. As young seasonal employees note, it is difficult to take seriously an organization that provides its retirees "Golden Ears" instead of gold watches after 20 or more years of service. All newcomers are aware that the label "Disneyland" has both an unserious and artificial connotation and that a full embrace of the Disneyland role would be as deviant as its full rejection. It does seem, however, because of the corporate imagery, the recruiting and selection devices, the goodwill trainees hold toward the organization at entry, the peer-based employment context, and the smooth fit with real student calendars, the job is considered by most ride operators to be a good one.

The University of Disneyland, it appears, graduates students with a modest amount of pride and a considerable amount of fact and faith firmly ingrained as important things to know (if not always accept).

Matters become more interesting as new hires move into the various realms of Disneyland enterprise. There are real customers "out there" and employees soon learn that these good folks do not always measure up to the typically well mannered and grateful guest of the training classroom. Moreover, ride operators may find it difficult to utter the prescribed "Welcome Voyager" (or its equivalent) when it is to be given to the 20-thousandth human being passing through the Space Mountain turnstile on a crowded day in July. Other difficulties present themselves as well, but operators learn that there are others on-stage to assist or thwart them.

Employees learn quickly that supervisors and, to a lesser degree, foremen are not only on the premises to help them, but also to catch them when they slip over or brazenly violate set procedures or park policies. Because most rides are tightly designed to eliminate human judgment and minimize operational disasters, much of the supervisory monitoring is directed at activities ride operators consider trivial: taking too long a break; not wearing parts of one's official uniform such as a hat, standard-issue belt, or correct shoes; rushing the ride (although more frequent violations seem to be detected for the provision of longer-than-usual rides for lucky customers); fraternizing with guests beyond the call of duty; talking back to quarrelsome or sometimes merely querisome customers; and so forth. All are matters covered quite explicitly in the codebooks ride operators are to be familiar with, and violations of such codes are often subject to instant and harsh discipline. The firing of what to supervisors are "malcontents," "trouble-makers," "bumblers," "attitude problems," or simply "jerks" is a frequent occasion at Disneyland, and among part-timers, who are most subject to degradation and being fired, the threat is omnipresent. There are few workers who have not witnessed firsthand the rapid disappearance of a co-worker for offenses they would regard as "Mickey Mouse." Moreover, there are few employees who themselves have not violated a good number of operational and demeanor standards and anticipate, with just cause, the violation of more in the future.[3]

In part, because of the punitive and what are widely held to be capricious supervisory practices in the park, foremen and ride operators are usually drawn close and shield one another from suspicious area supervisors. Throughout the year, each land is assigned a number of area supervisors who, dressed alike in short-sleeved white shirts and ties with walkie-talkies hitched to their belts, wander about their territories on the lookout for deviations from park procedures (and other signs of disorder). Occasionally, higher level supervisors pose in "plainclothes" and ghost-ride the various attractions just to be sure everything is up to snuff. Some area supervisors are well-known among park employees for the variety of surreptitious techniques they employ when going about their monitoring duties. Blind observation posts are legendary, almost sacred, sites within the park ("This is where Old Man Weston hangs out. He can see Dumbo, Storybook, the Carousel, and the Tea Cups from here"). Supervisors in Tomorrowland are, for example, famous for their penchant of hiding in the bushes above the submarine caves, timing the arrivals and departures of the supposedly fully loaded boats making the 8½ minute cruise under the polar icecaps. That they might also catch a submarine captain furtively enjoying a cigarette (or worse) while inside the conning tower (his upper body out of view of the crowd on the vessel) might just make a supervisor's day—and unmake the employee's. In short, supervisors, if not foremen, are regarded by ride operators as sneaks and tricksters out to get them and representative of the dark side of park life. Their presence is, of course, an orchestrated one and does more than merely watch over the ride operators. It also draws operators together as cohesive little units who must look out for one another while they work (and shirk).

Supervisors are not the only villains who appear in the park. The treachery of co-workers, while rare, has its moments. Pointing out the code violations of colleagues to foremen and supervisors—usually in secret—provides one avenue of collegial duplicity. Finks, of all sorts, can be found among the peer ranks at Disneyland, and although their dirty deeds are uncommon, work teams on all rides go to some effort to determine just who they might be and, if possible, drive them from their midst. Although there is little overt hazing or playing of pranks on newcomers, they are nonetheless carefully scrutinized on matters of team (and ride) loyalty, and those who fail the test of "member in good standing" are subject to some very uncomfortable treatment. Innuendo and gossip are the primary tools in this regard, with ridicule and ostracism (the good old silent treatment) providing the backup. Since perhaps the greatest rewards working at Disneyland offers its ride operator personnel are those that come from belonging to a tight little network of like-minded and sociable peers where off-duty interaction is at least as vital and pleasurable as the on-duty sort, such mechanisms are quite effective. Here is where some of the most powerful and focused emotion work in the park is found, and those subject to negative sanction, rightly or wrongly, will grieve, but grieve alone.

Employees are also subject to what might be regarded as remote controls. These stem not from supervisors or peers but from thousands of paying guests who parade daily through the park. The public, for the most part, wants Disneyland employees to play only the roles for which they are hired and costumed. If, for instance, Judy of the Jets is feeling tired, grouchy, or bored, few customers want to know about it. Disneyland employees are expected to be sunny and helpful; and the job, with its limited opportunities for sustained interaction, is designed to support such a stance. Thus, if a ride operator's behavior drifts noticeably away from the norm, customers are sure to point it out—"Why aren't you smiling?" "What's wrong with you?" "Having a bad day?" "Did Goofy step on your foot?" Ride operators learn swiftly from the constant hints, glances, glares, and tactful (and tactless) cues sent by their audience what their role in the park is to be, and as long as they keep to it, there will be no objections from those passing by.

> I can remember being out on the river looking at the people on the Mark Twain looking down on the people in the Keel Boats who are looking up at them. I'd come by on my raft and they'd all turn and stare at me. If I gave them a little wave and a grin, they'd all wave back and smile; all ten thousand of them. I always wondered what would happen if I gave them the finger? (Ex-ride operator, 1988)

Ride operators also learn how different categories of customers respond to them and the parts they are playing on-stage. For example, infants and small children are generally timid, if not frightened, in their presence. School-age children are somewhat curious, aware that the operator is at work playing a role but sometimes in awe of the role itself. Nonetheless, these children can be quite critical of any flaw in the operator's performance. Teenagers, especially males in groups, present problems because they sometimes go to great lengths to embarrass, challenge, ridicule, or outwit an operator. Adults are generally appreciative and approving of an operator's conduct provided it meets their rather minimal standards, but they sometimes overreact to the part an operator is playing (positively) if accompanied by small children. A recent study of the Easter Bunny points out a similar sort of response on the part of adults to fantasy (Hickey, Thompson, & Foster, 1988). It is worth noting too that adults outnumber children in the park by a wide margin. One count reports an adult-to-children ratio of four-to-one (King, 1981).

The point here is that ride operators learn what the public (or, at least, their idealized version of the public) expects of their role and find it easier to conform to such expectations than not. Moreover, they discover that when they are bright and lively others respond to them in like ways. This Goffmanesque balancing of the emotional exchange is such that ride operators come to expect good treatment. They assume, with good cause, that most people will react to their little waves and smiles with some affection and perhaps joy. When they do not, it can ruin a ride operator's day.

With this interaction formula in mind, it is perhaps less difficult to see why ride operators detest and scorn the ill-mannered or unruly guest. At times, these grumpy, careless, or otherwise unresponsive characters insult the very role the operators play and have come to appreciate—"You can't treat the Captain of the USS Nautilus like that!" Such out-of-line visitors offer breaks from routine, some amusement, consternation, or the occasional job challenge that occurs when remedies are deemed necessary to restore employee and role dignity.

By and large, however, the people-processing tasks of ride operators pass good naturedly and smoothly, with operators hardly noticing much more than the bodies passing in front of view (special bodies, however, merit special attention as when crew members on the subs gather to assist a young lady in a revealing outfit on board and then linger over the hatch to admire the view as she descends the steep steps to take her seat on the boat). Yet, sometimes, more than a body becomes visible, as happens when customers overstep their roles and challenge employee authority, insult an operator, or otherwise disrupt the routines of the job. In the process, guests become "dufusses," "ducks," and "assholes" (just three of many derisive terms used by ride operators to label those customers they believe to have gone beyond the pale). Normally, these characters are brought to the attention of park security officers, ride foremen, or area supervisors who, in turn, decide how they are to be disciplined (usually expulsion from the park).

Occasionally, however, the alleged slight is too personal or simply too extraordinary for a ride operator to let it pass unnoticed or merely inform others and allow them to decide what, if anything, is to be done. Restoration of one's respect is called for and routine practices have been developed for these circumstances. For example, common remedies include: the "seatbelt squeeze," a small token of appreciation given to a deviant customer consisting of the rapid cinching-up of a required seatbelt such that the passenger is doubled-over at the point of departure and left gasping for the duration of the trip; the "break-toss," an acrobatic gesture of the Autopia trade whereby operators jump on the outside of a norm violator's car, stealthily unhitching the safety belt, then slamming on the brakes, bringing the car to an almost instant stop while the driver flies on the hood of the car (or beyond); the "seatbelt slap," an equally distinguished (if primitive) gesture by which an offending customer receives a sharp, quick snap of a hard plastic belt across the face (or other parts of the body) when entering or exiting a seat-belted ride; the "break-up-the-party" gambit, a queuing device put to use in officious fashion whereby bothersome pairs are separated at the last minute into different units, thus forcing on them the pain of strange companions for the duration of a ride through the Haunted Mansion or a ramble on Mr. Toad's Wild Ride; the "hatch-cover ploy," a much beloved practice of Submarine pilots who, in collusion with mates on the loading dock, are able to drench offensive guests with water as their units pass under a waterfall; and, lastly, the rather ignoble variants of the "Sorry-I-didn't-see-your-hand" tactic, a savage move designed to crunch a particularly irksome customer's hand (foot, finger, arm, leg, etc.) by bringing a piece of Disneyland property to bear on the appendage, such as the door of a Thunder Mountain railroad car or the starboard side of a Jungle Cruise boat. This latter remedy is, most often, a "near miss" designed to startle the little criminals of Disneyland.

All of these unofficial procedures (and many more) are learned on the job. Although they are used sparingly, they are used. Occasions of use provide a continual stream of sweet revenge talk to enliven and enrich colleague conversation at break time or after work. Too much, of course, can be made of these subversive practices and the rhetoric that surrounds their use. Ride operators are quite aware that there are limits beyond which they dare not pass. If they are caught, they know that restoration of corporate pride will be swift and clean.

In general, Disneyland employees are remarkable for their forbearance and polite good manners even under trying conditions. They are taught, and some come to believe, for a while at least, that they are really "on-stage" at work. And, as noted, surveillance by supervisory personnel certainly fades in light of the unceasing glances an employee receives from the paying guests who tromp daily through the park in the summer. Disneyland employees know well that they are part of the product being sold and learn to check their more discriminating manners in favor of the generalized countenance of a cheerful lad or lassie whose enthusiasm and dedication is obvious to all.

At times, the emotional resources of employees appear awesome. When the going gets tough and the park is jammed, the nerves of all employees are frayed and sorely tested by the crowd, din, sweltering sun, and eye-burning smog. Customers wait in what employees call "bullpens" (and park officials call "reception areas") for up to several hours for a 3½ minute ride that operators are sometimes hell-bent on cutting to 2½ minutes. Surely a monument to the human ability to suppress feelings has been created when both users and providers alike can maintain their composure and seeming regard for one another when in such a fix.

It is in this domain where corporate culture and the order it helps to sustain must be given its due. Perhaps the depth of a culture is visible only when its members are under the gun. The orderliness—a good part of the Disney formula for financial success—is an accomplishment based not only on physical design and elaborate procedures, but also on the low-level, part-time employees who, in the final analysis, must be willing, even eager, to keep the show afloat. The ease with which employees glide into their kindly and smiling roles is, in large measure, a feat of social engineering. Disneyland does not pay well; its supervision is arbitrary and skin-close; its working conditions are chaotic; its jobs require minimal amounts of intelligence or judgment; and asks a kind of sacrifice and loyalty of its employees that is almost fanatical. Yet, it attracts a particularly able workforce whose personal backgrounds suggest abilities far exceeding those required of a Disneyland traffic cop, people stuffer, queue or line manager, and button pusher. As I have suggested, not all of Disneyland is covered by the culture put forth by management. There are numerous pockets of resistance and various degrees of autonomy maintained by employees. Nonetheless, adherence and support for the organization are remarkable. And, like swallows returning to Capistrano, many part-timers look forward to their migration back to the park for several seasons.

The Disney Way

Four features alluded to in this unofficial guide to Disneyland seem to account for a good deal of the social order that obtains within the park. First, socialization, although costly, is of a most selective, collective, intensive, serial, sequential, and closed sort.[4] These tactics are notable for their penetration into the private spheres of individual thought and feeling (Van Maanen & Schein, 1979). Incoming identities are not so much dismantled as they are set aside as employees are schooled in the use of new identities of the situational sort. Many of these are symbolically powerful and, for some, laden with social approval. It is hardly surprising that some of the more problematic positions in terms of turnover during the summer occur in the food and concession domains where employees apparently find little to identify with on the job. Cowpokes on Big Thunder Mountain, Jet Pilots, Storybook Princesses, Tour Guides, Space Cadets, Jungle Boat Skippers, or Southern Belles of New Orleans Square have less difficulty on this score. Disneyland, by design, bestows identity through a process carefully set up to strip away the job relevance of other sources of identity and learned response and replace them with others of organizational relevance. It works.

Second, this is a work culture whose designers have left little room for individual experimentation. Supervisors, as apparent in their focused wandering and attentive looks, keep very close tabs on what is going on at any moment in all the lands. Every bush, rock, and tree in Disneyland is numbered and checked continually as to the part it is playing in the park. So too are employees. Discretion of a personal sort is quite limited while employees are "on-stage." Even "back-stage" and certain "off-stage" domains have their corporate monitors. Employees are indeed aware that their "off-stage" life beyond the picnics, parties, and softball games is subject to some scrutiny for police checks are made on potential and current employees. Nor do all employees discount the rumors that park officials make periodic inquiries on their own as to a person's habits concerning sex and drugs. Moreover, the sheer number of rules and regulations is striking, thus making the grounds for dismissal a matter of multiple choice for supervisors who discover a target for the use of such grounds. The feeling of being watched is, unsurprisingly, a rather prevalent complaint among Disneyland people and it is one that employees must live with if they are to remain at Disneyland.

Third, emotional management occurs in the park in a number of quite distinct ways. From the instructors at the university who beseech recruits to "wish every guest a pleasant good day," to the foremen who plead with their charges to, "say thank you when you herd them through the gate," to the impish customer who seductively licks her lips and asks, "what does Tom Sawyer want for Christmas?" appearance, demeanor, and etiquette have special meanings at Disneyland. Because these are prized personal attributes over which we normally feel in control, making them commodities can be unnerving. Much self-monitoring is involved, of course, but even here self-management has an organizational side. Consider ride operators who may complain of being "too tired to smile" but, at the same time, feel a little guilty for uttering such a confession. Ride operators who have worked an early morning shift on the Matterhorn (or other popular rides) tell of a queasy feeling they get when the park is opened for business and they suddenly feel the ground begin to shake under their feet and hear the low thunder of the hordes of customers coming at them, oblivious of civil restraint and the small children who might be among them. Consider, too, the discomforting pressures of being "on-stage" all day and the cumulative annoyance of having adults ask permission to leave a line to go to the bathroom, whether the water in the lagoon is real, where the well-marked entrances might be, where Walt Disney's cryogenic tomb is to be found,[5] or—the real clincher—whether or not one is "really real."

The mere fact that so much operator discourse concerns the handling of bothersome guests suggests that these little emotional disturbances have costs. There are, for instance, times in all employee careers when they put themselves on "automatic pilot," "go robot," "can't feel a thing," "lapse into a dream," "go into a trance," or otherwise "check out" while still on duty. Despite a crafty supervisor's (or curious visitor's) attempt to measure the glimmer in an employee's eye, this sort of willed emotional numbness is common to many of the "on-stage" Disneyland personnel. Much of this numbness is, of course, beyond the knowledge of supervisors and guests because most employees have little trouble appearing as if they are present even when they are not. It is, in a sense, a passive form of resistance that suggests there still is a sacred preserve of individuality left among employees in the park.

Finally, taking these three points together, it seems that even when people are trained, paid, and told to be nice, it is hard for them to do so all of the time. But, when efforts to be nice have succeeded to the degree that is true of Disneyland, it appears as a rather towering (if not always admirable) achievement. It works at the collective level by virtue of elaborate direction. Employees—at all ranks—are stage-managed by higher ranking employees who, having come through themselves, hire, train, and closely supervise those who have replaced them below. Expression rules are laid out in corporate manuals. Employee time-outs intensify work experience. Social exchanges are forced into narrow bands of interacting groups. Training and retraining programs are continual. Hiding places are few. Although little sore spots and irritations remain for each individual, it is difficult to imagine work roles being more defined (and accepted) than those at Disneyland. Here, it seems, is a work culture worthy of the name.

Notes

1. The quote is drawn from a transcript of a speech made to senior managers of Hurrah's Club by Bill Ross, Vice President for Human Relations at Disneyland, in January 1988. Elsewhere in

this account I draw on other in-house publications to document my tale. Of use in this regard are: "Your Role in the Show" (1982), "Disneyland: The First Thirty Years" (1985), "The Disney Approach to Management" (1986), and Steven Birnbaum's semi-official travel guide to Disneyland (1988). The best tourist guide to the park I've read is Sehlinger's (1987) adamantly independent *The Unofficial Guide to Disneyland*.

2. This account is drawn primarily on my three-year work experience as a "permanent part-time" ride operator at Disneyland during the late 1960s. Sporadic contacts have been maintained with a few park employees and periodic visits, even with children in tow, have proved instructive. Also, lengthy, repeated beach interviews of a most informal sort have been conducted over the past few summers with ride operators (then) employed at the park. There is a good deal written about Disneyland, and I have drawn from these materials as indicated in the text. I must note finally that this is an unsponsored and unauthorized treatment of the Disneyland culture and is at odds on several points with the views set forth by management.

3. The author serves as a case in point for I was fired from Disneyland for what I still consider a Mickey Mouse offense. The specific violation—one of many possible—involved hair growing over my ears, an offense I had been warned about more than once before the final cut was made. The form my dismissal took, however, deserves comment for it is easy to recall and followed a format familiar to an uncountable number of ex-Disneylanders. Dismissal began by being pulled off the ride after my work shift had begun by an area supervisor in full view of my cohorts. A forced march to the administration building followed where my employee card was turned over and a short statement read to me by a personnel officer as to the formal cause of termination. Security officers then walked me to the employee locker room where my work uniforms and equipment were collected and my personal belongings returned to me while an inspection of my locker was made. The next stop was the time shed where my employee's time card was removed from its slot, marked "terminated" across the top in red ink, and replaced in its customary position (presumably for Disneylanders to see when clocking on or off the job over the next few days). As now an ex-ride operator, I was escorted to the parking lot where two security officers scraped off the employee parking sticker attached to my car. All these little steps of status degradation in the Magic Kingdom were quite public and, as the reader might guess, the process still irks. This may provide the reader with an account for the tone of this narrative, although it shouldn't since I would also claim I was ready to quit anyway since I had been there far too long. At any rate, it may just be possible that I now derive as much a part of my identify from being fired from Disneyland as I gained from being employed there in the first place.

4. These tactics are covered in some depth in Van Maanen (1976, 1977) and Van Maanen and Schein (1979). When pulled together and used simultaneously, a people processing system of some force is created that tends to produce a good deal of conformity among recruits who, regardless of background, come to share very similar occupational identities, including just how they think and feel on the job. Such socialization practices are common whenever recruits are bunched together and processed as a batch and when role innovation is distinctly unwanted on the part of the agents of such socialization.

5. The unofficial answer to this little gem of a question is: "Under Sleeping Beauty's castle." Nobody knows for sure since the immediate circumstances surrounding Walt Disney's death are vague—even in the most careful accounts (Mosley, 1983; Schickel, 1985). Officially, his ashes are said to be peacefully at rest in Forest Lawn. But the deep freeze myth is too good to let go of because it so neatly complements all those fairy tales Disney expropriated and popularized when alive. What could be more appropriate than thinking of Walt on ice, waiting for technology's kiss to restore him to life in a hidden vault under his own castle in the Magic Kingdom?

5

Breakfast at Spiro's:
Dramaturgy and Dominance

MICHAEL ROSEN

Preamble

An approach is presented here for analyzing the relationship between cultural and social action in bureaucracy.[1] Symbols and power are understood as the primary variables of sociocultural study, where symbolic forms and techniques are manipulated by asymmetrical groups in the articulation of basic interests. Through their interrelationship the organizational conditions of production are reproduced or transformed. Social drama is the processual unit through which power relations, symbolic action, and their interaction are played out and social structure is made evident. This perspective is applied to data from an ethnographic study of an advertising agency.

What follows, stripped of its original theoretical clothing and some of its corpus, was first published as a short ethnographic study in a special issue of the *Journal of Management,* (Rosen, 1985) edited by Peter Frost.

The social drama around which this study is based, a business breakfast, involved the members of Spiro and Associates, a Philadelphia advertising agency. For ten months in 1982 I did participant observation research in this agency, which then employed an average of 104 people.

AUTHOR'S NOTE: Reprinted with permission from the *Journal of Management,* 1985, 11(2), 31-48

Spiro and Associates billed approximately 44.8 million dollars for the fiscal year ending June 30, 1982, second among Philadelphia agencies.

The Annual Agency Breakfast

In early September all employees of Spiro and Associates attend the annual "Agency Breakfast." Attendance is required.

The event is held in the Main Ballroom of one of Philadelphia's luxury class hotels. For the 1982 event 12 large round tables were arranged throughout the room, with a speaker's podium at one end. Two slide projectors had been placed directly in front of the podium. Immediately behind it was a large viewing screen.

Each table was set with fine china and flatware. Pastries were on each table, and at each setting a piece of carved melon stuffed with strawberries had been placed. As guests arrived and were seated they were served coffee or tea. People were dressed formally, the men in ties and business suits and the women in business suits or dresses.

Breakfast was served almost exactly at 8:30 a.m., one hundred or so Eggs Benedict marched in by suited waiters in synchronization. Nine down at a table, nine down at the next.

"Coffee or tea for you?"

"Are you finished, sir? Would you like more coffee?" Code for letting them take your near empty plate.

Walter Spiro, Chairman of the Board, 59 years old, about five feet seven inches tall, balding, a slight German accent, walked to the podium at nine o'clock. He began by speaking of the agency's "record year." They should all be proud. The Breakfast carried on from there. Each department head gave a speech. Some were serious and some were funny. Some were both. Some people received awards, others were promoted. Many stood and were applauded. Music was played and slides were shown. When it was all done the employees of Spiro and Associates went to work for the day. Or at least to the office. As will be seen, they were already "at work."

In the same way that the various members of Spiro and Associates exert a measure of influence on other people's behaviors through the manipulation of their ideas via advertising, the messages encoded in and enacted through the Breakfast influence the practice of the members of Spiro and Associates themselves in a manner likely to recreate the relations of domination inherent to the bureaucratic form, if not essentially the form itself. Although the manifestations of contradiction—conflict through dissent and struggle— are not foreign to the bureaucratic terrain, re-creation of the power order inherent to the form nevertheless is primary. Re-creation is largely accomplished through manipulation of the symbolic order, reimpregnating the bureaucratic consciousness with meaning sufficient to largely re-create the lived order.

Some Symbolic Techniques

The Breakfast's significance derives not from its uniqueness, but from the normal affirmations, reaffirmations, and transformations which occur in and through this drama. The Breakfast is important and efficacious precisely because it is accepted by those involved with its performance as part of the natural order of things.

An encompassing technique of the Breakfast is commensality. That agency members all sit and eat together in one room as one body transforms formally unifunctional, contractual relationships to one another and the agency into an arena for multifunctional relations of communion and amity. At the same time, group identity and exclusiveness is signified by the body "breaking bread together." Those inside the ballroom are Spiro and Associates. Those outside are not.

The type of food eaten by the group signifies its image of itself in a particular role, or at least the elite's image of itself and the organization. In this instance the food fundamentally signifies "American gourmet," or *haute cuisine*—those eating this food are at a special event and are themselves high (Goody, 1982). The opulent surroundings of the hotel, the main ballroom, the fine china, and so on, intend the same message.

The techniques of "opulent" hotel, ballroom, china, food, and so on also serve an additional function. On the basis of their salaries the majority of members cannot normally afford such aspects of high culture. The fine surroundings reinvest the goal with meaning, saying that at least by association members can now afford part of "the good life." If they continue participation more will be theirs in the future.

Dress may be used to camouflage or define identity, or to accomplish both. Such was the dual function of dress at the Breakfast. The primary bifurcation in a typical advertising agency, both socially and culturally, is between the creative and business roles. This distinction extends to dress at Spiro and Associates, where there is an explicit dress code for those performing business functions, but none for those performing creative functions. The dress code, in fact addressed only to business males, states that suits (of appropriate color, tailoring, and color—not polyester, for example) must be worn at work. Female business clothing norms have yet to be formally codified, although women are expected to dress according to variations on the theme of formality.

The difference in dress norms between roles in the agency corresponds to its power hierarchy. The clerical workers and most creative people are not in the main contest for wealth and power and hence are not as socially constricted in their behavior. By contrast, the behavior of the business people is highly circumscribed. Clothing, hairstyles, expressed values and goals, friendships, verbal patterns, social club memberships, and other presumed ideational expressions are more closely restricted. Through these closures the borders of the powerful are in part maintained.

In congruence with the meaning of the Breakfast everyone came in business dress. The Breakfast is here equated with business. People did not come attired in black tie wear, for example, nor in leisure clothing. In this instance dress is used to camouflage distinct intra-organizational role identity, and hence power and status differences, to create a communion among disparate groups. At the same time, the dress standard is that of the powerful, legitimating their terrain and defining group identity on their ground.

The form of commensality at the Breakfast is as critical for accomplishing the symbolic function as is the specific types of food eaten. Unlike the buffet conditions of other formal agency ceremonials, food at the Breakfast is served. Being served creates a stratification between servers, who are standing, mobile, and providing, and consumers, who are sitting, immobile, and consuming; a leisure class is objectified in an arena of heightened elegance (Goody, 1982). The high culture pursued in the Breakfast necessitates this level of formality: a dominant class image of a group limited communion is sought.

An understanding of the "lavishness" message communicated by this and other Spiro and Associates social dramas that include commensality is enhanced through comparison to its opposite, fasting and abstinence. Pursuing a life of strict personal restraint, including abstinence, frequent fasting, avoidance of luxurious clothing, jewelry, and so on is understood in many systems as a means to grace and holiness (Goody, 1982). The social relations of business in general, and Spiro and Associates in particular, provides the opposite message. This is fundamentally the realm of the mundane. Personal appearance, including hair, hygiene, jewelry, and clothing and indulgence in food, alcohol, and sex are considered compatible and perhaps synonymous with the material logic of bureaucratic relations.

The Speeches

The technique of rhetoric is conspicuous during the Breakfast drama. A number of speeches are given by prominent managers, who discuss many different aspects of the agency's operations. A major segment of this phase will be recounted to provide an insight into agency process.

> *When Walter Spiro walked to the podium at 9:00 a.m., he began his talk by reminding those present of the "tradition" behind the Breakfast, saying that it is an annual event which everyone is expected to attend. He stated that it is held directly after Labor Day because this time period is the end of summer, and people at the agency "should be rested."*
>
> *Walter said that "immediately after the Breakfast" the agency is "releasing to the press" a note that "Spiro and Associates had a record billing in the past fiscal year a [1982] of $44.8 million dollars, an 18% increase over last year. We are clearly the number two agency in town." His remark was met by a small amount of applause. "The economy is bad," he said. "This often results in internal conflict in the agency . . . But we're all a part of this. It's called Spiro and Associates . . . Normally only I speak at the Breakfast, but today the Associate Directors [agency officers and department heads] will also speak. Before that, however, I'd like to give an overview of the agency's progress this year."*
>
> *"I would say that the Creative Department is in very good shape, and is under very good leadership . . . Hotels and Travel is doing well . . . So much for improved departments . . ."*
>
> *"Public Relations and Traffic have had problems this year . . . Public Relations . . . has had some problems with people and attitudes. We've made some changes in personnel there, and expect things to get better."*
>
> *"We got some important new accounts last year. 'X' is a new account. We like them. We especially like the color of their money."*
>
> *Walter continued. "We lost business too, and in each case I'll tell you why. We lost the Playboy Hotel and Casino. You all know that . . . It was basic incompatibility . . ."*
>
> *"Four outside agencies came into Philadelphia this past year. They will get clients, but if it were up to me they wouldn't. When we leave here we have to be more aggressive, more caring. And we will reward it."*

Of note is Walter's statement that people's "attitudes" in Public Relations have presented problems this past year. A deviation in attitude is a potential threat to hegemony, for control is efficacious to the degree it controls the totality of attitudes, beliefs, and behavior (Edwards, 1979). During the past year a significant ideational deviation was understood to have occurred in the Public Relations department. It could not be tolerated by top management, and steps were taken to negate the perceived cause.

Walter's discourse on the clients that had been lost and gained is a clear case of posturing. The agency is shown to handle important and prestigious accounts. By association, as these clients are important so is the agency and its employees. It does not matter that Walter is exaggerating and the members are to varying degrees aware of it, as long as the basic parameters are accepted.

The next phase of the drama concerned gift giving. Spiro and Associates has a tradition of presenting members with "gifts" each time they complete a five-year period of employment, up till their 25th year.

> At the Breakfast two members had just completed their tenth year of employment, and as Walter was starting to present their gifts he said, "I'd like to introduce some new people here, Jack Bithrow and Jose Hill." Jack Bithrow, an Art Director, was called to the podium first, and presented with a gift wrapped box. Jose Hill, the agency's "odd jobs" person, was called up next, accompanied by overwhelming applause. In response Walter announced "Jose is the most popular person in the agency," further increasing the applause.
>
> After the gifts were presented Walter read the names of those employed from five to ten years. He asked each individual to stand as his or her name was called, and asked the audience to hold its applause until he finished. Approximately fifteen people were met with a polite applause. Walter then announced those employed from ten to twenty years. Six people were named, and each was applauded individually as she or he rose. The same process was repeated for two employed for more than twenty but less than twenty five years, and again for one person, Harry Egbert, who had been with the agency for thirty seven years. Walter noted that Harry Egbert "keeps coming back to haunt us. He thinks he's eighteen and acts like he's twelve." People laughed, and Harry, the agency's "patriarch," rose to a loud applause. At this point over twenty five percent of the employees were standing. Walter asked everyone to applaud themselves, and people responded loudly.

Gift giving is related to the long-run orientation of bureaucratic control, of socialization to the rules, values, and assumptions constituting this form. The "loyal" employee is likely more valuable to the employer than is the new, nonsocialized employee. The conditioned worker has internalized the rules of the form—control appearing as freedom—and through practice has likely increased skills, client relationships, and so on. As the employee becomes skilled and loyal, she or he can be given tasks of greater value, with increasing return to the organization. Within this arena, therefore, it is functional to reward seniority. Although only a small part of this reward is constituted by public gift giving, these ritualized offerings are not insignificant. They conspicuously signify gratitude from the realm of moral bonding, applying to each socialized within the agency. The publicness of this exchange, whereby a loyal member is recognized, accepts a gift, is applauded and so on signifies and recreates.

As noted, when Walter had finished calling the names of those employed at least five years over twenty five percent of all members were standing, a physical symbol of valued seniority. When Walter asked everyone to applaud themselves, all were subject to the clapping and swelling of noise encompassing the room and saying "we have all achieved," "we are good," "I am good," "the agency is good," and "I belong."

> *Those standing sat, and Walter started talking about the "things the agency does for all of us." He mentioned that expenses rose by "eighteen percent during the past year, but the pension fund is fully funded. It's very expensive, but all of you have worked for it. Bill Walker [the one agency retiree present at the Breakfast] and Mort Koshlin [the other retiree, not present] know it's helpful . . ."*
>
> *"We're building from within. It's the Spiro way. We only go outside [the agency to hire] when it's absolutely necessary. I'm therefore happy to announce the following promotions . . . Herb Smith has been promoted to Senior Vice President [from Vice President] and Ed Shields has been promoted to Vice President [he was not previously an officer]. Congratulations to each of you. I'm happy to announce that Gerry Oakes has been promoted to Executive Vice President [from Senior Vice President]. Congratulations Gerry!" At the announcement of Gerry Oakes' promotion there was a loud round of applause.*

Walter's remarks concerning the pension plan are revealing, because the agency is postured as a benevolent and somewhat suffering provider. Pension fund money is connoted to be not all realized by members' labor, and thus as not belonging to them. Instead, the agency provides even though it has to bear perhaps inequitable financial pain. The agency is magnanimous: "It's [the pension fund] very expensive." Here the notion of gift is evoked, couched in parental terms. Workers are "good," so top management will reward them. The circumstances of appropriation are inverted in presentation. The theme of altruism is extended by connoting the retirees' pensions as gifts not fully earned.

Title promotions are rewarded on the combined basis of tenure, performance, and projected worth, and are valued because they increase one's organizational and personal status. However, they do not normally result in increases in remuneration, nor change one's task function. Title promotions signify recognition, but do not directly result in an increase in authority or responsibility. The major exception here was the promotion of Gerry Oakes to Executive Vice President, which represented formal recognition of his membership in the top circles of management.

Repeating the long-run theme of bureaucracy, Walter Spiro notes that the agency rewards tenure, loyalty, and dedication through promotions. Little could more readily undermine this theme than to consistently hire, and admit the hiring of, top level managers at the expense of promoting from within.

> *Finished announcing promotions, Walter began to explain why Spiro and Associates has two Creative Department Directors. The members sharing this responsibility are "two different people, as different as can be. One is from Creative and the other is from Copy." During this time the two Directors had walked to the podium. They were similarly dressing in light blue seersucker suits, light yellow Oxford shirts, dark blue ties, like shoes, and metal rimmed glasses. Standing on either side of Walter, one said, "Hi, I'm Isaac," and the other said "Hi, I'm Bob." They began to speak about advertising awards the agency had received during the year. They then showed a series of slides of each individual from the Creative Department. Each photograph was humorously posed, with members standing on their desks making faces, and so on. Then, to the accompaniment of the theme song from the movie "Star Wars," Bob and Isaac displayed slides of each award winning advertisement. After the show ended and the lights were turned back on, Bob noted that the agency won forty percent of the competitions they had entered, and then Isaac read the name of each member of the Creative Department, including Bob and himself. He asked people to stand as their names were called, and when all were standing he said, "Give these people a hand. They deserve it." The Creative Department members were applauded, and returned to their seats.*

The playfulness of the Creative Department's presentation draws attention to the norms governing business behavior. The two Creative Directors, dressed in light blue and white seersucker suits with similar accessories—standing on either side of Walter, who was dressed in a dark conservative suit, French-style cuffed shirt, sizable gold cuff links, and so on—are playing their role of agency jester, where the jester is funny by testing and mocking norms. The same taunting occurs in Bob and Isaac's comic introduction.

In the picture, Creative Department members are shown asleep at their desks, wearing outlandish clothing, making silly faces, standing on their desks, and so on. That the pictures were considered funny rather than offensive indicates an understood burlesque of norms, bringing all members together in sharing a slightly "naughty" experience. Further, the very nature of a slide show, a performance occurring in a dark room with all occupied in the same task, contributes to the shared experience, as do the accompanying slides of the "award winning" advertisements. The "Star Wars" score was met with laughter and applause, in appreciation of the Creative Department's deviant courage. Creative's performance was truly enjoyed by many, where the work of advertising, their work, was made fun of by portraying it in an inverted form. Imagine the Creative Department Directors dressing alike in foppish clothing and appearing to "pitch" a new business account by introducing themselves by "Hi, I'm Bob" and "Hi, I'm Isaac." Further, although potential clients are often shown a "best of Spiro and Associates" advertisement portfolio, this would not normally be done to the accompaniment of such overly dramatic music as the "Star Wars" score. Further, it is beyond the norms of standard business behavior for members to stand on their desks wearing outlandish clothing, and so on. In each of these instances members have mocked normative conduct by "distancing" their portrayals from acceptable role behavior (Goffman, 1961). Further, the inversion that occurs by not going "too far" makes known the deep rules of satisfactory action.

> Walter went to the podium and said "We now come to a subject of great importance to our community. We have good jobs, a good company, and good clients, but there are those less fortunate than us. I am speaking, of course, of the United Way. We are a 'pace setting' agency, giving early in the campaign, before others, to set an example."
>
> "I want to underscore the importance of this," said Walter. I hope you won't brush aside the responsibility. It's an important thing in this country and this city to support the United Way. I'll certainly do my part, and I'm sure you'll do yours."

The role of public service work is evoked here. Throughout this phase the agency is referred to in terms denoting unity. The interests of all are realized in a situation of mutual benefit.

Designating the agency as a "pace setter," with a corporate goal twenty-three percent above the previous year's, is an elite act of power. During a time when the agency is delaying salary increases and the overall economy is depressed, requesting members to make economic sacrifices significant on an individual level is an act which, in a zero-sum situation, primarily benefits corporate interests through the re-creation of bureaucracy. This form of centralized forced giving is an act of power for an additional reason. The average member has limited means. By giving to United Way, an institutionalized corporate charity, his or her economic means to contribute to other charities is subsequently reduced. As she or he meets the corporate goal she or he might be contributing to causes not personally desired, and forcibly ignoring those consciously wanted (see Rosen, 1984). He or she will likely donate through the agency's United Way drive, however. Since giving has directive overtones beyond that of a request, the goal will likely be met or exceeded, as it has been in past years.

> *Walter then introduced the topic of profit sharing and bonuses. He said that other Philadelphia agencies purport to have profit sharing and bonuses, but they are really "delayed pension and Christmas funds. Here at Spiro and Associates we share profits after retained earnings, the money coming from the past fiscal year. But management decisions have to be tempered by considerations of today's economy. Other companies may put away money for retained earnings for a rainy day. However, we've decided to give our money in the most generous possible way. It's been a difficult year, with expenses up. Almost everyone will receive as much of a bonus, if not more, than they did last year." Walter then described the employee bonus system, and said that each employee would meet with his or her department head by the end of that week and receive a copy of his or her performance evaluation. These are decided upon by Walter, Norman, Gerry Oaks, and each employee's department head.*
>
> *"Up to this year," Walter continued, "we did something we knew was a mistake. All of you received your profit sharing and bonuses at the same time you received your salary adjustments. But profit sharing and bonuses look backward to your and our performance over the past year. Salary adjustments look forward, and looking forward by September 15, with only July's accounting figures [from the new fiscal year the Accounting Department can compile only July's figures by the time management decides on salary increases] is difficult, and July's figures were not good. Therefore, on January first we'll announce the new salary adjustments. This decision isn't a salary freeze. From now on bonuses will be given after Labor Day [no longer at the Breakfast] and salary adjustments [cost of living increases and pay raises] will be given on January*

first. Everyone, from me to the lowest person here, will not receive a salary adjustment till January."

"We have a policy at Spiro and Associates of not laying off people. With the account losses we've sustained other agencies would lay off people, but we won't here. You can go back to sleep, because the next speaker is Norman Tissian." People laughed.

After the fiscal year ends the agency pays "bonuses" to members, which must be distributed no later than two-and-a-half months after the last day of the fiscal year. The agency also has a pension program. The money contributed to both programs is a tax deductible business expenses.

According to Gerry Oaks, the agency's chief financial officer, Walter Spiro has exaggerated the munificence of management. While Spiro and Associates pays a bonus "rewarding" workers' yearly performances, some other Philadelphia advertising agencies instead distribute "Christmas bonuses," considered as seasonal gifts. These are smaller than a salary bonus. Here Walter Spiro highlights the difference between these schemes to favorably cast his remunerative practices. However, Gerry Oakes reported that other comparable agencies pay higher base salaries, the agency performance bonus merely making their remuneration more competitive.

Walter's comment concerning the relationship between retained earnings and the bonus plan is worth examination for its illustration of social structure. According to Gerry Oakes, under Walter's direction the amount of funds credited to retained earnings is disproportionately large for a firm of its size and nature. By diverting funds to "profit" and consequently to retained earnings, Gerry noted, top management is primarily depriving general members of income realizable here through bonuses. Gerry termed this practice "a selfish one," and Walter's discourse over bonuses a "Walterism." It is "selfish," Gerry noted because the buyout price management will eventually receive is increased by this distribution of funds otherwise likely dispersed to general members as income. Thus, at least according the agency's top financial officer, Walter's statement that "other companies may put away money for retained earnings for a rainy day. However, we've [management] decided to give our money in the most generous possible way," is not reflective of Spiro and Associates practice: the opposite occurs. Where munificence is declared appropriation exists, clouded against a background of familial caring for the "we-ness" that is proposed as Spiro and Associates.

At 9:00 a.m. that morning Walter announced that the agency experienced record billings. One hour later a message of austerity mixed with benevolence is communicated. All salaries are to be frozen, but this freeze "isn't a salary freeze." Considering inflation, real wages have been cut. However, from Walter "to the lowest person here" all will suffer, implying a normatively equitable condition. Management's increased equity value and dividend return is not included. This is presumably an immaculate marginal return on capital.

It is not uncommon for agencies to experience seasonal fluctuations in expenditures as old clients leave and new ones are found. While Spiro and Associates did lose some major accounts during the past year, it also acquired other major ones, according to some managers, thus at least striking a balance. Because most members are unaware of the specific financial repercussion of any particular loss or gain, claiming account losses is an inherently vague argument appearing concretely grounded.

Considering management's long-run revenue projections, it is unlikely that they would base salaries even primarily on one month's accounting figures. Further, Walter's argument is misleading, for at any point raises are decided on the future, which remains unknowable. If raises are now to be given at the end of January, they will cover the last half of the current fiscal year and the first half of the next, not previous performance, as Walter implies. Management may use any number of previous months' financial figures to project performance. However, if the giving of raises is kept to the Breakfast, management may use any number of previous months' financial figures to project future performance, which is nevertheless unknowable absolutely but with a level of probability in the general condition equal to the proposed January decision date.

Norman Tissian walked to the podium. "You are in the advertising business because it's the only way for you to express yourself. You are in this agency because Spiro and Associates is the best shop in town, where you are pushed harder and can go farther. I can only speak of myself, but this year I will work longer hours. I will travel more. I will try harder to make my work, and this agency, into the best it can be . . . I want everyone here to stand, and to applaud ourselves for the great work we have done, and for what we have accomplished."

After the applause ended and people sat down, Walter Spiro asked for the lights to be turned off and showed a slide of the words "Tell/Listen" in large letters. He said, "If everyone in this agency told and listened, we'd have fifteen percent more revenue . . . If people told others what they need to know, and if people listened when they are being given information . . . and we would all be much better off."

He then projected another slide of the image "Me/We," and said, " 'Me/We,' they belong together. Me, I want more money. Me, I want more success. Me, I want more recognition. If we can get all of the ambitions of the Me under the We, Spiro and Associates could add another fifteen to twenty percent to our revenues. If we would think of all of us as a team, we would all be much better off."

The third slide Walter Spiro showed was of the words "Drive/Win," and he continued, "Winning is the objective. To give the best marketing plan . . . To have the most creative idea . . . To write the best public relations story."

"Laid back people have no place in this agency. Other agencies have laid back people, but ask them if they have profit plans, ask them if they have bonuses . . . ask them if they have the profit record and growth record that we have."

"Drive is what it takes to win. Have drive or get out of the kitchen. Or get it."

"I want driven people back at the agency. I want people who want to win, who want to listen, who want to tell, who want to think of this agency. Thank you, and let's get back to work."

Norman Tissian's speech, like Walter Spiro's, is at one level a "pep" talk. Here it is designed to reinforce the motivation to work hard, to reinforce relations of unity of purpose among members. These two performances create and project an ontology of hard work, success, and communitas.

More fundamentally, however, these performances reinforce the institutionalization of bureaucratic knowing and being, backgrounding that which is a contested terrain. It is not necessary that individuals will accept the surface exhortations, and will rather see these as "pep rallies." Instead, behind each speaker's particular phrases there exists an implicitly stated model of social structure. To the degree either speaker reinforces the acceptance of these models capitalist relations in and of production are re-created. Managerial domination in practice is maintained not by an excited audience rushing back to the agency to work energetically, but by a workforce accepting the defined terrain. Culture, creating, and being the terrain for consciousness here is a mechanism for control.

Note

1. Tony Tinker (Baruch College-CUNY) and Cheryl Lehman (Hofstra University) encouraged me to find that water well under the bridge. Joanne Martin asked me to look for it. Peter Frost was silly enough to let me publish this the first time. Thank you.

6

On the Naming of the Rose:
Interests and Multiple Meanings
as Elements of Organizational Culture

ED YOUNG

Two Models and an Interface

A quick glance into any academic bookshop will reveal that the study of
organizational culture is booming. Texts abound, how-to-do-it manuals
offer quick solutions, veteran managers publish their memoirs, shelves
heave.

Yet as this book suggests, much of this material is rooted in a distorted
theoretical focus. Most studies adopt, and sometimes advocate, a unitary
perspective in which diverse organizational interests are either ignored or
assumed to be fused in common agreement. The difficulties and methodological assumptions of this integration paradigm (cf. Martin & Meyerson,
1988) can be usefully contrasted with approaches that highlight the analytical value of recognizing pluralistic, differentiated interests.

Both integration and differentiation models offer insights and raise
questions. We should be wary however of viewing them as opposites.
Indeed awareness of the interdependence between these processes throws

AUTHOR'S NOTE: Excerpted with permission from "On the Naming of the Rose: Interests
and Multiple Meanings as Elements of Organizational Culture", by Ed Young, 1989. *Organization Studies,* 10(2) 187-206. © by Walter de Gruyter. Berlin. New York. ISSN 0170-8406/89

light on how values and issues are negotiated between organizational participants such that social events are attributed meaning.

Once we view organizations in this way, some interesting questions about the relationship between meanings and organizational interests come into view. Rather than something which an organization somehow has, that vacuous "way we do things around here," for instance, organizational culture emerges as sets of meanings constructed and imputed to organizational events by various groups and interests in pursuit of their aims. The analysis shifts from an appraisal of the content of meanings toward identifying how meanings are constructed and imposed in order to mobilize interest group support (Martin & Powers, 1983b; Young, 1986). Similarly, this link between putative meanings and mobilization suggests that events will receive diverse interpretations, several varying attributions of meanings simultaneously, as different groups seek to define their boundaries and membership (Feldman & March, 1981). Ambiguity then, an elision between integration and differentiation, between unity and distinctiveness, has utility as a means for constructing social identity.

I want to illustrate these themes by means of an account of shop-floor relationships in a small manufacturing firm. In this company, the existence of solidary values was explicitly marked by widely-held views concerning the firm, assertions of its unique qualities, and regular statements of collective identity by shop-floor groups. These were also the features of company culture proclaimed by its managers. Yet a closer appraisal suggests that precisely these statements of collectivity also constitute the vehicles whereby different interests amongst shop-floor workers asserted superiority and celebrated sectional boundaries. Unity and division existed in tandem.

Viewing Proteus

Proteus Rainwear Limited (PRL) occupies a small site on the edge of a decaying factory estate in a major manufacturing city in northern Britain. The firm has for several years specialized in producing sewn raincoats, hats, and industrial clothing, all largely made from imported fabrics and for major retailing companies.

Over a period of some 10 months, I regularly visited PRL while I was assisting in the design of post-graduate programs at the Manchester School. During this period I utilized a mix of informal interviewing and conversation throughout the shop floor. To record comments from machinists,

Job Description	Number of Employees
Management	6
Supervision	7
Office	6
Shop Floor	61
Warehouse/Dispatch	11
Design	1

Figure 6.1. PRL Stall Distribution

supervisors, and managers, I took rapid notes in a notebook, usually on the spot, or sometime behind piles of sewn rainwear. My efforts at "pure" participant observation floundered with my ineptitude before sewing machines, but I became effective at packing finished items in the Packing/Despatch Section (see Figure 6.2). I maintained an unstructured interviewing format, allowing machinists and supervisors to elaborate on any theme they wished. As various issues recurrently emerged—not all noted in this chapter of course—from the views of these workers, I increasingly sought elaboration on them, focusing more specific questions and sometimes seeking direct clarification. In this way, I was attempting to follow the broad outlines of "grounded theory" as discussed by Glaser and Strauss (1967).

Operating from a single large machining floor with adjoining office and warehouse space, the PRL factory is a noisy, cluttered place, with piles of fabric lining the machine shop floor, rows of sewing machines loudly stitching throughout the day, and the machinists bent over various repetitive stitching tasks. The firm retains a small management group of six directors, managing some 80 to 100 largely female employees, the precise numbers varying with work levels. Figure 6.1 details the functional distribution of the workforce at the point of my study, with the shop-floor machinists clearly in the majority.

"A Unique Little World of Its Own Down There"

The most significant feature of PRL for our interest here was the perception held by both management and the workforce that the company retained a distinctive culture. These values centered around the themes of long-standing employee involvement and a concern by the management to provide steady employment. Statements that employees held particular

loyalty to PRL and that the firm had retained long employment relationships with a large core of staff, found frequent expression:

> See, most of the people in 'ere 'ave been in the company for years. It's like that.
> Like a family really, with the management trying to 'old onto the ones who they
> know 'ave the skills and can work. (Machinist, PRL shop floor)

> I'd say that a lot of the ones down there are very committed to the firm. They've
> been here for years and they know the management will look after them. So you'll
> find that most people here are very positive about the place. (Warehouse Supervisor)

This picture of stability and established ties was believed to be epitomized
by the shop-floor machinists. Both the machinists and other PRL employees
emphasized the existence of common values uniting the shop floor, values
which found regular expression and which marked out the distinctive identity
of this section of the workforce. Among the machinists, a unique company
culture was believed to be most salient and most imbued with collective
sentiment:

> Everyone says 'ow we're all different down 'ere on the floor. . . . See, there's a
> very close atmosphere. All the girls 'ave known one another for years, and we've
> worked in the firm for ages too. So down 'ere you get the feeling that we all stick
> together like, whereas in other parts they don't so much. (Machinist, PRL shop-
> floor)

> It's on the shop floor, amongst the machinists that all that's really in evidence.
> There's real identification with the firm there, and a solid sense of team spirit. There
> are various events, you know, that they all organize which mark them out espe-
> cially. (PRL Managing Director)

> Oh I'll tell you, it's a unique little world of its own down there. They all have their
> own little events which they organize, and they've got their own lot of interests.
> You should see them all wearing roses on St. George's Day. (PRL Production
> Director)

Roses, Royals, and Outings

Roses

Three recurring events were felt to capture these themes. The most
frequently cited of these was the wearing of St. George's Day roses. On
the prescribed day each year, all of the shop-floor machinists would wear

a red rose, purchased by collections among themselves, with the roses handed out by supervisors on the floor. For participants and other PRL employees alike, this event held the significance of a ritual of collective unity, an expression of common identity in relation to other work groups in the firm:

> It's just something the girls have always done. Just a way we have of being friendly with one another and showing it. (Supervisor, PRL shop floor)

> Out there (i.e., the shop floor) all the girls wear red roses on St. George's Day; it's a real sight. But they're the only ones. Out here there isn't so much of a common spirit, so that sort of thing doesn't get organized. (Office worker, PRL Main Office)

> It's the way they've got of showing how they're the real old part of the firm, the ones where it all started. (PRL Marketing Director)

Royals

This patriotic theme was continued elsewhere. Among the machinists, an enthusiasm for the Royal Family was marked. Located on one wall of the machining room was a board edged with Union Jack flags that was visible across the whole factory floor. This was loaded with photographs of the Royals, newspaper clippings about the Royal Family, rosettes from employees who had watched royal processions, and so on. Pride of place was held by a menu from Buckingham Palace donated by a machinist who had attended a royal charity lunch.

Consistent efforts were made to maintain the "Monarchy Board," as it was called, with a rota of people responsible for keeping it tidy, providing new clippings and photographs, and so forth. These concerns reached fever pitch during royal weddings (there were two during the period of my study). On these occasions, machinists produced skillfully sewn and embroidered rainwear in their leisure time for the royal brides. A shop-floor collection provided money for gifts donated in the name of the PRL machinists. One of the supervisors arranged for a shop-floor viewing of videos of the royal weddings. The Monarchy Board groaned with new photographs, letters from the Palace expressing gratitude, and letters from machinists to the new princesses.

Outings

Lastly, the organization of informal events among the machinists was also viewed as marking the common ties uniting this group. Several groups of machinists met regularly in their leisure time, visiting theaters and restaurants together. Over thirty had travelled abroad together the previous summer for a fortnight. Special occasions, weddings, retirements and so on found groups of machinists organizing celebrations and events specific to themselves and largely independent of other PRL employees.

From the viewpoint of the management, these events were viewed as summarizing a collective identity among the machinists, which by fostering a sense of team spirit oiled the wheels of everyday output and task performance. General supervisory and management policy consequently was toward the tacit encouragement of these activities, a recognition of their potential value.

> Well see, the photo's on the Board and all that, these are ways to keep up team spirit you see, keep up interest. It makes the job easier. (Production Director)

> Frankly, there isn't much job satisfaction for the machinists, or at least I don't see how there could be. But the supervisors encourage all sorts of ways to keep up morale and provide an interest. The Board down there's one example. (Managing Director)

> You've got to understand the girls if you want to get them to work well. So the roses and the little outings occasionally are important to bring people together. (Supervisor, Shop floor)

Unity Manifest

So here was that ideal depicted in managerial studies of organizational culture. Explicit and solidary values informed the PRL workforce, expressing their sense of collectivity and common interest. PRL employees regularly noted their long-standing ties with the company, their joint experiences, and their unique qualities. More specifically, an array of organized activities among the shop-floor machinists—easily the majority of the workforce remember—were viewed as both marking their common identity as celebrating it. Roses and Royals captured agreed sentiments and the distinctiveness of the shop floor within the whole firm.

Work-Wear

Cutting Room	Initial sewing to	Final sewing	Finish/
4 Cutters	asembled item	and assembly	Quality control
	13 Machinists	14 Machinists	9 Machinists
1 Supervisor		1 Supervisor	1 Supervisor

Bags

Packing/Despatching
11 Operatives
+ 2 Supervisors

Assembly Group 1
(Cutting, sewing,pleating, etc.)
7 Machinists + 1 Supervisor

Assembly Group 2
(Cutting, sewing, pleating, etc.)
7 Machinists + 1 Supervisor

Figure 6.2. PGL "Work-Wear" and "Bag" Production Lines

The Origins of Division: Task and Domestic Life Cycle

If we view social relationships among the PRL machinists more closely, it is clear that these events not only expressed collectivity, but also provided for the statement of division between elements within this apparently solidary group.

First, although the shop-floor workers were a distinct category in the sense of sharing a common location and their involvement in broadly similar jobs, in practice different work tasks associated with the products of this firm divided the machinists into two different groups. The PRL shop floor was organized into two production lines: "work-wear" and "bags," each producing different commodities.

Work-Wear

In the work-wear line, machinists stitched and assembled pieces of material into overalls and laboratory jackets ordered by industrial companies and government agencies. Production flows in the work-wear line are depicted in Figure 6.2. Pre-cut materials were progressively stitched together and assembled, then put through to final finish and packing.

The work-wear machinists were paid on an individual piecework basis, their tasks largely comprising repetitive stitching and assembly jobs. Workloads in each of the sections were heavy, with constant customer demands for large quantities. The high division of labor in the work-wear line, the fragmentation of tasks into a small number of activities recurrently performed by individual machinists, meant that although the line was divided into sections, in practice the tasks required little cooperation between individuals. Each machinist, assembler, or packer worked largely independently of others, with the section supervisors responsible for coordinating the flow of work between individuals.

Bags

By contrast, machinists in the bag line were engaged in sewing and lining small pieces of material together to create various handbag and toilet-bag products. Rather than the highly specialized tasks of the work-wear line, individual bag machinists undertook the whole production task, from initial sewing of basic materials through to insertion of clipping devices, labels, and so forth. Figure 6.2 charts the bag line work flow. Thus work tasks in the bag line entailed machinists individually applying several stitching operations on an item through to its completion, without the need for cooperative efforts between themselves. The bag machinists also were paid on piecework performance, but the unstable customer demand for these products meant that the whole bag line went through peaks and troughs of activity. Consequently, in contrast with the regular employment available to the work-wear machinists, the bag line was subject to periodic redundancies, and sometimes shrank to only the supervisors and a core of remaining machinists seeking out the trickle of work.

These task variations in turn were reinforced by demographic and attitudinal differences between the two machinist groups. In work-wear, the majority of women retained a long familiarity with one another over time, based on lengthy employment in PRL and the work-wear line specifically. Many had joined the firm at an earlier period, left to raise families, and then gradually returned through part-time and then full-time employment. Most had circulated through all the work-wear section over time, so that the whole group had an intimate knowledge of the tasks associated with the line. Most of these women continued to hold child rearing and domestic responsibility to some degree.

The combination of these two factors, extensive common employment in the firm and family obligations beyond it, prompted specific work attitudes within this group. These centered around a concern for income maximization coupled with the perception that long experience in PRL had invested them with considerable machining skills. For the work-wear machinists, regular employment in PRL provided valued income for domestic expenditure, such that work tasks were continually sought after, yet this appetite for work was simultaneously seen as itself fostering and marking expertise:

> Oh no, I need to earn my money see. You've got to be ready to take a job, because you can't earn your money otherwise. . . . We're all like that see, that's why on this side (i.e., work-wear) everyone 'as good sewing skills. We've all done different jobs. (Work-Wear Machinist)

> In this Section the girls all look for the work. Oh course, that's mainly because they need the money. But they also know that the more experience they get, the more skills they get, the more they can take on any job. (Work-Wear Supervisor)

The social structure of the bags machinists group was quite different. These women generally were younger than their work-wear counterparts and most were unmarried or without domestic ties. Few retained lengthy employment experience in the firm, because with the fluctuation in orders for bags this group was subject to frequent redundancies and dissolution.

This combination of employment conditions and nonwork social roles also fostered different attitudes to the task and the company. Critical and hostile responses to PRL management and its policies were much more common among the bag machinists, and contrasted sharply with the deferent views prevailing in work-wear. Again, for the bag workers, employment in PRL was not prompted by income maximization, but rather the concern to secure a sufficient minimum wage to provide cash for weekend leisure pursuits. Once this minimum had been reached the bag machinists tended to view continued high performance as superfluous:

> Once you 'ave enough just to go out like, I don't try too much after that, because I don't really like the work, an' I can't see the point of jus' workin' away for nothin'. (Bags Machinist)

> I like to keep to a minimum level really, but once I get to that I like to be a bit choosy. You learn see, that you get laid off whether you work 'ard or not, whereas all the old ones over there are always lookin' for work, 'cos they need the money. (Bags Machinist)

The young ones here are a problem, yes. They only want cash for the weekend, so it's difficult to keep them at the machine, turning out good quality. With the ones over on work-wear, you can basically leave 'em at it an' they'll earn their money. But on this side they're not like that. (Bags Supervisor)

Summary of Differences

We can now summarize some of the social characteristics of these two groups. On one hand, in the work-wear line, a core of established and experienced machinists were concerned with maximizing earnings to meet domestic expenditures. Work flows here were both heavy and stable. In contrast, the bag line comprised of much younger women with few domestic ties prompted a concern for sufficient income for immediate personal expenditures. Employment in this line was unstable, and comprised complete production of a finished item. Although the work-wear machinists represented the core PRL shop floor workforce, the bag section retained the characteristics of a secondary labor force within the firm.

Division Stated: "That Lot Over There!"

The underlying distinctions between the two groups of machinists had gradually found open expression over time. Each of these groups asserted its superiority from the other and sought to establish and define its boundaries.

Among the work-wear machinists, for instance, a rhetoric claiming superior machining skills and the poor abilities apparent in the bag line was pervasive. The bag machinists were readily depicted as a marginal social group, poorly motivated, uncommitted to PRL, and largely incapable of effort:

> That lot over there! Oh, there's no skills over there. They're all young girls really, without much machining skills. All they've got to do is sew in a square really, whereas in work-wear it's more complicated. (Work-Wear Machinist)

> In the bags it is difficult to motivate. . . . They only want the quick cash you see, and there's no real commitment to the firm. You've got to watch them all the time, because they're quite happy to sit around over the machines and talk, or turn out rubbish work. (Work-Wear Supervisor)

For their part, the bag machinists would refute these claims and assert that in fact they were required to display superior skills, given the nature of their task. Emphasis here fell on the intricate machining skills required to complete this product. The bag machinists also sought to refute attributions of marginal status. In their view, the work-wear line comprised a stagnant group, maintaining "snobbish" attitudes but largely out-moded to present conditions in the firm.

> They all say we're rubbish, but I think the real skills are over this side, where you've got tiny little pieces which all have to be sewn together just right. It's because they're all old Proteus people really, an' they just don't like we new ones. (Bag Machinist)

> All the old ones over there are just old women really. They all love this place, they think it's marvelous. But I don't; I reckon it's useless. They like to make you think that they're all good machinists an' that, but we've got better ones on this side in my opinion. (Bag Machinist)

Far from a solidary category then, the PRL shop-floor machinists were divided into these two broad camps, each engaged in claim and counter-claim regarding their mutual superiority and depicting the social distance between them. We should be clear that these sentiments were not merely rhetorical outbursts of intergroup hostility. Rather the existence of these boundaries had practical outcomes on social processes on the shop floor, including processes of management control. Let me illustrate this quickly with reference to the issue of the transferability of machinists between the two production lines.

Given the pace of orders in work-wear, the machinists here were invariably fully stretched, such that transfer to tasks in the bag line hardly ever occurred. With the fluctuation in work levels in bags, however, bag machinists were frequently idle. In these circumstances, the bag machinists represented a potential labor reserve to supplement the hard-pressed work-wear lines. In practice, however, this direct transfer across the production lines rarely occurred. Instead, surplus bag machinists were allocated tasks in the final packing section, which was common to both lines (see Figure 6.2). Once there, the younger bag machinists were carefully scrutinized over several weeks by the two packing supervisors—both ex-work-wear—as to their "suitability" for transfer into the work-wear line.

The criteria underlying this scrutiny represented a set of both formal and informal values, in that while upholding official management standards concerning work standards, speed of work, and so forth, these values also expressed sentiments informing the work-wear group. Evaluating the bag entrants, the supervisors—and from a distance the other work-wear machinists—maintained a series of "telling" categories (Burton, 1978) that were believed to signal compliance with the characteristics and views of the work-wear group.

> I look for things which I know are important. They've got to have a flexible attitude so that they want to learn new skills and will accept supervision. You keep a check on how quickly they cope with speed of the machine. How they'll accept instructions. Most of these young ones are surly and won't take the discipline. (Supervisor, Packing Section)

> You've got to watch them really closely. I've found that most from the bags are rubbish. The younger ones don't 'ave an interest really; they'd rather sit with their friends an' talk. They wait for work to arrive. . . . I can't abide that; I pull 'em up sharp. But we shouldn't 'ave to do that, not with the good ones. (Supervisor, Packing Section)

Predictably, surplus bag machinists ultimately transferred to work-wear were those most closely aligned to the work-wear model of the "good worker." These were older women, usually with families, who displayed a willingness to accept the values and hierarchies prevalent in the work-wear line. As we have seen, these represented a minority within the bag group. The younger women, concerned primarily with income maintenance alone, invariably were judged intractable and "not wanting to work." They would either be transferred back to the bag line, if work existed, or laid off.

From this perspective then, the packing section of these two production lines represented a locus of boundary maintenance between the two groups. Potential transfers between work-wear and bags were carefully filtered by sets of informal values that both asserted and reinforced the status claims of the former. The outcome was the displacement of the "espoused" management policies emphasizing labor flexibility by the "theories-in-use" (Schön, 1971) maintained by the supervisors which echoed the status claims of the different work groups.

Ritual as Boundary Maintenance

It is against this context that the significance of what appeared to be statements of collectivity among the PRL shop-floor workers needs to be understood. We have seen that at one level, the wearing of the St. George's Rose, the maintenance of the Monarchy Board, the organized leisure

outings, and so forth were viewed as statements of shop-floor distinctiveness and identity.

Once we recognize the cleavages between the shop-floor groups, however, these same activities emerge as simultaneously expressing division
between these interests. Let us take each of these events in turn from this
perspective, starting with those red roses. Although virtually all of the
machinists did wear a rose on the appointed day, it was significant that the
collection of money and the distribution of the flowers was organized
separately across the work-wear and bag lines. Work-wear and bags collected their own funds and pinned on their own blooms.

This sense that this highly visible and apparently collective event contained within it the expression of difference between the two production
lines was widely recognized.

> Course, it's really only on this side like, that we all collect together for our roses.
> There's not enough common feeling like, over amongst all them bag girls, 'cos
> they couldn't really care less so long as they get their money. (Machinist, Work-
> Wear)

> We collect for it by ourselves see. Organize amongst ourselves. Because all that
> lot are so stand-offish and think they're better workers an' that. So we do ours just
> around this part of the factory. (Machinist, Bags)

The Monarchy Board too, showed a similar pattern. Although the board
was open to all on the shop floor, in practice, its decoration and contributions were drawn exclusively from work-wear. The rota for tidying the
board was drawn only from work-wear staff. Among the bag machinists,
the Monarchy Board was widely viewed as a prerogative of work-wear and
one further statement of their claimed superiority.

> All that stuff over on the board, that's all the old biddies really. They do all that.
> It's their way of sayin' 'ow special they think they are; 'ow they've been 'ere
> longest an' all that. Just sort of tryin' to put all the others down. (Machinist, Bags).

Lastly, the social events confirmed this theme. Although PRL machinists
certainly did meet in large groups in leisure time, these events were
invariably organized within work-wear, and involved only work-wear staff.
Indeed, the recurring redundancies characterizing the bag line and the rapid
turnover among the machinists curtailed the formation of social ties that
spanned the work-nonwork setting. Characteristically, the organized out-

ings of the work-wear machinists were viewed by some bag staff as another statement of distinctiveness:

> There's a group of 'em, mainly the old ones on work-wear who go out together an' that, to shows and things. But they don't let anyone else go. They keep it all in their group. It's their way of sayin' they're superior see, showin' their service in the factory.

These three events, while apparently instances of collective ritual, emphasizing group unity, also contained within them the seeds of discord between sectional interests. Stated collectivity also asserted division.

7

Multiple Constituencies
and the Quality of Working Life:
Intervention at FoodCom

JEAN M. BARTUNEK

MICHAEL K. MOCH

Much of the research exploring organizational culture distinguishes organizations on the basis of their single more-or-less internally consistent cultures. Often, however, organizations embrace multiple cultures: different and even incompatible beliefs, values, and assumptions held by different groups (e.g., Gray, Bougon, & Donnelly, 1985; Louis, 1985; Martin & Meyerson, 1988; Meyerson & Martin, 1987). There is little documentation of this phenomenon, however, despite its obvious importance. For example, when organizations embrace multiple cultures, strategies for planned change may have to consider simultaneous multiple and interdependent changes within and between culturally heterogeneous groups.

In this chapter we introduce the reader to the cultural heterogeneity that confronted external change-agents in a medium-sized unionized commercial bakery located in the southern United States. The change-agents were commissioned to improve productivity and the quality of employees' working lives (QWL) in the bakery, one of several operated by a multinational firm we call "FoodCom." As evaluators, we were on-site at the plant at frequent intervals throughout a 2½ year period. An intern for the QWL

AUTHORS' NOTE: Both authors contributed equally to this chapter.

project, one of whose duties was to collect observational data about the intervention, was present the entire time. When we were at the plant we sat in on meetings, interviewed employees, administered surveys, and generally observed the day-to-day activities that occurred. We paid attention to the types of language the various participants used (cf. Moch & Fields, 1985), to certain patterns of behavior (such as seating arrangements in the cafeteria), and to how participants addressed work problems.

As we observed events over time, it became clear that there were multiple constituencies in the plant, each of which had its own understanding of events. These differences appeared to be cultural—rooted in differing beliefs, values, and assumptions. The differences caused problems for the plant-wide QWL intervention. They also affected a broader range of work activities. In this chapter we provide an overview of the perspectives of many of the constituencies (the consultants, corporate management, plant management, line employees, and the machinists) by describing ways these groups carried out and/or responded to the intervention. A more complete analysis of the intervention is available elsewhere (Moch & Bartunek, 1990).

QWL Program Consulting Staff: The Cooperative Perspective

The change effort was designed to improve productivity and the quality of working life by encouraging greater labor-management cooperation. A joint labor-management committee was established to encourage cooperative efforts directed toward achieving common goals. Committee members were to share responsibility for addressing shared labor-management concerns that went beyond the scope of the bargaining contract (Drexler & Lawler, 1977). They also were to generate subcommittees designed to address specific QWL issues and to staff them with representatives from potentially affected groups.

The consultants attempted to encourage a cooperative atmosphere in a variety of ways. For example, when the newly established labor-management committee met for the first time, management and union members assumed traditional adversarial positions on opposing sides of the table. The consultant, whom we call Tim Deigh, turned his chair around so his back was to the group and remained silent until the representatives redistributed themselves so that management and labor representatives were intermingled. Then he led them in an exercise designed to demonstrate the superiority of consensus decision making. At one point during the intervention, the QWL consulting staff also supported the suggestion that the company consider implementing a gain-sharing program.

Top Management: The Control Perspective

Top corporate management of FoodCom seemed most concerned about control, and illustrated this concern in numerous ways. From the outset of the QWL program, top managers expressed concern that the program not get out of control. For example, they did not allow us to visit the plant until the program had been officially initiated. We had to check in at the plant manager's office each time we visited the bakery. We were told that we could publish nothing without the company's explicit and prior approval. Since this was unacceptable to us, we negotiated an alternative. However, it took months to conclude an acceptable agreement.

The control orientation also was evident in top management's response to a proposed plant-wide employee survey, a component of many QWL interventions. The survey would require a minimum of 30 minutes from each employee. Local management was not willing to absorb this time in their productivity figures. On the other hand, we, as assessors, were convinced that if employees were asked to fill out the questionnaire on their own time there would be a very low response rate. The issue was addressed during a meeting between senior FoodCom executives and Tim Deigh. The executives objected to allocating work time for the question-naire, because expenses for this activity had not been stated in the initial project proposal, and their superior, Frank Struthers, was unwilling to incur unanticipated costs. After the meeting Deigh wrote a memorandum to the senior executives in which he complained that "the pressure for 'efficiency no matter what' had already begun to create (undue) pressures on the effort to bring about meaningful change . . . such pressures from 'on high' make real progress extremely difficult."

Struthers called a meeting to resolve the issue. He opened the meeting by stressing that (1) the QWL experiment was of critical importance to the company and (2) the emphasis on cost control should not be compromised. After considerable debate and a search for less costly alternatives, Struthers announced that the company would pay to have employees complete the questionnaire on company time. He reinforced his com-mitment to the QWL experiment, saying "It's got Frank Struthers' name on it, and it's going to succeed!" He also reinforced his commitment to cost-minimization, leaving little doubt that by conceding on the survey issue he was not likely to approve other unanticipated expenditures.

Top management's concern with minimizing costs was institutionalized in a strict accounting control system. In this system company personnel developed schedules detailing the number of units of each product to be produced each week. The company then calculated standards specifying the number of baking and packaging labor hours needed to produce the scheduled products. Figures reflecting the number of labor hours used relative to this standard were calculated and circulated throughout the company on a weekly basis.

Variances from standard labor hours were extremely difficult to get approved, both for hourly employees and for supervisors. Line employees and supervisory personnel attended the joint labor-management committee meetings. The time spent in these meetings, however, was included in the calculations of labor hours. It took several months to approve a variance that would allow department heads to allocate time for line employees to a category which would not detract from their cost figures. Such a variance was never obtained for supervisors. Rather, the time they spent on QWL program activities was simply absorbed by department heads, who subsequently came under fire for declining productivity.

Local Plant Management: The Paternalistic Perspective

The assessment team spent much of its first few days in the bakery interviewing employees. The interviews and subsequent observations revealed frequent use of family, especially paternalistic, imagery. There were frequent allusions to plant management as "parents" and to employees as "children." For example, one baker was frustrated, because "The administration is playing parent. They tell supervisors what they want supervisors to make us do, 'cause we're always wrong. Well, that game comes back on top, because we want to play parent and make them kids!" The business agent of the union local believed that the plant and the QWL program should be managed the same way a parent should manage his or her children. "It's gotta be done on a gradual, firm, constructive approach. And I'm saying it should be done just like you would raise your child. I'm not saying they're children; I'm saying, you know, that sometimes you gotta police it like they were children."

Paternalism also characterized the attitude of plant management. It seemed to involve at least two dimensions: a concern about control somewhat similar to that of corporate management (cf. Feldman, 1986), and an assumption that plant management had ultimate responsibility for plant-level decision making. The plant manager, Roger Matson, vigorously defended his right to exercise control over the outside consultants and the assessors, as well as the activities of the joint labor-management commit-tee. To do this, he often enacted rituals of power and domination (Mock & Huff, 1983). Soon after we had begun interviewing employees, the assess-ment coordinator (Mike Moch) was called to a telephone on the bakery floor. It was Deigh calling from his office on the East Coast. He had just received a call from FoodCom headquarters complaining that the assessors were dirty and unshaven. The assessment coordinator explained that those conducting interviews on the bakery floor had dressed casually in order to help respondents feel at ease. Male members of the team had trimmed their beards before coming to the plant. After a second conversation with the head of labor relations (calling from his office at World Headquarters of FoodCom), the assessment coordinator went to talk with Matson. It was obvious that Matson had contacted World Headquarters to complain about the assessors' dress.

Walking past the secretary, the assessor could see the top of Matson's head as he was bent over his desk. It was a large highly polished desk at the far end of a long rectangular office. It was the only carpeted room in the building and had fine wood paneling. With some trepidation, the assessment coordinator walked in unannounced and standing directly in front of Matson's desk, said, "I hear you wanted to see me."

Matson looked up as though he had been accosted by an intruder and, pointing to a chair off to his right, demanded that the assessor sit in it. The assessor did. Matson then returned to his work, leaving the assessor to await his next move. After what seemed to the assessor to be a very long time but which probably was no more than a minute, Matson rolled his chair back a couple of feet and swiveled it so he could look directly at the assessor. Leaning back, he took off his tie and threw it on the floor. He was not wearing a jacket. He then unbuttoned and untucked his shirt. Under-neath he wore a sleeveless undershirt. Matson then turned up his shirt collar; messed up what little hair he had left so that much of it stood straight up or out an various unseemly angles, slouched in his chair and, in a demanding tone, asked, "Do you respect me?" The assessor, somewhat shaken, said something to the effect that well-dressed people often are accorded respect. Pointing directly at the assessor, Matson literally shouted, "Exactly!!! From now on you and your people will wear ties in my plant!!!" After attempting some conciliatory remarks which he could not recall later, the assessor left the room.

Matson also seemed to assume that the plant's new labor-management committee should act in ways supportive of management prerogatives. Several weeks after the assessment team concluded its initial interviews, we met with members of the newly formed plant labor-management committee to begin identifying problem areas in the plant. In preparation for this meeting we had forwarded a list of issues employees had raised during our interviews. This meeting had no sooner gotten underway when Matson burst in red-faced and visibly very angry. He had just received a copy of our list.

In strident tones Matson complained bitterly that he had not been given his right to view all documents before they were publicly distributed. Looking directly at members of the new committee, he literally yelled, "I pay your salary here and don't you forget it! I will sign and approve any communications, and I'll be the first to see them!" He then stormed out of the room.

Matson's concern about maintaining responsibility for decision making was communicated through his response to many of the joint labor-management committee's initiatives. One of these initiatives involved committee members' attempts to obtain better food in the cafeteria. Rather than working with the committee on this request, Matson pressured the committee to focus on redecorating the cafeteria, a project he had advocated before the intervention began. Another initiative involved new uniforms for some of the employees. The company had already decided to replace these uniforms. However, Matson treated the new uniforms as a labor-management committee project. Finally, Matson decided that one of the projects of the labor-management committee should be a type of autonomous work group: coordination across all the functional areas working on one particular assembly line. The labor-management committee in the plant believed this was a management initiative, not an initiative of theirs. However, Matson insisted that the joint committee accept this project as one of its own and continued for the duration of the intervention to treat it as such, even though he subsequently ignored many of the labor-management committee's recommendations concerning the project.

Line Employees: The Dependence Perspective

We suggested above that plant management seemed to act as "parents" while line employees acted as "children" in the plant. As children, the line employees seemed to depend on others, especially management, to solve their problems and satisfy their desires. This was illustrated in multiple ways throughout the intervention. We became aware of it during our initial interviews with employees. On this occasion, we were inundated by requests and complaints. First, line employees asked for a large number of amenities, such as improved food in the cafeteria, new shower heads for showers, new clocks, athletic facilities, new uniforms, more social activities, and a repaved parking lot. Many of the employees seemed to expect that the labor-management committee could obtain these for them. In fact, contrary to the usual prescriptions of QWL interventions (cf. Drexler & Lawler, 1977), obtaining amenities became a primary focus of the QWL intervention at FoodCom.

In addition, after several interviews it also became clear that line employees viewed the QWL program as an opportunity to counter past or present grievances. They seemed to expect that the outside consulting staff should change the attitudes of plant and union management. They also had many complaints about the 90 or so maintenance personnel, mostly machinists, associated with a different union. A sample of employee complaints follows:

> There's massive thievery. It's in the maintenance department and includes supervisors. But we can't tell, 'cause then we get in trouble.

> Our damn union don't represent us. They just stand still.

> Slow the lines down. They've got us working like machines here. . . . The union doesn't do anything about it.

> (Supervisors) talk to you like you're a criminal. Then the next day they want you to speak to them.

> Machinists here. You call one and he won't know what to do. Only one does all the work. They all get paid for it. They should teach all the machinists what they're supposed to know.

> Machinery trouble. A lot of problems stem from equipment and the attitude of the machinists.

About three supervisors here are terrible. You can't relate to them. They talk to you like you're dirt under their feet. . . . They use people like guinea pigs. They give you an inferiority complex.

These statements suggest an awareness, one we shared, that there were many problems between groups in the plant. They also suggested the absence of a sense of responsibility for the problems: an expectation that someone else (such as the consultants or plant management) was responsible for addressing them.

Employees' dependence on others to solve problems was reflected not only in the initial interviews, but also in the actions of the labor-management committee. One of the concerns the committee addressed was security in the plant's parking lot. Initially, a parking lot subcommittee took a considerable amount of initiative in facing and addressing the problem. However, the plant manager demanded that the committee develop documented cost estimates, blueprints, and specific recommendations for the proposed structural changes. These tasks were quite difficult, and seemed to the subcommittee to be an unreasonable requirement. The subcommittee members therefore decided that actually doing the work to develop the proposal was the responsibility of plant management. Not gaining his cooperation, the subcommittee instead enlisted and received the support of a corporate and national union level oversight group that visited the plant. Subsequently, the subcommittee left all implementation decisions to the plant manager. Its members took no responsibility for the actual process of implementing changes they had proposed.

Machinists: The Competitive Perspective

The machinists in the bakery were members of a very independent local of what we call the International Machinists Union (IMU). They viewed themselves as in competition with other groups in the bakery, especially the line employees. Several of the quotes presented earlier reflect the generally contentious relations between the machinists and the line workers and, particularly, machinists and female line employees.

The machinists once had been members of the line employees' union, what we call the Food Workers International Union (FWIU). As a minority of this larger group, they had failed in attempts to maintain their significant pay differential over bakers, packers, and other FWIU members. They simply were outvoted when it came to determining the union's bargaining position. Consequently they had left the FWIU and joined the IMU. This move allowed them to maintain their relative pay advantage. However, they frequently expressed concern that the FWIU would attempt to "recapture" them by forcing a plant-wide unionization vote.

Machinists in the plant frequently expressed particular disdain for female employees. Most of the packing department employees in the bakery were women, and packing had the greatest number of employees. As the majority, these women could control the FWIU local. For years they had pressed successfully for bargaining positions advocating absolute rather than percentage raises. Consequently, female FWIU members were paid almost as much as their male counterparts in the baking department, a condition considered unacceptable by most machinists.

The machinists occupied the most desirable position in the cafeteria, a position under the only bank of windows in the room. From their advantaged position, they would evoke images of their superior status. One story, told on several occasions in our presence, compared machinists' tool boxes with women's purses. One machinist would tell another that he owned his own work tools. He then would ask how much the other machinist thought these tools were worth. After several low estimates, the first machinist would proclaim that his work tools were worth several thousand dollars. The machinists would then change roles, the second asking the first how much his tools were worth. After the second machinist proclaimed the true value of his tools, the first machinist would ask the second, "And what do the silly bitches carry in their purses?" Together the two participants would call out "Kotex!" Those listening, usually under the windows in the cafeteria, would smile and nod approval.

The workflow exacerbated tensions between the predominantly female FWIU employees and the machinists. Those packing the product would be the first to experience a mechanical breakdown. However, asking a machinist for help, even if he were in the immediate vicinity, would only delay the repair process. As Whyte (1948) observed in his study of restaurants, employees can respond negatively when those they feel have lower status initiate interaction with them. So it was with the machinists. Requests for repair, however minor, had to be referred up the chain of command until a level commensurate with the machinists' job scheduler was found. At that point the problem could be scheduled and, in time, addressed. Since the technology created sequential interdependencies, this could cause considerable downtime through the production line.

On one occasion, FWIU members petitioned management to move a scheduled holiday from a Thursday to a Friday. By doing so, they argued, employees could benefit from a three-day weekend and the company could save costs associated with firing up the bake shop ovens for only one day of production. Plant management and FWIU representatives approached the officers of the IMU local who rejected the proposal on procedural grounds. Acknowledging that it was a good idea, the IMU officers argued that it had to be rejected, because they had not initiated it. The proper procedure, they argued, was for individual employees to make the suggestion to IMU representatives. Then the IMU could make a formal request of plant management. To do otherwise would be to violate the established procedure for such decisions and expose IMU members to the possibility of having to acquiesce to proposals made by those with whom they had little in common. If they agreed to this particular proposal, they might find themselves outvoted on other issues with which they had substantive disagreement. They were particularly angry with plant management for having violated established practice, because they would very much have appreciated the proposed three-day weekend. The proposal, accordingly, was dropped.

The machinists refused to participate in the QWL program, for fear they might be co-opted by plant management and the FWIU members. Consequently, the QWL program encountered problems similar to those frequently faced by the FWIU. FWIU members, through the local labor-management committee, could propose projects. However, because many of these projects involved requests for physical amenities, the projects usually relied on the machinists for implementation. But projects initiated by the local committee often violated the machinists' understanding of the plant's status hierarchy.

Machinists accepted some of the local committee's proposals. For example, they accepted a new scooter and tool cabinet that were proposed for their own department. However, they changed and/or simply never implemented some other proposals that might have been of more benefit to other departments. One of these proposals was for a no-smoking area in the cafeteria. The machinists installed the area in the space traditionally used by black employees, smokers and non-smokers alike. A second proposal was for more and better synchronized clocks. There had been several problems due both to an inadequate number of clocks and a lack of synchronization of the already existing clocks, and these had caused FWIU members a number of problems. Consequently, the plant's labor-management committee had proposed that new clocks be ordered and that all the clocks be synchronized. The plant manager approved the project.

When new clocks came in, however, the machinists used them to replace existing older clocks.

Conclusion

This description illustrates the presence of cultural heterogeneity in the workplace. Outside consultants, top management, plant management, line supervisors, and machinists held widely differing values, beliefs, and behavioral predispositions. Analysts seeking to understand the bakery's culture would be hard-pressed to identify a single set of pervasive cultural predispositions. Rather, the social system contained a variety of cultures reinforced by physical, social, and occupational barriers among groups. Analysts therefore would do well to identify these subcultures and the barriers that maintain them. Those responsible for managing planned change in culturally heterogeneous systems like FoodCom likewise would be ill-advised to assume a shared set of values and beliefs. Rather, they should seek to identify culturally disparate groups as an initial step in developing a strategy of planned change.

Section IC
The Fragmentation Perspective

According to Martin and Meyerson, the hallmark of a fragmentation study is its attention to the ambiguities of contemporary organizational life. These ambiguities have a variety of sources. For example, organizational ambiguities emerge from complex, apparently unsolvable problems, such as pollution, drug abuse, and poverty. Ambiguities also arise from the multiplicity of vantage points and belief systems represented in today's culturally diverse organizations. The fragmentation perspective also attends to the confusion associated with complex, imperfect systems, loosely coupled technologies, and emergent, unclear expectations. Furthermore, the fragmentation perspective does not assume that cultural members have similar reactions to these ambiguities and therefore it does not focus on shared expressions, for example, of approval or disapproval. According to the fragmentation perspective, if cultural research is to capture the experience of contemporary organizational life, it cannot exclude ambiguity.

Fragmentation studies examine cultural manifestations that are neither clearly consistent nor clearly inconsistent with each other. Relationships among espoused values, formal practices, informal norms, rituals, stories, and physical arrangements are seen as blurred—impossible to decipher, open to a myriad of interpretations. From the fragmentation perspective, consensus fails to coalesce on an organization-wide or subcultural basis, except in transient, issue-specific ways.

Some of the ambiguity that is so central to the fragmentation viewpoint is attributable to ignorance—presumably resolvable by the provision of more information. Other aspects of this ambiguity are inescapable and apparently unresolvable. For example, a paradox is a kind of ambiguity that draws attention to underlying tensions between opposites. These tensions cannot be reconciled in some unifying synthesis or partial compromise. The fragmentation perspective on cultural research is relatively new and so exemplars are relatively rare. Three studies are included here.

The first study, Chapter 8, by Karl E. Weick examines the difficulties that complicated decision making one night at the Tenerife Airport. The fog was exceptionally thick, one flight crew (due to flight time regulations) was in a rush, and it was very difficult to turn around large 747 jets on the small runways. Language difficulties, a shortage of trained controllers, and broken runway lights created an environment that fostered confusion, miscommunication, and—ultimately—a collision. According to this study, these circumstances caused different individuals to construe the evening's events in quite different ways. This was not an inconsequential ambiguity; over 500 passengers were killed.

In Chapter 9, Debra E. Meyerson studies hospital social workers. Whereas at Tenerife an unusual confluence of ambiguities combined to foster a disaster, some social workers, according to Meyerson, experience ambiguity as a normal attribute of their work. For example, some of the social workers in her study had no clear definition of their occupation; its boundaries with other related occupations (nursing, psychological counselors, the clergy) were unclear and permeable. Some social worker reacted with dismay, seeking ways to clarify the ambiguous aspects of their jobs. Others accepted the ambiguity without either marked positive or negative affect. A few reveled in the freedom they saw as a concomitant of their occupation's lack of clarity. Some social workers fluctuated among a variety of reactions to ambiguity. At some level, all agreed that ambiguities pervaded their working lives.

The final empirical chapter in this section, Chapter 10, by Martha S. Feldman, like the study of social work described above, focuses on a context that was seen as highly ambiguous: the work of policy analysts at the Department of Energy in Washington, DC. These analysts wrote policy papers that might not be read and, if they were read, might not influence policy decisions. Even the most cogent policy analysis could be overridden by changes in the balance of power in Congress, the political climate of the country, the international arena, or a change in presidential administrations. Here, as in the study of social work, analysts' reactions to this uncontrollable ambiguity varied from dismay to delight; different kinds of ambiguity held different meanings for different individuals.

Rather than the clear unity of the integration perspective, or the clear conflicts of the differentiation viewpoint, these fragmentation studies focus on that which is unclear. Other examples of research predominantly congruent with the fragmentation perspective are listed at the end of Part I.

8

The Vulnerable System:
An Analysis of the Tenerife Air Disaster[1]

KARL E. WEICK

There is a growing appreciation that large scale disasters such a Bhopal (Shrivastava, 1987) and Three Mile Island (Perrow, 1981) are the result of separate small events that become linked and amplified in ways that are incomprehensible and unpredictable. This scenario of linkage and amplification is especially likely when systems become more tightly coupled and less linear (Perrow, 1984).

What is missing from these analyses, however, is any discussion of the processes by which crises are set in motion. Specifically, we lack an understanding of ways in which separate small failures become linked. We know that single cause incidents are rare, but we don't know how small events can become chained together so that they result in a disastrous outcome. In the absence of this understanding, people must wait until some crisis actually occurs before they can diagnose a problem, rather than be in a position to detect a potential problem before it emerges. To anticipate and forestall disasters is to understand regularities in the ways small events can combine to have disproportionately large effects.

The purpose of the following analysis is to suggest several processes that amplify the effects of multiple small events into potentially disastrous outcomes. These processes were induced from an analysis of the Tenerife

AUTHOR'S NOTE: Reprinted with permission from the *Journal of Management, 16*(3), 571-593, 1990.

air disaster in which 583 people were killed. The processes include the interruption of important routines, regression to more habituated ways of responding, the breakdown of coordinated action, and misunderstandings in speech-exchange systems. When these four processes occur in the context of a system that is becoming more tightly coupled and less linear, they produce more errors, reduce the means to detect those errors, create dependencies among the errors, and amplify the effects of these errors.

These processes are sufficiently basic and widespread to suggest an inherent vulnerability in human systems that, up to now, has been overlooked.

Description of Tenerife: Disaster[2]

On March 27, 1977, KLM flight 4805, a 747 bound from Amsterdam to the Canary Islands, and Pan Am flight 1736, another 747 bound from Los Angeles and New York to the Canary Islands, were both diverted to Los Rodeos airport at Tenerife when the Las Palmas airport, their original destination, was closed because of a bomb explosion. KLM landed first at 1:38 p.m. followed by Pan Am which landed at 2:15 p.m. Because Tenerife is not a major airport, its taxi space was limited which meant that the Pan Am plane had to park behind the KLM flight in such a way that it could not depart until the KLM plane left (see Figure 8.1). When the Las Palmas airport reopened at 2:30, the Pan Am flight was ready to depart because its passengers had remained on board. KLM's passengers, however, had left the plane so there was a delay while they reboarded and while the plane was refueled to shorten its turnaround time at Las Palmas. KLM began its taxi for takeoff at 4:56 p.m. and was initially directed to proceed down a runway parallel to the takeoff runway. This directive was amended shortly thereafter and KLM was requested to taxi down the takeoff runway and at the end, to make a 180 degree turn and await further instruction.

Pan Am was requested to follow KLM down the takeoff runway and to leave the takeoff runway at taxiway C-3, use the parallel runway for the remainder of the taxi, and then to pull in behind the KLM flight. Pan Am's request to hold short of the takeoff runway and stay off it until KLM had departed, was denied. After the KLM plane made the 180 degree turn at the end of the takeoff runway, rather than hold as instructed, they started moving and reported, "we are now at takeoff." Neither the air traffic controllers nor the Pan Am crew were certain what this ambiguous phrase meant, but Pan Am restated to controllers that they would report when they

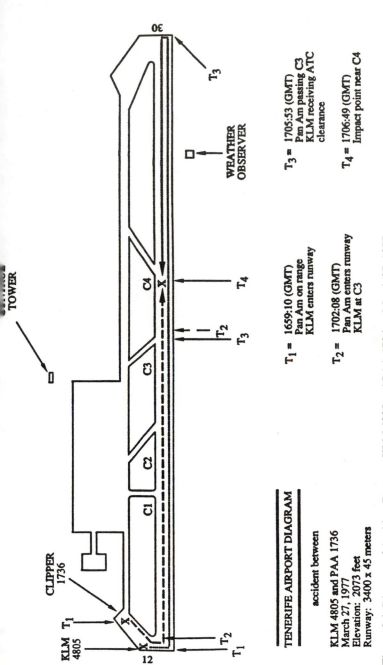

TENERIFE AIRPORT DIAGRAM

accident between

KLM 4805 and PAA 1736
March 27, 1977
Elevation: 2073 feet
Runway: 3400 x 45 meters

T_1 = 1659:10 (GMT)
Pan Am on range runway
KLM enters runway

T_2 = 1702:08 (GMT)
Pan Am enters runway
KLM at C3

T_3 = 1705:53 (GMT)
Pan Am passing C3
KLM receiving ATC
clearance

T_4 = 1706:49 (GMT)
Impact point near C4

Figure 8.1. Diagram of Accident Between KLM 4805 and PAA 1736 on March 27, 1977

119

were clear of the takeoff runway, a communique heard inside the KLM cockpit. When the pilot of the KLM flight was asked by the engineer, "Is he not clear then, that Pan Am?", the pilot replied "yes" and there was no further conversation. The collision occurred 13 seconds later at 5:06 p.m. None of the 234 passengers and 14 crew members on the KLM flight survived. Of the 380 passengers and 16 crew members on the Pan Am plane, 70 survived although 9 died later, making a total loss of 583 lives.

A brief excerpt from the Spanish Ministry of Transport and Communication's investigation of the crash, described interactions among the KLM crew members immediately before the crash. These interactions, reconstructed from the KLM cockpit voice recorder (CVR), are the focus of the remainder of our analysis.

As the time for the takeoff approached, the KLM captain

> seemed a little absent from all that was heard in the cockpit. He inquired several times, and after the copilot confirmed the order to backtrack, he asked the tower if he should leave the runway by C-1, and subsequently asked his copilot if he should do so by C-4. On arriving at the end of the runway, and making a 180 degree turn in order to place himself in takeoff position, he was advised by the copilot that he should wait as they still did not have an ATC clearance. The captain asked him to request it, which he did, but while the copilot was still repeating the clearance, the captain opened the throttle and started to takeoff. Then the copilot, instead of requesting takeoff clearance or advising that they did not yet have it, added to his read-back, "We are now at takeoff."

The tower, which was not expecting the aircraft to take off as it had not given clearance, interpreted the sentence as, "We are now at takeoff position." (When the Spanish, American, and Dutch investigating teams heard the tower recording together and for the first time, no one, or hardly anyone, understood that this transmission meant that they were taking off.) The controller replied: "o.k., . . . stand by for takeoff . . . I will call you." Nor did the Pan Am crew, on hearing the "We are now at takeoff," interpret it as an unequivocal indication of takeoff. However, in order to make their own position clear, they said, "We are still taxiing down the runway." This transmission coincided with the "Stand by for takeoff . . . I will call you," causing a whistling sound in the tower transmission and making its reception in the KLM cockpit not as clear as it should have been, even though it did not thereby become unintelligible.

The communication from the tower to the PAA [Pan Am] requested the latter to report when it left the runway clear. In the cockpit of the KLM, which was taking off, nobody at first confirmed receiving these communications until the Pan Am responded to the tower's request that it should report leaving the runway with an "o.k., we'll report when we're clear." On hearing this, the KLM flight engineer asked: "Is he not clear then?" The captain didn't understand him and he repeated: "Is he not clear that Pan American?" The captain replied with an emphatic "Yes" and, perhaps influenced by his prestige, making it difficult to imagine an error of this magnitude on the part of such an expert pilot, both the copilot and flight engineer made no further objections. The impact took place about 13 second later (Span., p. 71).

Tenerife as a Stressful Environment

Stress is often defined as a relation between the person and the environment as in Holroyd's and Lazarus's (1982) statement that "psychological stress requires a judgment that environmental and/or internal demands tax or exceed the individual's resources for managing them" (p. 22). Their use of the word "judgment" emphasizes that stress results from an appraisal that imposes meaning on environmental demands. Typically, stress results from the appraisal that something important is at stake and in jeopardy (McGrath, 1976).

There were several events impinging on people at Tenerife that are likely to have taxed their resources and been labeled as threatening. These events, once appraised as threatening, had a cumulative, negative effect on performance (George, 1986). After we review some of the more prominent of these events, we will look more closely at which concepts used in the stress literature help us most to make sense of the Tenerife disaster. It is these concepts that deserve closer attention in subsequent research on how crises are mobilized. The concepts to be discussed include size of discrepancy between demands and abilities, regression to first learned responses, and interruption as the occasion for stress. First, however, we review the demands at Tenerife.

Environmental Demands at Tenerife

The KLM crew felt growing pressure from at least three sources: Dutch law, difficult maneuvers, and unpredictable weather. Since the accident took place near the end of March, members of the KLM crew were very near the limits of time they were allowed to fly in one month. This was more serious than a mere inconvenience because, in 1976 Dutch enacted a tough law on "Work and Rest Regulations for Flight Crews" (ALPA, p.

14) which put strict limits on flight and duty time. The computation of these limits was complex and could no longer be done by the captain nor did the captain have any discretion to extend duty time. Therefore, the KLM crew faced the possibility of fines, imprisonment, and/or loss of pilot license if further delays materialized. The crew was informed that if they could leave Las Palmas by 7 p.m. their headquarters thought they could make it back to Amsterdam legally, but headquarters would let them know in Las Palmas.

Further pressure was added because the maneuver of turning a 747 around (backtracking) at the end of a runway is difficult, especially when that runway is narrow. It takes a minimum width of 142 feet to make a 180 degree turn in a 747 (ALPA, p. 19). The Tenerife runway was 150 feet.

Finally, the weather was unpredictable and at Tenerife, that creates some unique problems. Tenerife is 2,073 feet above sea level and the sea coast is just a few miles away which means that clouds rather than fog float into the airport. When KLM's crew backtracked they saw a cloud 3,000 feet down the runway moving toward them at 12 knots (ALPA, p. 12), concealing the Pan Am plane on the other side. Pan Am was taxiing inside this cloud and passed its assigned runway exit because it could not see it. KLM entered that same cloud 1,300 feet into its takeoff roll and that is where the collision occurred. The tower didn't see the collision or the resulting fire because of the cloud, nor could the firemen find the fire at first when they were summoned. The density of the cloud is further shown by the fact that when the firemen started to put out the fire on one plane, the KLM plane, they didn't realize that a second plane was on fire nearby because they couldn't see it (Span., pp. 117-119).

The KLM crew was not the only group that was under pressure. Controllers at Tenerife were also under pressure because they were short-handed, they did not often handle 747s, they had no ground radar, the centerline lights on the runway were not operating, they were working in English which was a less familiar second language, and their normal routines for routing planes on a takeoff and landing were disrupted because they had planes parked in areas they would normally use to execute these routines.

Regression in Responding

The stressful environment at Tenerife is important because it seems to be an unusually clear example of the much discussed, but seldom pursued idea that stress can produce regression to first learned responses (Allnutt,

1982, p. 11; Barthol & Ku, 1959). If there is a "key" to understanding the Tenerife disaster, it may lie in this principle.

The pilot of KLM 4805 was Head of the Flight Training Department of KLM. He was a training captain which meant that the flights he was most familiar with were those which followed a script, had fewer problems, and were shorter in duration. Furthermore, he had not flown on regular routes for 12 weeks. The importance of this background becomes evident in the context of a footnote in the Spanish report:

> Although the captain [KLM captain] had flown for many years on European and intercontinental routes, he had been an instructor for more than 10 years, which relatively diminished his familiarity with route flying. Moreover, on simulated flights, which are so customary in flying instruction, the training pilot normally assumes the role of controller: that is, he issues takeoff clearances. In many cases no communications whatsoever are used in simulated flights, and for this reason takeoff takes place without clearance. (Span., p. 121)

Pressure leads people to fall back on what they learned first and most fully which, in the case of the KLM pilot, was giving himself clearance to takeoff. Giving clearance is what he had done most often for the last 10 years when sitting at the head of a runway and is the response he may have reverted to as pressures mounted at Tenerife.

Both the Pan Am crew and the air traffic controllers seem also to show evidence of regression. The Pan Am captain wanted to hold short of the active runway, but he was asked to proceed down the active runway by a ground controller who spoke with a heavy accent and who did not seem to comprehend fully what Pan Am was requesting. Rather than attempt a potentially more complex negotiation to get permission to hold short, the Pan Am captain chose the more overlearned option of compliance with the controller's directive. Controller communiques also became more cryptic and harder to understand as controllers tried to cope with too many aircraft that were too big. These pressures may have made their use of English, a language which they used less frequently, more tenuous and increased the likelihood that more familiar Spanish language constructions would be substituted.

The more general implication of the disruptive effects of regression is that more recently learned complex rationales and complex collective responses are more vulnerable to disruption than are older, simpler, more overlearned, cultural and individual responses. Requisite variety (Zeleny, 1986) is much harder to achieve than it looks. When people acquire more complex responses so that they can sense and manage more complex environments, they do not become more complex all at once. Instead, they develop their complexity serially. Under pressure, responses acquired more recently and practiced less often should unravel sooner than those acquired earlier, which have become more habitual. Thus, requisite variety may disappear right when it is most needed. Hypothetically, the KLM pilot had high requisite variety because he was both a training pilot and a line pilot. In reality, however, his more recent habits of line flying disappeared under pressure and were replaced by his older habits of flying under training conditions.

The Breakdown of Coordination Under Stress

The phrase "operator error" is misleading in many ways, but among the most subtle problems is the fact that the term is singular (Hayashi, 1985). An operator error is usually a collective error (e.g., Gardenier, 1981), but it is only recently that efforts have been made to understand the ways in which team interaction generates emergent potentialities for and remedies of local failures (e.g., Hirokawa, Govran, & Martz, 1988). The crew in the KLM cockpit provides a unique glimpse of some ways in which crises become mobilized when crew interaction breaks down.

Individualism in the Cockpit

The setting in the KLM cockpit was unusual, not only because the captain was the head of flight training and a member of the top management team, but also because this captain had given the co-pilot (first officer) his qualification check in a 747 just 2 months earlier. This recently certified first officer made only two comments to try to influence the captain's decision during the crucial events at the head of the runway. The ALPA report of the crash described those comments this way:

> The KLM first officer was relatively young and new in his position and appeared to be mainly concerned with completing his tasks so as not to delay the captain's timing of the takeoff. He only made two comments in order to try to influence the captain's takeoff decision. When the captain first began pushing up the thrust levers, he said, "Wait a minute, we do not have an ATC clearance." The captain, rather than admitting to an oversight, closed the thrust levers and responded by saying, "No, I know that, go ahead and ask." The second occurrence was at the

end of the ATC clearance readback. The KLM first officer observed that the captain had commenced the takeoff and finished the ATC clearance readback by stating, "We are, uh, taking off" or "We are at takeoff" over the radio. After many hours of replaying the tapes, it is difficult to be sure what statement the first officer made. For this reason, we assume that neither the approach controller nor the Pan Am crew were positive about what was said. The Study Group believes that this ambiguous statement by the first officer was an indication that he was surprised by the KLM captain's actions in commencing the takeoff. We believe the first officer thought something was wrong with the takeoff decision by the captain, and tried to alert everyone on frequency that they were commencing takeoff. The KLM captain did not comment on his first officer's radio transmission but rather became immediately involved in setting takeoff power and tracking the runway centerline. (ALPA, p. 18)

Team Immunity to Stressful Environments

These several observations suggest that the KLM crew acted less like a team (Hackman, 1987) than like three individuals acting in parallel. That difference becomes important in the context of an important generalization suggested by Hage (1980):

Micro-sociological hypotheses usually require limits. The human scale is much smaller than the organizational one—at least as far as hypotheses are concerned. Beyond this the "world" of the individual appears to be dominated by normal curves where too much of a good thing is as bad as too little. In contrast, linearity appears to be a good first approximation in the organizational "world". (p. 202)

When we move from individual to group, we move from micro in the direction of macro and should expect to find fewer curvilinear relationships and more linear relationships. For example, the recurrent finding that the relationship between stress and performance is curvilinear, holds for individuals, but when it is examined as a group phenomenon, the relationship is found to be more linear (Lowe & McGrath, 1971). Thus, as we move from individual to group, increases in stress should lead to increases not decreases in performance. However, this shift is dependent on whether individuals coalesce into a team, which is a distinctive entity exhibiting distinctive functional relationships, or whether they merely act in the presence of another and respond and fall apart, more like individuals than like groups.

A KLM crew that is not a team is subject to curvilinear relationships, whereas a crew that is a team is more subject to linear relations. It is conceivable that more stress improves team performance while it degrades individual performance, because teamwork lowers task complexity. A well functioning team may face a simpler task than a poorly functioning team. And research on the Yerkes-Dodson law (e.g., Bregman & McAllister, 1982) shows that performance of simple tasks is less susceptible to the disruptive effects of arousal than is performance of complex tasks.

Speech-Exchange Systems as an Organizational Building Block

KLM as an airline is in large part constituted by its speech exchanges. When people employed by KLM talk among themselves and with outsiders, they not only communicate within an organization, but also construct the organization itself through the process and substance of what they say. As their talk varies, the solidity and predictability of the organization itself varies. Conversations with headquarters about duty time, conversations with the KLM agent at Las Palmas about ways to hasten the departure, conversations (or the lack of them) among crew members which construct the hypothesis that the runway is empty, all are the building blocks out of which the order and disorder that is the hallmark of organized activity is built.

The unfolding of the Tenerife disaster reminds us that macroprocesses such as centralization are made up of repetitive microevents that occur frequently and in diverse locations. Organizations are built, maintained, and activated through the medium of communication. If that communication is misunderstood, the existence of the organization itself becomes more tenuous.

The Tenerife disaster was built out of a series of small, semi-standardized misunderstandings among which were the following:

1. KLM requested two clearances in one transmission (we are now ready for takeoff and are waiting for ATC clearance) which meant that any reply could be seen as a comment on both requests.
2. The Controller, in giving a clearance, used the words "after takeoff" ("maintain flight level niner zero right after takeoff proceed with heading zero four zero until intercepting the three two five radial from Las Palmas") which could have been heard by the KLM crew as permission to leave. The ATC Manual (7110.650, October 25, 1984) clearly states, under the heading "Departure Terminology" that controllers should "Avoid using the term 'takeoff' except to actually clear an aircraft for takeoff or to cancel a takeoff clearance. Use such terms as 'depart,' 'departure,' or 'fly' in clearances when

necessary" [heading 4-20, p. 4-5]. Thus, the Tenerife controller could have said "right turn after departure" or "right turn fly heading zero four."

3. As we have seen, the phrase "We are now taking off" is nonstandard and produced confusion as well as safe assumptions as to what it meant.

4. When the controller said to KLM, "Okay . . . stand by for takeoff . . . I will call you," there was a squeal for the last portion of this message which changed the timbre of the controller's voice. This may have led the KLM crew to assume that a different station was transmitting and that the message was not intended for them.

5. The controller did not wait to receive an acknowledgment (e.g., "Roger") from KLM after he had ordered them to "standby for takeoff," and had he done so, might have discovered a misunderstanding (Hurst, 1982, p. 176).

6. Shortly before the collision, for the first and only time that day, the controller changed from calling the Pan Am plane "Clipper 1736" to the designation "Pappa Alpha 1736." This could sound like the controller is referring to a different plane (ALPA, p. 22).

The point to be emphasized is that speech exchange and social interaction is an important means by which organization is built or dismantled. This is not to say that social interaction is a local, self-contained production that is unaffected by anything else in the setting. There clearly are "noninterpretational foundations of interpretation in social interaction" (Munch & Smelser, 1987, p. 367). The interpretation process is shaped by shared language, authority relationships that assign rights of interpretation, norms of communication, and communication. The meanings that actors co-construct are not self-created. So micro analysis cannot go it alone without macro input. As Mead put it, people carry a slice of society around in their heads (Alexander & Giesen, 1987, p. 9). But to acknowledge that slice, is also to acknowledge the carrier, and the fact that the slice is realized, made visible, and given shape in discourse.

Hierarchical Distortion in Speech-Exchange Systems

The likelihood that crises impose hierarchical constraints (Stohl & Redding, 1987) on speech-exchange systems, is a straightforward extrapolation from the finding that stress leads to centralization (see Staw, Sandelands, & Dutton, 1981). This finding traditionally has been interpreted in a way that masks a potentially key cognitive step that allows us to understand Tenerife more fully. Before stress creates centralization, it must first increase the salience of hierarchies and formal authority, if it is to lead to centralization. It is the increased salience of formal structure that transforms open communication among equals into stylized communications between unequals. Communication dominated by hierarchy activates a different mindset regarding what is and is not communicated and different dynamics regarding who initiates on whom. In the cockpit, where there is a clear hierarchy, especially when the captain who outranks you is also the instructor who trained you, it is likely that attempts to create interaction among equals is more complex, less well-learned, and dropped more quickly in favor of hierarchical communication when stress increases.

What is especially striking in studies of communication distortion within hierarchical relationships (Fulk & Mani, 1985) is that the "types of subordinate message distortion [to please the receiver] are quite similar to the strategies used to address message overload. They include gatekeeping, summarization, changing emphasis within a message, withholding, and changing the nature of the information" (Stohl & Redding, 1987, p. 481). The similar effects of hierarchy and overload on communication suggests that one set of distortions can solve two different problems. A mere change in emphasis in a communication upward can both reduce message overload and please the recipient. The mutually reinforcing "solutions" to two distinct problems of crises—overload and centralization—should exert continuing pressure on communication in the direction of distortion and away from accuracy.

Interactive Complexity as Indigenous to Human Systems

As the day unfolded at Tenerife after 1:30 in the afternoon, there was a gradual movement from loosely coupled events to tightly coupled events, and from a linear transformation process to a complex transformation process with unintended and unnoticed contingencies. Human systems are not necessarily protected from disasters by loose coupling and linear transformation systems, because these qualities can change when people are subjected to stress, ignore data, regress, centralize, and become more self-centered.

Thus it would be a mistake to conclude from Perrow's (1984) work that organizations are either chronically vulnerable to normal accidents or chronically immune from them. Perrow's (1984) structural bias (p. 63) kept him from seeing clearly that, when you take people and their limitations into account, susceptibility to normal accidents can change within a relatively short time.

Several events at Tenerife show the system growing tighter and more complex.

1. Controllers develop ad hoc routing of two jumbo jets on an active runway because they have no other place to put them. (ALPA, p. 8).
2. Controllers have to work with more planes than they have before, without the aid of ground radar, without a tower operator, and with no centerline lights to help in guiding planes.
3. Controllers keep instructing pilots to use taxiway "Third Left" to exit the active runway, but this taxiway is impossible for a 747 to negotiate. It requires a 148 degree left turn followed by an immediate 148 degree right turn onto a taxiway that is 74 feet wide (ALPA, p. 19). Thus, neither the KLM pilot nor the Pan Am pilot is able to do what the controller tells him to do, so both pilots assume that controller really means that they use some other taxiway. Nevertheless, the KLM pilot may have assumed that the Pan Am pilot had exited by taxiway third left (ALPA, p. 24).
4. The longer the delay at Tenerife, the higher the probability that all hotel rooms in Las Palmas would be filled, the higher the probability that the air corridor back to Amsterdam would be filled with evening flights occasioning other air traffic delays, and the greater the chance for backups at Las Palmas itself, all of which increased the chances that duty time would expire while the KLM crew was in transit.
5. Throughout the afternoon there was the continuing possibility that the terrorist activities that had closed Las Palmas could spread to Tenerife. In fact, when the tower personnel heard the KLM explosion, they first thought that fuel tanks next to the tower had been blown up by terrorists (ALPA, p. 8).

Stress paves the way for its own intensification and diffusion because it can tighten couplings and raise complexity. Each of the several effects of stress that we have reviewed up to this point either increase dependencies among elements within the system or increase the number of events that are unnoticed, uncontrolled, and unpredictable. For example, the same stress that produces an error due to regression paves the way for that error to have a much larger effect by increasing the complexity of the context in which the error first occurred. As stress increases perception narrows, more contextual information is lost, and parameters deteriorate to more extreme levels before they are noticed, all of which leads to more puzzlement, less meaning, and more perceived complexity. Not only does stress increase the complexity, it also tightens couplings. Threat leads to centralization, which tightens couplings between formal authority and solutions that will be influential, even thought the better solutions may be in the hands of those with less authority. Notice how the same process that produces the error in the first place also shapes the context so that the error will fan out with unpredictable consequences.

Normally, individual failures stay separate and unlinked if they occur in a linear transformation system where they affect only an adjacent step and if they occur in a loosely coupled system where that effect may be indeterminate. (Perrow, 1984, characterizes "airways" as linear, modestly coupled systems in Figure 3.1, p. 97.) If the couplings become tighter (e.g., slack such as excess duty time is depleted) and if the linear transformation process becomes more complex through the development of a greater number of parallel events having unknown but multiple logical entailments (Douglas, 1985, p. 173), then more failures can occur and they can affect a greater number of additional events.

The point of these details is that "normal accidents" may not be confined to obvious sites of technical complexity such as nuclear power plants. Instead, they may occur in any system that is capable of changing from loose to tight and from linear to complex. As we have suggested, any system, no matter how loose and linear it may seem, can become tighter and more complex when it is subject to overload, misperception, regression, and individualized response. Small details can enlarge and, in the context of other enlargements, create a problem that exceeds the grasp of individuals or groups. Interactive complexity is likely to become more common, not less, in the 1990s. It is not a fixed commodity, nor is it a peculiar pathology confined to nuclear reactors and chemical plants. It may be the most volatile linkage point between micro and macro processes we are likely to find in the next few years.

Notes

1. Early abbreviated versions of this article were presented at the dedication of the Stanford Center for Organizational Research, at the School of Library and Information Management at Emporia State University, and at the Strategic Management Research Center at the University of Minnesota. Animated discussions with people at all three locations contributed immeasurably to the final product and I deeply appreciate the interest and help of those people.

2. All details concerning the Tenerife disaster are taken from two sources. The first source was the report of the Spanish Ministry of Transport and Communication, summarized in consecutive issues of *Aviation Week and Space Technology:* November 20, 1978, pp. 113-121; November 27, 1978, pp. 69-74. Reference to this report are abbreviated Span. The second source was Roitsch, P. A., Babcock, G. L., & Edmunds, W. W. (1979), *Human factors report on the Tenerife accident*. Washington, DC: Airline Pilots Assn. References to this report are abbreviated ALPA.

9

"Normal" Ambiguity?
A Glimpse of an Occupational Culture

DEBRA E. MEYERSON

Traditionally, the study of culture has been the study of how a community of people solves its shared everyday problems (e.g., Schein, 1985b; Swidler, 1986). Whether the community is a society, an organization, or an occupation, its cultural boundaries strictly depend on how members themselves define who's in and who's out (Van Maanen & Barley, 1984). This perspective defines culture in terms of those boundaries that members can agree on and defines as cultural those problems and solutions that members can concur are shared. It assumes that cultural members share common—and clear—understandings and identities. This conception virtually precludes the possibility that cultural members routinely live with ambiguities.

This chapter brings ambiguity experiences into the study of culture.[1] In some cultures, members do not agree on clear boundaries, cannot identify shared solutions, and do not reconcile contradictory beliefs and multiple identities. Yet, these members contend that they belong to a culture. They share a common orientation and overarching purpose, face similar problems, and have comparable experiences.[2] However, these shared orientations and purposes accommodate different beliefs and incommensurable technologies, these problems imply different solutions, and these experiences have multiple meanings.

AUTHOR'S NOTE: I am indebted to Martha Feldman, Peter Frost, Meryl Reis Louis, Larry Moore, and Karl Weick for their very helpful comments on an earlier draft. I am especially grateful to Joanne Martin who made innumerable suggestions on the dissertation from which this chapter was developed.

For example, this chapter describes the occupational culture of hospital social work (Meyerson, 1989). Members share a common orientation—they work in organizations dominated by the medical profession—and they share a common purpose—to "help" people. Yet, in different contexts, to different audiences, or at different times, social workers vary in their beliefs about their medical orientation, how to "help," and even what it means to "help."

In this way, cultures can embody ambiguities. Members may still share an overarching orientation and purpose, they may face similar problems and experiences, but how they interpret and enact these may vary so radically as to make what is shared seem vacuously abstract (Martin & Meyerson, 1988). Thus, at least for some cultures, to dismiss the ambiguities in favor of strictly what is clear and shared is to exclude some of the most central aspects of members' cultural experience and to ignore the essence of their cultural community.

In this chapter I describe some of the sources of ambiguity in hospital social work. I also discuss how and why members in distinct cultural contexts experience and interpret ambiguities differently. I suggest that much can be gleaned about a culture by understanding its ambiguities, how these experiences are interpreted, and why these experiences figure prominently in some contexts but not in others. Before describing these ambiguity experiences, I will overview the study from which this portrait is derived.

Methods

Sample

I studied hospital social work because of the ambiguities that seemed to characterize this occupation. Using several qualitative methods, I studied 59 social workers in five San Francisco Bay Area hospitals. Two of the five hospitals were private and three were public. In addition, two of the hospitals, one public and one private, were teaching facilities. The hospitals ranged in size from 437 to 745 beds and all had separate social service departments. Four of the five hospitals were acute care facilities; one was a chronic care hospital, oriented primarily toward rehabilitation.

All but 6 of the 59 social workers in the study held Masters of Social Work (MSW) degrees, the professional certification of social work. In addition, I interviewed 8 social work supervisors (at least one in each of five hospitals), 2 social work professors at a large university, and 10 first-year MSW students at the same university.

Methods and Data Sources

Because I was interested in developing theory about how social workers experienced ambiguity, I needed methods suitable to inductive, interpretive research (e.g., Glaser & Strauss, 1967; Miles & Huberman, 1984; Miles, 1979; Mintzberg, 1979). I therefore used an assortment of qualitative methods, including 14 months of participant observation, in-depth semi-structured interviews, and a written exercise. All interviews were tape-recorded and transcribed. Drawing conclusions entailed moving back and forth between fieldwork and data analysis. Periodic analysis throughout the project let me refine my questions and observations to fit the emergent theory.

To observe social workers, I followed them as they conducted their daily routines; I attended workshops, weekly staff meetings, parties, retreats, and lunches. In addition, I conducted 59 interviews in the five hospitals. These became increasingly structured after each stage of analysis as I developed a better grasp of the theory. Participants were also asked to complete an exercise which asked them to draw their experiences of ambiguity and burnout on paper. The shape of their drawings and their accompanying descriptions provided rich data on what these experiences meant to them.[3]

Ambiguities and Hospital Social Work

In hospital social work, ambiguities exist at two levels: within the occupational community as a whole and within individuals' cultural experience. The community experiences ambiguity when multiple interpretations or beliefs across members cannot be easily reconciled. This ambiguity is equivalent to diffuseness or lack of consensus within the collective. An individual experiences ambiguity when he or she experiences ambiguity in the structure of his or her work or when he or she holds multiple beliefs about the same problem. I describe each of these two sources of ambiguity in turn and then address why ambiguities are experienced differently by individuals in different cultural contexts.

Ambiguities Within the Occupational Community

Ambiguities arise in the collective experience because different social workers assume disparate beliefs and apply different solutions to some fundamental problems. Some of these differences can be traced to cultural factors that varied across the organizations, but some fundamental beliefs also varied randomly across individuals in the same organization or even the same role. For example, the problem of purpose or identity varied among social workers who shared the same role in an organization. Not only did many social workers find it was often difficult to define what being a social worker meant, but among those who had clear ideas, their interpretations were often quite distinct. To some, being a social worker meant helping people with the "gutsy stuff":

> We don't deal with things that are numbers and facts and figures, we deal with the gutsy stuff, and figures are not facts in the same way that feelings are facts.

These people tended to define their work, including what making a difference means, in terms of vague outcome criteria:

> I feel I've made a difference when I can get a family to communicate together when they haven't done that in the past. This moment of crisis when somebody is dying. I feel that I've made a difference when I've done the smallest of interventions or something that has been monumental, even after the fact.

To others, being a social worker meant being a discharge planner. Yet even the meaning of discharge planning varied among individuals. Some viewed discharge planning as the task of moving people out of the hospital as efficiently as possible. Their goals were clear: "The first thing we look at when a patient comes in the door is how can we get him out." Others, who were sometimes in the same organization, viewed discharge planning as a process of helping people through all sorts of difficult physical, social, and psychological transitions. They defined their role in terms of processors rather than specific outcomes.

> The other human being in contact with the social worker has to participate in the process. Otherwise you are a teacher or a doctor or a nurse, or a secretary or someone else who's doing unto others. Social workers are passing out skills in learning how to manage life under duress. And that's a process.

These are distinct interpretations of the same underlying role: the former views discharge planning as moving patients out of the hospital efficiently; the latter sees it as helping patients make effective transitions. The former is defined by the hospital's goals, the latter by the patient's needs.

The social workers also applied different solutions to the problem of authority. Although a belief in egalitarianism lies at the heart of social work's core ideology, the social workers displayed a range of beliefs about the legitimate structure of authority. Some supported egalitarianism, while others clearly endorsed hierarchy; still others showed signs of ambivalence. These beliefs were expressed in a number of ways. For example, the processes the social work supervisors used to recruit informants for this study revealed their beliefs about authority. Some supervisors suggested that I explain the study and ask for volunteers, others explained it themselves and "encouraged" volunteers, and one simply ordered her staff to participate.

The supervisor who mandated that her staff participate in my study demonstrated her preference for hierarchy in other decision-making processes as well. For instance, the decision to substitute outside nurses for internal social workers for special discharge planning jobs was made unilaterally, even though all members were affected by the decision. However, another supervisor who asked for volunteers for this study believed that one of her central responsibilities was to include others in decisions. For example, the decision on how to staff the hospital during a slow down from a nursing strike was made by developing a consensus. She claimed that she believed in and abided by egalitarianism:

> I think success is allowing participation in problem solving. I personally would not feel successful if I had to go in and make a unilateral decision that affects all of us . . . I think when you have to use authority that is a sense of failure. I would feel a sense of failure if I hadn't incorporated the people with whom I work or included them in decision making.

In this way, social workers differed in what they believed to be the legitimate structure of authority. These differences surfaced across as well as within departments. For example, some social workers who belonged to the department with the more authoritative supervisor expressed their dissatisfaction with their supervisor's "heavy hand" and authoritative style. Others thought that her authoritative approach and adherence to hierarchy brought the department credibility. Thus, even though egalitarianism is pivotal in social work's core ideology, belief in this value, and adherence to it, seemed to vary considerably (and unpredictably) across and within social work departments.

Structural Ambiguities in Individuals' Experience

Individual social workers experience ambiguity in their structures, including their boundaries, technologies, goals, and evaluation criteria (e.g., Huntington, 1981). Boundaries seem unclear because the occupation of social work includes a wide range of tasks and responsibilities, many of which are performed by members of other occupations. In a hospital, social work can include everything from concrete discharge planning, such as placing an individual in a nursing home, to less well defined clinical work with patients and families. Yet nurses also plan discharges; psychologists counsel; and members of the clergy coordinate community resources. Thus, insiders, as well as outsiders, hold diffuse ideas about what social work is and about who is and is not a social worker. In addition, technologies seem ambiguous because what one does as a social worker (e.g., talk to clients) seems only loosely related to what results (e.g., how clients behave).

The experience of structural ambiguity, particularly the experience of unclear boundaries and loose technologies, became apparent immediately at one field setting. During my first meeting at one hospital, people talked all at once, came and went as they pleased, and held phone calls as if no one else were there. As recorded in my fieldnotes, "it was madness." The informal processes and "free for all" meeting structure seemed to reflect a high level of ambiguity in their roles and the permeable boundaries around the group and between its members. Apparently, I was not the only one to whom the setting seemed chaotic. Some of the social workers joked openly about the confusion and chaos. One mentioned that this fluid structure had contributed to her satisfaction working in this department. Others spoke enthusiastically about the department's effectiveness and a few even attributed their success to the loose structure. At this same meeting, the supervisor acknowledged the group's apparent comfort with this high level of confusion:

Supervisor 2: Hey people, control yourself. We have someone evaluating our communication.
Debra (me): I'm completely confused.
Supervisor 2: Then you are getting the point.

Others in this hospital openly admitted their experience of ambiguity:

You're studying social work? It's so diffuse. It's really not clear what it is we do. It's sort of everything and anything. Whatever anyone wants to tell us to do. How can you study us?

The supervisor at another hospital more reluctantly admitted her experience of ambiguity:

I know I should say yes ['Can others without social work training do your work?'], there's lots we do that others can't, but I've seen people perform social work functions superbly without a day of training as a social worker. So I'll have to say no, I guess not.

Another described the experience of ambiguous boundaries with an evocative metaphor:

One day I was feeling real scattered and I was trying to get a good image of what that meant for me. Tom said 'It sounds like you're trying to find a place to stand in the middle of a kaleidoscope.' And he just captured what I was feeling.

In addition to living with unclear boundaries, social workers also experience ambiguity in their technologies, goals, and evaluation criteria. In one hospital it was perhaps their tacit agreement about their ambiguous boundaries that enabled them to accept and even thrive on disparate and loosely structured technologies. Some of the social workers spoke proudly about their idiosyncratic (person-specific) technologies. For example, one confessed that the admission process they used was wildly idiosyncratic: "We are inconsistent as hell regarding who gets in. That makes it a more human process." Others agreed that their technology depended on the specific qualities of the caregiver:

Let's say there's one gentleman (the client) and Gene goes to see him and does an intervention and I go to see him and do another intervention. Because of who we are they are going to be different. The client's experience is going to be different. Nobody can do my job for me. We have jobs where who we are makes a major difference in how things are going to get done and how our process is going to be.

Some suggested that they experienced ambiguity in their goals and outcome criteria:

Person 1: We take the unfixable. Like hospice care is really process oriented. It focuses on quality of life on a day-to-day basis. That's what we want to focus on.

Person 2: Here there's an awful lot that can be fixed. There are some tangible outcomes, but you know the fundamental problem doesn't generally get fixed.

Such unclear goals and outcomes make it difficult to evaluate performance:

Debra: Can you give me an example of a time when you felt like you made a difference?

Person 3: That's a hard thing in social work in a hospital. You know doctors can see their difference, but for us it's hard to figure out what that difference is and how much you had to do with it.

One supervisor summed up how she felt about these ambiguities: "When they (other social workers) come to me for a simple, clear solution, I tell them: 'Life is gray. If you want black and white go to Macy's. Black and white are in this year.' "

This experience of structural ambiguity, which initially seemed like chaos, enabled many of the social workers to interpret their roles as they saw fit. However, as I will discuss in a subsequent section, others experienced ambiguities differently.

Ideological Ambiguities in Individuals' Experience

In addition to structural ambiguities, individual social workers also experience ambiguities that arise from felt contradictions within their belief system. Most fundamentally, social workers embrace contradictory beliefs about the dominant institution of health care: the profession of medicine. The profession of medicine, or the "medical model," embraces an ideology of cure: fix what's broken; treat the disease; and most important, focus on outcomes (Freidson, 1970; Starr, 1982). The doctor, who is trained in treating disease (and often very specific forms of disease), is usually granted authority over the patient's health care (Larson, 1977; Starr, 1982). This authority comes with a strong endorsement of hierarchy and at the expense of a more interdisciplinary approach. Moreover, this medical ideology favors methods that are objective, emotionally detached, and universalistic (Merton, 1976). In short, the medical ideology places great faith and authority in science, the scientific method, and the scientist, which in a hospital is synonymous with the physician (Freidson, 1970, 1986).

In contrast, the "psychosocial model" underlies the occupational culture of social work. This model endorses an ideology of care: treat the whole person including her psychological, social, and economic condition; empower the client by giving her as much control as possible; value emotions and behave empathetically; and focus on process as well as specific outcomes (Huntington, 1981). The model values egalitarianism and stresses the importance of interdisciplinary professional teams. Given the occupation's respect for empathy and emotion, and its belief in the importance of the individual client relationship, social work theoretically accepts that its technologies and goals are subjective, idiosyncratic, and loosely connected to each other.

To varying extents, social workers in hospitals must embrace contradictory beliefs. They must adhere both to their own ideology of care and to the dominant ideology of medicine if they want to maintain their own legitimacy (Huntington, 1981). Consequently, individual social workers in hospitals are, as one described, "caught in between": "The medical model is more technology based, and the psychosocial is more dealing with people's strengths and with kind of helping the person. It really seems that medicine deals with problems and deals with fixing things. We're sort of caught in between."

These contradictory beliefs about the medical model surfaced in a number of specific domains. For example, many of the indicators of professionalism—technical jargon, a highly specialized knowledge base, emotional detachment, and "professional uniform"—are consistent with (and one could argue emerge from) medicine's ideology (Freidson, 1970; Larson, 1977; Starr, 1982). Social workers consider professionalization desirable insofar as it helps them attain control over both the services they offer and the market for those services. Yet, many of the trappings of professionalism undermine the core values of social work. Theoretically, to most social workers, the nitty gritty of their work entails rolling up their sleeves and talking with people in the people's own language. Using technical jargon, putting people in abstract categories, or wearing a tie detracts from "real social work." In this manner, social workers face a fundamental contradiction between professionalism and professional social work. Insofar as medicine is the prototypical profession, this specific tension arises from their more general ambivalence towards the medical model.

Individuals' contradictory beliefs about professionalism surfaced in discontinuities in their everyday expressive behaviors. For instance, one social worker usually dressed "funky social work," but on a particular day looked, as the supervisor pointed out, "really professional." The contrast between the two styles of dress, and, perhaps more revealing, the supervisor's reaction to the disjuncture, expressed the tension between professionalism and professional social work.

Contradictions in other symbolic forms, such as office decor, also expressed ambivalence about professionalism. For example, one social worker's office appeared strikingly void of social work books, journals, or paraphernalia. Novels and magazines occupied the bookshelves and comics adorned the walls. The occupant had a personal stereo on one shelf and an assortment of food on another. Yet a framed diploma was displayed prominently above her desk. The incongruity between the diploma and the rest of her office expressed the same underlying tension about professionalism

Contradictory beliefs about the medical model also surfaced in social workers' attitudes about social reform. As an occupation, social work rest on a tradition of system level reform and individual level advocacy (Ehrenreich, 1985; Huntington, 1981). One social worker mentioned that being "the elbow in the system's side" was her professional responsibility. Others viewed themselves as the patient's advocate. However, because social workers work in organizations in which they have little formal power, they must comply with and even become exemplars of the system to gain legitimacy. Some admitted that their job was to uphold, even "grease" the system:

> There's a commitment in social work to change the system, to make it better smooth out the process. We are the grease in the wheel. We are the ones that make sure that the system works. Our job is to play the system so it works for patients

This tension was described by one as a delicate balancing act:

> It just seems to me like social workers are always a little bit on the fringe; they're part of the institution, but they're not. You know they have to be part of the institution in order to really get what they need for their clients, but basically they're usually at odds with the institution. You have to remain affiliated with the institution in order to work the system. So it's like we are in the institution but not of it.

Thus, although some social workers believed that their role was to change or resist the status quo, they also believed that to be effective they must work within and thereby perpetuate the status quo. Social worker must simultaneously advance reforms and preclude them, critique the medical model and enforce it.

Some members expressed their contradictory feelings about "the system" and their role within it through their cynical sense of humor. For some cynicism was a pragmatic response to the contradictions between what they did and what they believed. Cynicism enabled them to recognize the contradictory nature of their work lives without have to resolve the contradictions. To some, cynicism was a highly adaptive response to the ambiguities they experienced:

> I get a bit cynical about the VA system, but less cynical than I am about the hospital care system in general. I think I have enough healthy cynicism which sometimes is just what I need. As a social worker you always have to look for solutions even if they are not there.

Cynicism was also a legitimate expression of felt, but unspoken, ambiguities in group settings. During social work staff meetings at one hospital, cynicism would surface precisely when discussions became most tense. Cynicism defused the felt ambiguity that erupted from seemingly unsolvable problems (e.g., when a patient refuses to cooperate with his rehabilitation), from irreconcilable differences (e.g., when the attending physician ignores seemingly essential emotional factors), and most frequently from situations in which social workers lacked the clarity or authority to take action (e.g., when they are faced with incomprehensible "red tape"). By acknowledging and suspending the ambiguity with a cynical remark, the cynic enabled the conversation to proceed without premature closure: allowing unsolvables, irreconcilables, and untenables to remain unresolved.

Thus, individuals' contradictory beliefs about the medical model were expressed through many forms of expressive behaviors, from the social workers' choice of dress and office decor to their cynical sense of humor. Moreover, this fundamental tension about the medical model surfaced in a number of different domains, including, but not limited to, their beliefs about professionalism and social reform.

Interpretations of Ambiguity: A Cultural Explanation

In the previous few sections I have shown how various ambiguities manifested at the occupational and individual levels. For simplicity, I have implied that social workers in different organizational settings had comparable levels and types of ambiguity experiences. This was not the case. In particular, the social workers in the one rehabilitation or chronic care hospital ("Chronic") seemed to experience ambiguity differently than their colleagues in the other four hospitals. They tended to talk more openly about their ambiguity experiences and to interpret these experiences as "normal" rather than "abnormal."

These differences cannot be explained simply by differences in the nature of their work roles (e.g., some roles simply are "more ambiguous" than other roles) because many roles across the five hospitals were comparable in their level of specificity. Moreover, my observations, particularly of some group meetings in one of the acute care hospitals, uncovered extensive evidence of structural and ideological ambiguities. Ambiguities were expressed, for example, in their dress, office decor, humor, and stories. Yet despite these expressions of ambiguity, in interviews the social workers in the acute care settings often shied away from talking about their ambiguity experiences. When they did discuss ambiguities, they generally did so in the process of explaining why and how they tried to control or avoid such experiences. For example, some tried to avoid ambiguity because it enabled others to "dump" on them:

> Sometimes I feel it's unclear to others what the social worker does. In other words, if there's a drunk person who's bugging the doctor they call me. This happened the other day. It was just a dump. Sometimes we'll get referrals, dump referrals like "we can't deal with this guy so send him to a social worker. Have the social worker fix him."

Insofar as ambiguity gave others more latitude to "dump" on social workers, it was experienced as highly undesirable and thus a state to try to avoid or control.

In contrast, the social workers in Chronic readily admitted their experiences of ambiguity in interviews and freely expressed ambiguities in their informal and symbolic behaviors. To them, ambiguity seemed to be a normal and sometimes desirable condition:

> The social worker is really like the bastard who could go in anywhere. The social worker gets in between them all and can do it all. That's one of the advantages. It's certainly not a limitation. It is a flexibility that is phenomenal.

Some of these differences in how ambiguity was interpreted can be explained by the values and the norms of the medical and psychosocial models and how they were enacted in each setting.[4] As discussed above, based on the assumptions of science, the medical model values objectivity and clarity (Freidson, 1970; Larson, 1977). In valuing that which is clear and objective, the medical model devalues and directs people's attention away from that which is ambiguous. In contrast, the psychosocial model values empathy and subjectivity and is based on very "nonscientific" technologies. In valuing that which is subjective and often idiosyncratic, the psychosocial legitimates that which is ambiguous. Moreover, the medical model tends to formulate various individual states and experiences as pathologies that should be cured. The psychosocial model tends to formulate states as conditions with which one should learn to live.

The medical model, although institutionally prevalent in all five hospitals, was much less so in the one chronic care facility. In Chronic, the legitimacy of the ideology of medicine, or cure, was challenged simply because patients in this facility could not, by definition, be cured. (Despite this fact, medicine is so dominant an institution in health care that its legitimacy was still quite potent.) Consequently, in Chronic, where the psychosocial ideology carried some legitimacy, the social workers tended to view ambiguity as a normal experience, one with which they simply learned to live. However, in the other hospitals where the medical model unequivocally dominated, the social workers tended to view ambiguity as a pathological experience, one they had to control or cure. In this way, how the social workers interpreted their experiences of ambiguity reflected the particular cultural mix in that setting.

Conclusion

I have tried to demonstrate that experiences of ambiguity are prevalent in some settings of hospital social work and have suggested that these experiences at the occupational and individual levels should be included in any cultural portrait of the occupation. Some social workers even suggested that the unique contribution of the occupation of social work to medicine lies precisely in its focus on, and acceptance of, the "inherent" ambiguities of health care. However, how social workers experienced ambiguities and what these experiences meant varied in ways revealing of the cultural mix of the context in which the social workers were embedded. Here, whether individuals freely admitted these experiences and whether they experienced ambiguities as pathological or normal depended in part on the relative mix of the medical and psychosocial ideologies in a setting.

This view of ambiguity, as an experience that has different meaning and legitimacy under different cultural conditions, departs from traditional treatments where ambiguity is an exogenous state that is experienced to greater and lesser extents. Most treatments of ambiguity examine how it affects a range of individual and organizational processes (e.g., Eisenberg,

1984; Feldman, 1985; March & Olsen, 1976) and have underplayed what ambiguities mean to those who experience them (see Feldman in this volume as an exception). Even the research that touts the benefits of ambiguity (e.g., March, 1976; Weick, 1979) pays little attention to how cultural forces shape what these experiences mean or whether or not they are perceived as legitimate.

It should be noted that social work is not the only occupational culture that embodies ambiguities. Our own academic community includes a diverse body of individuals who somehow manage to come together to discuss related, although not completely shared, problems in a common language, which masks disparate political agendas, idiosyncratic solutions, irreconcilable epistemologies, and incommensurable methods. Many of us have no illusion that we will find much of interest to agree on, yet our occupation is still a cultural entity. An entity exists because we share a sense of sameness and overarching purpose with other members and experience a sense of difference between ourselves and nonmembers.

So why then do investigators of culture tend to ignore ambiguities and concentrate instead on that which is agreed upon and clear? When expressions of ambiguity are not apparent, we should ask "why not?" We can learn much about the cultures we are studying if we look beyond single meanings and clear responses at the surface to multiple meanings and confusions, sometimes at the surface, sometimes beneath it. Moreover, the exclusion of ambiguity from the study of culture may be as much an artifact of our own community's values and beliefs as it is of the cultures we study. Not coincidentally, like many of the social workers in my study, we too tend to construct ambiguities as pathologies—as conditions to control or "cure" (Meyerson, 1989). Thus, to include ambiguity in the study of culture is to challenge our definition of culture and to question the ideology underlying that definition.

Notes

1. See Martin and Meyerson (1988) and Meyerson and Martin (1987) for earlier treatments of the topic.

2. I am indebted to Martha Feldman for these observations (personal communication, February 12, 1990).

3. For lack of space, I cannot explain the nuances of this exercise and the specific patterns of experience it revealed. However, this exercise is explained in a bit more detail in Chapter 18.

4. Meyerson (1989) has a detailed analysis of differences in how these ideologies were enacted in each setting.

10

The Meanings of Ambiguity:
Learning from Stories and Metaphors

MARTHA S. FELDMAN

Many students of organization have attended to issues of ambiguity in organizations.[1] Some people have studied the effects on individuals of ambiguity at the individual level or role ambiguity. They have suggested that such ambiguity is an important source of job related stress (Kahn et al., 1964) and that it is related to job dissatisfaction, turnover, and tension (Bedeian & Armenakis, 1981; Hall, 1972; Rizzo, House, & Lirtzman, 1970).

Other people have studied the relationship of ambiguity at the organizational level to organizational dynamics. For example, Smith has related the pervasiveness and importance of the social influence process to the level of organizational ambiguity (Smith, 1973). Weick has also connected the process of sense-making in organizations to the issue of dealing with equivocality, a notion closely related to ambiguity (Weick, 1979). Other, more specific, processes have also been studied. The effects of organizational ambiguity on decision making, for example, has been extensively explored (Brunsson, 1985; Cohen & March, 1986; March & Olsen, 1976; Sproull, Weiner, & Wolf, 1978). The effects of organizational ambiguity on management and leadership have also received some attention (Cohen & March, 1986; House, 1971; Sproull, Weiner, & Wolf, 1978).

More recently, Martin and Meyerson (1988) have studied the relationship of organizational culture to ambiguity. This work begins to explore the effects of organizational ambiguity on individuals within the organization. However, as the authors note, the work is restricted by the lack of appropriate research. What is particularly missing is an examination of the meaning of ambiguity to organizational members. In this chapter I explore the reactions of nonmanagement level professionals to a situation characterized by a high level of ambiguity. I examine the effects of these reactions on their attitudes about the performance of tasks and on their loyalty to the organization.

Before proceeding any further, a discussion of the term "ambiguity" is in order. Ambiguity occurs when there is no clear interpretation of a phenomenon or set of events. It is different from uncertainty in that it cannot be clarified by gathering more facts (Feldman, 1989). The facts that are or could be available support more than one interpretation. Thus, March and Olsen (1976) talk about the ambiguity of intention in which the actions taken by an organization and the statements made about its goals and preferences do not clearly support any one purpose or plan of action. In this case, it is hard to make a statement to the effect that "X, Y, or Z is what this organization is about." This is ambiguity.

The meaning of ambiguity is not the same as the ambiguity itself. The meaning may vary from person to person and from setting to setting. People may, for instance, find ambiguity exhilarating or they may find it depressing. They may think of it as an unnecessary or necessary evil or as an essential and beneficial feature of their work environment. The meaning of ambiguity for any individual is complex and influenced by historical, biographical, and sociological factors. To the extent that reactions to ambiguity are common among members of the organization, the interpretation may indicate a collective understanding about ambiguity and its effects. This collective understanding is a part of the culture of that organization (Van Maanen & Barley, 1985).

In this chapter I explore some data I gathered about organizational members' attitudes in an organization characterized by a high level of ambiguity. In the first section I present some information about the organization and the methods used to study the organization. In the second section I discuss the nature of the ambiguity that characterized the organization and present data in the form of stories and metaphors told to me by the members of the organization. The stories and metaphors illustrate the range of interpretations of ambiguity displayed by these people. In the third section I discuss briefly the relation between interpretations of ambiguity and organizational culture.

The Organization and the Methods

The organization I studied was the policy office of the U.S. Department of Energy. This office had responsibility for the development of policy for the Department of Energy (DOE) and for oversight of program offices. It consisted of about 140 people.[2] Just over 50% of these people are professional, nonmanagerial staff members. About 35% are clerical and support staff. Just over 10% are managers.

The professional nonmanagerial staff are the focus of this chapter. Their responsibilities were to provide information and make recommendations to aid their hierarchical superiors in policy making. They were highly educated, with an average of just over two college degrees per person. Most had master's degrees and several had doctorates. They had been employed by the organization for an average of 4 years and had held the positions they were in for an average of two years.[3] Their average age was 36.[4]

Although the basis of the research is participant observation, much of the data presented in this chapter was gathered through interviews with members of the policy office. I interviewed 39 policy office staff members. This sample is one half of the staff members from each division of the policy office. In other words, if a division had two staff members, I interviewed one; if it had eleven, I interviewed six. Five of the individuals interviewed worked in administrative divisions, and are excluded from the following analysis. Although they belong to the same organization and may display similar attitudes, they are not policy analysts, and their inclusion would be inappropriate here. The resulting sample size is 34. I conducted the interviews between September 23, 1981 and December 7, 1981. Because I had been studying the organization for a lengthy period prior to conducting the interviews, I used the interviews primarily to measure how widespread the phenomena that I had observed were and to explore the attitudes of the staff members in depth.[5] In this chapter quotations are drawn from these interviews. Each quotation is accompanied by a number identifying the respondent.

Organizational Ambiguity

Many features of an organization may be ambiguous. March and Olsen have identified four features (March & Olsen, 1976). They relate to what the organization intends to do, what is appropriate for the organization to do, what the organization has done in the past and why, and who in the organization is responsible for what the organization does. March and Olsen have referred to these as the ambiguities of intention, understanding, history, and organization. In the Department of Energy during the period of study, these four sources of ambiguity can be easily identified.

The Ambiguity of Intention

An organization is characterized by ambiguity of intention if it appears to have ill-defined preferences. In the Department of Energy there was little agreement about what the organization did or should do, and many people thought that the organization did nothing that was worthwhile. Debate and criticism about the department were widespread in the media (*Newsweek,* 1979; *New York Times,* 1979a, 1979b; *Time* 1979).

These problems were evident not only to observers, but also to members of the organization. Members of the policy office acknowledged that the department which they represented was generally perceived as ineffective, and that there was a lot of controversy over what role the organization ought to play. In fact, there was little agreement among the respondents themselves about what their organization was supposed to do.

Policy analysts are charged with the responsibility of evaluating policies and programs that the department endorses or carries out. One of the criteria for evaluation is whether or not the policy or program is consistent with what the organization as a whole is trying to do. Thus, more than in other parts of the organization, one would expect the policy analysts to be in touch with the organization's goals or mission. When I asked the policy analysts about DOE's mission, however, there was little agreement in their responses. No more than 8 out of 34 people agreed on any general formulation of the mission of the department. This, in itself, indicates a lack of an agreed upon goal. This perception is supported by the fact that 10 people claimed that the department did not have a mission at all. This was the most common response given. People made such statements as: "DOE does not have a mission I can describe right now . . ." (#7)[6] and "mission, what mission?" (#17).

Further support for the perception that the policy analysts did not have a clear sense of the purpose of the organization was provided by cynical responses. They took two forms. One form was to say that the department's mission was to promote technologies, especially nuclear technologies, that they had no part in and of which they were not in favor. Eight people made statements of the following nature:

". . . develop technology that is far enough advanced and too expensive for private
     industry . . ." (#4)
". . . subsidize nuclear industry—make thermonuclear warheads . . ." (#16)

The other form of cynical response was to say that the department's
mission was to go out of business. The following are two of the four
statements to this effect:

". . . to get out of the energy business . . ." (#13)
". . . to go out of business as an organization . . ." (#28)

Thus, both observers and members of this organization were confused
about what the goals of the organization were. They were clear, however,
that the organization was not doing a very good job at whatever it was
supposed to be doing. Both of these opinions contributed to the ambiguity
of intention.

Stories and metaphors told by members of the organization capture their
perceptions and reactions to this ambiguity. For instance, one person
referred to the organization as a "sinking ship" (#14), and another said it
was like "lifeboats with people being thrown aboard" (#12).

Another person told about his experience trying to make a contribution
to energy policy.

[The] thing I remember most: The National Energy Plan . . . [we were] very
successful at connecting with [the relevant] group at the White House. . . . [We]
provided a lot of analytical background. [We] had input to policies. [I felt] part
of a team. [You] had a chance to make your case. . . . There was lots of transpor-
tation-related activity I felt like I was having an impact on. The process continued
in-house and then nothing ever happened when it moved to the Senate. [It] was
taken out of the hands of [our] group. The President lost interest in the problem.
He flip-flopped on natural gas and lost liberal support" (#22).

From these examples we can see that people were not sure what the
organization was supposed to be doing or what they were supposed to be
doing for the organization. They engage in actions that seem normal for
their positions, but the purpose of these actions is not clear.

The Ambiguity of Understanding

Where there is ambiguity of understanding there are many interpretations of how the organization should do what it does and of how to understand

the feedback from the environment. In other words, there are competing ideas of what it is appropriate for the organization to do. The ambiguity of understanding occurred in the DOE because the role of this department and of government, in general, in energy policy was not well understood (*National Journal,* 1979; 1980). It was never clear, for example, whether the DOE should be leading Congress or following it. When the department was first established, many envisioned it having a large role in the development of policies. It was supposed to coordinate old programs and policies and integrate them with new ones. As time passed, however, the whole notion of government intervention in this area became less and less popular and Congress became less and less sanguine about the contributions of the department.

This ambiguity was compounded by a lack of consensus about the appropriate technology for accomplishing energy goals (*National Journal,* 1980). Even when there was agreement about what the organization should do (e.g., increasing the supply of available domestic energy), it was not clear what technology the department should use to accomplish the goal. Should it be promoting regulation, pursuing research and development projects, providing grants to private interests to pursue research and development, making contingency plans for future emergencies, developing models of energy use, or some mix of these? Similarly, it was not clear whether the department should be most concerned with short-, medium-, or long-term issues.

Again stories and metaphors relate the perceptions of organization members of this ambiguity. For example, one person described the vacillation in the approaches taken by the DOE. "There are two schools of thought: (1) regulatory—generate a government entity to intervene; and (2) let the market take care of it. When there is a crisis, everybody says, 'Do something; activate school number one.' When the crisis is over, 'Activate school number two' " (#6).

The metaphors people used were more evocative. One of them suggests that some people found the lack of a common understanding acutely distressing: "A lot of people trying to do a little bit of good, bumping into each other. [They are] all on a little bit different wave length, within the same echo system. [They are] going crazy [hearing the other wave lengths]" (#20). By contrast, other people found the situation, at least potentially, liberating. One member (27) expressed the sense that there were few boundaries on how to understand what the organization was. He described the organization as "a vehicle that can be ridden for awhile with great joy." He went on to say that the vehicle could also just "be endured.

One would hope it's a vehicle that can be steered—though a lot of able people have dashed their hopes on that one." He expressed a similar sentiment with another metaphor: "a mirror in which you see what you want to see and do what you want do—not an effectively functioning organization."

The Ambiguity of History

The ambiguity of history occurs because what happened and why may be difficult to understand. The ambiguity of history was evident in the DOE in the movement of the organization from being the "new shining star" to being the "bad kid on the block." Less than two years after the department went into business, the first Secretary of Energy resigned. James R. Schlesinger left office in July 1979 in the midst of a gasoline shortage and adverse public opinion about the federal government's handling of energy policy. The arrival of the second Secretary, Charles Duncan, brought many changes in personnel and new approaches to the energy problem. A reorganization announced on the department's second anniversary, October 1, 1979, marked both of these changes. Less than a year later, however, Reagan was calling for the dismantling of the department as part of his presidential campaign. After he won the election, he appointed James Edwards as Secretary of Energy. A month after his appointment, Edwards announced another reorganization of the department. Consistent with campaign promises, the activities of many parts of the department were discontinued or transferred to other organizations.

In less than four years, then, the department had come into existence and had been partially dismantled. It had gone from being championed as the solution to a troubling problem to being derided as both a problem itself and the source of energy problems. The many possible sources of explanation for this downfall only contributed to the confusion. The energy situation had changed, comprehension of what it would mean to do something about the energy situation had changed, Schlesinger and Carter had been less than adept politically, and the politics of energy had been more complicated than anyone had envisioned. While any or all of these explanations may have been correct, none of them provided a sufficient sense of what people should, or even could, do to ameliorate the situation. The result was the ambiguity of history.

Many of the stories that people told have a perplexed quality to them. There is a sense that they don't understand how the events they are relating could have happened. This confusion is associated with the ambiguity of history. This sense was expressed in a story about a friend who had been laid off (riffed)[7] in a particularly uncaring manner.

> When [he was] riffed, [he felt] angry and hurt. [His] wife urged him to hustle and get to work. He and some other guys pulled together and got together a package [resumes, etc.] and hustled. All this time [he was] angry about being let go and [about] the politics of being riffed, [but he was also] excited about finding something challenging with a promotion. [Then] DOE came to him and asked him to come to work [and] took him off the RIF rolls. The same organization that riffed him hired him back. He could have been spared all the bother and anger (#3).

A more mundane story simply relates the inability to fulfill simple requests. One person related that he "got an assignment with a 'buck slip' (a form used to delegate responsibility for an assignment to another employee) that had five different colors of ink and five different circled names with arrows (indicating that responsibility had been passed) down to the next level of the bureaucracy. All the person had wanted was a copy of a report. [It] took five weeks to get it to him" (#19).

Another story is about double payment on a contract. "[One part of DOE 'let' a] contract for $13 billion for two years for studies on alternative nuclear systems. Between [the times of] money allocation and contract letting, the job changed. [Now the job was] to examine alternative nuclear technologies. One office was contracting it out [and was] getting paid twice. It could have been a joint contract. [I] found out by accident" (#21).

Metaphors used that relate to the ambiguity of history implied both that there was something wrong and that the analysts were implicated in it. The phrases "things associated with World War II" and "guilt by association" (#14) for example, were used by one analyst. The implication gave rise to a particularly poignant remark by another. "Normally, when I'm with friends, people will ask me what I do at DOE. I tell them about [my] study. A lot of them, they think it's a joke" (#4).

The Ambiguity of Organization

The ambiguity of organization occurs because people are differently involved in the organization at different times. Frequent reorganizations contributed to the ambiguity of intention and also promoted an ambiguity of organization in which there was confusion about what roles existed in the organization and who fulfilled them. The policy office, for example, had three different forms during the four years from its inception to the end of this study—October 1977 to December 1981. In the first form, functions were emphasized. There was, for instance, a Deputy Assistant Secretary for Planning and Evaluation, for Development and Competition, and for Policy Analysis. By contrast, in the second form fuels were emphasized. The Deputy Assistant Secretaries in the second organization were for Oil and Gas; Coal, Nuclear, and Electric Systems; Conservation and Renewable Resources; and Systems Analysis. The significance of this change is not completely captured by these titles. The reorganization occurred because Secretary Schlesinger resigned and a new Secretary of Energy took over. This change took place, in part, because Schlesinger and the department had been severely criticized (*National Journal,* 1979). Thus, an effort was made to change what the department was focusing on and the reorganization reflects this effort.

The third form that the policy office took was similar to the first in its emphasis on functions. The purpose of these functions, however, was heavily influenced by the change in administration from the Carter to the Reagan presidency. The new administration had very different ideas about what role the Department of Energy should play in making energy policy and about what role energy policy should play at all.

For analysts of the policy office, these shifts meant changes in location, supervisors, and approaches to problems. Their comments reveal that for all the changes there did not appear to be much progress on the substantive problems confronting the department. One analyst likened the energy problem to the "nine-headed hydra, where every time you cut off one head, another one grew. . . . We have chased so many problems in so many ways that we're back to the original approach. I have done some of the same things in 1974, [again in] 1977-78 and again in 1980-81" (#10). Another person commented on the number of times he had moved. After recounting four changes of location and supervisor, he said finally that he "recycled back to the same place and back to the same bosses and continued the same functions throughout" (#29).

Thus, in four years the department underwent three major shifts in emphasis. The position of people in the department changed accordingly. Although this may be an understandable part of the development of a new organization, it could hardly help but contribute to confusion about who is supposed to be doing what. The perception of this ambiguity, expressed in numerous stories and comments, was that management was poor and that the bosses in this organization, in general, were not people whom you could look up to. They lacked integrity, they were laughable.

One person, for instance, said that "every 'reorganization' supposedly offered better management. The expectation was never fulfilled. From the Secretary on down, the quality of management in Policy is poor. . . . [Those hired are] not necessarily the best qualified. [DOE hires] known quantity, not the best, [because this is] low risk. Position descriptions [are] inflated, distorted, and falsified" (#31). Another claimed that "[there are] people at the higher grades in the Policy Office who wouldn't last a day in the private sector. You wouldn't believe the people I work with. . . . [There are] a lot of people at the ceiling who are useless" (#5).

A not uncommon story was told of the boss's inability to stand up for what "was right." "The [contractor's final] report didn't come up with anything about alternative nuclear systems. [The report showed that] current [systems were] least costly. People at DOE knew that this is what Congress wanted them to come up with. They didn't rock the boat. [I] sent memos but they did not get past my boss's boss—couldn't stand up to Joe, who had a lot of clout" (#21).

The policy analysts even had metaphors for their bosses. "Our old boss—we had a standing joke about him. [We] called him the balloonman because he looked like he should be selling balloons. He's short and chubby, with a round face. [The balloon man metaphor] reflects his personality and how adept he was at the job" (#26).

Ambiguity and Organizational Culture

Discussing the relation between ambiguity and organizational culture requires some definition of organizational culture. As others have noted (Martin & Meyerson, 1988; Van Maanen & Barley, 1985) culture does not necessarily imply a uniformity of values. Indeed quite different values may be displayed by people of the same culture. In such an instance, what is it that holds together the members of the organization? I suggest that we look to the existence of a common frame of reference or a shared recognition of relevant issues. There may not be agreement about whether these issues *should* be relevant or about whether they are positively or negatively valued. For example in Chapter 9, the members of the organization all recognize "traditional" approaches to social work as a relevant issue. They array themselves differently with respect to that issue, but whether positively or negatively they are all oriented to it.

In policy work there is a conception of the role of analysis that has this central relevance. A simple version of the conception is as follows: Analysts are supposed to analyze relatively well-defined problems and produce solutions that can be implemented by politicians (Feldman, 1989). The responsibility for selecting problems lies jointly with the politicians and the analyst's hierarchical superiors or bosses. Bosses are also supposed to insure that politicians use the analyses produced by the analysts. In the policy office of the DOE, this frame of reference was embraced by virtually every member of the organization.

This frame of reference accounts for the predominantly negative tone of the stories and metaphors used by the members of the policy office of the DOE to describe their organization. The ambiguities disrupt the possibility of such a smooth flow between analysis and politics. Analyses do not lead to positions that are promoted through politics. Analyses do not even support positions chosen by politicians. Analyses are being produced, but it is not clear for what or for whom. As a result, the stories are mostly about what's not working. One analyst said, "all my stories are about how DOE misses doing the right thing" (#16). The metaphors also are mostly pretty grim. One person summed up his impression of DOE as "a mixture of the Three Stooges Comedy Act, Ringling Brothers' Barnum and Bailey, and 5-year-olds playing with matches in a nitroglycerin factory" (#10).

This frame of reference, however, only goes so far in explaining the interpretations of ambiguity expressed by members of this organization. Not only was the negative tone not universal, but there was also great variety among generally negative responses. Each person had his or her own interpretation. Often there was considerable diversity even within one person's interpretation. A final metaphor illustrates this phenomenon and, to the extent that any single quote can, provides an apt summary of the interpretations of ambiguity in this organization.

> Working in the Department of Energy is like traveling across Alaska on foot. Sometimes it is very rewarding, [but] often [you're] in a swamp with mosquitoes and mud and [it's] cold or [there's] too close proximity to bears. [The] ratio of beauty to risk and discomfort is low (#7).

Notes

1. I am indebted to Joanne Martin and Debra Meyerson for helpful comments on this chapter.

2. The number of people in the office varied over the time of observation.

3. The experience of people in organizations that were incorporated into the Department of Energy was included in these figures. Thus, a person could have been in the same organization for longer than the Department of Energy had existed.

4. See Feldman (1989), *Order Without Design,* for a more complete description of the office and the staff.

5. The questions were, for the most part, open-ended. I analyzed the data using a text analysis program (TEXTAN) that allows the researcher to assign categories to responses and maintain verbatim text (Sproull & Sproull, 1982). This program is particularly useful for examining responses to open-ended questions, because people often make several responses to one question. TEXTAN allows the researcher to separate these responses and place them in appropriate categories.

6. Informants are numbered and names are disguised to protect anonymity.

7. The term *riffed* comes from the military acronym for Reduction in Force.

ID
Conclusion:
Taking a Three-Perspective Approach

Martin and Meyerson have argued, using data from a variety of case studies, that any cultural context contains elements that can be understood only when all three perspectives are used.[1] For example, Meyerson and Martin (1987) studied the Peace Corps/Africa, using each perspective in turn. When this organization was viewed from an integration perspective, the values espoused by President Kennedy and implemented by his appointees took center stage. Peace Corps/Africa was seen as an ideologically motivated cadre of fervently committed staff and volunteers. When the same organization was viewed from a differentiation perspective, attention was drawn to the relationships among various subcultures, such as the top management team in Africa, the staff and volunteers assigned to the various African nations, and project assignments (such as teaching English, building sanitation facilities) shared by volunteers working in different countries.

From a fragmentation perspective, each volunteer's relative isolation from other U.S. citizens became salient. Because of the two-year limitation on most volunteers' commitment, turnover was high. These factors contributed to widespread ignorance and confusion, particularly given the difficulties of adjusting to a new language and foreign ways. Under these conditions, according to the fragmentation viewpoint, consensus developed only on an issue-specific, transient basis. For example, issues such as the danger of contagious illness or the appropriateness of love affairs with Africans would generate intense interest, some agreement, and some disagreement, and then would fade from view. Another issue would arouse a different pattern of involvement, agreement, and disagreement. From this fragmentation point of view, the ability to live with these ambiguities was essential for any Peace Corps member. As this brief summary of part of the Peace Corps/Africa study indicates, a three-perspective approach to the study of culture can offer insights inaccessible to any single perspective.

The need for a three-perspective approach becomes even more evident when the process of cultural change is considered. An integration study must acknowledge the conflicts that accompany any change. A differentiation study must be able to cope with the possibility that a dissenting subculture might win the struggle to become dominant (Would they try to establish a new, organization-wide consensus?). Conversely, the dissenting subculture might be defeated (Would the clarities of the old struggle become clouded with doubts and ambiguities?). A fragmentation study would have to acknowledge that change requires some forms of clarity, consistency, and consensus, if coordinated action is to be accomplished. As these examples indicate, a single perspective view of the cultural change process is misleadingly incomplete. For these reasons, Martin and Meyerson insist that, at any point in time, a culture can be viewed usefully from all three perspectives.

A common response to this argument is: "But in the organization I studied, one of the three perspectives was more 'accurate' than the other two." This argument makes the assumption that the perspectives are objectively "true" descriptions of particular contexts. This assumption is implicit in the language used in some of the chapters that compose Part I. Some authors (and, in some cases, their informants) report that they have observed organization-wide consensus, subcultural differentiation, or fragmentation. Authors who rely on informants' perceptions are reporting those perceptions as accurately as they can.

Martin and Meyerson, like some of the chapter authors in Part I of this book, take a more subjectivist, "sociology of knowledge" position. They argue that the three perspectives are subjective points of view that people (both researchers and organizational members) use to understand and interpret the meaning of what they see and experience. This means that three people might observe the same events in the same cultural context and describe what they see differently because each person views the experience from a different perspective. These people are not being dishonest; they simply see things differently. For example, they may pay attention to different aspects of what is going on; they may bring a different subjective frame of mind or a different theoretical framework to what they see, so they interpret it differently. When the perspectives are conceptualized as subjective points of view, it becomes possible to view the same context from all three points of view, with no one perspective considered more "objectively accurate" than the others.

Some people are used to thinking predominantly within a single perspective. Others move more easily from one perspective to another. If some people do habitually use only one perspective, why is this so? The reasons may differ, depending on whether one is a cultural member or a researcher.

Martin and Meyerson argue that some cultural members may find one perspective more comfortable than the others, in part because of their position within an organization. Higher ranking managers tend to see the world with integrationist glasses, perhaps because the integration perspective may be congruent with managers' desires to see their values shared and their policies implemented with enthusiasm. Blue-collar workers and others clustered at the lower levels of a hierarchy are somewhat more likely to express views congruent with a differentiation perspective, perhaps because their status puts them at a distance from (and perhaps in conflict with) a managerial perspective. Finally, newcomers, employees whose jobs seem ambiguous, and individuals with a high tolerance for ambiguity tend to see their work from the fragmentation perspective.

According to Martin and Meyerson, research often relies on a single perspective because of limitations in the ways culture is defined and cultural members are "sampled." When culture is defined in terms of consistency, clarity, and organization-wide consensus, and when primarily high ranking managers are studied, evidence congruent with the integration perspective is more likely to be found. Similarly, if a study works from a definition of culture that encompasses subcultures and conflict, and if primarily disempowered, lower status employees are studied, the differentiation perspective is more likely to receive empirical support. If a study focuses on occupations and events characterized by unusually high levels of ambiguity awareness, and if ambiguity is defined as an inescapable and centrally important component of culture, support for the fragmentation viewpoint is more likely to be found. To some extent, then, research finds what it is looking for.

These single-perspective preferences are emotionally and politically grounded. People vary in the extent to which they are comfortable with homogeneity, conflict, and ambiguity. Furthermore, certain political ideologies are more congruent with one perspective than another. For example, the integration perspective's homogenizing claims of unity enshrine and support an established authority. The differentiation perspective implicitly challenges established authority, as it attempts to articulate alternative points of view, stresses the importance of difference, and sometimes acknowledges the dynamics of power, conflict, and oppression. The fragmentation perspective undermines the unifying claims of any established authority and any group that would try to establish an alternative authority.

In recognizing the ambiguities that emerge from multiple viewpoints, the fragmentation perspective attempts to legitimate differences in interpretation.

Some researchers, some individual cultural members, and even some organizations have a "home" perspective that is more comfortable and seems a more obvious, accurate, and appropriate way to view culture. However, Martin and Meyerson insist that it is essential to remember that any single perspective can tell only part of a cultural story. In any context, at any time, the other two perspectives explain aspects of the culture that are ignored or misrepresented by the home perspective. When two of the three perspectives are suppressed, one of the suppressed viewpoints is usually fairly easily accessible ("Of course, I should have seen that"); the other perspective is usually deeply repressed because its acknowledgment would be threatening to current arrangements and understandings. In cultural research, as in psychoanalysis, the more a perspective is repressed, the greater the potential growth in understanding if the relevance of that perspective can be understood.

Each of the three perspectives, in some sense, denies the validity of the others. Martin and Meyerson argue that the oppositions among these perspectives cannot and should not be resolved in some grand unifying synthesis. Pressures toward assimilation across perspectives would undermine each perspective's oppositional stance toward the others, threatening its integrity. A multi-perspective approach to cultural understanding must vacillate among the three viewpoints, perhaps presenting each in turn.

It is cognitively and emotionally difficult to adopt a three-perspective approach. One strong rationale for undertaking this difficult task is captured in the adage "know thine enemy." For example, if your goal is clarity, it is essential to know where ambiguities lie. If your goal is creating an organization where the disempowered become empowered, some form of organization-wide consensus might be needed. If you see organizational life as riddled with ambiguities that people are denying, it would be helpful to know which claims of clarity need to be challenged. For all of these reasons, researchers and cultural members need to learn to use all three perspectives, not just one.

Martin (in press) extends the three-perspective framework, using it to analyze a case study of a single cultural context (a large corporation) and to delineate the overlaps, disjunctions, and blindspots of contemporary organizational culture research. This book attempts to use the three perspective framework to understand differences, without creating pressures towards meta-theoretical homogenization or assimilation. When used in this way, the three-perspective framework can help elucidate what has been learned from the last decade of organizational culture research and what might be learned in the future.

One way to see if the three-perspective approach can be useful to you, as a reader or as a researcher, is to review your reactions to the empirical chapters in Part I of this volume: Which chapters did you prefer and why? Do you have a home perspective? What predictable blindspots might be associated with your preferences?

Note

1. The three-perspective framework was first articulated in relation to the organizational change literature in Martin and Meyerson (1987) and in relation to ambiguity research in Martin and Meyerson (1988). The distinction between the integration and differentiation perspectives was first developed in Martin and Siehl (1983) and Martin, Sitkin, and Boehm (1985). The three-perspective framework is elaborated and extended in a book (tentatively) titled *Harmony, Conflict, and Ambiguity in Organizational Cultures* (Martin, in press).

Selected Readings Congruent With Different Perspectives

Integration Perspective

Clark, B. (1972). The organizational saga in higher education. *Administrative Science Quarterly, 17,* 178-184.

Deal, T. E., & Kennedy, A. A. (1982). *Corporate cultures: The rites and rituals of corporate life.* Reading, MA: Addison-Wesley.

Denison, D. P. (1990). *Corporate culture and organizational effectiveness.* New York: John Wiley.

Lincoln, J. R., & Kallberg, A. L. (1985). Work organization and workforce commitment: A study of plants and employees in the U.S. and Japan. *American Sociological Review, 50*(12), 738-760.

Martin, J., Feldman, M. S., Hatch, M. J., & Sitkin, S. B. (1983). The uniqueness paradox in organizational stories. *Administrative Science Quarterly, 28,* 438-453.

Martin, J. (1982). Stories and scripts in organizational settings. In A. H. Hastorf & A. M. Isen (Eds.), *Cognitive social psychology.* New York: Elsevier-North Holland.

Ouchi, W. G. (1981). *Theory Z: How American business can meet the Japanese challenge.* Reading, MA: Addison-Wesley.

Ouchi, W. G., & Wilkins, A. L. (1985). Organizational culture. *Annual Review of Sociology, 11,* 457-483.

Pascale, R. T., & Athos, A. G. (1981). *The art of Japanese management: Applications for American executives.* New York: Simon & Schuster.

Peters, T. J., & Waterman, R. H. (1982). *In search of excellence: Lessons from America's best-run companies.* New York: Harper & Row.

Pettigrew, A. (1979). On studying organizational culture. *Administrative Science Quarterly, 24*, 570-581.

Rohlene, T. (1974). *The basic form of the company. For harmony and strength: Japanese white-collar organizations in anthropological perspective.* Berkeley: University of California Press.

Sathe, V. (1985). *Culture and related corporate realities: Text, cases, and readings on organizational entry, establishment, and change.* Homewood, IL: Richard D. Irwin.

Schein, E. H. (1985). *Organizational culture and leadership.* San Francisco, CA: Jossey-Bass.

Selznick, P. (1957). *Leadership and administration.* Evanston, IL: Row & Peterson.

Differentiation Perspective

Barley, S. (1986). Technology as an occasion for structuring: Evidence from observations of CT scanners and the social order of radiology departments. *Administrative Science Quarterly, 31*, 78-108.

Brunsson, N. (1986). Organizing for inconsistencies: On organizational conflicts, depression, and hypocrisy as substitutes for action. *Scandinavian Journal of Management Studies,* May, 165-185.

Christensen, S., & Kreiner, K. (1984). *On the origin of organizational cultures.* Paper prepared for the first International Conference on Organizational Symbolism and Corporate Culture. Lund, Sweden.

Feldman, S. P. (1985). Culture and conformity: An essay on individual adaptation in centralized bureaucracy. *Human Relations, 38*(4), 341-356.

Friedman, S. (1983). *Cultures within cultures? An empirical assessment of an organization's subcultures using projective measures.* Unpublished manuscript, Institute for Social Research, University of Michigan, Ann Arbor.

Gregory, K. L. (1983). Native-view paradigms: Multiple culture and culture conflicts in organizations. *Administrative Science Quarterly, 28*, 359-376.

Jermier, J. (1985). When the sleeper wakes: A short story extending themes in radical organization theory. *Journal of Management, 11*, 67-80.

Louis, M. R. (1983). *Cultures: Yes; Organization: No!* Paper presented at the 1983 Academy of Management Meeting. Dallas, Texas.

Louis, M. R. (1985). An investigator's guide to workplace culture. In P. J. Frost, L. F. Moore, M. R. Louis, C. C. Lundberg, & J. Martin (Eds.). *Organizational culture.* Beverly Hills, CA: Sage.

Lukas, R. (1987). Political-cultural analysis of organizations. *Academy of Management Review, 12*, 144-156.

Martin, J., & Siehl, C. (1983). Organizational culture and counterculture: An uneasy symbiosis. *Organizational Dynamics,* Autumn, 52-64.

Martin, J., Sitkin, S. B., & Boehm, M. (1985). Founders and the elusiveness of a cultural legacy. In P. J. Frost, L. F. Moore, M. R. Louis, C. C. Lundberg, & J. Martin (Eds.), *Organizational culture.* Beverly Hills, CA: Sage.

Riley, P. (1983). A structural account of political cultures. *Administrative Science Quarterly, 28*, 414-437.

Smircich, L. (1983). Organizations as shared meanings. In L. R. Pondy, P. J. Frost, G. Morgan, & T. C. Dandridge (Eds.), *Organizational symbolism.* Greenwich, CT: JAI.

Smircich, L., & Morgan, G. (1982). Leadership: The management of meaning. *Journal of Applied Behavioral Science, 18*(3), 257-273.

Sunesson, S. (1985). Outside the goal paradigm: Power and structured patterns of non-rational-
    ity. *Organization Studies, 6*(3), 229-246.
Trice, H., & Morand, D. (in press). Organizational subcultures and countercultures. In G. Miller
    (Ed.), *Studies in organizational sociology*. Greenwich, CT: JAI.
Turner, B. A. (1986). Sociological aspects of organizational symbolism. *Organizational Studies,
    7*(2), 101-115.
Van Maanen, J., & Barley, S. (1984). Occupational communities: Culture and control in
    organizations. In B. Staw & L. Cummings (Eds.), *Research on organizational behavior*
    (Vol. 6). Greenwich, CT: JAI.
Van Maanen, J., & Barley, S. (1985). Cultural organization: Fragments of a theory. In P. J. Frost,
    L. F. Moore, M. R. Louis, C. C. Lundberg, & J. Martin (Eds.), *Organizational culture*.
    Beverly Hills, CA: Sage.
Van Maanen, J., & Kunda, G. (1989). "Real feelings": Emotional expression and organizational
    culture. In L. Cummings & B. Staw (Eds.), *Research in Organizational Behavior, 11*,
    43-103. Greenwich, CT: JAI.
Weston, K., & Rofel, L. B. (1984). Sexuality, class, and conflict in a lesbian workplace. *Signs,
    9*(4), 623-646.

Fragmentation Perspective

Arac, J. (Ed.). (1986). *Postmodernism and politics*. Minneapolis: University of Minnesota Press.
Becker, H. S. (1982). Culture: A sociological view. *Yale Review, 71*, 513-527. Boston, MA:
    Beacon.
Brunsson, N. (1985). *The irrational organization*. New York: John Wiley.
Calas, M., & Smircich, L. (1987). *Post-culture: Is the organizational culture literature dominant
    but dead?* Paper presented at the International Conference on Organizational Symbolism
    and Corporate Culture, Milan, Italy.
Calas, M., & Smircich, L. (1989). *Voicing seduction to silence leadership*. Paper presented at
    the International Conference on Organizational Symbolism and Corporate Culture, Fon-
    tainebleau, France.
Clifford, J., & Marcus, G. E. (1986). *Writing culture*. Berkeley: University of California Press.
Cohen, D., March, J. G., & Olsen, J. P. (1972). A garbage can model of organizational choice.
    Administrative Science Quarterly, 17, 1-25.
Derrida, J. (1976). *Speech and phenomenon*. Evanston, IL: Northwestern University Press.
Grafton-Small, R., & Linstead, S. (1987). *Artefact as theory: All roses lead to Milan*. Paper
    presented at the International Conference on Organizational Symbolism and Corporate
    Culture, Milan, Italy.
Krackhardt, D., & Kilduff, M. (1987). *Diversity is strength: A social network approach to the
    constructs of organizational culture*. Unpublished manuscript, Cornell University, Ithaca,
    NY.
Levitt, B., & Nass, C. (1989). The lid on the garbage can: Institutional constraints on decision
    making in the technical core of college-text publishers. *Administrative Science Quarterly,
    34*, 190-207.
March, J., & Olsen, J. (1976). *Ambiguity and choice in organizations*. Bergen, Norway:
    Universitetsforlagert.
Martin, J. (1990). Deconstructing organizational taboos: The suppression of gender conflict in
    organizations. *Organizational Science, 1*(4), 339-359.

Martin, J., & Meyerson, D. (1988). Organizational culture and the denial, channeling, and acknowledgment of ambiguity. In M. Moch, L. Pondy, & H. Thomas (Eds.), *Managing ambiguity and change*. New York: John Wiley.

Rosaldo, R. (1989). *Culture & truth: The remaking of social analysis*. Boston, MA: Beacon.

Sabrosky, A. N., Thompson, J. C., & McPherson, K. A. (1982). Organized anarchies: Military bureaucracy in the 1980s. *Journal of Applied Behavioral Science, 18*(2), 137-153.

Schultz, M. (1989). *Postmodern pictures of culture*. Unpublished manuscript, Copenhagen School of Economics and Social Science, Copenhagen, Denmark.

Sproull, L., Weiner, S., & Wolf, D. (1978). *Organizing an anarchy*. Chicago, IL: University of Chicago Press.

Starbuck, W. (1983). Organizations as action generators. *American Sociological Review, 48*, 91-102.

Van Maanen, J. (1988). *Tales of the field*. Chicago, IL: University of Chicago Press.

Weick, K. E. (1979). *The social psychology of organizing*. Reading, MA: Addison-Wesley.

PART II

RESEARCHING ORGANIZATIONAL CULTURE

THE NAMING OF CATS

The Naming of Cats is a difficult matter,
　　It isn't just one of your holiday games;
You may think at first I'm as mad as a hatter
When I tell you, a cat must have THREE DIFFERENT NAMES.
First of all, there's the name that the family use daily,
　　Such as Peter, Augustus, Alonzo or James,
Such as Victor or Jonathan, George or Bill Bailey—
　　All of them sensible everyday names.
There are fancier names if you think they sound sweeter,
　　Some for the gentlemen, some for the dames:
Such as Plato, Admetus, Electra, Demeter—
　　But all of them sensible everyday names.
But I tell you, a cat needs a name that's particular,
　　A name that's peculiar, and more dignified,
Else how can he keep up his tail perpendicular,
　　Or spread out his whiskers, or cherish his pride?
Of names of this kind, I can give you a quorum,
　　Such as Munkustrap, Quaxo, or Coricopat,
Such as Bombalurina, or else Jellylorum—
　　Names that never belong to more than one cat.
But above and beyond there's still one name left over,
　　And that is the name that you never will guess;
The name that no human research can discover—
　　But THE CAT HIMSELF KNOWS, and will never confess.
When you notice a cat in profound meditation,
　　The reason, I tell you, is always the same:
His mind is engaged in a rapt contemplation
　　Of the thought, of the thought, of the thought of his name:
　　　　His ineffable effable
　　　　Effanineffable
Deep and inscrutable singular Name.

—T. S. ELIOT

Introduction

The bureaucratization of scientific research proceeds on the assumption that the task of research is one which is amenable to the same kind of hierarchical division of labor as are tasks in manufacturing industry or in official administration. This view of research is reinforced by much of the abstract and elaborate edifice of 'research methodology' which the social sciences have generated, (Willer & Willer, 1974; Zetterberg, 1954; Hage, 1972) and which has generated its own momentum and its own autonomy as an area of abstract learning. But there is an obscurity about how the detailed and rule-bound practices advocated for the definition of concepts and for the construction of theory related to the actual process of ongoing research. Such writings, while pursuing theoretical and logical rigour, produce systems of abstraction with normative undertones—this is how research should be done—whilst retaining a problematic relationship to the processes which they claim to explicate. In a similar manner, as we shall see, attempts to absorb the new emphasis upon qualitative research into existing orthodoxies of research methodology produce an illusory clarity, for they do not look closely enough at the research process.

—SILVIA GHERARDI & BARRY TURNER
(*Real Men Don't Collect Soft Data*, 1987)

How is organizational culture researched? What does one include in one's mindscape when one decides to conduct empirical research on culture? What influences the choices one makes, the content one includes and excludes as the research process is engaged? Are there patterns of thinking and acting in the research arena that we can identify and learn from? Have these changed over time or is this a process that is generalizable across time and space? In Part I, we outlined, discussed, and showcased three different frames for conceptualizing organizational culture. Researchers, we pointed out, may use one or more of these perspectives (or others) for modeling their studies. Such choices can be made to focus a study or to interpret its results. They can be made rationally or intuitively or using both modes of understanding. They will be influenced by the socialization and prior professional experiences of the researchers.

In Part II we are interested in exploring what assumptions about research are made when investigators study organizational culture. We are not focusing here on operational issues, choice points, or criteria for making choices. These are identified in most discussions of methodology in books on the research process (cf. Mowday & Steers, 1979). The logic behind such discussions has been that the choices a researcher makes will influence the quality of the study and its results. For the most part, the influences considered have been explicit, conscious choices. More recently, ontological and epistemological choices have been added to the discussions. As a result, researchers now are frequently reminded to make explicit and test the appropriateness of their assumptions about the nature of phenomena under study as they embark on culture research. This is essentially the question of what the writers of the chapters in Part II are doing as they discuss organizational culture.

In Section IIA several authors discuss William Foote Whyte's research in *Street Corner Society* (1943). We invite you to read the reprinted excerpt from the Appendix of the 1955 edition of Whyte's book as essential context to the assessments and Whyte's response written for the present volume.

In Section IIB a number of contemporary organizational culture researchers describe their respective approaches to studying the topic. Harrison M. Trice comments on these descriptions and adds his own views on doing organizational culture research.

In Section IIC the chapter "Masquerade: Organizational Culture as Metafiction" challenges the whole notion of doing organizational culture research as a systematic, orderly progression of activities, created uniquely by identifiable individuals. The authors convey a perspective on organizational culture that is very different from most others in the book.

In Section IID we spin from the earlier chapters of Part II and weave our own story about what influences the way organizational culture is done.

IIA
Exploring an Exemplar of Organizational Culture Research

Every mythological theme has in every period been the subject of a number of different stories, each of them variously conditioned by the place, time, and artistic powers of the narrator.

—C. KERENYI
(*The Gods of the Greeks*, 1951, p. 9)

Contemporary research in the social sciences contains ingredients of earlier work in the field. That work, particularly when seen as exemplary, serves as a source of ideas and ways of doing research for others who come later to the same issues. Early works are inevitably influenced by the context of their time and the perspectives of the researchers themselves. Exemplars may be reinterpreted and repositioned when examined from the orientations and assumptions of a different era. Nevertheless, studies that endure as significant contributions to knowledge do have an impact on what is believed to be important by researchers and what is communicated to new scholars in a field.

Perhaps the most well known and recognized early study of organizations as cultures is *Street Corner Society* (Whyte, 1943). Whyte's Appendix to the 1955 edition of the book constitutes a fascinating and rare depiction of how one novice researcher discovered and dealt with the many epistemological issues that were encountered in that pioneering attempt to do research in the phenomenological domain of organizational culture. Further details of that process are reported in the 1981 edition of the book.

Street Corner Society together with the 1955 Appendix have without doubt had a major impact in influencing the research designs of a couple of generations of sociologists and, more recently, organizational culture researchers. As we noted in the opening paragraph, all such studies are to an extent bounded in time and Whyte, as a researcher, would have been influenced by his own personal characteristics and his assumptions about the way the world works as well as by the level and scope of his training and background knowledge. What he accomplished with the resources available to him at that time is truly remarkable and we can learn much from his work.

In Part IIA, we have three objectives. First, an excerpted portion of the Appendix to *Street Corner Society* (1955) has been reproduced in Chapter 11, not only as an exemplar of an organizational culture research project, but also as an epistemological account, in the researcher's own words, of how the foundations on which he built came to be. Second, we have asked four contemporary researchers of organizational culture, (Jones, Bryman, Riley, and Jermier) to read the excerpt of the Appendix, to reflect on the epistemological significance of *Street Corner Society* from their own (somewhat diverse) backgrounds and perspectives and to delineate and comment on issues that emerged as they thought about the meaning of this work. Finally, W. F. Whyte was invited to respond to these four authors.

As an exemplar, a piece of research such as *Street Corner Society* may be expected to inform and guide other research efforts which follow. Often, the influence of an exemplar can be traced in fields of study only laterally related to the central concern of the exemplar. Moreover, the influence of an exemplar frequently persists forward through time, providing structure and form to subsequent (and often more sophisticated) theoretical and empirical efforts. Metaphorically, then, an exemplar can be seen as a benchmark, a stepping stone, or a conceptual road map. The commentaries to follow each illustrate in different ways how Whyte's *Street Corner Society* has influenced contemporary thinking and research on the cultural aspects of organizational life.

For Michael Owen Jones, a folklorist, Whyte's account of the use and importance of symbols and traditions and their effect on organizational action, interaction, and sentiments highlights the potential of field research in generating inferences and insights leading to better organizational understanding, planning, and change. In Chapter 12, Jones goes well beyond *Street Corner Society* to provide a cameo portrayal of W. F. Whyte's background, including the identification of some of the people who influenced his formative thinking.

Does *Street Corner Society* represent exemplary methodology? In Chapter 13 Alan Bryman explores this question, examining the research against several criteria. He focuses particular attention to Emerson's (1987) four criteria for evaluating an ethnographic study. In contrast to Whyte's lengthy and sustained personal immersion in his investigation, Bryman believes that there may be a current tendency for "short consultancy-style investigation" with an overemphasis on application.

While conceding that this exemplar constitutes a landmark ethnographic study, in Chapter 14 Patricia Riley notes that cultural descriptions are subjective narrations and thus are at least partially fictional. The observer (ethnographer) is in the position of creating culture. From Riley's post-modern perspective, this produces a "reflective" account, bound and shaped by whatever descriptive words and language forms the narrator selects. Riley notes in particular that research narration (for political and other reasons) is often couched in elitist academic jargon, raising questions of representation and privileged understanding. Furthermore, she argues, there is a need to revise earlier research accounts in light of emerging theories and insights. Her point of view suggests that every work is in one sense located in the context of its time and in another sense is liable to revision or reinterpretation when viewed from a different era.[1]

John M. Jermier's critical essay, Chapter 15, identifies a number of limitations in *Street Corner Society* and points out some important issues, such as institutionalized racism and immigrant inequality, which were neglected in Whyte's analysis. Jermier reminds us that culture is subjective reality, thus value neutrality in social research is not possible. What is possible, though, is a mode of inquiry that continually examines one's moral bases and political interests.

In responding to the four commentators on *Street Corner Society* in Chapter 16, William Foote Whyte adds further insights into the history and development of this work. He directs his attention to three categories which contain their major concerns: the role of culture in field studies of organizations and communities; research methods; and the nature of science in social research. Whyte's final brief description of his recent work with the Mondragon cooperative complex in Spain clarifies the nature of his own political commitments in his work and serves to remind us that research in the arena of organizational culture can be a powerful springboard for social change.

In conclusion, we are reminded that the primary function of an exemplar is to provide an example that will stimulate further inquiry. An inquiry need not slavishly emulate the exemplar, which may, in itself, be incomplete. The challenge for present researchers is to venture into realms where no road maps or guideposts exist. This means we must be prepared to back-track or take a new tack when necessary.

Note

1. Readers might be interested in a forthcoming Special Issue of the *Journal of Contemporary Ethnography* (April 1992, Vol. 21 No. 1) devoted to *Street Corner Society*. Among other papers is one by Marianne Boelen, "Street Corner Society Revisited," which challenges Whyte's findings and interpretations in the study and one by Whyte in which he gives his rejoinder to her critique.

11

Street Corner Society:
Excerpts from the Appendix to the 1955 Edition

WILLIAM FOOTE WHYTE

First Efforts

When I began my work, I had had no training in sociology or anthropology. I thought of myself as an economist and naturally looked first toward the matters that we had taken up in economics courses, such as economics of slum housing. At the time I was sitting in on a course in slums and housing in the Sociology Department at Harvard. As a term project I took on a study of one block in Cornerville. To legitimize this effort, I got in touch with a private agency that concerned itself in housing matters and offered to turn over to them the results of my survey. With that backing, I began knocking on doors, looking into flats, and talking to the tenants about the living conditions. This brought me into contact with Cornerville people, but it would be hard now to devise a more inappropriate way of beginning a study such as I was eventually to make. I felt ill at ease at this intrusion, and I am sure so did the people. I wound up the block study as rapidly as I could and wrote it off as a total loss as far as gaining a real entry into the district.

Shortly thereafter I made another false start—if so tentative an effort may even be called a start. At that time I was completely baffled at the problem of finding my way into the district. Cornerville was right before me and yet so far away. I could walk freely up and down its streets, and I

AUTHOR'S NOTE: Reprinted with permission from *Street Corner Society* (288-308, 356-358) W.F. Whyte (2nd ed., 1955), Chicago, IL: University of Chicago Press.

had even made my way into some of the flats, and yet I was still a stranger in a world completely unknown to me.

At this time I met a young economics instructor at Harvard who impressed me with his self-assurance and his knowledge of Eastern City. He had once been attached to a settlement house, and he talked glibly about his associations with the tough young men and women of the district. He also described how he would occasionally drop in on some drinking place in the area and strike up an acquaintance with a girl, buy her a drink, and then encourage her to tell him her life-story. He claimed that the women so encountered were appreciative of this opportunity and that it involved no further obligation.

This approach seemed at least as plausible as anything I had been able to think of. I resolved to try it out. I picked on the Regal Hotel, which was on the edge of Cornerville. With some trepidation I climbed the stairs to the bar and entertainment area and looked around. There I encountered a situation for which my adviser had not prepared me. There were women present all right, but none of them was alone. Some were there in couples, and there were two or three pairs of women together. I pondered this situation briefly. I had little confidence in my skill at picking up one female, and it seemed inadvisable to tackle two at the same time. Still, I was determined not to admit defeat without a struggle. I looked around me again and now noticed a threesome: one man and two women. It occurred to me that here was a maldistribution of females which I might be able to rectify. I approached the group and opened with something like this: "Pardon me. Would you mind if I joined you?" There was a moment of silence while the man stared at me. He then offered to throw me downstairs. I assured him that this would not be necessary and demonstrated as much by walking right out of there without any assistance.

I subsequently learned that hardly anyone from Cornerville ever went into the Regal Hotel. If my efforts there had been crowned with success, they would no doubt have led somewhere but certainly not to Cornerville.

For my next effort I sought out the local settlement houses. They were open to the public. You could walk right into them, and—though I would not have phrased it this way at the time—they were manned by middle-class people like myself. I realized even then that to study Cornerville I would have to go well beyond the settlement house, but perhaps the social workers could help me to get started.

As I look back on it now, the settlement house also seems a very unpromising place from which to begin such a study. If I had it to do over again, I would probably make my first approach through a local politician or perhaps through the Catholic church, although I am not myself Catholic. John Howard, who worked with me later, made his entry very successfully through the church, and he, too, was not a Catholic—although his wife was.

However that may be, the settlement house proved the right place for me at this time, for it was here that I met Doc. I had talked to a number of the social workers about my plans and hopes to get acquainted with the people and study the district. They listened with varying degrees of interest. If they had suggestions to make, I have forgotten them now except for one. Somehow, in spite of the vagueness of my own explanations, the head of girls' work in the Norton Street House understood what I needed. She began describing Doc to me. He was, she said, a very intelligent and talented person who had at one time been fairly active in the house but had dropped out, so that he hardly ever came in any more. Perhaps he could understand what I wanted, and he must have the contacts that I needed. She said she frequently encountered him as she walked to and from the house and sometimes stopped to chat with him. If I wished, she would make an appointment for me to see him in the house one evening. This at last seemed right. I jumped at the chance. As I came into the district that evening, it was with a feeling that here I had my big chance to get started. Somehow Doc must accept me and be willing to work with me.

In a sense, my study began on the evening of February 3, 1937, when the social worker called me in to meet Doc. She showed us into her office and then left so that we could talk. Doc waited quietly for me to begin, as he sank down into a chair. I found him a man of medium height and spare build. His hair was a light brown, quite a contrast to the more typical black Italian hair. It was thinning around the temples. His cheeks were sunken. His eyes were a light blue and seemed to have a penetrating gaze.

I began by asking him if the social worker had told him about what I was trying to do.

"No, she just told me that you wanted to meet me and that I should like to meet you."

Then I went into a long explanation which, unfortunately, I omitted from my notes. As I remember it, I said that I had been interested in congested city districts in my college study but had felt very remote from them. I hoped to study the problems in such a district. I felt I could do very little as an outsider. Only if I could get to know the people and learn their problems first hand would I be able to gain the understanding I needed.

Doc heard me out without any change of expression, so that I had no way of predicting his reaction. When I was finished, he asked: "Do you want to see the high life or the low life?"

"I want to see all that I can. I want to get as complete a picture of the community as possible."

"Well, any nights you want to see anything, I'll take you around. I can take you to the joints—gambling joints—I can take you around to the street corners. Just remember that you're my friend. That's all they need to know. I know these places, and, if I tell them that you're my friend, nobody will bother you. You just tell me what you want to see, and we'll arrange it."

The proposal was so perfect that I was at a loss for a moment as to how to respond to it. We talked a while longer, as I sought to get some pointers as to how I should behave in his company. He warned me that I might have to take the risk of getting arrested in a raid on a gambling joint but added that this was not serious. I only had to give a false name and then would get bailed out by the man that ran the place, paying only a five-dollar fine. I agreed to take this chance. I asked him whether I should gamble with the others in the gambling joints. He said it was unnecessary and, for a greenhorn like myself, very inadvisable.

At last I was able to express my appreciation. "You know, the first steps of getting to know a community are the hardest. I could see things going with you that I wouldn't see for years otherwise."

"That's right. You tell me what you want to see, and we'll arrange it. When you want some information, I'll ask for it, and you listen. When you want to find out their philosophy of life, I'll start an argument and get it for you. If there's something else you want to get, I'll stage an act for you. Not a scrap, you know, but just tell me what you want, and I'll get it for you."

"That's swell. I couldn't ask for anything better. Now I'm going to try to fit in all right, but, if at any time you see I'm getting off on the wrong foot, I want you to tell me about it."

"Now we're being too dramatic. You won't have any trouble. You come in as my friend. When you come in like that, at first everybody will treat you with respect. You can take a lot of liberties, and nobody will kick. After a while when they get to know you they will treat you like anybody else—you know, they say familiarity breeds contempt. But you'll never have any trouble. There's just one thing to watch out for. Don't spring [treat] people. Don't be too free with your money."

"You mean they'll think I'm a sucker?"

"Yes, and you don't want to buy your way in."

We talked a little about how and when we might get together. Then he asked me a question. "You want to write something about this?"

"Yes, eventually."

"Do you want to change things?"

"Well—yes. I don't see how anybody could come down here where it is so crowded, people haven't got any money or any work to do, and not want to have some things changed. But I think a fellow should do the thing he is best fitted for. I don't want to be a reformer, and I'm not cut out to be a politician. I just want to understand these things as best I can and write them up, and if that has any influence. . . ."

"I think you can change things that way. Mostly that is the way things are changed, by writing about them."

That was our beginning. At the time I found it hard to believe that I could move in as easily as Doc had said with his sponsorship. But that indeed was the way it turned out.

While I was taking my first steps with Doc, I was also finding a place to live in Cornerville. My fellowship provided a very comfortable bed-room, living-room, and bath at Harvard. I had been attempting to commute from these quarters to my Cornerville study. Technically that was possible, but socially I became more and more convinced that it was impossible. I realized that I would always be a stranger to the community if I did not live there. Then, also, I found myself having difficulty putting in the time that I knew was required to establish close relations in Cornerville. Life in Cornerville did not proceed on the basis of formal appointments. To meet people, to get to know them, to fit into their activities, required spending time with them—a lot of time day after day. Commuting to Cornerville, you might come in on a particular afternoon and evening only to discover that the people you intended to see did not happen to be around at the time. Or, even if you did see them, you might find the time passing entirely uneventfully. You might just be standing around with people whose only occupation was talking or walking about to try to keep themselves from being bored.

On several afternoons and evenings at Harvard, I found myself consid-ering a trip to Cornerville and then rationalizing my way out of it. How did I know I would find the people whom I meant to see? Even if I did so, how could I be sure that I would learn anything today? Instead of going off on a wild-goose chase to Cornerville, I could profitably spend my time reading books and articles to fill in my woeful ignorance of sociology and social anthropology. Then, too, I had to admit that I felt more comfortable among these familiar surroundings than I did wandering around Cornerville and spending time with people in whose presence I felt distinctly uncomfortable at first.

When I found myself rationalizing in this way, I realized that I would have to make the break. Only if I lived in Cornerville would I ever be able to understand it and be accepted by it. Finding a place, however, was not easy. In such an overcrowded district a spare room was practically nonexistent. I might have been able to take a room in the Norton Street Settlement House, but I realized that I must do better than this if possible.

I got my best lead from the editor of a weekly English-language newspaper published for the Italian-American colony. I had talked to him before about my study and had found him sympathetic. Now I came to ask him for help in finding a room. He directed me to the Martinis, a family which operated a small restaurant. I went there for lunch and later consulted the son of the family. He was sympathetic but said that they had no place for any additional person. Still, I liked the place and enjoyed the food. I came back several times just to eat. On one occasion I met the editor, and he invited me to his table. At first he asked me some searching questions about my study: what I was after, what my connection with Harvard was, what they had expected to get out of this, and so on. After I had answered him in a manner that I unfortunately failed to record in my notes, he told me that he was satisfied and, in fact, had already spoken in my behalf to people who were suspicious that I might be coming in to "criticize our people."

We discussed my rooming problem again. I mentioned the possibility of living at the Norton Street House. He nodded but added: "It would be much better if you could be in a family. You would pick up the language much quicker, and you would get to know the people. But you want a nice family, an educated family. You don't want to get in with any low types. You want a real good family."

At this he turned to the son of the family with whom I had spoken and asked: "Can't you make some place for Mr. Whyte in the house here?"

Al Martini paused a moment and then said: "Maybe we can fix it up. I'll talk to Mama again."

So he did talk to Mama again, and they did find a place. In fact, he turned over to me his own room and moved in to share a double bed with the son of the cook. I protested mildly at this imposition, but everything had been decided—except for the money. They did not know what to charge me, and I did not know what to offer. Finally, after some fencing, I offered fifteen dollars a month, and they settled for twelve.

The room was simple but adequate to my purposes. It was not heated, but, when I began to type my notes there, I got myself a small oil-burner.

There was no bathtub in the house, but I had to go out to Harvard now and then anyway, so I used the facilities of the great university (the room of my friend, Henry Guerlac) for an occasional tub or shower.

Physically, the place was livable, and it provided me with more than just a physical base. I had been with the Martinis for only a week when I discovered that I was much more than a roomer to them. I had been taking many of my meals in the restaurant and sometimes stopping in to chat with the family before I went to bed at night. Then one afternoon I was out at Harvard and found myself coming down with a bad cold. Since I still had my Harvard room, it seemed the sensible thing to do to stay overnight there. I did not think to tell the Martinis of my plan.

The next day when I was back in the restaurant for lunch, Al Martini greeted me warmly and then said that they had all been worried when I did not come home the night before. Mama had stayed up until two o'clock waiting for me. As I was just a young stranger in the city, she could visualize all sorts of things happening to me. Al told me that Mama had come to look upon me as one of the family. I was free to come and go as I pleased, but she wouldn't worry so much if she knew of my plans.

I was very touched by this plea and resolved thereafter to be as good a son as I could to the Martinis.

At first I communicated with Mama and Papa primarily in smiles and gestures. Papa knew no English at all, and Mama's knowledge was limited to one sentence which she would use when some of the young boys on the street were making noise below her window when she was trying to get her afternoon nap. She would then poke her head out of the window and shout: "Goddam-sonumabitcha! Geroutahere!"

Some weeks earlier, in anticipation of moving into the district, I had begun working on the Italian language myself with the aid of a Linguaphone. One morning now Papa Martini came by when I was talking to the phonograph record. He listened for a few moments in the hall trying to make sense out of this peculiar conversation. Then he burst in upon me with fascinated exclamations. We sat down together while I demonstrated the machine and the method to him. After that he delighted in working with me, and I called him my language professor. In a short time we reached a stage where I could carry on simple conversations, and, thanks to the Linguaphone and Papa Martini, the Italian that came out apparently sounded authentic. He liked to try to pass me off to his friends as *paesano mio*—a man from his own home town in Italy. When I was careful to keep my remarks within the limits of my vocabulary, I could sometimes pass as an immigrant from the village of Viareggio in the province of Tuscany.

Since my research developed so that I was concentrating almost exclusively upon the younger, English-speaking generation, my knowledge of Italian proved unnecessary for research purposes. Nevertheless, I feel certain that it was important in establishing my social position in Cornerville—even with that younger generation. There were schoolteachers and social workers who had worked in Cornerville for as much as twenty years and yet had made no effort to learn Italian. My effort to learn the language probably did more to establish the sincerity of my interest in the people than anything I could have told them of myself and my work. How could a researcher be planning to "criticize our people" if he went to the lengths of learning the language? With language comes understanding, and surely it is easier to criticize people if you do not understand them.

My days with the Martinis would pass in this manner. I would get up in the morning around nine o'clock and go out to breakfast. Al Martini told me I could have breakfast in the restaurant, but, for all my desire to fit in, I never could take their breakfast of coffee with milk and a crust of bread.

After breakfast, I returned to my room and spent the rest of the morning, or most of it, typing up my notes regarding the previous day's events. I had lunch in the restaurant and then set out for the street corner. Usually I was back for dinner in the restaurant and then out again for the evening.

Usually I came home again between eleven and twelve o'clock, at a time when the restaurant was empty except perhaps for a few family friends. Then I might join Papa in the kitchen to talk as I helped him dry the dishes, or pull up a chair into a family conversation around one of the tables next to the kitchen. There I had a glass of wine to sip, and I could sit back and mostly listen but occasionally try out my growing Italian on them.

The pattern was different on Sunday, when the restaurant was closed at two o'clock, and Al's two brothers and his sister and the wives, husband, and children would come in for a big Sunday dinner. They insisted that I eat with them at this time and as a member of the family, not paying for my meal. It was always more than I could eat, but it was delicious, and I washed it down with two tumblers of Zinfandel wine. Whatever strain there had been in my work in the preceding week would pass away now as I ate and drank and then went to my room for an afternoon nap of an hour or two that brought me back completely refreshed and ready to set forth again for the corners of Cornerville.

Though I made several useful contacts in the restaurant or through the family, it was not for this that the Martinis were important to me. There is a strain to doing such fieldwork. The strain is greatest when you are a stranger and are constantly wondering whether people are going to accept you. But, much as you enjoy your work, as long as you are observing and interviewing, you have a role to play, and you are not completely relaxed. It was a wonderful feeling at the end of a day's work to be able to come home to relax and enjoy myself with the family. Probably it would have been impossible for me to carry on such a concentrated study of Cornerville if I had not had such a home from which to go out and to which I might return.

Beginning with Doc

I can still remember my first outing with Doc. We met one evening at the Norton Street House and set out from there to a gambling place a couple of blocks away. I followed Doc anxiously down the long, dark hallway at the back of a tenement building. I was not worried about the possibility of a police raid. I was thinking about how I would fit in and be accepted. The door opened into a small kitchen almost bare of furnishings and with the paint peeling off the walls. As soon as we went in the door, I took off my hat and began looking around for a place to hang it. There was no place. I looked around, and here I learned my first lesson in participant observation in Cornerville: Don't take off your hat in the house—at least not when you are among men. It may be permissible, but certainly not required, to take your hat off when women are around.

Doc introduced me as "my friend Bill" to Chichi, who ran the place, and to Chichi's friends and customers. I stayed there with Doc part of the time in the kitchen, where several men would sit around and talk, and part of the time in the other room watching the crap game.

There was talk about gambling, horse races, sex, and other matters. Mostly I just listened and tried to act friendly and interested. We had wine and coffee with anisette in it, with the fellows chipping in to pay for the refreshments. (Doc would not let me pay my share on this first occasion.) As Doc had predicted, no one asked me about myself, but he told me later that, when I went to the toilet, there was an excited burst of conversation in Italian and that he had to assure them that I was not a G-man. He said he told them flatly that I was a friend of his, and they agreed to let it go at that.

We went several more times together to Chichi's gambling joint, and then the time came when I dared to go in alone. When I was greeted in a natural and friendly manner, I felt that I was now beginning to find a place for myself in Cornerville.

When Doc did not go off to the gambling joint, he spent his time hanging around Norton Street, and I began hanging with him. At first, Norton Street meant only a place to wait until I could go somewhere else. Gradually, as I got to know the men better, I found myself becoming one of the Norton Street gang.

Then the Italian Community Club was formed in the Norton Street Settlement, and Doc was invited to be a member. Doc maneuvered to get me into the club, and I was glad to join, as I could see that it represented something distinctly different from the corner gangs I was meeting.

As I began to meet the men of Cornerville, I also met a few of the girls. One girl I took to a church dance. The next morning the fellows on the street corner were asking me: "How's your steady girl?" This brought me up short. I learned that going to the girl's house was something that you just did not do unless you hoped to marry her. Fortunately, the girl and her family knew that I did not know the local customs, so they did not assume that I was thus committed. However, this was a useful warning. After this time, even though I found some Cornerville girls exceedingly attractive, I never went out with them except on a group basis, and I did not make any more home visits either.

As I went along, I found that life in Cornerville was not nearly so interesting and pleasant for the girls as it was for the men. A young man had complete freedom to wander and hang around. The girls could not hang on street corners. They had to divide their time between their own homes, the homes of girl friends and relatives, and a job, if they had one. Many of them had a dream that went like this: some young man, from outside of Cornerville, with a little money, a good job, and a good education would come and woo them and take them out of the district. I could hardly afford to fill this role.

Training in Participant Observation

The spring of 1937 provided me with an intensive course in participant observation. I was learning how to conduct myself, and I learned from various groups but particularly from the Nortons.

As I began hanging about Cornerville, I found that I needed an explanation for myself and for my study. As long as I was with Doc and vouched for by him, no one asked me who I was or what I was doing. When I circulated in other groups or even among the Nortons without him, it was obvious that they were curious about me.

I began with a rather elaborate explanation. I was studying the social history of Cornerville—but I had a new angle. Instead of working from the past up to the present, I was seeking to get a thorough knowledge of present conditions and then work from present to past. I was quite pleased with this explanation at the time, but nobody else seemed to care for it. I gave the explanation on only two occasions, and each time, when I had finished, there was an awkward silence. No one, myself included, knew what to say.

While this explanation had at least the virtue of covering everything that I might eventually want to do in the district, it was apparently too involved to mean anything to Cornerville people.

I soon found that people were developing their own explanation about me: I was writing a book about Cornerville. This might seem entirely too vague an explanation, and yet it sufficed. I found that my acceptance in the district depended on the personal relationships I developed far more than upon any explanations I might give. Whether it was a good thing to write a book about Cornerville depended entirely on people's opinions of me personally. If I was all right, then my project was all right; if I was no good, then no amount of explanation could convince them that the book was a good idea.

Of course people did not satisfy their curiosity about me simply by questions that they addressed to me directly. They turned to Doc, for example, and asked him about me. Doc then answered the questions and provided any reassurance that was needed.

I learned early in my Cornerville period the crucial importance of having the support of the key individuals in any groups or organizations I was studying. Instead of trying to explain myself to everyone, I found I was providing far more information about myself and my study to leaders such as Doc than I volunteered to the average corner boy. I always tried to give the impression that I was willing and eager to tell just as much about my study as anyone wished to know, but it was only with group leaders that I made a particular effort to provide really full information.

My relationship with Doc changed rapidly in this early Cornerville period. At first he was simply a key informant—and also my sponsor. As we spent more time together, I ceased to treat him as a passive informant. I discussed with him quite frankly what I was trying to do, what problems were puzzling me, and so on. Much of our time was spent in this discussion of ideas and observations, so that Doc became, in a very real sense, a collaborator in the research.

This full awareness of the nature of my study stimulated Doc to look for and point out to me the sorts of observations that I was interested in. Often when I picked him up at the flat where he lived with his sister and brother-in-law, he said to me: "Bill, you should have been around last night. You would have been interested in this." And then he would go on to tell me what had happened. Such accounts were always interesting and relevant to my study.

Doc found this experience of working with me interesting and enjoyable, and yet the relationship had its drawbacks. He once commented: "You've slowed me up plenty since you've been down here. Now, when I do something, I have to think what Bill Whyte would want to know about it and how I can explain it. Before, I used to do things by instinct."

However, Doc did not seem to consider this a serious handicap. Actually, without any training he was such a perceptive observer that it only needed a little stimulus to help him to make explicit much of the dynamics of the social organization of Cornerville. Some of the interpretations I have made are his more than mine, although it is now impossible to disentangle them.

While I worked more closely with Doc than with any other individual, I always sought out the leader in whatever group I was studying. I wanted not only sponsorship from him but also more active collaboration with the study. Since these leaders had the sort of position in the community that enabled them to observe much better than the followers what was going on and since they were in general more skillful observers than the followers, I found that I had much to learn from a more active collaboration with them.

In my interviewing methods I had been instructed not to argue with people or pass moral judgments upon them. This fell in with my own inclinations. I was glad to accept the people and to be accepted by them. However, this attitude did not come out so much in interviewing, for I did little formal interviewing. I sought to show this interested acceptance of the people and the community in my everyday participation.

I learned to take part in the street corner discussions on baseball and sex. This required no special training, since the topics seemed to be matters of almost universal interest. I was not able to participate so actively in discussions of horse-racing. I did begin to follow the races in a rather general and amateur way. I am sure it would have paid me to devote more study to the *Morning Telegraph* and other racing sheets, but my knowledge of baseball at least insured that I would not be left out of the street corner conversations.

While I avoided expressing opinions on sensitive topics, I found that arguing on some matters was simply part of the social pattern and that one could hardly participate without joining in the argument. I often found myself involved in heated but good-natured arguments about the relative merits of certain major-league ball players and managers. Whenever a girl or a group of girls would walk down the street, the fellows on the corner would make mental notes and later would discuss their evaluations of the females. These evaluations would run largely in terms of shape, and here was glad to argue that Mary had a better "build" than Anna, or vice versa. Of course, if any of the men on the corner happened to be personally attached to Mary or Anna, no searching comments would be made, and I, too, would avoid this topic.

Sometimes I wondered whether just hanging on the street corner was an active enough process to be dignified by the term "research." Perhaps I should be asking these men questions. However, one has to learn when to question and when not to question as well as what questions to ask.

I learned this lesson one night in the early months when I was with Doc in Chichi's gambling joint. A man from another part of the city was regaling us with a tale of the organization of gambling activity. I had been told that he had once been a very big gambling operator, and he talked knowingly about many interesting matters. He did most of the talking, but the others asked questions and threw in comments, so at length I began to feel that I must say something in order to be part of the group. I said: "I suppose the cops were all paid off?"

The gambler's jaw dropped. He glared at me. Then he denied vehemently that any policemen had been paid off and immediately switched the conversation to another subject. For the rest of that evening I felt very uncomfortable.

The next day Doc explained the lesson of the previous evening. "Go easy on that 'who,' 'what,' 'why,' 'when,' 'where' stuff, Bill. You ask those questions, and people will clam up on you. If people accept you, you can just hang around, and you'll learn the answers in the long run without even having to ask the questions."

I found that this was true. As I sat and listened, I learned the answers to questions that I would not even have had the sense to ask if I had been getting my information solely on an interviewing basis. I did not abandon questioning altogether, of course. I simply learned to judge the sensitiveness of the question and my relationship to the people so that I only asked a question in a sensitive area when I was sure that my relationship to the people involved was very solid.

When I had established my position on the street corner, the data simply came to me without very active efforts on my part. It was only now and then, when I was concerned with a particular problem and felt I needed

more information from a certain individual, that I would seek an opportu
nity to get the man alone and carry on a more formal interview.

At first I concentrated upon fitting into Cornerville, but a little later
had to face the question of how far I was to immerse myself in the life c
the district. I bumped into that problem one evening as I was walking dow
the street with the Nortons. Trying to enter into the spirit of the small tal
I cut loose with a string of obscenities and profanity. The walk came to
momentary halt as they all stopped to look at me in surprise. Doc shoo
his head and said: "Bill, you're not supposed to talk like that. That doesn
sound like you."

I tried to explain that was only using terms that were common on th
street corner. Doc insisted, however, that I was different and that the
wanted me to be that way.

This lesson went far beyond the use of obscenity and profanity. I learne
that people did not expect me to be just like them; in fact, they wer
interested and pleased to find me different, just so long as I took a friendl
interest in them. Therefore, I abandoned my efforts at complete immersion
My behavior was nevertheless affected by street corner life. When Joh
Howard first came down from Harvard to join me in the Cornerville stud
he noticed at once that I talked in Cornerville in a manner far different from
that which I used at Harvard. This was not a matter of the use of profanit
or obscenity, nor did I affect the use of ungrammatical expressions. I talke
in the way that seemed natural to me, but what was natural in Cornervill
was different from what was natural at Harvard. In Cornerville, I foun
myself putting much more animation into my speech, dropping termina
g's, and using gestures much more actively. (There was also, of course, th
difference in the vocabulary that I used. When I was most deeply involve
in Cornerville, I found myself rather tongue-tied in my visits to Harvar
I simply could not keep up with the discussions of international relation:
of the nature of science, and so on, in which I had once been more or les
at home.)

As I became accepted by the Nortons and by several other groups, I trie
to make myself pleasant enough so that people would be glad to have m
around. And, at the same time, I tried to avoid influencing the grou
because I wanted to study the situation as unaffected by my presence a
possible. Thus, throughout my Cornerville stay, I avoided accepting offic
or leadership positions in any of the groups with a single exception. At on
time I was nominated as secretary of the Italian Community Club. M
first impulse was to decline the nomination, but then I reflected that th
secretary's job is normally considered simply a matter of dirty work–

writing the minutes and handling the correspondence. I accepted and found that I could write a very full account of the progress of the meeting as it went on under the pretext of keeping notes for the minutes.

While I sought to avoid influencing individuals or groups, I tried to be helpful in the way a friend is expected to help in Cornerville. When one of the boys had to go downtown on an errand and wanted company, I went along with him. When somebody was trying to get a job and had to write a letter about himself, I helped him to compose it, and so on. This sort of behavior presented no problem, but, when it came to the matter of handling money, it was not at all clear just how I should behave. Of course, I sought to spend money on my friends just as they did on me. But what about lending money? It is expected in such a district that a man will help out his friends whenever he can, and often the help needed is financial. I lent money on several occasions, but I always felt uneasy about it. Naturally, a man appreciates it at the time you lend him the money, but how does he feel later when the time has come to pay, and he is not able to do so? Perhaps he is embarrassed and tries to avoid your company. On such occasions I tried to reassure the individual and tell him that I knew he did not have it just then and that I was not worried about it. Or I even told him to forget about the debt altogether. But that did not wipe it off the books; the uneasiness remained. I learned that it is possible to do a favor for a friend and cause a strain in the relationship in the process.

I know no easy solution to this problem. I am sure there will be times when the researcher would be extremely ill advised to refuse to make a personal loan. On the other hand, I am convinced that, whatever his financial resources, he should not look for opportunities to lend money and should avoid doing so whenever he gracefully can.

If the researcher is trying to fit into more than one group, his fieldwork becomes more complicated. There may be times when the groups come into conflict with each other, and he will be expected to take a stand. There was a time in the spring of 1937 when the boys arranged a bowling match between the Nortons and the Italian Community Club. Doc bowled for the Nortons, of course. Fortunately, my bowling at this time had not advanced to a point where I was in demand for either team, and I was able to sit on the sidelines. From there I tried to applaud impartially the good shots of both teams, although I am afraid it was evident that I was getting more enthusiasm into my cheers for the Nortons.

When I was with members of the Italian Community Club, I did not feel at all called upon to defend the corner boys against disparaging remarks. However, there was one awkward occasion when I was with the corner

boys and one of the college boys stopped to talk with me. In the course of
the discussion he said: "Bill, these fellows wouldn't understand what I
mean, but I am sure that you understand my point." There I thought I had
to say something. I told him that he greatly underestimated the boys and
that college men were not the only smart ones.

While the remark fitted in with my natural inclinations, I am sure it was
justified from a strictly practical standpoint. My answer did not shake the
feelings of superiority of the college boy, nor did it disrupt our personal
relationship. On the other hand, as soon as he left, it became evident how
deeply the corner boys felt about his statement. They spent some time
giving explosive expressions to their opinion of him, and then they told me
that I was different and that they appreciated it and that I knew much more
than this fellow and yet I did not show it.

My first spring in Cornerville served to establish for me a firm position
in the life of the district. I had only been there several weeks when Doc
said to me: "You're just as much of a fixture around this street corner as
that lamppost." Perhaps the greatest event signalizing my acceptance on
Norton Street was the baseball game that Mike Giovanni organized against
the group of Norton Street boys in their late teens. It was the old men who
had won glorious victories in the past against the rising youngsters. Mike
assigned me to a regular position on the team, not a key position perhaps
(I was stationed in right field), but at least I was there. When it was my
turn to bat in the last half of the ninth inning, the score was tied, there were
two outs, and the bases were loaded. As I reached down to pick up my bat,
I heard some of the fellows suggesting to Mike that he ought to put in a
pinch-hitter. Mike answered them in a loud voice that must have been
meant for me: "No, I've got confidence in Bill Whyte. He'll come through
in the clutch." So, with Mike's confidence to buck me up, I went up there,
missed two swings, and then banged a hard grounder through the hole
between second and short. At least that is where they told me it went. I was
so busy getting down to first base that I did not know afterward whether I
had reached there on an error or a base hit.

That night, when we went down for coffee, Danny presented me with a
ring for being a regular fellow and a pretty good ball player. I was
particularly impressed by the ring, for it had been made by hand. Danny
had started with a clear amber die discarded from his crap game and over
long hours had used his lighted cigarette to burn a hole through it and to
round the corners so that it came out a heart shape on top. I assured the
fellows that I would always treasure the ring.

Perhaps I should add that my game-winning base hit made the score 18-17, so it is evident that I was not the only one who had been hitting the ball. Still, it was a wonderful feeling to come through when they were counting on me, and it made me feel still more that I belonged on Norton Street.

As I gathered my early research data, I had to decide how I was to organize the written notes. In the very early stage of exploration, I simply put all the notes, in chronological order, in a single folder. As I was to go on to study a number of different groups and problems, it was obvious that this was no solution at all.

I had to subdivide the notes. There seemed to be two main possibilities. I could organize the notes topically, with folders for politics, rackets, the church, the family, and so on. Or I could organize the notes in terms of the groups on which they were based, which would mean having folders on the Nortons, the Italian Community Club, and so on. Without really thinking the problem through, I began filing material on the group basis, reasoning that I could later redivide it on a topical basis when I had a better knowledge of what the relevant topics should be.

As the material in the folders piled up, I came to realize that the organization of notes by social groups fitted in with the way in which my study was developing. For example, we have a college-boy member of the Italian Community Club saying: "These racketeers give our district a bad name. They should really be cleaned out of here." And we have a member of the Nortons saying: "These racketeers are really all right. When you need help, they'll give it to you. The legitimate businessman—he won't even give you the time of day." Should these quotes be filed under "Racketeers, attitudes toward"? If so, they would only show that there are conflicting attitudes toward racketeers in Cornerville. Only a questionnaire (which is hardly feasible for such a topic) would show the distribution of attitudes in the district. Furthermore, how important would it be to know how many people felt one way of another on this topic? It seemed to me of much greater scientific interest to be able to relate the attitude to the *group* in which the individual participated. This shows why two individuals could be expected to have quite different attitudes on a given topic.

As time went on, even the notes in one folder grew beyond the point where my memory would allow me to locate any given item rapidly. Then I devised a rudimentary indexing system: a page in three columns containing, for each interview or observation report, the date, the person or people interviewed or observed, and a brief summary of the interview or observation record. Such an index would cover from three to eight pages. When it came time to review the notes or to write from them, a five- to ten-minute perusal of the index was enough to give me a reasonably full picture of what I had and of where any given item could be located.

Reflections on Field Research

As I carried through the Cornerville study, I was also learning how to do field research. I learned from the mistakes I made. The most important of these I have described fully. I learned from the successes that I had, but these were less spectacular and more difficulty to describe. It may therefore be worth while to try to summarize the main characteristics of the research.

Of course, I am not claiming that there is a one best way to do field research. The methods used should depend upon the nature of the field situation and of the research problem. I am simply trying to fit together the findings of the study and the methods required to arrive at such findings.

In the first place, the study took a long time. This was due in part to the fact that I had had no previous field experience and very little educational background that was directly relevant to my problem. But that was not all. It took a long time because the parts of the study that interest me most depended upon an intimate familiarity with people and situations. Furthermore, I learned to understand a group only through observing how it changed *through time*.

This familiarity gave rise to the basic ideas in this book. I did not develop these ideas by any strictly logical process. They dawned on me out of what I was seeing, hearing, doing—and feeling. They grew out of an effort to organize a confusing welter of experience.

I had to balance familiarity with detachment, or else no insights would have come. There were fallow periods when I seemed to be just marking time. Whenever life flowed so smoothly that I was taking it for granted, I had to try to get outside of my participating self and struggle again to explain the things that seemed obvious.

This explains why my research plans underwent such drastic changes in the course of the study. I was on an exploration into unknown territory. Worse than unknown, indeed, because the then existing literature on slum districts was highly misleading. It would have been impossible to map out at the beginning the sort of study I eventually found myself doing.

This is not an argument against initial planning of research. If his study grows out of a body of soundly executed research, then the student can and should plan much more rigorously than I did. But, even so, I suspect that he will miss important data unless he is flexible enough to modify his plans as he goes along. The apparent "tangent" often turns out to be the main line of future research.

Street Corner Society is about particular people and situations and events. I wanted to write about Cornerville. I found that I could not write about Cornerville in general without discarding most of the data I had upon individuals and groups. I was a long time before I realized that I could explain Cornerville better through telling the stories of those individuals and groups that I could in any other way.

Instead of studying the general characteristics of classes of people, I was looking at Doc, Chick, Tony Cataldo, George Ravello, and others. Instead of getting a cross-sectional picture of the community at a particular point in time, I was dealing with a time sequence of interpersonal events.

Although I could not cover all Cornerville, I was building up the structure and functioning of the community through intensive examination of some of its parts—*in action.* I was relating the parts together through observing events between groups and between group leaders and the members of the larger institutional structures (of politics and the rackets). I was seeking to build a sociology based upon observed interpersonal events. That, to me, is the chief methodological and theoretical meaning of *Street Corner Society.*

12

On Fieldwork, Symbols, and Folklore in the
Writings of William Foote Whyte

MICHAEL OWEN JONES

*It is said that the most important things to know about a group of people
are the things they themselves take for granted. Yet it is precisely those
things that the people find most difficult to discuss.*

—WILLIAM FOOTE WHYTE
(*Men at Work,* 1961, p. 57)

Whyte's report of doing fieldwork is an engaging and insightful account
of what actually happens when one person attempts to study others by
observing and interviewing them in the course of their daily lives. As such,
it offers lessons for field-workers today. In addition, certain concepts and
assumptions underlie the research for *Street Corner Society,* which Whyte
later made explicit in his studies of other social settings, especially industrial ones. Labeled variously "event process analysis," "interaction theory," and "interactionism," Whyte's orientation foreshadowed the interest
in and importance attributed to symbols at work, which gained currency in
the late 1970s and the early 1980s.

In this article I briefly consider aspects of fieldwork as a human process
implicit in the appendix to the second edition of Whyte's *Street Corner
Society.* Then I examine some concepts with which Whyte approached
social issues, whether in a slum, restaurant, or factory. These are interaction, activities, sentiments, and symbols. Finally, I suggest another direc-

tion, implicit in Whyte's theory and research, which organizational symbolism and culture studies might take. This approach involves documenting and analyzing folklore in organizational settings.

By "folklore" I mean those symbolic forms and processes that are generated in people's face-to-face interactions and that are repeated, emulated, or reproduced so as to become "traditions" or "traditional" (Georges, 1985, p. 134). Narrating, ritualizing, using figurative language, personalizing work space, and so on can reveal much about individuals' perceptions, feelings, and ways of dealing with problems (Jones, 1990a; Jones, Moore, and Snyder, 1988). This, I believe, is one of the legacies of Whyte's research, beginning with his field-based study of street corner society in the late 1930s.

Background

First, some biographical data. William Foote Whyte aspired to be a writer. In his senior year in high school he covered his school for the *Bronxville Press,* a village newspaper published twice a week, and also wrote a column called "The Whyte Line." His first fieldwork of note was when, still in high school, he carried out extensive observations in the local elementary school and interviewed teachers, publishing a series of articles in 1931 (Whyte & Whyte, 1984, pp. 12-14).

Following graduation he accompanied his father, a language teacher in the New York City college system, to Germany for a sabbatical year. He wrote a weekly column, "Personally Conducted," from Europe. "I got personal stories of experience from young people of my generation who had grown up in the bleak years for Germany of the 1920s and early 1930s" (Whyte & Whyte, 1984, p. 13).

These "personal stories of experience" may be similar to what folklorists have labeled Personal Experience Narratives or Personal Narratives (Brandes, 1975; Robinson, 1981; Stahl, 1975, 1977, 1985, 1989; Stanley, 1979). Such stories are told by people based on their own experiences. Not traditional in the usual sense, the stories are, however, a creative response to experience and the tradition of narrating (Santino, 1983; Stahl, 1989).

After attending Swarthmore College (1932-1936) where he majored in economics, Whyte was awarded a three-year fellowship to study at Harvard University. Elton Mayo, with whom he had a course, stimulated Whyte's interest in industry (Whyte, 1969, p. 22). Mayo was then director of the Harvard Business School's research program at the Western Electric Company, which began in the late 1920s to study the effects of varying physical conditions on worker productivity. The program is legendary for the "Hawthorne effect." Named after the plant where it was observed, this term refers to a rise in productivity resulting from the subjects feeling they are receiving special recognition and gaining prestige by participating in the experiments rather than from (or in addition to) any actual improvement in working conditions.

"The Mayo group also coined the term 'informal organization,' to point to the tendency of human beings, when thrown together in an organization, to develop relations with each other that are not specified by the formal organization structure and that sometimes seemed to develop in opposition to these formal channels" (Whyte, 1961, p. 10; see also Whyte, 1961, p. 539; 1978, p. 131). These subcultures with their own folkways and lore are, in the words of Chester I. Barnard (1938) in his classic treatise on organization, "necessary to the operation of formal organizations as a means of communication, of cohesion, and of protecting the integrity of the individual" (p. 123; see also Jones, 1988b).

Whyte was influenced by another junior fellow at Harvard, Conrad M. Arensberg, a social anthropologist who had recently returned from fieldwork in rural Ireland (Whyte & Whyte, 1984, pp. 14-15). With Eliot D. Chapple, Arensberg developed what would become known as "interaction theory," which they first presented in a monograph in 1940 called *Measuring Human Relations: An Introduction to the Study of the Interaction of Individuals* (Whyte, 1959, p. 158). Interaction theory was first applied to industrial organizations in a study on morale by Arensberg and Douglas McGregor published in *Applied Anthropology* in 1942 (Whyte, 1961, p. 15).

Acquaintance with Arensberg and Chapple as social anthropologists "led me to an interest both in their methods of research and theories and to an interest in the study of industry," writes Whyte (1969, p. 22). "I used the Chapple-Arensberg approach in my first field study in an urban slum district and have later applied it to all of my work in industry" (Whyte, 1961, p. 15).

In 1940 Whyte moved to Chicago where he began formal graduate work. He wanted to study under W. Lloyd Warner, a social anthropologist. Although "for some months I described myself as a social anthropologist," he writes, Whyte opted for a doctorate in sociology with a minor in social anthropology (Whyte & Whyte, 1984, p. 15).

Whyte began industrial research in 1942 (Whyte, 1961, p. 10; 1969, p. 22). While teaching at the University of Oklahoma he also did fieldwork at the Phillips Petroleum Company in Oklahoma City (Whyte & Whyte, 1984, p. 15). By 1944 he was back at the University of Chicago where he joined the Committee on Human Relations in Industry, which was started and chaired by Warner in 1943 (Whyte, 1961, p. 10). Whyte worked on a project concerning human relations in the restaurant industry (Whyte 1969, p. 23) and then he supervised an action-research project in a large hotel (Whyte & Whyte, 1984, p. 16). In 1948 he moved to Cornell University where he continues to hold a faculty position in the School of Industrial and Labor Relations.

Fieldwork

The term *fieldwork* designates the act of inquiring into the nature of phenomena by studying them firsthand in the environments in which they naturally exist or occur (Georges & Jones, 1980, p. 1). In research on human behavior, this usually entails observation and intensive interviewing rather than reliance on questionnaires. It may also include participating in the activities and round of life studied as well as gathering life history information and documenting customs, traditions, and material culture (Jones, 1985b, 1987a, 1987d, 1988c, 1989).

Although he later employed survey techniques (Whyte & Whyte, 1984, p. 295), William Foote Whyte has been known generally as a participant observer using what he called "anthropological methods" (Whyte, 1961, p. 16; 1969, p. 22; Whyte & Whyte, 1984, p. 20), that is, "fieldwork." At the time Whyte conducted his research on a slum in the late 1930s, little had been published on how to do fieldwork. Indeed, the justification for "On the Evolution of *Street Corner Society,*" the appendix that Whyte added to his book in 1955, was that it might shed light on the process of observing and interviewing people while living and interacting with them.

In the last 30 years numerous guides have been published dealing with the mechanics of fieldwork. Most imply that projects evolve sequentially through clearly defined steps from hypothesis formation to establishing rapport, systematic observation, controlled interviewing, and the impersonal presentation of results. Whyte's account suggests otherwise.

For example, whatever the alleged "scientific" reasons for undertaking a study, often there is a close correlation between one's personal history and the kinds of plans formulated for fieldwork. As Whyte indicates, he was motivated to study a slum for a number of personal reasons, from wanting to enlarge his experiences as a basis for writing novels or plays to having a commitment to social reform (Whyte & Whyte, 1984, pp. 14, 19; see also Whyte, 1955, pp. 280-283).

Like many other field-workers, once he had chosen a research site Whyte grappled for an appropriate means of gaining entry into what he regarded as an alien community. There were numerous false starts, including intrusions into people's lives through a study about living conditions and attempts to follow the lead of a young economics instructor who bragged about dropping in on a bar, striking up an acquaintance with a girl, and getting her to tell him her life story. Turning to the settlement houses, Whyte finally found a social worker who seemed to understand what he wanted and who told him about Doc.

Whyte's description of his and Doc's initial encounter and exchange is a miniature study in the dynamics of establishing relationships and negotiating rights and responsibilities. In their initial meeting, Whyte gave Doc a lengthy and overly academic explanation of his research. Doc listened politely and then simplified it all by asking if Whyte wanted to see the high life or low. He warned Whyte to say only that he and Doc were friends, and not to spring people (pay for drinks, etc.) lest he be taken for a sucker. He gave Whyte pointers should they be arrested. He began to define his role to Whyte and himself, for example, telling Whyte he would "stage an act" so that Whyte could find out gang members' philosophy of life.

In soliciting Doc's assistance, Whyte implicitly requested permission to assume, and indicated his willingness to accept, a relatively subordinate, dependent status. Doc's listening to Whyte state his aims and aspirations led Doc to develop his own expectations, the expression of which caused Whyte to clarify his motives and means. In stipulating the terms for establishing a working relationship, Doc outlined the rights and responsibilities of the two men, specifying numerous do's and don'ts.

Like other field-workers before and after him, Whyte repeatedly discovered a need to clarify and compromise as his research developed. He abandoned his earlier ambition of writing a study of the entire Cornerville community, instead focusing on selected aspects of social structure, for example, a gang and an ethnic club. At the outset he viewed Doc as "simply a key informant—and also my sponsor." But the relationship changed, with Whyte depending on Doc as confidant, observer, interpreter, collaborator, and friend (see also Georges & Jones, 1980, pp. 34-36, 68-74).

As Whyte's experiences demonstrate, fieldwork entails more than merely knowing what to observe and how to record, process, and present it. The field-worker must explain his or her presence and purpose to others, gain their confidence and cooperation, and develop and maintain mutually acceptable relationships. These requirements create dilemmas, produce confrontations, demand clarifications and compromises, and evoke reflection and introspection that one can neither fully anticipate nor prepare for in advance. Worthwhile projects may fail. Research strategies frequently must be modified or abandoned as researchers and subjects interact. Unexpected opportunities, fruitful leads, and important insights can blossom as fieldwork develops. Contrary to what is implied in most manuals, the "results" of fieldwork include not only the tangible and impersonal in the form of reports and presentations but also the intangible and the personal, such as Whyte and Doc's friendship (Georges & Jones, 1980, pp. 2-3, 135-136). Finally, as Whyte contends, researchers' ideas rarely if ever occur in a systematic, structured way. Rather, they tend to develop "out of our immersion in the data and out of the whole process of living" (Whyte, 1955, p. 280; see also Whyte & Whyte, 1984, p. 20).

Symbols

Throughout his career, writes Whyte, interaction theory has guided what he has been looking for and at (Whyte, 1961, p. 15). Arguably he often has *had* to do fieldwork rather than rely on questionnaires and other quantitative methods. By participating in events, observing behavior firsthand, and interviewing people in depth he has been able to obtain information directly about interactions and activities through which he could uncover social processes (see, for example, Whyte, 1953, p. 22; 1961, p. 16).

Whyte claims that Eliot D. Chapple and Carleton Stevens Coon's *Principles of Anthropology* (1942) and George C. Homans's *The Human Group* (1950) most influenced his own symbolic interaction approach (Whyte, 1949b, p. 13; 1959, p. 158; 1961, pp. 10, 15; 1969, p. 22; Whyte & Whyte, 1984, pp. 14-15). Four concepts loom large. These are *interaction, activities, sentiments,* and *symbols.* Whyte writes that he defines the first two much as Homans, who was a fellow student at Harvard in the late 1930s (Whyte, 1959, p. 158), does in *The Human Group* (1950). Whyte's definition of "sentiments" is less inclusive; also, Whyte notes that he later added two environmental forces not considered by Homans, the legal and the economic (Whyte, 1959, p. 159). Whyte defines symbols almost exactly as Chapple and Coon do (cf. Chapple & Coon, 1942, p. 465; Whyte, 1951, p. 160; 1959, p. 173; 1961, pp. 24, 37, 141).

According to Whyte *interaction* refers to people's contacts—with special emphasis on their frequency, duration, and origination. Interactions are both observable and quantifiable (Whyte, 1949b, p. 13; 1951, p. 159; 1959, p. 156; 1961, p. 18).

Activities—which Whyte initially labeled "actions" (1949, p. 13)—"refer to the things that people do" (1951, p. 161), that is, "the physical acts they perform" (1959, p. 157). These include, for example, working on the job, horseplay at work, drinking coffee and smoking a cigarette during the morning break, and playing cards with friends during lunch (Whyte, 1961, pp. 17-18). "These activities can be objectively described and even to some extent measured" (1961, p. 18). Unlike interactions, many activities can be carried out by one person alone (Whyte, 1961, p. 22).

"*Sentiments* refer to the way people feel about themselves, other people, their work, their organization, and so on" (Whyte, 1951, p. 161; see 1949b, p. 13 where he also includes as sentiments of people "the moral standards in which they believe"). Sentiments are not directly observable but may be inferred from what people say and do. They contain three elements: an idea, emotional content, and a propensity to recur on "presentation of the same symbols that have been associated with the sentiment in the past" (Whyte, 1959, p. 157).

Symbols "are words, objects, conditions, acts, or characteristics of persons which refer to (or stand for) the relations among men, and between men and their environment" (Whyte, 1961, p. 24). Symbols can be phrases in conversation, objects (Whyte, 1949b, p. 13), and emblems of rank or status established through technology and work process (Whyte, 1969, p. 296). Also, "the physical arrangements of the workplace, the cleanness or dirtiness of the plant, and quality of the materials worked on, among other things, may serve to place the organization in social space" (Whyte, 1969, p. 591).

Symbols may express sentiments, trigger certain activities and interactions (Whyte 1961, p. 24), provide personal identity (Whyte, 1969, p. 588), or serve as vehicles for introducing organizational change (Whyte, 1961, pp. 575, 594). An individual's actions and words may be taken as symbolic and treated as a basis on which others assess their relations with that person (Whyte, 1961, p. 26). "A symbolic act may also serve to bring people closer together, to open up increasing opportunities for interaction, and to pave the way for the development of positive sentiments" (Whyte, 1961, p. 26).

Whyte has stated that interactions, activities, sentiments, and symbols are mutually dependent. "That means that a change in any one of the four categories leads to changes in the other three" (Whyte, 1951, p. 162). It is not possible therefore to state that any one of these is primary or that change begins with one in particular, "because the life of an organization is a continuous process, and the beginning point we select is just a matter of convenience" (1951, p. 163). In fact, however, Whyte has tended to concentrate on documenting and analyzing interactions and activities, and by this emphasis to imply that they are particularly important (in Whyte, Hamilton, & Wiley, 1964, p. 183ff., Whyte dropped symbols from the list of four concepts and made sentiments a dependent variable that responds to changes in interactions and activities). This is not surprising, given his identification of himself as a sociologist and his desire to observe or elicit "interpersonal events" in order to infer social process (e.g., Whyte, 1953).

Despite a bias toward social relations and processes rather than beliefs, aesthetics, and expressive behavior, Whyte has written extensively about symbols, used them as sources of information, and employed them as a vehicle of communication. For example, he allocated two chapters in a book on labor-management relations to symbolism (Whyte, 1951). One chapter concerned the impact of "verbal symbols" on negotiations in collective bargaining. The other considered the role of money as it affects the activities and sentiments of workers and the interactions of workers and managers (a subject considered more fully in Whyte, Dalton, Roy, & Sayles, 1955). Whyte relegated two thirds of an introductory chapter of another book to explaining and illustrating the concept of symbol, providing examples of symbolic acts, and discussing the situational determinants of what symbols mean (Whyte, 1961, pp. 24-37). This chapter is as viable today as it was 30 years ago, and should be essential reading in organizational symbolism study.

Whyte also devoted an entire article on interviewing for organizational research to discussing and illustrating how he elicited stories from one man, trying "to move from sentiments to specific interpersonal events" (Whyte, 1953, p. 20). He often mentions stories in his writings, quoting people's oral accounts at length (Whyte, 1948, pp. 8-9; 1953; 1969, p. 591; Whyte & Gardiner, 1945, pp. 7, 8, 12, 23). He refers to his own case studies as "stories" (Whyte, 1961, p. 527; Whyte & Whyte, 1984, p. 187). And he organizes books, chapters, or essays by "telling" a story first and then abstracting principles about social processes (Whyte, 1944, p. 1; 1949b, p. 6; 1951; 1955, p. 6; 1961, pp. 198, 393, 395, 589; 1969, pp. 277-299).

Just as he paved the way in doing fieldwork and presenting it as a human process, Whyte pioneered in utilizing the constructs of interaction, activities, sentiments, and symbols. Other than Whyte's work little had been published on symbols in organizations until a few years ago. A survey of major texts in the field of organizational behavior, reported in 1980, "establishes clearly that there are virtually *no* references" to "organizational symbolism," defined as "those aspects of an organization that its members use to reveal or make comprehensible the unconscious feelings, images, and values that are inherent in that organization" (Dandridge, Mitroff, & Joyce, 1980, p. 77; see also Pondy, Frost, Morgan, & Dandridge, 1983). Although a spate of works on organizational culture has appeared in recent years, there still are few publications about organizational symbolism.

Nevertheless, as some of Whyte's work suggests (e.g., Whyte, 1953; 1961, pp. 24-37), the symbolic infuses organizational life. Much of organizational symbolism, in turn, is traditional, expressive behavior, that is, "folklore."

Folklore in Organizational Settings

The Concept of Folklore

The term *folklore* was coined in England in 1846 to replace "popular antiquities" and "oral traditions" used in previous centuries. Other designations include the French *traditions popularies;* the German *Volkskunde,* coined in 1803; and the Swedish *folkliv,* or "folklife," in use since at least 1847 (Bronner, 1984; Dorson, 1972; Dundes, 1965).

Some of the "genres" of folklore are celebrations, festive events, parties, ceremonies, rituals, rites of passage, customs, and social routines; recreation, games, and play; traditional sayings, proverbs, nicknaming, jargon, and argot; gossip and rumors; anecdotes, legends, and myths; jokes and kidding; costuming, the making of personal items at work, and the personal decoration of space (Collins, 1978; Jones, 1984, 1988a, 1989, 1990a; Jones, Moore, & Snyder, 1988; Nickerson, 1976; Schwartzman, 1983). Students of folklore have identified and discussed dozens of kinds of stories from exempla to sagas, floating legends, memorates, and personal experience narratives; and there are many types of rites and rituals (Brunvand, 1978; Dégh, 1972; Dorson, 1983; Oring, 1986, 1989; Toelken, 1979). In addition, folklorists have labeled and investigated such phenomena as ethnic display events, small group festive gatherings, and the proto-festival.

The forms and processes called folklore have three things in common. First, they are examples of symbolic communication and interaction. "Attack the problem, not the person" "If you want people to tell you the truth, then 'don't shoot the messenger,' " "If you want to get to know someone, walk a mile in his shoes" and other proverbs and traditional sayings communicate basic precepts by calling forth vivid, metaphorical images. Evoking strong images, emotions, and physiological sensations in teller and listener alike, narrating is a dramatic performance that highlights and selectively portrays some aspects of an event. Rituals are repeated acts invested with special significance recalling a host of associations and dramatically conveying sentiments and values. In each instance, something visible (and vivid, evocative, and memorable) stands for the invisible—particularly ideas, qualities, and feelings (Abrahams, 1968a, 1968b; Allen

& Montell, 1981; Arora, 1988; Dégh, 1972; Sackmann, 1989; Trice & Beyer, 1984; Trice, Belasco, & Alutto, 1969). Even customs are symbolic; as "our" way of doing things, they define behavior and express identity.

Not all symbols are folklore. The company pin or ashtray with its logo, for example, is a manufactured item rather than a handmade object and it is a product of the formal organization rather than an outcome of spontaneous expression or informal organization. As one employee remarked about "official" ceremonies: "They seem too much like work." The second feature of folklore, therefore, is that it is generated in firsthand interaction, not legislated, and its character and meaning(s) are determined in large measure by the immediate context of participants and their experiences, attitudes, and relationships (Bauman, 1986; Georges, 1969).

Finally, folklore forms and processes are considered "traditional" or "traditions." By being repeated, emulated, or reproduced, examples of folklore have both an historical and a social character, manifesting continuities through time and consistencies in space in regard to values, sentiments, and ways of doing things.

Various forms and examples of folklore express aspirations and concerns, serve as a means of characterizing perceptions, transmit conceptions and interpretations of events, occupy leisure, or teach and reinforce norms and values (Georges, 1985, p. 135). They also project anxieties, express joy and satisfaction, provide meaning, and in other ways help people make sense of their world, cope, and act (Jones, 1990b; Jones et al., 1988). This is so in organizations just as it is in other social settings (cf. Bronner, 1984; Dandridge, 1976; Dorson, 1973, 1981; Jones, 1981, 1984, 1987c, 1988a; Pondy et al., 1983; Santino, 1990; Wilkins, 1984). An understanding of organizations is incomplete, therefore, if it does not include knowledge of the traditional, symbolic interaction and communication that pervades people's activities and relations (Beyer & Trice, 1987; Trice & Beyer, 1984).

Folklore in Organizations

To some, culture is simply "how things are done around here" (Deal & Kennedy, 1982). Others conceive of it as customs and traditions on the one hand, and values on the other (Louis, 1983a). Culture also has been said to be basic assumptions that determine espoused values which then are expressed in visible artifacts (Schein, 1985b; for overviews of culture, see Smircich, 1983a, 1985a). All these conceptions point to the fact that inferences about a culture are based on something that can be perceived and interpreted.

Because much of behavior in any social setting is traditional and symbolic, inferences about culture in organizations must be derived from
customs, folkways, stories, dress, decor, figurative language, and other
expressive forms and processes whether conscious or unconscious. However, basic guides ignore symbolic behavior (e.g., Sathe, 1985) or caution
against using "myths, legends, stories, and charters" as sources of information about organizational assumptions and values (Schein, 1983, p. 125;
although he seems to be concerned with *printed* accounts espousing *ideal*
values and behavior rather than with folklore forms and processes per se).

To illustrate how folklore may serve as a source of information about
culture, social relations, and psychological states, I would mention two
studies of work group traditions. In the mid-1970s, Bruce Nickerson and
Camilla Collins undertook extensive research on occupational traditions
in, respectively, an urban factory in the North and a hosiery mill in the
South. They found that people personalized their work space, engaged in
games and horseplay, told stories about local characters and work experiences, celebrated events, and joked. But there were differences.

Nickerson (1976) discovered that much of the lore of machinists in the
northern factory embodied antagonism toward supervisors, expressed suspi-
cion of and hostility toward the larger formal organization and its representatives, and revealed a propensity to institutionalize unsanctioned behavior and
to ritualistically defy rules. Although prohibited by the union, obscenities were
so rife as to become hackneyed clichés. Sarcastic and derogatory nicknames
abounded. Obscene and scatological epithets adorned restroom walls. Many
of the stories focused on accidents at work. An example is the account of a
worker who lost a finger. On returning to his work station he was asked by the
plant safety manager how the accident occurred. The machinist replied, "I was
just working like this and. . . . Whoops! There goes another one!" (p. 132).

This story is traditional, having been recorded many times in many places,
usually as a "numbskull joke." In this company the account often contained a
statement to the effect that when the worker reports to the plant dispensary he
is asked immediately whether he was wearing his safety glasses and shoes at
the time of the accident. "In this instance," writes Nickerson about the
storyteller, "the worker is convinced that the company does not care for him
as an individual, but is only concerned with their insurance premiums"
(Nickerson, 1976, p. 145).

The Sains Hosiery Mill in North Carolina, studied by Camilla Collins,
(1978) was established in 1912. Like the northern aircraft parts factory, the
mill paid wages for piecework, had a seniority system, and maintained various
levels of supervision. Hosiery mill workers received lower pay, however, and

did not have formal retirement, insurance, or other benefits programs (workers' needs were taken care of informally as they arose). Nor were there many of the status markers at the hosiery mill that were found in the northern factory, for example, supervisors wearing ties, deferential terms of address, preferential parking, varied length of lunch breaks, differentiated eating areas, differing degrees of mobility and freedom to interact, and so on.

The folklore at the hosiery mill differed in tone, theme, content, and even form from the lore of the urban factory. There was no ritualization of beating the system, no institutionalization of forbidden behavior, no denigration of the formal organization. In addition, two forms of folklore that were not reported at the Widget prevailed at Sains: foodsharing and the celebration of people's birthdays and of minor holidays. Finally, the themes and tone of stories and social routines at the hosiery mill were harmonistic as opposed to the antagonistic quality of lore in the urban factory.

According to Collins (1978), it was customary to welcome employees joining the company. Evincing "a careful and concerned acceptance, the current hands do not play pranks on the new members of a department," lest it cause dissension and confusion (p. 91). Compare this to the hazings at Widget and the reference to many trainees as "losers" (Nickerson, 1976, p. 103).

Whatever the causes of the differences in the lore, it is apparent that folklore was generated in both the northern factory and the southern mill as a vehicle of communication and a basis for interaction. It reflected some realities as well as created others and provided a sense of identity, in one case that of a subgroup and in the other instance that of an organization as a whole. The presence or absence of particular forms, and the content and themes of the lore, grew out of prevailing conditions.

Through analyzing the folklore, Nickerson and Collins were able to learn much about the nature of the work, the organization, the relations among people, and the assumptions, values, and attitudes that various individuals held but took for granted. Folklore, therefore, can be a source of information about the culture or serve consciously and systematically as a basis for inferring a culture.

Besides ascertaining precepts and values, the researcher who documents and analyzes examples of folklore can discover fundamental social and psychological processes in human beings, uncover sources of stress and conflict in an organization, and diagnose the climate of a work place. The purpose of researching folklore may be to increase understanding of human behavior and organizations generally or to apply inferences and insights in order to plan and implement changes in a particular organization.

Conclusion

Increasingly more organizational researchers are utilizing methods pioneered by William Foote Whyte, such as observing firsthand what newcomers to an organization learn (Siehl & Martin, 1988; Van Maanen & Schein, 1979) as well as participating in the daily round of activities to document in detail what people actually say and do (Jones, 1990b; Jones, et al., 1988; Wallace, 1986). By being present in situations in which phenomena naturally exist or occur, these field-workers become privy to the customs and traditions of informal organization as well as witness examples of spontaneous festivity, narrating, the use of figurative language, joking and kidding, social routines, and ritualistic interaction. Whether or not their research paradigms include the concept of folklore or they explore folkloristic issues, recent field-workers must be, like William Foote Whyte long has been, deriving inferences and insights about organizations from traditional, symbolic forms and processes (cf. Whyte, 1944).

The documentation and analysis of stories, metaphors, and sayings, ceremonies, rituals, customs, and other forms of folklore in organizations can help uncover fundamental values as well as discover attitudes and feelings and some of the reasons for them. It also can assist in diagnosing problems and eliciting possible solutions. As considered more fully elsewhere, folklore has implemental value in enhancing communication and cooperation, easing organizational changes, and helping members cope with the vicissitudes of work life (Jones, 1987a, 1988a; Sackmann, 1989; Stewart, 1989; Tommerup, 1990; Wells, 1988; Wilkins, 1984; Wilson, 1988).

The most important things to know about a people, wrote William Foote Whyte three decades ago, are things that they take for granted and find most difficult to discuss (Whyte, 1961, p. 57). Guided by the concepts of interaction, activities, sentiments, and symbols as well as relying on extensive fieldwork, Whyte has recorded stories, metaphors, and other examples of oral communication (see also Whyte, 1944; 1949a). He has utilized them as sources of information or as vehicles of communication.

All people tell stories. They celebrate, ritualize, play, and use figurative language. They participate in traditions that convey meanings, recall past experiences, and act as symbols. One solution to the dilemma noted by Whyte, therefore, is to document a people's traditional, symbolic behavior in order to discover what they take for granted or find it difficult to discuss. Whyte often has done this himself, albeit without calling it folklore.

13

Street Corner Society as a Model for
Research into Organizational Culture

ALAN BRYMAN

On the face of it, even though *Street Corner Society (SCS)* is a "masterpiece of sociological fieldwork" (Van Maanen, 1988, p. 39), its relevance to the methodology of organizational culture research would appear to be limited, since the book is to all intents and purposes a study of a slum area. However, the adoption of such a view would be misguided for a number of reasons. First, there is a sense in which the slum was conceived of by Whyte as a form of organization in the more general sense of an entity with social structure. Indeed, Whyte was at pains to disabuse readers of the prevalent view of a slum as disorganized and lacking coherence. The articulation of the culture of this area was one of Whyte's manifest aims. Second, there is much in the book about the culture of specific organizations, like Chick Morelli's Italian Community Club and the S. and A. Club. In these studies of specific organizations, Whyte was concerned to uncover their internal cultures and often to relate these to the wider cultures of Cornerville itself. However, it is in the third sense that Whyte's book has the greatest importance for modern research into organizational cultures, namely as a model for the way in which such research can and perhaps should be conducted. This third theme will provide the chief focus for the present contribution. Most studies of organizational culture fall within the tradition of qualitative research, although the desirability of this apparent affinity has been questioned (Martin, 1990a, pp. 33-36). Initially, *SCS* will be examined in terms of how far it exhibits the features of qualitative research. It will then be explored in terms of its adequacy as a piece of qualitative research. Some implications of *SCS* for organizational culture research will then be addressed.

Street Corner Society and Qualitative Research

One of the reasons why *SCS* is so often regarded as a classic piece of sociological fieldwork is that it represents one of the first studies to reveal many of the characteristics of modern fieldwork. Whyte's book was by no means the first attempt to investigate a sociological issue using what has become the quintessential qualitative research method, participant observation or ethnography as it is more popularly known today. The Chicago school sociologists were making considerable use of the method in their investigations, but in terms of both bringing participant observation to wider attention and allowing the method's possibilities to be appreciated, *SCS* is probably more influential. It is very much in the mold of the modern style of ethnographic research.

In what ways can the distinctive features of modern qualitative research be discerned in *SCS*? Qualitative research can be construed as a style of research with a cluster of characteristics that distinguish it markedly from the familiar quantitative model that has long prevailed in the social sciences. In the context of studying the culture of Cornerville, Whyte was clearly skeptical about the potential of quantitative research, preferring the more direct approach of participant observation. In conducting his research with this method, Whyte revealed many of the characteristics of modern qualitative research. In order to elucidate these characteristics, it is proposed to draw upon Bryman (1988a).

Probably, the most fundamental ingredient of qualitative research is the preference for *seeing through the eyes* of one's subjects. In a sense this is the *sine qua non* of qualitative research. That Whyte did indeed examine Cornerville life from the point of view of his subjects is evident from just about every page of the book. On page after page we are given detailed accounts of things that happened and how they were interpreted by the actors concerned. There is even a sense that he may have gone too far in this regard and almost gone native, as when he remarks that he found himself "becoming almost a nonobserving participant" (Whyte, 1955, p. 321), a comment that catches the imagination of my students year after year.

Whyte recognized that in order to adopt the perspective of the people he was studying, it was necessary to get *close* to them. There was little point in remaining aloof and distant, since he would not be able to appreciate fully what was going on and to gain the confidence of the people of Cornerville. He decided, therefore, to live in the area: "Only if I lived in Cornerville would I ever be able to understand and be accepted by it" (p. 293). Also useful to Whyte in gaining "an intimate familiarity with people and situations" (pp. 356-357) was his decision to learn Italian. This did not prove essential, since he concentrated his attentions increasingly on younger, English-speaking people in Cornerville. However, it was symbolically important, since his preparedness to learn Italian established his sincerity and perhaps allowed greater proximity to his subjects than could have occurred otherwise. Although Whyte does not appear to have intended to learn Italian for this reason, there is an interesting lesson in field relations to be learned from this experience.

There is a predilection in much contemporary qualitative research for *descriptive detail,* which can be seen in *SCS.* Throughout the book there is rich description of structures, situations, and people. The chapter on racketeering, for example, provides enormous detail about the mechanics of this activity. Description is an important component of the craft of qualitative research because it provides the material for the *contextual understanding* of action and what people say. Whyte says at one point: "I realized that I could explain Cornerville better through telling the stories of those individuals and groups than I could in any other way" (p. 357). Such data provide the kind of information that is required for understanding what goes on and the people involved in the specific context being studied. The intricate elucidation of something as apparently mundane as bowling becomes a backcloth to the appreciation of leader-follower relations among the Nortons that was to catch the attention of Homans (1950). Such detail is an essential prerequisite of the development of what we nowadays see as the study of meaning in context (Mishler, 1979) and which is an essential ingredient of seeing through the eyes of those that are studied.

Yet a further feature is that Whyte exhibits the concern among many modern qualitative researchers with *process.* In contrast to the static tendency in much social scientific research, a virtue of participant observation is that because of the researcher's sustained involvement in a setting for an appreciable period of time, a dynamic quality can be introduced. Whyte recognized this when he wrote: "Instead of getting a cross-sectional picture of a community at a particular point in time, I was dealing with a time-sequence of interpersonal events" (*SCS,* 1955, p. 358). This ability of the participant observer to expose processual matters points to a possible advantage of the method over other techniques of qualitative data collection, such as unstructured interviewing. (Bryman, 1989, p. 160).

Finally, Whyte's research exhibits a further virtue that is often claimed for qualitative research, namely, it is *flexible*. To a certain extent, this characteristic is an inevitable product of the qualitative researcher's concern to let contact with the field at least in part determine what is important and what should be investigated. However, it also points to a tactical advantage of qualitative research, since it implies that the researcher is able to capitalize upon issues and topics that occur to him or her after an initial formulation of research plans. In Whyte's case, he says that he had been 18 months in the field before he fully knew the direction in which his research was going (*SCS*, 1955, p. 321). He also points out that research should be flexible and that the "apparent 'tangent' often turns out to be the main line of future research" (*SCS*, 1955, p. 357).

An equally interesting question to the one posed at the outset is to ask: In what ways does *SCS* depart from contemporary qualitative research? One way is that Whyte seems to have relied almost exclusively upon observation in the collection of data, whereas many modern ethnographers prefer to conduct formal interviewing and possibly collect other data in conjunction. By contrast, Whyte did very little formal interviewing (*SCS*, 1955, p. 302). Ironically, Whyte has become a major spokesman for the advantages of integrating research methods, including those typically associated with quantitative research (e.g., Whyte & Whyte, 1984). This instance is almost a natural outcome of his view that "the methods used should depend upon the nature of the field situation and of the research problem" (*SCS*, 1955, p. 356). This methodological eclecticism means that Whyte distinguishes himself from many advocates of qualitative research who have become wedded to a particular style of research above all else. Fortunately, the organizational culture literature displays a preparedness among its practitioners to consider the integration of methods (e.g., Schall, 1983; Siehl & Martin, 1988).

A further distinguishing aspect of Whyte's research is the use of observation for a formal delineation of relationships among individuals in a group. In a sense, this aspect of *SCS* could be viewed as the employment of a separate method, but I would argue that it was in fact an essential ingredient of the style of participant observation he had learned from Arensberg (*SCS*, 1955, pp. 286-287). This work allowed Whyte to understand the structure of relationships in Cornerville in much more intricate detail than would otherwise be possible, but his readers also gained a better feel for the area and its inhabitants too. Perhaps the kind of mapping that

Whyte undertook could be accorded greater consideration by organizational researchers as a means of understanding patterns of influence and their connections with culture.

Does *Street Corner Society* Represent Good Ethnography?

In a symposium that is meant at least in part to be eulogistic, perhaps it may seem perverse to ask the question that heads this section. However, in his writings on research methodology, Whyte has repeatedly committed himself to a belief in the need for open-minded evaluation of techniques and a reflective stance to his own work. As such, there is no need to draw back from asking such a question.

Emerson (1987) has implicitly provided some interesting criteria for evaluating an ethnographic study. Drawing upon his experience as an editor of *Urban Life* (now *Journal of Contemporary Ethnography*), Emerson enunciated four ways of improving ethnographic fieldwork. These may be used fruitfully as yardsticks for evaluating a study such as *SCS*. First, Emerson proposes that many field-workers need to *spend more time in the field*. He detects a tendency for many fieldwork projects to be of very short duration, even just a few weeks, and for participation to be episodic. *SCS* is manifestly not guilty of this charge. Whyte was a participant observer for 3 years, which is about as long as can reasonably be expected for many people. As he recognized, the method becomes increasingly difficult to implement as one gets older, since the researcher's home and work commitments are likely to inhibit the kind of prolonged and sustained immersion that occurred in Cornerville. It may be that the increasingly brief, episodic examples of fieldwork that Emerson describes are in large part a product of the growing difficulty researchers experience of finding the space in their home and work lives for prolonged immersion. The reasons for preferring prolonged immersion relate to issues covered in the previous section: the researcher's ability to look at social life through the eyes of the subjects will be enhanced, there is greater opportunity for a flexible research strategy (rather than one that possibly closes off potentially interesting lines of inquiry prematurely), processes can be more readily etched, and so on.

Emerson's second charge is that *much ethnographic work exhibits poor conceptualization and inadequate theoretical focus*. He goes further than many exponents of qualitative research in suggesting that the predilection for letting data generate theoretical issues should be given less prominence and that many studies should start out with a clear theoretical focus. The latter point is controversial, since there is a widespread concern among qualitative researchers that an explicit a priori theoretical focus may simply be imposed on the subjects of a study and thereby contaminate in advance their point of view (Bryman, 1988a, pp. 85-87). In other words, the second part of Emerson's criterion is controversial, whereas the first—the accusation that much ethnographic research is atheoretical—is a common concern and is of greater interest in the context of *SCS*. Whyte's research shows a preference for delaying making theoretical inferences from his data. The influential theoretical elaboration in the Conclusion of his findings for an understanding of leader-follower relations are an indication of this facility with the theoretical level.

Third, Emerson (1987, p. 75) criticizes many ethnographic studies for *failing* sufficiently to *"attend to the categories and meanings actually recognized and used by those under study."* As Emerson recognizes, this accusation sits uneasily with the previous charge, because the development of a priori theoretical schemes may actually contribute to the neglect of members' meanings. Nonetheless, the point has considerable importance, since it relates to a central motif of ethnographic research. Here again, *SCS* is not guilty; Whyte consistently related his ideas to the ways in which Cornerville's inhabitants view the world. The book is rich in illustrations drawn from Cornerville life and in transcripts of conversations both with Whyte and others. It is clear that Whyte forged his understanding of what went on in Cornerville out of how Doc, Chick, and the others viewed their lives. Indeed, the very notion, which is presented in both the Introduction and the Conclusion, that a slum is inappropriately understood if it is viewed as a disorganized community, is a testament to the importance of qualitative research as a means of correcting potentially misleading assumptions through attention to the ways in which members understand their situation.

The fourth and final problem with much modern ethnography is that it *fails to "specify the actual interactional and textual practices that produce ethnography"* (Emerson, 1987, p. 77). There are two points here: that ethnographers often fail to provide information about fieldwork relations and that they give insufficient attention to how the ethnographic account itself is constructed. The first edition of *SCS* was probably guilty as charged in respect of the first point, but the addition of the influential appendix in 1955 provides ample detail of how Cornerville was chosen, how Doc was first contacted, problems of getting access to certain situations, and so on. It is hard to believe that there could be much that is missing.

However, the second aspect of this point is an especially interesting one because it relates to a growing area of concern among anthropologists, namely, the writing practices that are associated with the rendering of an alien culture to an academic audience. This cluster of concerns has a number of different components, such as the strategies used by ethnographers to convey to their readers a sense of having rendered an authoritative account of the cultures that they claim to have penetrated. The bulk of this concern has developed in the context of anthropology (e.g., Clifford, 1983; Clifford & Marcus, 1986), but Van Maanen (1988) has introduced ethnographers exploring features of their own societies to the problems identified by anthropologists. Van Maanen distinguishes between different styles of writing ethnography of which there are three main types.

First, there is what might be termed the traditional approach, the realist tale, which presents the "findings" as an authoritative account which anyone in the ethnographer's situation would have seen and concluded. What is most striking about realism as a genre is the absence of the subject (the ethnographer) in the ethnographic product. Emerson's point seems to be that too much modern ethnography is written within this realist mode. Second, there is the confessional tale which tells of the problems and vicissitudes of being an ethnographer—the mistakes, false starts, personal problems that have to be endured, and so on. This genre makes it clear that the ethnography is a product in which the field-worker is inextricably involved. Third, Van Maanen distinguishes the impressionist tale which tells in great detail of incidents in the field in which the field-worker was directly implicated and which are regarded as being of special significance. These genres can co-exist in any study.

It is easy to view early ethnographic studies like *SCS* as predominantly realist and many of Van Maanen's illustrations are from this era. Indeed, *SCS* is cited on at least two occasions in relation to the realist tale (Van Maanen, 1988, pp. 47, 68). There is certainly much to support this view, since a great deal of *SCS* entails the recounting of the nature of Cornerville life. The realism is underscored by a feature of the book that is rarely remarked upon—the absence of bibliographical references. This is quite an unusual feature in a book that claims to relate to sociological concerns and it cannot be easily explained away by suggesting that there was no literature to which Whyte could have referred, since there were quite a few studies of the nature of urban life and leadership even in the early 1940s that could have been cited. However, *SCS* also contains elements of both the confessional and the impressionist tale. The Appendix to the second edition is in many ways the archetypal confessional tale and has been much

emulated. Indeed, Bell and Newby (1977, p. 12) in their letter to the
contributors to a book of accounts of what sociological research is really
like suggested that the Appendix provided a model for the sort of chapter
that they wanted. Thus, although not cited by Van Maanen as an example
of a confessional tale, it not only exemplifies most of the ingredients he
identifies, it has also served as a paradigm for many others. But *SCS* reveals
many aspects of the impressionist tale as well. Van Maanen (1988, p. 107)
cites the case of Whyte "stuffing the ballot box in a Cornerville election,"
but there are many other illustrations. Most notably the story of a bowling
match in which he participated (and won) is used as a lengthy vignette
through which the significance of bowling for an understanding of leadership processes can be revealed.

If we employ Emerson's four criteria, there is evidence that *SCS* does
not exhibit the flaws that they identified in recent work. Even the criticism
which Emerson (1987, p. 80) identified which is a product of very recent
concerns—the tendency to "suppress the presence and the person of the
observer as an active, relevant force in recounted events and incidents"—is largely inappropriate.

Implications of *Street Corner Society* for the Study of Organizational Culture

SCS is significant for the view that it conveys of the nature of culture.
One aspect that it conveys is that culture is something that is constantly
changing in response to the everyday adjustments introduced by those
individuals who are related to it. As Becker (1982, p. 521) has observed,
"people create culture continuously." This continuous process of culture-
creation occurs as individuals confront new situations to which they must
adjust; the ensuing solutions directly affect their shared understandings
which constitute the culture's bedrock. This sense of culture pervades
much of *SCS*. By taking a processual view of Cornerville, Whyte was able
to demonstrate that culture is both something that frames what people do
and is also continuously affected by them. One does not get the sense of
the culture of Cornerville or of its organizations as inert objects to which
people passively respond. It is striking how different this conception is
from much research on organizational culture, particularly investigations
with a strong emphasis on applied issues. In this literature much of the
research projects a sense of an organizational culture as something that is
formulated by the top leadership and culture-change consultants who

impose it on the workforce. Culture is thus seen as something that can be consciously created and enforced and members will then passively and automatically respond to its precepts. This emphasis can be seen in much of the practitioner-led research (Barley et al., 1988) and in many investigations working within what Martin and Meyerson (1988) call an integration paradigm. Whyte implicitly rejected such a view on the last page of the presentation of the findings of *SCS* (p. 276). Instead, he views culture as something that is in relative flux and as emergent. Surely this is exactly what the understanding of any culture should reflect and in this respect organizational culture research should be no exception?

The influence of practitioner-led issues in organizational culture research can be discerned in connection with another issue, namely, how culture is conceptualized. The *Business Week* article (1980) that stimulated much of the current interest in corporate culture gave an impression that culture is something that is eminently visible and can readily be captured by sobriquets such as "customer service" and "teamwork" at Delta, "service philosophy" at IBM, and so on. Such notions are consistent with the "quick fix" solutions that pervade much of the field, but it is hard to believe that they are really what culture is all about. Culture goes much deeper than such relatively superficial characteristics denote. If we treat culture, as Becker (1982) does, as shared understanding, then we must recognize a need to penetrate the more superficial manifestations. Schein (1983, p. 14) acknowledged this point when he wrote that organizational culture comprises "the assumptions that underlie . . . values and determine not only behavior patterns, but also such visible artifacts as architecture, office layout, dress codes, and so on." This level of approaching the study of culture is more or less precisely the one at which Whyte was conducting his investigations into Cornerville. He was concerned to elucidate not just patterns of behavior, but to show how these meshed with, and were underpinned by, the wider culture that he was investigating. Moreover, such research should be sensitive to subcultural variations that relate to the kind of differentiation to which Martin and Meyerson (1988) have drawn attention. Whyte did precisely this in his characterization of the divergent world views of the corner and college boys.

He needed 42 months in which to conduct this work. In part, this can perhaps be explained by the 18 months that were needed to figure out what he was doing, but even this still leaves two full years of research after the initial problem-formulation. It is difficult not to be struck by the contrast that this represents with most organizational culture research. There are some examples of sustained and prolonged involvement (e.g., Rohlen,

1974; Rosen, 1986), but they are few and far between. Instead, we typically find fairly short periods of immersion of the kind described by Emerson (1987) or intermittent involvement. Alternatively, there is the employment of methods, like interviewing, which possibly limit the field researcher's ability to penetrate the deeper levels to which Schein refers. It may be that the strong influence of practitioner-led issues, usually concerned with the control of organizational culture, has produced a tendency for short consultancy-style investigations. An applied focus does not inevitably lead to the absence of sustained research of the kind exhibited by *SCS*. Not only has Whyte exhibited a life-long concern with the application of the social sciences which has invariably entailed detailed studies of specific milieux (Whyte, 1987), it is possible to argue that *SCS* was itself concerned with matters of practice. Perhaps the problems of access that many organizational researchers report (Bryman, 1988b) mean that such prolonged periods of involvement are impractical. Also, as suggested earlier, researchers' work lives may not readily permit prolonged immersion. However, we must recognize that if *SCS* is truly a paradigm for organizational culture research, certain features of its methodology are often not being adhered to.

Conclusion

The bulk of researchers concerned with organizational culture see the most appropriate style of investigation as being one which is located within the qualitative style of research or in combination with quantitative research. There are some studies which have used quantitative methods exclusively (e.g., Gordon, 1985), but these do not seem to have found favor. *SCS* exhibits many of the characteristics of the qualitative research approach that is currently popular. In fact, its significance as a classic qualitative study probably means that it has exerted a profound influence on contemporary qualitative research. Moreover, Whyte's research can be used as a model, in that some qualitative research seems to have departed from the good practices that he exhibited. Specifically, in the area of organizational culture research, it has been argued that the field would benefit greatly from greater use of the general approach employed by Whyte, since it would engender research that manifests more rounded depictions of its primary object.

14

Cornerville as Narration

PATRICIA RILEY

It was a long time before I realized that I could explain Cornerville better through telling the stories of those individuals and groups than I could in any other way.

—WILLIAM FOOTE WHYTE
(*Street Corner Society,* 1943d, p. 357)

Conceived in a reformist spirit, guided by an intense curiosity about human action, goaded by a sort of middle-class anomie, and funded by a Harvard fellowship, W. F. Whyte's *Street Corner Society* (1943d) stands today as a gifted analysis of social organization. His account of this project (in the "here is my story" Appendix in the 1955 edition now ubiquitous in ethnographic studies) was as compelling as the study itself. The historical impact of his work, positioned at the forefront of sociological analyses of group and organizational culture, is one reason. Another is that his confessional narrative evokes this sense that I am watching a morality play about lessons learned in the field, and understanding more clearly how these lessons become enmeshed in theoretical constructions. As if that were not sufficient, there is a cast of both eminent and eccentric characters: distinguished scientists, an affable, earnest, intellectual hero with his good-timing gambling sidekick, real-life racketeers, and a caring, swearing Italian mama. And while the pace is rather patient—a lot of hanging around—the plot is suffused with enough primal tension emerging from conflicts about group acceptance, personal ethics, class struggles, and self-awareness that an engaging tale develops; one that belies the difficulty of cultural analysis.

Two questions guide my reflections on Whyte's study and organizational culture research in general: First, in what way(s) is *Street Corner Society* the product of a particular time and place in organizational culture analysis? Second, how might my reading of Cornerville differ from Whyte's? By way of answering these questions, this chapter is divided into three sections: (a) Cornerville as ethnography, (b) Organizational culture as representation, and (c) Cornerville as narration. It is critical to remember that this analysis is equally bound by time, space, and theoretical constraints as well as local understanding.

Cornerville as Ethnography

Ethnography—which literally means folk ("ethno") description ("graphy")—is the study of culture. Several textbooks required for my graduate seminar in field research identify *Street Corner Society* as a premier example of ethnographic analysis (e.g., Werner & Schoepfle, 1987, although they misspell Whyte).

In its most generic sense, ethnography describes a social group, usually small (though not in this case), using participant observation, conversation, and interview techniques (see Spradley's texts, 1979, 1980; and Van Maanen, 1988, for thorough descriptions). Ethnography is not a new concept—Herodotus in ancient Greece was an early observer of other cultures (Sanday, 1979)—but it was Franz Boas' (1948) fieldwork at the start of this century that established the model of a long residence in another culture in order to improve the researcher's ability to illuminate day-to-day routines and practices that might otherwise go unnoticed. Typically, the ethnographer is also trained to take field notes—to record, categorize, and code what is observed. Thus although *Street Corner Society* is not archetypal in the tradition of Eskimo studies or the rites and rituals of Tahitian natives, it exemplifies the ethnographic paradigm. Specifically, Whyte was immersed for several years in Cornerville and his upper middle-class background provided a stark contrast to the "slum" he chose to study, and he presumably obtained a vantage point not available to a "native" observer.

There is, of course, more than one ethnographic method (i.e., Werner and Schoepfle's 1987 typology of ethnographies; Sanday's 1979 discussion of three distinct ethnographic styles: holistic, semiotic, and behavioristic; and Van Maanen's 1988 categories: realist, confessional, impression-ist, critical tales, formal tales, literary tales, and jointly told tales). In addition, little is simple or uncomplicated when doing ethnography and studies of *Street Corner Society's* scope and duration merely magnify this condition.

A number of research difficulties are readily apparent. For organiza-tional culture researchers, the time commitment for ethnography often appears at best intimidating, at worst impossible. This approach requires complete dedication to a project, both physically and emotionally, as the researcher becomes intimately involved in the culture being studied and with the people who produce and reproduce that culture. She or he also simultaneously strives to maintain enough distance to examine both the acculturation process and its results. Whether this distance is possible is debatable; clearly the researcher becomes both the "knower" and the "known" in doing ethnography (see Rorty, 1979, for a detailed discussion of this phenomena). For Whyte, it was apparent he had become part of his observation the night Mama waited up for him and his embeddedness increased until he was an active change agent in Cornerville (see p. 336 of Whyte's 1955 Appendix).

Other research difficulties, however, are less obvious and create numer-ous intriguing dilemmas within which analysts of social or organizational cultures must operate. Although an enumeration of these problems would be quite lengthy, a good example is Van Maanen's distinction between first order "facts" of an ethnographic investigation and the second order "the-ories" used to organize and explain these facts (1979, p. 540).

In social and organizational research today, questions about our basic assumptions regarding facts (or fictions) are being hotly debated. The following discussion briefly positions ethnography or other types of organ-izational culture in the ongoing discourse regarding the nature of "know-ing," and then addresses the implications of this debate for organizational research.

Organizational Culture as Representation

It is widely believed that the social sciences developed out of an Enlightenment notion of human betterment; that with improved knowledge about our world (especially "nature") and increased abilities to make rational decisions, we will be able to design a world fit to live in. It is this conception of the social sciences that appears to characterize *Street Corner*

Society, given Whyte's concerns about slums and his self-reported reformist attitude.

Ethnography, historically situated in naturalistic inquiry, takes as basic assumptions issues such as cultural relativism and subjective understanding. Cultural relativism holds that values, customs, practices, and so forth are embedded in a particular milieu and cannot be judged or compared to another culture as higher or lower, better or worse. The widely known practice of attempting to understand culture from the point of view of its members is commonly referred to as subjective understanding. Through such assumptions, traditional ethnographers attempted to give the most accurate representation possible to the culture under investigation. Although the subjectivity of the researcher was understood to be problematic, Whyte and others were constantly in pursuit of theories or methods to allow them to be more objective (see p. 287 in Whyte's 1955 Appendix).

Although some researchers have continued in this tradition, most notably those in cognitive ethnography or ethnoscience, the 1960s and 1970s played host to a burgeoning critique of culture as representation. A major figure in this critique, Clifford Geertz, has been a vocal advocate that cultural descriptions, filtered through the ethnographer, are actually second or third order fictions ("fictions" in the sense of something made) (Sanday, 1979). His most recent concept is that ethnography is actually a "kind of writing" (Geertz, 1988b, p. 1) in the literary sense. In *Writing Culture: The Poetics and Politics of Ethnography* (Clifford & Marcus, 1986), it is argued that the various blindnesses, evasions, and fictions that were created in order to produce ethnographic insights essentially required new vocabularies and new modes for describing the social and cultural worlds being studied. Stated simply, there is no culture or organization "out there" to be accurately represented by observers; instead the observer creates cultural or organizational fictions in the process of the investigation.

Indeed, other more radical critiques of the social sciences have posited the notion that the modern world itself, built on principles of knowledge derived from the Enlightenment, is obsolete as we once conceived of it (e.g., Lyotard, 1984). Very briefly, the postmodern world is characterized by a deconstruction of epistemology in the traditional sense—authors are not privileged as having special knowledge (an interesting issue for culture researchers who supposedly know what they know because they have "been there"), no theory or concept is any better or any worse than another, and there are no longer any grand narratives (e.g., saving humanity) to give purpose or focus to social research (see Cooper & Burrell, 1988, for a detailed examination of these issues).

There are varieties of postmodernism, of course, and the recommendations that emerge from postmodern critiques are varied; however, I want to appropriate the spirit of these revolutionaries to look for alternative means of conceptualizing organizational culture. My perspective does not denigrate social scientific knowledge, but simply accepts its reflexive nature. Anthony Giddens (1990) best explains this concept when he notes that the skepticism of knowledge claims that characterize the post-modern dismissal of objectivity, determinism, representation, and so forth is actually a feature of our modern world (or Modernity). The position is that our culture (Western civilization) continually supplants old knowledge with the new, and that everything we "know" could easily be revised or discarded as soon as better information is made available (Giddens, 1990). This hermeneutic notion of knowledge is important; it focuses attention on the cultural issues of reflexivity such as modes of discourse, argumentative forms, and cultural rules.

The position I am taking is not that the postmodernism debate about epistemology is incorrect, merely that it is not a call to end organizational culture research. Richard Rorty has been most influential in my thinking about these matters. Not privileging a particular voice is important because we as researchers are in but a certain stage of a conversation—"a conversation which once knew nothing of these issues and may know nothing of them again" (1979, p. 391). In this light, theoretical constructions, methodological guidelines, and personal imperatives are seen as results of historical accident, as turns the conversation has taken. "It [Western thought] has taken this turn for a long time, but it might turn in another direction without human beings thereby losing their reason or losing touch with 'the real problems' " (Rorty, 1979, p. 392).

When ethnography, or any other method of organizational culture analysis, is the practice of "normal science" (to adopt a Kuhnian phrase), it uses the patterns of discourse of that method which were "adopted for various historical reasons and as the achievement of objective truth, where 'objective truth' is no more and no less than the best idea we currently have about how to explain what is going on" (Rorty, 1979, p. 385).

Whyte had a multitude of ideas about what was going on in groups including the relationship between social structure and bowling scores (see p. 319 in Whyte's 1955 Appendix), as well as the influence of patterns of interaction on mental health (see p. 328 in the Appendix). Some of these ideas have proved more heuristic than others but they should be viewed as a particular conversation, bound in time and space by the rules governing their production. This notion of a "conversation" can be valuable to organizational culture researchers when it is viewed epistemologically within a narrative analysis.

Cornerville as Narration

I think one of the best ideas we have right now to study organizational culture is narrative analysis. Again, of course, there is more than one approach to narration. Two of the primary schools of thought will be covered briefly in this section. Both perspectives share a repudiation of technical rationality, although Lyotard (1984) is decidedly postmodern in philosophy, whereas Fisher (1987) is probably best described as a late modernist.

It should be noted that the approaches to narrative discussed here differ extensively from the research done by Joanne Martin and others who focus on the functions of storytelling in organizations (e.g., Martin, Feldman, Hatch, & Sitkin, 1983; Mumby, 1987). In such studies, the focus is often on stories as manifestations of particular cultures—for example, the founder who started the company in his garage, or stories as legitimators of organizational power—not on narrative as a fundamental formulation of knowledge.

Lyotard (1984) claims that narration is the quintessential form of customary knowledge. First, narratives allow the society in which they are told to both define its criteria of competence (e.g., success and failure) and evaluate according to those criteria what can or cannot be performed (Lyotard, 1984, p. 20). Second, he argues that the narrative form allows a wide variety of language games (e.g., denotative statements, deontic statements, evaluative statements, implied interrogatives, etc.). Third, narration usually follows rules that guide transmission—what one must say in order to be heard, what one must listen to in order to speak, and what role one must play to be the object of a narrative (p. 21). Fourth, narrative form is believed to have a "rhythm" that contextualizes time. "They [narratives] thus define what has the right to be said and done in the culture in question, and since they are themselves a part of that culture, they are legitimated by the simple fact that they do what they do" (p. 23).

Fisher (1987) articulates a narrative paradigm (to be read in opposition to the "rational world" paradigm) which postulates that humans, above all, are storytellers. In this paradigm, the mode of human decision making is "good reasons," which vary in form among situations, genres, and communication media. Also, the production and practice of good reasons are "ruled by matters of history, biography, culture, and character along with . . . [the] language action paradigm. And, rationality is determined by the nature of persons as narrative beings—their inherent awareness of "narrative probability," what constitutes a coherent story, and their constant habit of testing "narrative fidelity," whether or not the stories they experience ring true with the stories they know to be true in their lives . . . (p. 5). Finally, in this perspective the world is a set of stories that must be chosen among in order to live life (Fisher, 1987, p. 5).

These perspectives position narrative as both fundamental to knowing and to living, doing, and deciding based on the rules that govern narration. Issues about what is right to say, what can and cannot be performed, how to be heard in the culture, and how decisions are made are the "stuff" or organizational culture research. Organizational culture from this vantage point, however, is less about structure and leaders and networks, a la Whyte, and more about discourse and rules and power.

Following Lyotard, if the Appendix to *Street Corner Society* is read from a narrative perspective, then Whyte (1955) is engaged in a number of different conversations, each with its own rules. For example, the language game of the Harvard Fellow requires adherence to fundamental social science guidelines regarding fieldwork, the need to continue to participate in the academic community, writing case studies that serve as evidence for Fellowship renewal, and not getting caught doing anything that would embarrass the University (see p. 315 in the Appendix). Whyte's story grants legitimacy to the academic game (e.g., keeping the Harvard world and Cornerville separate so the conversational rules could remain distinct) and clarifies the nature of success (e.g., having a one-year Fellowship renewal was actually not a failure because there is no real endpoint when studying a social community). The elite rules of academic conversation, so matter-of-factly noted in the Appendix, are replicated, to some degree, in the research, for example, wanting to start with the leader of some group in order to figure it out (see p. 325 in the Appendix), the mostly invisible role of women (e.g., the "girls" and discussions of their builds, akin in Cornerville to discussing baseball).

Whyte's other conversations with the Nortons, the racketeers, in politics, and with other groups similarly have rules particular to these smaller cultures as well as those that are more universal in application. In addition, Whyte's observation that he was taking a moving picture, not a snapshot, exemplifies the way narratives have a rhythm and an internal coherence.

A narrative analysis is not about functioning parts, but about streams of discourse; and change does not happen over time so much as the narrative creates time. Thus typical features of analysis such as organizational life-cycles, leaders, and values are less the focus of a narrative analysis than are the ways in which organizations or communities cohere through knowledge of the narrative form and understanding the sensibilities of those who participate in the discourse. Complexities in organizing, decision making, and environmental pressures, for example, are thus features of the language games of the respective cultures (see Riley, Hollihan, & Freadhoff, in press). Understanding the language game, according to Lyotard (1984), is one key to understanding how power is manifested in a given culture.

In addition, this analysis does not privilege the stories of executives over line workers, men over women, or group leaders over group members. And analyzing the tension between rules that are more globally reproduced and those that are more local in their application is critical to understanding the intersections of the different conversations.

Street Corner Society is an icon of modern ethnography. Our conception of ethnography, however, is being revisited in the modernity/postmodernity debate. This revision questions fundamental epistemological assumptions that guide cultural research in organizations—questions of representation and of privileged understanding. That numerous types of ethnography, as well as other means of analyzing organizational culture, have developed is not a surprise. A postmodern interpretation of these alternatives is not chaos but a natural progression to accepting many "authors." A late modernist, however, would remind researchers that our reflexive nature requires that we revise what we know in light of new information (read: theories, ideas, fictions, or whatever). This assumes we are part of the discourse, and telling our own stories. Did you hear the one about . . . ?

15

Critical Epistemology and the Study of Organizational Culture: Reflections on *Street Corner Society*

JOHN M. JERMIER

Street Corner Society: **Fifty Years Later**

William Foote Whyte's splendid classic, *Street Corner Society (SCS)*, has become the best-selling sociological monograph in history (D'Antonio, 1984). Whyte has achieved legendary status based on his presumed adventuresomeness in gaining hard-won knowledge of another culture (Van Maanen, 1988). What accounts for the powerful impact of this book? In the age of skinheads, rockers, punks, and other street corner predators (who make Whyte's subjects seem genteel by comparison), is *SCS* still relevant? What theory of the nature of knowledge (epistemology) underwrote Whyte's work? How does Whyte's approach relate to a critical epistemology of social science? What promise does critical epistemology hold for contemporary studies of organizational culture? This chapter consists of reflections on these questions.

The Impact of SCS

In some areas of North American cities, street corners have been colonized by violent "punks" (Baron, 1989; Kontash, 1987). Their main activity is "hanging out." To live, they beg, panhandle, run scams on unsuspecting outsiders, steal and fence, roll people, sell drugs, turn tricks (prostitution), and exploit the street scene in numerous other ways. Their life styles are antithetical to the dominant culture. From the viewpoint of the latter, the lives of the urban street punks are twisted and meaningless. Their profoundly deviant ways of living make them seem primitive and alien.

One thing we have learned from interpretive cultural analysis is that people practicing bizarre life styles, like those living more conventionally, imbue their worlds with meaning. They react to the fundamental conundrums of existence by creating elaborate symbolic worlds that shield them from the experience of meaninglessness. In diverse ways, alienated labor is alleviated, everyday boredom and interpersonal anxiety are offset, and existential dread is overcome as human actors socially construct their realities.

The domain of culture studies involves examination of the symbolic worlds of human actors. The products of this work are representations of different patterns and ways of life, rendered from the perspectives of the actors. In the tradition of interpretive social science, cultural analysis is aimed at unpacking, examining, and illustrating alternative worlds of meaning, whether they are found in the exotic Trobriand Islands, in a crowded Italian-American slum district of Boston, in the hypermodern control room of a phosphate manufacturing plant in Tampa, or in any other location.

Fifty years have passed since Whyte followed his social reformist tendencies into what appeared to be a setting overrun with social problems and overwhelmed by social chaos. With little formal training in fieldwork methodology, he entered a world that may have seemed primitive and alien to him. Perhaps it seemed as primitive and alien as the deviant urban street culture does now to the average university professor from an elite background. He lived among its natives for over three years, gaining their acceptance.

The primary triumph of this work rests on the fact that Whyte began to unpack the cultural practices whereby Cornerville residents established meaning and purpose in their lives. The study's appeal is closely tied to Whyte's ability to persuade readers that their naive assumptions about the chaotic nature of urban slums were unfounded. He showed ways in which Cornerville life was "highly organized and integrated" (p. xvi). His portrayal emphasized the planned, orderly, rule-governed nature of Cornerville's underlife. Some of the study's vast popularity can be accounted for by recognizing that denial of common sense, taken-for-granted assumptions is interesting (cf. Davis, 1971).

To understand the rise of *SCS* to the level of a classic, it is also necessary to consider rhetorical factors (cf. Davis, 1986). For example, readers are made aware of one of the shocking consequences of ethnic inequality and discrimination: high-density, deviant, and dangerous neighborhoods in close proximity to affluent and "respectable" people. This representation may have excited readers' fears that hard-core poverty was spreading (or at least that its effects were spreading), leading to moral panic. However, Whyte left readers with hope that there were ways of controlling problems associated with ethnic inequality (e.g., assigning and promoting members of the ethnic subculture to positions of authority so they could serve as role models and instill faith in social mobility). According to Davis (1986), each of these rhetorical factors (highlighting a new or neglected problem affecting many aspects of modern society; exciting the audiences' fears that this problem may be spreading into more and more areas of life; and elevating hope by positing solutions) is important in the emergence of a classic.

In addition, *SCS* is multi-layered, ambiguous, and incomplete enough to appeal to both generalists and specialists (cf. Davis, 1986). On the surface, Cornerville is memorable for its patterns of order: unified residents, organized life styles, and strong, informal leadership. Culture studies specialists are equally impressed, however, by Whyte's sophisticated representations of subcultural diversity and conflict (corner boys vs. college boys, the Nortons vs. the Italian Community Club, cliques within the gangs, intergenerational strains and tensions, etc.). And they appreciate his emphasis on the temporariness of gang structure, the state of flux of the community, and the sensitivity of social organizing to temporal effects. Although it is possible to interpret *SCS* in simple images, it is a complex work with ambiguous passages and incomplete renderings which add to its rhetorical appeal.

Finally, the study's impact has been heightened by the story-life character of the representations. Whyte (1955, p. 357) remarked: "It was a long time before I realized that I could explain Cornerville better through telling the stories of those individuals and groups than I could in any other way." In noting that only a few studies really persuade, Van Maanen (1990a) argued that factual detail and theory per se do not determine impacts. Narrative devices and writing skill separate good (memorable) accounts from forgettable ones. In his view, studies that have impact, ". . . create a narrative using theory to abbreviate, organize, and embed certain features of the account such that a convincing story could be told." (p. 5). Whyte succeeded in displaying Cornerville's culture (and subcultures) in an

engaging, reportorial style (Van Maanen, 1988). *SCS* is a good read, and
it is memorable.

The Contemporary Relevance of SCS

Like all scientific works, *SCS* is a product of its time. The conceptual
framework that guided Whyte's observations was interaction theory. The
book is full of descriptions of action-reaction sequences, reports of reciprocal exchanges, and diagrams of informal group structures. Whyte resisted the influence of Harvard's sociometricians of the day. He did not
conduct the planned study of friendship patterns among Cornerville's
people, finding that he could examine social structure more directly by
observing people in action. Had he focused on quantitative summaries of
interaction dynamics (perhaps consequently titling the book *A Sociometric
Analysis of Interaction Patterns in a Depressed Community*), it seems
likely that the study of Cornerville would have become another volume
anal-retentive librarians fantasize about—one that stays on the shelf in its
assigned place. To his credit, Whyte creatively conveyed aspects of the
cultural practices of Cornerville residents while straightjacketed by interaction theory.

During the 1960s, emphasis in the human sciences shifted away from
documentation of behavior and social structure toward interpretive understanding of social life. In sociology and anthropology, culture studies
emerged focused on systems of shared meanings, symbols, and language
(Marcus & Fischer, 1986). Of course, *SCS* contains no explicit symbolic
analysis, limiting its potential to inform contemporary theorizing about the
deeper realms of culture. However, Whyte did present a substantial amount
of conversational evidence, allowing readers to grasp partially native
points of view.

During the 1960s and 1970s, Marxist-informed social theory became
viable, sensitizing social researchers to consider the reciprocal effects
between capital accumulation imperatives and aspects of social life. In
sociology and anthropology, culture studies emerged that focused on
interactions between exploitative material forces and ideological domination (cf. Marcus & Fischer, 1986). Although *SCS* deals extensively with
patterns of stratification, occasionally inserting family background and
education into the analysis (e.g., p. 255), there is no connection made
between Cornerville's working-class culture and institutionalized racism,
extraction of surplus value in production and unemployment, or reproduction of inequality and the capitalist labor process. It seems apparent that

Cornerville's youth socially constructed "resistance subcultures" to deal with the harsh realities of their class situation. Whyte's neglect of the class basis of Cornerville's culture and, to a lesser extent, structural patterns of ethnic discrimination, limits the potential of *SCS* to inform discussions of injuries associated with class membership or radical social change. However, it is worth noting that one of Whyte's primary motives for studying Cornerville was to facilitate social reform. Presently, he is well-known as an advocate of social research aimed at improving human welfare, especially the lot of poor people (Whyte & Whyte, 1988).

No good cultural study ever becomes obsolete. At a minimum, detailed description of varied cultural practices heightens awareness of historical alternatives. This is beneficial in resisting cultural homogenization. With *SCS,* Whyte foreshadowed interpretive and radical sociology. Also, a careful reading reveals that he displayed aspects of Cornerville's culture in a manner that parallels in sophistication much contemporary culture research. For these reasons, *SCS* remains relevant.

The Influence of Traditional Epistemology and Ethnography on SCS

Whyte conducted his fieldwork for *SCS* in the late 1930s and published the first edition in 1943. In the appendix to the second edition of *SCS* (1955), Whyte made it clear that he was constrained in this research by more than interaction theory. His work also reflected a strong influence from the natural science model of research (positivism) favored by his colleagues and mentors at Harvard. This was visible in the text in several places where he chose to mention that Cornerville residents viewed him as a neutral outsider (e.g., p. 166). However, it is most pronounced in the appendix itself in his lamentations about missing a golden opportunity to record quantitative bowling scores (pp. 319-320) and in his recounting of the orientations of Harvard professors Arensberg, Chapple, Mayo, Henderson, and others (pp. 286-288).

The appendix to the second edition of *SCS* was written in the early 1950s after Whyte completed graduate study and a research associateship at the University of Chicago (Whyte, 1976, Whyte & Whyte 1984). This was around the time when second generation Chicago field-workers turned toward more marginal, objective roles in participant observation, emphasizing detachment (Adler & Adler, 1987a, 1987b). Although *SCS* is marked by the powerful influence of Chicago School epistemology and the broader pressures of positivism, Whyte practiced fieldwork and wrote ethnography in a subtle subjectivist style that was ahead of his time.

Critical Epistemology and Social Science

> The elevation of the quest for the Grail over the Grail itself, the acceptance that all that is solid *has* melted into air, that reality and morality are not givens but imperfect human constructs, is the point from which fiction begins. (Rushdie, 1990)

Years of heated "positivism bashing" by social theorists (borrowing the term from Van Maanen, 1990b) have finally melted this icy foundation of social research. Vienna Circle verificationism, Popperian falsificationism, and the other classic epistemological specifications of the conditions for the possibility of knowledge (see Adorno, Popper, Dahrendorf, Habermas, Albert, & Pilot, 1976) do not inspire dispassionate inquiry with the same zeal they once did. The counter-positivist Zeitgeist liberates experimentation, but has produced a crisis of representation in the human sciences (see Marcus & Fischer, 1986). In summarizing this crisis, Geertz (1988a, p. 32) captured the dispirited moment: "What is at hand is a pervasive nervousness about the whole business of claiming to explain enigmatical others on the grounds that you have gone about with them in their native habitat or combed the writings of those who have."

However, the experience of epistemological dread is not universal and has not paralyzed production of images of others. Despite important differences among counter-positivists, most have in common a position advocating the researcher's own subjectivity as a virtue. In some approaches, such as the everyday life sociologies (Adler, Adler, & Fontana, 1987), researcher subjectivity enables penetration of the fronts individuals and groups present which, in turn, permits deeper understanding of actors' perspectives and ways of living. In other approaches, such as Critical Theory (Bottomore, 1984), researcher subjectivity and partisanship are essential to overcoming technocratic domination and orienting the human sciences toward serving the interests of oppressed and disadvantaged groups. Thus, amidst the postmodern malaise, alternative epistemologies exist that ground knowledge in soul searching.

Habermas's (1971) theory of knowledge and human interests has been highly influential in critiquing objectivist social science and in formulating an alternative epistemology. The theory of knowledge and human interests has been reviewed in detail by Bernstein (1976), Held (1980), Wuthnow, Hunter, Bergeson, and Kurzwail (1984), and others and is widely circulated among contemporary social theorists. Therefore, it will be only briefly sketched here.

According to Habermas (1971), knowledge is produced intentionally by human actors to serve three different interests. The *technical interest* is oriented toward manipulating and controlling the natural and social worlds. This interest is best served by positivist epistemology and empirical-analytical methodology. Validity of the knowledge claims of this form of inquiry depends on the (presumed) objectivity and disinterestedness of theoretical formulations and on the technical quality of evidence supporting the theory. The *practical interest* is oriented toward achieving mutual understanding among human actors and is dependent on interpretation of the meanings of contextually situated interactions. This interest is best served by phenenomenological epistemology and hermeneutical (idiographic) methodology. Validity of the knowledge claims of this form of inquiry depends on the depth of understanding of the human condition that results. The *emancipatory interest* is oriented toward revealing sources of domination and oppression. It is aligned with a central purpose of promoting human emancipation, especially by unveiling hidden forms of power that exploit the democratic majority. This interest is best served by critical (partisan, anti-elite) epistemology. It is compatible with a range of methodologies, but probably is best served by social research and representation modes that reach society's disadvantaged and oppressed. Validity of the knowledge claims of this form of inquiry depends on the intensity of illumination of exploitive forces that results and, perhaps, the sense of empowerment experienced by oppressed individuals and groups in contact with the knowledge.

In my view, further articulation of a critical epistemology is essential to development of the human sciences. Too little progress has been made in providing critique of the conservative political content of social research underwritten by positivism; even less critique is available of social research underwritten by phenomenological epistemology. Often, researchers' assumptions of social consensus, claims of value-neutrality, and conclusions about serving the public interest are not challenged. More damaging still is the vast number of human studies implicitly assumed to be politically neutral despite tacit endorsement of existing social processes. Social research always serves interests, but its ideological content is not always apparent. As Blackburn (1972, p. 9) commented: ". . . ideology is by no means defined by the conscious choices made by the social theorist about how society works but rather precisely by those assumptions of which the theorist is least aware and about which he is least explicit."

In his landmark essays on critical epistemology, Horkheimer (1937/1972a, 1939/1972b) provided some guidelines for developing a critical science.

Central to the project is understanding that traditional theory assists in the process of social reproduction, but critical theory subverts it and is aimed at the abolition of distorted thinking and social injustice. Because no program of research or theory is without political and moral content, it is desirable to conduct social research and build theory *for the exploited* (cf. Morgan, 1986). However, it is equally important to avoid superficial fault-finding and piecemeal problem solving which give the illusion of social progress but, in effect, stabilize existing structures of domination. Social research has emancipatory potential (and meets the criterion of demarcation of critical science) only if it addresses foundational issues significant enough to challenge established power structures. Within its domain of analysis, it must define primary causes of domination and oppression, such as concentration of wealth, private property ownership, irreconcilable interests of capital and labor, inequalities in opportunities for employment and education, and technocratic rationality and ideologies of work, consumption, and leisure.

Critical Studies of Organizational Culture

Infusion of critical epistemology into social research is perhaps most crucial in the area of organization studies, much of which has been seen as excessively concerned with management control issues and the development of acceptable ideologies for established powers (Alvesson, 1987a; Baritz, 1960; Rose, 1975). Research analyzing organizations as cultures has been especially prone to elitist bias in assuming that organizations are, or have, a singular culture. This bias is even more pronounced among organization development specialists and management practitioners. They have reached new heights of enthusiasm about planned change based on the assumption that organization culture can (and should) be molded to support the interests of capital (Jermier, Slocum, Fry, & Gaines, in press). What is necessary to build a critical science of organizations as cultures?

First, it is necessary to reject the idea that culture is one of many subsystems in an organization in favor of an approach that promotes research on organizations *as* cultures. Acceptance of culture as a root metaphor for conceptualizing organizations leads to a view that culture is something an organization is, not something an organization has (see Smircich, 1983b). More precisely, an organization may be viewed as a specific cultural setting in which human actors, as carriers of broader cultural expressions (e.g., societal, regional, community, interorganizational, social class, occupational, ethnic, gender, age), construct social realities and negotiate meaning for their lives. Apart from official level expressions by top management, an organization is not a monolithic cultural form (Jermier et al., in press). Furthermore, its relationship with broader culture, as manifested in extra-organizational identities of its participants, cannot be dismissed.

Second, critical studies of organizational culture center analysis on processes whereby wealth created by labor activity is extracted and appropriated by owners and their agents. In capitalist economies, class struggle develops primarily as a result of problems associated with alienated labor—the condition in which labor's products become the property of capitalists in exchange for wages. Working class culture emerges in patterns of accommodation and resistance to the interests of capital, at the point of production and in the broader society (see Jermier, 1988).

Thus, organizational culture is a contested reality. It reflects, first and foremost, the divergent economic and political interests of capital and labor. Despite the strong tendency for actors to align with subcultures of resistance or accommodation based on class position, ambiguous class positions (Wright, 1984) and other identifications (e.g., gender, occupation) can lead to more than two subcultures. Also, subcultures vary considerably in the form and extent to which preferences of capital elites are challenged, modified, or replaced, and subcultural memberships can change. Riley (1983), Gray, Bougon, and Donnellon (1985), and Knights and Willmott (1987) have made valuable contributions in highlighting the precariousness of organizational culture without overlooking more stable, deep structural forces (also see Frost, 1987; Frost & Egri, 1991). However, the subtleties of the class-based cultural production and reproduction seem better represented with the concept of impermanence, not precariousness.

Third, a critical concept of culture is inseparable from the phenomenon of *reification,* defined as the "moment in the process of alienation in which the characteristic of thinghood becomes the standard of objective reality" (Berger & Pullberg, 1966, p. 198). In harnessing nature with their labor, human actors create themselves and their social worlds. Culture is the objectified product of the labor of human subjects. In reified consciousness, there is profound forgetting of the fact that the world is socially constructed and can be remade. It appears as a divine or natural order and is not challenged (see Jermier, 1981; 1985). Exploitative practices are mystified and concealed. Others refer to this as ideological or hegemonic domination (e.g., Burawoy, 1985). It is of central interest because it facilitates reproduction of labor processes and other structures of domination.

Fourth, an epistemology fully capable of underwriting critical studies of organizational culture can draw insight and inspiration from neo-positivist projects such as Whyte's *SCS*, but must be more explicit in its political commitments. Once false hope in the possibility of value neutrality in social research is suspended, it is possible (through subjective reflection) to examine the moral underpinnings of one's political interests. Ways in which they foster human emancipation can be identified. This enables inquiry oriented toward producing knowledge beneficial to society's underprivileged and oppressed. Studies aimed at demystifying ideologies that perpetuate exploitation of the working class are valuable, especially if they provide persuasive critique of these practices (see Jermier & Nord, 1991). Studies that uncover forms of critique and resistance indigenous to an oppressed group are valuable, especially if they enlighten others in similar circumstances and open up other alternatives (Marcus & Fischer, 1986), or if they are able to go beyond surface-level conflict to deep structures supporting capital accumulation in explaining problems (cf. Frost, 1987; Jermier & Nord, 1991).

Of course, there is some danger that any cultural knowledge can be used by elites in developing more dominating ideologies or in undercutting resistance (Said, 1989). Since critical epistemology promotes critiquing oppressive practices and imagining viable alternatives (in addition to rigorous description), the minds of some elites with access to the knowledge will be changed. The problem will not disappear, but can be further contained by representational decisions.

Fifth, critical studies of organizational culture can take advantage of a variety of methodologies and data. However, to penetrate fronts constructed by individuals and groups engaged in political struggles and to understand what actors have at stake in meaning-making contests involving deep subjectivities, it is necessary to become an insider. Usually, this requires months of fieldwork; at a minimum, it requires intimate, personal contact with several key informants. Sometimes, covert observation is necessary.

Quantitative data are important as well in critical research, especially if they can be gathered unobtrusively. Some cultural phenomena are material or tangible in nature even though they may stand for ideational phenomena (Geertz, 1973). Since some ideational phenomena can be estimated quantitatively (e.g., ideologies) and since most material phenomena (e.g., demographics, formal structures, behavior patterns) can be measured quantitatively, it seems unnecessary to exclude quantitative methods from culture studies. In fact, "paradigm wars" may deny authors of cultural reports without quantitative data access to journals and audiences they wish to reach. However, qualitative methods are essential to clarifying the meaning of numerical data and provide the most trustworthy depiction of the actors' worlds (cf. Willis, 1981).

Finally, it is important that scholars engaged in critical science recognize that mode of representation is not just an academic or theoretical quandary but is a political choice (Said, 1989). As stated earlier, *SCS* has a number of desirable rhetorical qualities, amplifying its impact. Good stories written in accessible language are important in building a critical theory of organizational culture. Obviously, demystifying insights and effective resistance strategies are not easily shared with working people and other oppressed groups in the stilted prose most academics learn to love. Van Maanen (1988) expanded understanding of the rich variety of cultural representation styles and recommended that field-workers refine their literary and aesthetic sensibilities and experiment with new, creative genres. In many important ways, in *SCS,* Whyte anticipated this poetic.

To the positivist, science ends at the point where researchers analyze a work's literary merits and political content. Bias is evident if numbers and brute description do not speak for themselves and if there is partisanship directed anywhere other than "the truth" itself. Critical epistemologists insist that truth lies in ever deeper levels of subjective reflection and disclosure and that science serves most when it serves the least. Contrary to the positivist's suspicions, this does not mean that anything goes. As Kaplan (1984, p. 25) noted: "Art criticism can be as demanding as a logical critique." Perhaps the circle is unbroken as soft-hearted, hard-headed cultural critique challenges hard-hearted, soft-headed positivist science.

16

Comments for the *SCS* Critics

WILLIAM FOOTE WHYTE

More than 50 years after I left the street corners of the North End of Boston, it is gratifying to find *Street Corner Society (SCS)* still receiving such appreciative attention. The critics, however, raise some interesting issues regarding the changing nature of field research and writing over the years, and those issues I will address.

What the Critics Overlooked

The critics have given serious attention to the book and have raised many interesting points of discussion, but unfortunately all of them limited their attention to the second edition (1955). The third edition (1981) contains the appendix on field methods and experience of the second edition but adds additional material that would have been relevant for some of the points raised by the critics.

The third edition adds to the methodological appendix "An Unnatural History of the Book." Bryman finds it hard to explain why *SCS* contains no review of the literature. Let me summarize my explanation from that section of the 1981 edition. At the time, Chicago required the doctoral thesis to be printed. I believed that some of the most prominent studies were highly misleading, I wanted the book to be widely read, and I did not want to clutter it up with material that I considered worse than useless. How did I get away with such a radical departure from academic custom? Running the gauntlet of a sociology department, some of whose members were affronted by this scholarly neglect, was not easy. Since I had gone into this study from an academic base of readings in social anthropology, I had not read any of the previous sociological studies of slum districts until I began formal graduate work at the University of Chicago. By the time I faced my thesis examination, I had read up on that sociological literature. While I consider myself fortunate not to have been misled by it when I was starting my field study, I now was well prepared to defend myself. Thanks to the skillful mediation of Everett C. Hughes, the department decided that they would award the degree but on condition that I write separately a review of the sociological literature on slum districts. They agreed that it would not have to be printed in the book but it would have to be bound in the one copy officially deposited in the university library. When, some months later two of my articles, "Social Organization in the Slums" and "A Challenge to Political Scientists," had been accepted for publication, Hughes persuaded the department to accept those publications as fulfilling the literature review requirement, without insisting on having them bound with the book in the library copy.

Jermier believes that "*SCS* is marked by the powerful influence of Chicago School epistemology." Whatever that means, it can hardly apply to *SCS*. As I reported (1981, p. 355), "I had arrived in Chicago to begin graduate work with the first draft of the thesis in my trunk." Between that point and publication, I did substantial rewriting to improve the style, and I had to condense the content as required by the publisher, but I can't recall any changes in interpretation and analysis during that rewriting period. Furthermore, on the advice of social anthropologist Conrad Arensberg, I went to Chicago to study with social anthropologist W. Lloyd Warner. There I also found a mentor in Everett C. Hughes, a sociologist who was also attracted to anthropology. (He later became active in the Society for Applied Anthropology and was elected its president.) Those most representative of the Chicago School of Sociology in that department were Louis Wirth, Herbert Blumer, and Ernest Burgess—and, in the thesis examination, I had to withstand the strong challenges of Wirth and Blumer.

The 1981 edition contains the list of all of my articles growing out of the North End study, including those mentioned above. Also relevant for the present discussion is "On Street Corner Society" (Whyte, 1964), which presents my own assessment of the book. Perhaps of further interest to critics would be my most popular reprint (1943c), "A Slum Sex Code," the one piece of my *SCS* writing that deals explicitly with the culture of the corner boys. This was later reprinted in Louis Coser's edited volume, *The Pleasures of Sociology* (1980). Perhaps I should have put this in *SCS,* but,

at the time, I did not think it would fit well with the overall organizationa
themes.

Finally, there was an unexpected dividend of my retirement ceremonies
an eloquent statement on "The Whyte Impact on an Underdog." Here
Angelo Ralph Orlandella (Sam Franco in *SCS*) describes how we worked
together on studies of the structure of the street corner gangs and how these
methods helped him in his later career.

Issues for Discussion

It seems that the issues raised by the critics sort themselves out into three
main categories: (1) the role of culture in field studies of organizations and
communities, including folklore; (2) research methods, involving the rela
tions between qualitative and quantitative research; and (3) the nature o
science in social research. That last category includes the issues regarding
objectivity versus subjectivity and critical epistemology.

On the Role of Culture in Organizational Studies

As the critics note, in *SCS* I never focus explicitly on the culture of the
community or of the street corner gang. On the other hand, I suppose the
whole book could be considered a study of that local culture. As Jones ha
noted, the only place in my early writing on industrial organizations that
focus explicitly on aspects of culture was in *Pattern for Industrial Peace*
(Whyte, 1951) and *Money and Motivation* (Whyte et al., 1955). I even go
into some folklore in the latter volume, especially in the tales told by
experienced workers about how some of their heroes had outwitted the
time study people. In the North End, I heard some tales about gang war
in the prohibition era, but those conflicts had long since subsided. I could
not see that they had any relevance to the scene that I was seeking to
understand.

Research Methods: What Do You Quantify?

The issue should not be qualitative versus quantitative research method
but rather what is to be quantified and how the measurements are to be
integrated with the descriptions and analyses of behavior. When sociolo
gists speak of quantification these days, nearly always they are thinking o
measuring attitudes, perceptions, and values through surveys—in other

words, focusing entirely on the subjective side of life. Early in my career, I had no use for surveys, but I later came to appreciate and use them, especially in combination with field observation and interviewing (Whyte, 1976; Whyte & Whyte, 1984).

On the other hand, although *SCS* contains very few numbers, major parts of the book are based on quantification, the measurement (albeit imprecise) of observed and reported behavior. When I reported that, over a period of months in 1937 and 1938, some or all of the members of the Norton Street gang could be observed on their corner five to six evenings a week, that was a quantitative statement. When I reported that, some months later, while some low ranking members of that group continued to congregate on the street corner, members of the leadership subgroup could no longer be seen there, that was also a quantitative statement. Putting the two statements together gives us a quantitative conclusion on changes in group and individual behavior. Similarly, when I report on how to identify the leader of a stable informal group, that method is based on quantitative observations: the leader frequently (but not always) proposes actions then performed by the group. When someone else proposes a change in activity, it does not take place unless the leader gives his assent or makes a move in the direction of the proposed change.

Perhaps the problem with recognizing that such reports are based on quantification arises because, in survey research, we never expect to find correlations of 1.0 and are frequently happy with correlations of .30, accounting for only 9% of the total variance. In contrast, I have stated behavioral uniformities that can be observed 100% of the time in a group that has a stable leadership pattern. Furthermore, if this pattern is not observed in the group under study, either the group has recently come together and a pattern has not developed and stabilized or else the group is undergoing change where there is competition for leadership. One of the most exciting experiences of my North End study occurred around the clarification of this issue. The previous night, in response to my suggestion, Ernest Pecci (Doc) and Angelo Ralph Orlandella (Sam Franco) were identifying the individual leaders in 10 of the groups of younger boys in the store front recreation center. In nine of those cases, each named the same individual. In the 10th case, they could not agree whether it was Tony or Al, with each observer recounting incidents that supported his own conclusion. The following morning, when Kathleen and I were at breakfast, we heard Orlandella thundering up the stairs to our flat. He burst in upon us with the news that, right after the center had closed the previous night, Tony and Al had got into a fight and now their gang had split into two parts, some going with Tony and some with Al.

On the Nature of Science and Social Research

It seems to me that attacks on positivism confuse us by failing to distinguish between what is objectively out there to observe and how the researcher interprets the organization observed. I think it is important to distinguish between observation/description and interpretation and to base our analysis primarily on observation/description. Observation/description can be made as objective as humanly possible whereas interpretation is much more a product of the particular personality and character of the researcher and thus must contain some elements of subjectivity. Suppose the task is to observe a group: who is present, what topics are discussed, who proposes a change in group activity, who supports or opposes that proposal, and how and in what direction the activity changes. It should be possible for two observers to make the same observations, with a minimum of error. Furthermore, with modern technology, if members of the group or organization being studied are willing, their interactions and activities can be tape-recorded or videotaped so that any number of observers can make their quantitative observations and measurements. On the other hand, if the researcher describes the attitudes, values and beliefs of the members of the community or organization, based upon interviewing as well as observation, necessarily a large personal element comes into the interpretation process. For those reasons, I reject the Geertz statement (1988, p. 1, quoted by Riley in Chapter 14) that "cultural descriptions, filtered through the ethnographer, are actually second or third order fictions." I also challenge the Geertz claim that "there is no culture or organization 'out there' to be accurately represented by observers." I argue that some important aspects of culture and organization *are* "out there" to be observed. If that were not the case, it would be difficult, if not impossible to establish a truly scientific basis for the behavioral sciences.

I also challenge Riley's statement that my conclusions on the sociology of bowling and the relationship between changes in the interaction pattern and mental health "have proved more heuristic than others but they should be viewed as a particular conversation, bound in time and space by the rules governing their production" (Chapter 14).

I claim that my report on how to determine the structure of an informal group can be applied to any group anywhere by anyone competent to make field observations of interactions and changes in group activity. My statement on the sociology of bowling proposed a relationship between ranking in an informal group and athletic performance on some activities of importance to the group. Years ago, this relationship was tested experimentally in a project directed by Muzafer Sherif (1953). A report by O. J. Harvey (1953) found evidence supporting the propositions I stated. On the relationship between changes in the interaction pattern and mental health, this was tested semi-experimentally when I suggested to Doc what social conditions needed to be created to solve Long John's mental health problems, and Doc very skillfully brought about those conditions. To be sure, a single case does not prove the validity of an hypothesis, but it does point to ways of gathering further empirical evidence.

I would also argue that my theme on "The Social Role of the Settlement House" (Whyte, 1941) is generalizable beyond time and place. With my permission, anthropologist Scudder Mekeel (1943) used that article (also a chapter in *SCS*) in analyzing relations between American Indians and the Bureau of Indian Affairs (BIA). He claimed he only had to substitute "BIA" for "settlement house" and "Indians" for "corner boys"; otherwise almost every word fitted what he had observed.

It seems to me that some critics have gone so far in attacking positivism as to eliminate the possibility of a scientific basis for social research. I have puzzled long over Jermier's statement in Chapter 15 that "truth lies in ever deeper levels of subjective reflection and disclosure and that science serves best when it serves the least." I can't make any sense out of that statement. How am I to demonstrate that my deeper levels of subjective reflection are yielding more valid conclusions than anybody else's deeper reflections? In the natural and physical sciences, we take it for granted that good research produces conclusions whose validity can be tested experimentally and whose findings can be adapted to practical purposes. Why should we settle for anything less in the behavioral sciences?

On Jermier's statements in Chapter 15 regarding critical epistemology, this seems to assume that a critical stance to one's own society necessarily involves some commitment to Marxist ideology. Does *SCS* really neglect the class basis of the problems of the slum dwellers or the existence of ethnic discrimination? It seems to me that the book deals with these issues in every way except simply labeling them.

Long ago, when I entered college, I considered myself a socialist and was attracted by Marxist ideology, without being a close student of those doctrines. I then believed in the classical socialist solution to economic and social problems in terms of government ownership and control of the means of production. Over the years, my studies and readings regarding the behavior of large bureaucratic organizations made me increasingly skeptical of that solution, long before the collapse of the command economies of Eastern Europe and the Soviet Union.

But that does not mean that I am unwilling to express my political commitments—in my work. I am committed to building the *applied* behavioral sciences. That means focusing my interest on ideas that individuals, groups, and organizations can act on, rather than speculating on global solutions for national economies.

In *SCS* I was illustrating the value of recognizing and working with indigenous leadership. In my industrial and rural development research, I was exploring the value of worker or small farmer or peasant participation in decision making, as a means of increasing productivity and benefiting the underdogs. Since 1970, I have been pursuing an interest in employee ownership and worker cooperatives, both in applied field research and in working with congressmen to develop the Small Business Employee Ownership Act of 1980.

It had long been believed that worker cooperatives were not likely to be viable economic organizations. When I learned of the Mondragón cooperative complex in the Basque country of Spain—the most impressive refutation of that condition—I had to go to Mondragón (first in 1975) to discover what could be learned from that case that might be applied elsewhere. Continuing research in Mondragón led to a book (Whyte & Whyte, 1988) that has attracted wide attention from practitioners as well as scholars interested in finding better ways to promote and develop employee ownership and worker cooperatives. Through this line of work, I have played a small role in a social movement spreading from industrialized nations of the west into Eastern Europe and the Soviet Union. Consultants familiar with the research literature in this field are now playing influential roles in Eastern Europe and the Soviet Union in seeking to develop openings for employee ownership and worker cooperatives. My political commitments have thus supported more far reaching changes in national economies than I would have thought possible when I began this work.

IIB
Current Inquiries About Organizational Culture

Where chaos begins, classical science stops. For as long as the world has had physicists inquiring in to the laws of nature, it has suffered a special ignorance about disorder in the atmosphere, in the turbulent sea, in the fluctuations of wildlife populations, in the oscillations of the heart and the brain. The irregular side of nature, the discontinuous and erratic side—these have been puzzles to science, or worse monstrosities.

—JAMES GLEICK
(*Chaos*, 1987, p. 3)

In the previous section we used a well known culture study from an earlier era to begin to access the way investigators think about and do their research. In Section IIB we attempt to widen and deepen the scope of this issue. We invited three scholars, Debra Meyerson, Michael Rosen, and Edgar H. Schein, whose empirical work was presented in Part II of the book, to share with us their thoughts on the research process. We also extended this invitation to two other scholars, Barbara Czarniawska-Joerges from Sweden and Harrison Trice. To Trice we entrusted the additional task of commentary on the papers in this section by the other four authors. Taken together, these voices on cultural research extend in interesting and thought-provoking ways the dialogue on doing cultural research in organizations.

Several points ought to be born in mind as you read these chapters. First, Meyerson, Rosen, and Schein's empirical work published in Part I of the book was specifically chosen to represent one of the three culture perspectives used in this book. It does not follow that the authors themselves necessarily limit themselves to that perspective. At any given time, or over time, these authors may work within more than one such perspective. This is most clearly illustrated in this volume in the two presentations by Rosen. "Breakfast at Spiro's: Dramaturgy and Dominance" in Part I illustrates a differentiation perspective. "Scholars, Travelers and Thieves: On Concept, Method, and Cunning in Organizational Ethnography" in this section of Part II reflects much more clearly what we have labeled the ambiguity perspective on culture. In fact, when we asked Rosen in August 1990 to give us his thoughts on research method, given his "Breakfast at Spiro's" study, he commented very quickly that his thinking and approach on cultural research had changed radically since that earlier work, which he now considers rather narrow and limiting.

We are not making that kind of evaluative judgment about any of the cultural perspectives. Rather, we want to be clear that researchers are not necessarily confined to any given theoretical frame for their work.

Second, we asked Meyerson, Rosen, Schein, and Czarniawska-Joerges to focus on broad scale issues of doing research on culture rather than on the nitty gritty of research technique. This provides an important context for Trice's comments about the attention these four authors gave to method in this book. They were not asked to focus on that aspect of research. Having said this, it is important to deliberate on Trice's observation that we need to document and explain more fully how we do research on organization culture so that others who follow us can see what it is we have done. Careful documentation of method aids both learning and re-examination of published work, although there are those among us who believe one can never repeat a study of organizational culture. One steps into a river of moving water and nothing we observe or experience is ever the same again. We note that the appendix that Whyte published of his *Street Corner Society* study (Whyte, 1955) meets some of Trice's concerns. Whyte, in addition, gave all his field notes to the Cornell University archives so that they would be available for subsequent examination over the decades.

Trice adds a discussion of the use of quantitative methods in organizational culture research. This is a valuable facet of the research issue that is not addressed elsewhere in this book.

17

What Is Culture?

EDGAR H. SCHEIN

Organizational culture as a concept has taken hold, but it is not yet clear whether it will survive as a useful and viable addition to the conceptual armamentarium of organization studies. And the issue, as I see it, revolves around the core definition, both from a formal conceptual point of view and from a practical applied point of view. We cannot build a useful concept if we cannot agree on how to define it, "measure" it, study it, and apply it in the real world of organizations.

Right now I see several competing approaches to the definition and study of organizational culture:

1. *The Survey Research Approach.* In this approach the passion to measure and quantify leads to the de facto definition of culture as something that is measurable through individual questionnaires (e.g., Hofstede, 1980; Hofstede & Bond, 1988; Kilmann, 1984). Interestingly, the proponents of this method start with "deep" conceptual definitions of culture as "mental models" or "underlying assumptions," but their subsequent attempts to measure it by questionnaires and the forcing of the data into dimensions derived a priori or by factor analysis implies that culture is definable at the surface attitude level. In this approach culture and "climate" become virtually synonymous concepts and it is not clear why one should retain the culture concept at all. What does it add?

AUTHOR'S NOTE: The material in this chapter is an expansion and elaboration of ideas originally presented in my 1985 book *Organizational Culture and Leadership*. The tables and figures are taken from that work (Schein, 1985a). Additional elaboration can be found in my recent article in the *American Psychologist* (Schein, 1990).

Furthermore, if one starts with a definition of culture as an aspect of the "deep structure" of an organization or some of its parts, it is highly unlikely that the pre-determined dimensions that lead to questionnaire construction adequately cover the conceptual terrain that culture deals with in human systems. This approach also presupposes that organizational cultures have common dimensions and that these dimensions are the most important aspect to study. Another possibility is that cultures, like personalities, are in part unique and that the power of the culture concept will ultimately lie in its ability to force us to look at the uniqueness of organizations rather than their common properties.

2. *The Analytical Descriptive Approach.* In this approach, as in the survey research approach, the dominant definitional force comes from the need to describe and measure culture. But in this approach one breaks culture down analytically into components that are empirically more tractable and settles for studies of those components (e.g., Harris & Sutton, 1986; Martin & Siehl, 1983; Schall, 1983; Trice & Beyer, 1984; Wilkins, 1983b). Thus the core concept remains implicit and often undefined, while its manifestations such as rites, rituals, and organizational stories, symbolic manifestations of the "deeper" phenomena, occupy center stage and become the de facto definition of culture.

As a research strategy this approach is very practical, but as a conceptual strategy it imposes a possibly undesirable bias and makes assumptions that may not be valid from other points of view. Specifically, this approach fractionates a concept whose primary theoretical utility may be to draw attention to the holistic and systemic aspects of organizational phenomena. And in this analytical decomposition one may lose validity in that the true meaning of the symbolic or behavioral manifestations may not be decipherable without understanding a deeper set of phenomena that tie those manifestations together.

3. *The Ethnographic Approach.* The ethnographic approach taken from anthropology and sociology starts with the assumption that there are deeper structures and that those structures cannot be unraveled or understood without intensive and extensive observation supplemented by interview data from cultural insiders (informants). Such research leads to what have been called "thick descriptions" (Geertz, 1973) that bring out the uniqueness and complexity of cultural phenomena very well, but paradoxically leave unexamined the conceptual and definitional problems of the concept of culture as applied to organizations and subunits of organizations. Instead such research has focused more on occupational communities and broader issues such as the "management of emotions" in all kinds of organizational

contexts (e.g., Barley, 1983; Van Maanen, 1988; Van Maanen & Barley, 1984; Van Maanen & Kunda, 1989).

One core assumption in this approach is that culture can ultimately only be deciphered as it is "enacted." In other words, the implication is that culture does not exist conceptually except in the observable behavioral manifestations enacted by the members of that culture. But when one examines the definitions that lie behind this observational strategy, one finds conceptually vague things like "the way we do things around here" or "common systems of meaning" that belie the "depth" of the observational methods.

Similarly, though conceptually the implication is that culture is a holistic systemic phenomenon, the ethnographic method often forces one to limit one's observations to some limited aspect of the group's behavior and explain that aspect in great detail without necessarily tying that entire behavioral set into other phenomena that may exist in that group.

Toward a Conceptual Resolution: Clinical/Analytic/Descriptive

Why do we need the concept of culture anyway? What does it add that concepts like norms, behavior patterns, and climate do not adequately convey? Why not just settle for the study of symbols and observed behavior patterns in their own right? Why do we need a conceptually "deeper" level? To answer these questions we should pause and ask ourselves a bit about the origin of the culture concept. Why was it taken out of the context of representing some of the more refined aspects of social phenomena into anthropology as a core concept for studying societies?

Culture implies stability. Without doing the necessary historical analysis, I will speculate that the concept was needed first of all to explain the fact that in most societies certain phenomena persisted over time and displayed remarkable stability even in the face of pressures toward change. This stability would be especially noticeable in some of the preliterate societies that had survived in a basically unchanged way for centuries. Culture, then, has something to do with long-range stability.

Culture emphasizes conceptual sharing. Secondly, I would speculate that what struck early ethnographers was the remarkable degree of similarity not only of manifest behavior but also the perceptions, cognitions, and feelings of the members of a given society, suggesting that there was something under the surface that new members learned that led to a high degree of similarity of outlook. Culture, then, has something to do with *sharing* or consensus among the members of a group. The most obvious aspect of such sharing is the common language and conceptual categories that are discovered whenever one studies a social group that has had any kind of history and shared experience. The study of socialization processes, especially their content, then became one of the primary ways of deciphering what the common underlying shared things were.

Culture implies patterning. Thirdly, I would speculate that what struck at least some anthropologists was the degree to which there were patterns evident in societies. The observed regularities reflected higher order phenomena that created patterns and paradigms, sometimes leading to premature formulations of cultural types. The fact that early typologies proved to be more stereotypic and ignored important variations among and within societies only reinforced the idea that *patterns* had to be studied carefully and were somehow at the crux of deciphering cultural phenomena.

Culture implies dynamics. How is one to explain the perpetuation of observed regularities and the ability of a group to perpetuate patterns over long periods of time and across many generations of membership? The analysis of culture pushes us to the analysis of how culture is created and perpetuated, thus leading to studies of the socialization process and a renewed emphasis on origins. Anthropologists had difficulty with cultural origins because one could not obtain historical data on the kinds of societies that were studied. Current attempts to apply culture to organizations do not suffer from this limitation because one can reconstruct historically the origin of organizations. In fact, some of the best cultural analyses in organization studies have been conducted by historians because they have been able to capture the dynamic, holistic patterning that is characteristic of cultures (e.g., Chandler, 1977; Dyer, 1986; Pettigrew, 1979; Westney, 1987).

Culture implies all aspects of group life. If one looks at early ethnographies, one is struck by the fact that cultural phenomena penetrate all of the aspects of daily life. There is virtually nothing that we do that is not colored by shared ways of looking at things. In analyzing culture, then, it becomes important not to develop simplistic models that rely only on a few key dimensions, but to find models that reflect the vastness that culture represents.

What we need is a model of culture that does justice to (a) what the concept connotes and (b) what has been its source of utility in other fields. Such a model comes out of an eclectic approach that draws on anthropology, sociology, and social psychology, and that reflects research methods broader than the traditional ones. Specifically, we need to add to other methods what I have called the "clinical perspective" (Schein, 1987) by which I mean what one learns when one is in a helper/consultant role (as contrasted with a researcher role). Sometimes one learns most about what culture is, how it operates, and what its implications are when one is helping an organization to solve real problems. At such times the insiders are more open, more willing to reveal what they really think and feel, and, thereby, make it more obvious what things are shared and how things are patterned. At such times one also begins to understand what it means to go to "deeper" levels.

A Formal Definition of Culture

Culture is:

1. A pattern of shared basic assumptions,
2. invented, discovered, or developed by a given group,
3. as it learns to cope with its problems of external adaptation and internal integration,
4. that has worked well enough to be considered valid, and, therefore,
5. is to be taught to new members of the group as the
6. correct way to perceive, think, and feel in relation to those problems.

The Definition Examined and Explained

Culture, in any of its meanings, is a property of a human group. If one cannot define the group, then one cannot define the culture of that group. It will not help us in the conceptual domain to do what is sometimes done, namely, to define the group as "all those people who share some common behavior or attitude." In other words, to define a group as a set of people who share a culture is to be circular and to remain unenlightened on what precisely it is that they share. So we must start with group definitions that are more objective—sets of people who have a history with each other, who have shared experiences together, where membership is sufficiently stable to have allowed some common learning to occur.

At the simplest conceptual level, then, we can say that culture is the shared common learning output. But this does not yet tell us what sorts of things groups learn, retain, and pass on, or why they do this. What this "model" does say, however, is that only what is *shared* is, by definition, cultural. It does not make sense, therefore, to think about high or low consensus cultures or cultures of ambiguity or conflict. If there is no consensus or if there is conflict or if things are ambiguous, then, by definition, that group does not have a culture in regard to those things. It may have subcultures, smaller groups that have a shared something, a consensus about something, but the concept of sharing or consensus is core to the definition, not something about which we have an empirical choice.

The next part of the definition draws more on social, cognitive, and dynamic psychology. When one observes new groups or studies the histories of new organizations, one observes that all such organizations have to deal with two fundamental sets of issues—external adaptation and internal integration—and that they deal with such issues at the behavioral, cognitive, and emotional level.

The problems of external adaptation and internal integration specify what the learning focus is. Analyzing these problems, the primary issues faced by all groups, gives us an important insight into the likely "content" of any given culture. In other words, a given group's culture will reflect what that group has learned in solving its particular problems in its own history. A different group that has had different problems and experiences will, by definition, have a culture with different content.

Common dimensions tend to be useful only at a fairly abstract level such as those shown in Table 17.1, and even those categories are subject to theoretical revision as we learn more about group histories. So the issues identified in Table 17.1 are only a first approximation at identifying the dimensions of culture based on the analysis of what issues any group must resolve both internally and externally. The breadth of these issues also reminds us that culture content can cover a very wide territory since it reflects all of a group's shared learning, not only the few dimensions that may be of interest to a hypothesis testing oriented researcher. If one were to determine all of the things a group has learned in all of the categories of Table 17.1, one would have a full blown ethnography, and only then could one claim to have described "the" culture of a group or organization.

If one wanted a more parsimonious theory of culture content, one could derive a higher order set of issues that are implied in almost all culture research, as shown in Table 17.2. However, at this level of abstractness one is at risk of not really capturing what is uniquely important in any group.

The next issue in defining culture is whether or not one should view culture as a set of shared behaviors, skills, perceptions, expectations, symbols, beliefs, values, attitudes, assumptions, feelings, or mental models. No doubt even other categories could be considered as candidates. Most of the current definitions seem to blur distinctions that have become

TABLE 17.1. The External and Internal Tasks Facing All Groups

External Adaptation Tasks	Internal Integration Tasks
Developing consensus on:	Developing consensus on:
1. The core mission, functions, and primary tasks of the organization vis-à-vis its environments.	1. The common language and conceptual system to be used, including basic concepts of time and space.
2. The specific goals to be pursued by the organization.	2. The group boundaries and criteria for inclusion.
3. The basic means to be used in accomplishing the goals.	3. The criteria for the allocation of status, power, and authority.
4. The criteria to be used for measuring results.	4. The criteria for intimacy, friendship, and love in different work and family settings.
5. The remedial or repair strategies if goals are not achieved.	5. The criteria for the allocation of rewards and punishments.
	6. Concepts for managing the unmanageable—ideology and religion.

Source: Adapted from *Organizational Culture and Leadership* (pp. 52, 56) by E. H. Schein, 1985a, San Francisco: Jossey-Bass. Copyright 1985 by Jossey-Bass. Adapted by permission.

very important within psychology. Thus to talk about "beliefs, attitudes, and values" in one breath is putting together a set of concepts that operate very differently in the psychic life of an individual. What then should culture be? All of the above?

To resolve such a problem conceptually, I have drawn on a dynamic model of how I believe the learning process proceeds in any new group or organization. Basically the founder of the new group starts with some beliefs, values, and assumptions about how to proceed and teaches those to new members through a whole variety of mechanisms. What is for him or her a basic reality becomes for the group a set of interim values and beliefs about which they have limited choice. The group then behaves in a certain way based on the founder's beliefs and values, and either succeeds or fails. If it fails, the group eventually dissolves and no culture is formed. If it succeeds, and this process repeats itself, what were originally the beliefs, values, and assumptions of the founders come to be validated in the shared experiences of the group.

This process always starts with beliefs and values that represent predictions about how things are (beliefs) and statements of how things ought to be (values). As they get validated for the group, what was originally a value comes to be gradually transformed cognitively into an assumption (a belief

TABLE 17.2. Some Underlying Dimensions of Organizational Culture

Dimension	Questions to Be Answered
1. The organization's relationship to its environment	Does the organization perceive itself to be dominant, submissive, harmonizing, searching out of niche?
2. The nature of human activity	Is the "correct" way for humans to behave to be dominant/pro-active, harmonizing, or passive/fatalistic?
3. The nature of reality and truth	How do we define what is true and what is not true; and how is truth ultimately determined both in the physical and social world? By pragmatic test, reliance on wisdom, or social consensus?
4. The nature of time	What is our basic orientation in terms of past, present, and future, and what kinds of time units are most relevant for the conduct of daily affairs?
5. The nature of human nature	Are humans basically good, neutral, or evil, and is human nature perfectible of fixed?
6. The nature of human relationships	What is the "correct" way for people to relate to each other, to distribute power and affection? Is life competitive or cooperative? Is the best way to organize society on the basis of individualism or groupsim? Is the best authority system autocratic/paternalistic or collegial/participative?
7. Homogeneity vs. diversity	Is the group best off it it is highly diverse or if it is highly homogeneous, and should individuals in a group be encouraged to innovate or conform?

Source: Adapted from *Organizational Culture and Leadership* (p. 86) by E. H. Schein, 1985a, San Francisco: Jossey-Bass. Copyright 1985 by Jossey-Bass. Adapted by permission.

about how things are, now based on experience, and therefore no longer in need of being tested). As the group builds up more common experience, it gradually transforms its values and beliefs into assumptions. If this is a shared process because of stable membership and common experiences, the group evolves a shared assumption set. The more these assumptions are validated, the more they come to be taken for granted and drop out of awareness.

Validation occurs both externally and internally. From an external point of view, it is measured by actual success in task accomplishment. From an internal point of view it is validated by reducing the anxiety that is associated with meaninglessness and unpredictability. Shared assumptions thus get their stability in part from the fact that they provide meaning, structure, and predictability to the members of the group.

If culture is something the group learns, how does this learning occur? Here we need to draw on learning theory and note that three kinds of learning promote unusual levels of stability of learned responses (Schein, 1983). One mechanism derives from Pavlovian conditioning and is based on the avoidance of pain. If a group has made mistakes that have led to failures, it will develop assumptions about what *not to do* that tend *not* to get tested because the testing produces very high levels of anxiety.

A second mechanism derives from Skinner's observation that partial random reinforcement can produce more stable behavior than regular predictable reinforcement. If something works all the time and then one day stops working, it is easier to unlearn than if something works most of the time in an unpredictable pattern.

A third learning mechanism derives from gestalt psychology, where one notes that whole conceptual patterns can shift at once, the phenomenon of "insight." Such patterns derive their stability from the fact that they are patterns, suggesting that if culture is a pattern of assumptions, one cannot expect any given isolated assumption to change unless the pattern as a whole changes.

If we are to understand the stability of shared assumption sets, we must investigate historically how the group learned those assumptions in the first place. Depending on the learning history, one would have different hypotheses about how stable any given cultural assumption actually was and how it could be unlearned, should that become desirable or necessary.

The definition emphasizes that unless such assumptions are passed on to new members one cannot define them as part of the culture. The passing on of assumptions through the socialization process is the test of sharedness and taken-for-grantedness. It distinguishes assumptions that are idiosyncratic from those that are a shared characteristic of the group.

Finally, the definition emphasizes that if we make basic assumptions about different aspects of reality, those assumptions will influence perceptions, thought, and feeling as well as overt behavior. But overt behavior is also influenced by local circumstances and immediate events, so if one is to define culture as a deeper phenomenon, one must define it in terms of deeper psychic categories. Behavioral regularities, in other words, could result from common environmental pressures, but common perceptions, thoughts, and feelings reflect more accurately a common learning process.

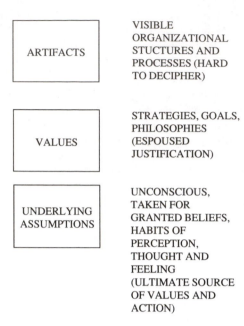

Figure 17.1. The Levels of Organizational Culture

Levels of Culture

Figure 17.1 summarizes these issues by acknowledging that culture is manifested at different levels and can therefore be studied at different levels provided one has understood the deeper levels. In other words, if I understand the pattern of shared basic assumptions of a group, I can decipher its espoused values and its behavioral rituals. But the reverse does not work. One cannot infer the assumptions unless one has done extensive ethnographic research.

How then can one study culture? Does one have to limit oneself to ethnographic studies? The answer is "no," because it turns out that if the members of an organization are motivated to study their own culture, one can provide them a process that reveals underlying assumption fairly readily.

This process relies on combining the observations of an outsider with the analyses of a group of insiders (Evered & Louis, 1981; Schein, 1985a).

The essence of the method is to give a motivated group of insiders a model such as is presented in Figure 17.1, and ask them as a group to brainstorm the contents of each box. By recording all of the artifacts the group comes up with, stimulated by questions and observations from the outsider/consultant, one can make visible the manifest side of the culture. One then pushes the group to name the values that are implied by these artifacts and, when those have been examined, pushes the group further to identify the shared underlying assumptions that lie behind the artifacts and values.

If one devotes a number of hours to such an exercise, one can go surprisingly far in surfacing even some of the deeper assumptions held by the group. By then extending this process to other representative groups within an organization, one can map out at least portions of the culture relevant to the issue that is motivating the group to do the analysis. Such issues usually have to do with examining strategic options, the potential resistances to change that a turnaround may encounter, the need to examine whether certain assumptions that have worked in the past are still well matched with environmental realities, the need to identify aspects of the culture that the group wants to preserve in a period of rapid change, and so on.

Summary and Conclusions

I have tried in this essay to lay out the conceptual issues involved in defining organizational culture. The definition proposed is an attempt to be very clear and explicit about the underlying model of culture that is implied. This model has the advantage that it (a) points clearly to the kinds of variables that have to be considered in studying culture, (b) shows why some of the methods currently in use fall short, and (c) provides enough face validity to enable practitioners to use the concept constructively in deciphering their own culture.

The process of deciphering a given group's culture is outlined, and it is pointed out that if an outsider using this model works with a motivated insider group, many of the most critical dimensions of a given group's culture can be deciphered in a fairly short period of time.

18

Acknowledging and Uncovering Ambiguities in Cultures

DEBRA E. MEYERSON

The notion that cultures embody many sources of ambiguity was put forth in Chapter 9. That chapter discussed several sources and expressions of cultural ambiguity and showed a variety of ways in which people might respond to ambiguities. It argued that in some cultures ambiguities may be experienced as "normal" and pervasive, whereas in others ambiguities may be experienced as "abnormal" and perverse. In some cultures ambiguities are openly expressed; in others ambiguities are normatively suppressed. More generally, my previous chapter argued that what experiences of ambiguity mean and how they are enacted in a given setting are constructions of culture.

Similarly, how we, as researchers of culture, treat ambiguities in our studies of culture is shaped by the values and norms of our own professional culture. I hinted at this idea in the previous chapter's conclusions: "The exclusion of ambiguity from the study of culture may be as much an artifact of our own community's values and beliefs as it is of the cultures we study. Thus, to include ambiguities in the study of culture is to challenge our definition of culture and to question the ideology underlying that definition."

This chapter takes up this challenge.[1] Although I was asked to write about the methods one might use to study ambiguities in culture, I thought it was first important to address why one might care about ambiguities in cultures and discuss some of the obstacles in our own profession to taking up this inquiry. I begin by discussing why most studies of culture tend to exclude ambiguities, and I examine how and why this exclusion, and thus our most accepted definitions of culture, has come to be viewed as legitimate and "normal." The section that follows addresses what is to be gained by acknowledging ambiguities in our studies of culture and discusses the theoretical, epistemological, and political implications of acknowledging ambiguities. Finally, in the last half of the chapter, I suggest some methods that enable researchers, who are inclined to do so, to uncover ambiguities, even in those cultures that tend to suppress them.

Before starting, it is worth reviewing what I mean by ambiguity. As described in more detail in my earlier chapter in this book, ambiguity can arise from lack of clarity or from multiple meanings or beliefs. For example, in a study of hospital social workers (Meyerson, 1989), lack of clarity stemmed from seemingly unclear structures, including amorphous role and occupational boundaries, loose connections between means and ends (what they did and what occurred), and unclear or irreconcilable goals and evaluation criteria. Multiple meanings and beliefs resulted from fragmented, contradictory, and unclear ideologies and interests. Insofar as the ambiguities were rooted in the values, beliefs, interests, and structures of the collective (organization or occupation), the ambiguities were inherently cultural. Yet these ambiguities can be enacted at the individual or collective levels of analysis. For example, an occupation's ideology may contain contradictory beliefs about an issue such as professionalism. These contradictions could surface in an individual's ambivalence about his or her professionalism or in contradictory beliefs across different members of the culture. Like the earlier chapter, this chapter speaks of ambiguities that are fundamentally cultural and enacted at both individual and collective levels of analysis.

Why Ambiguities Are Excluded from Studies of Culture

Why do students of organizational culture dislike ambiguities? Why do we tend to notice (and value) that which is clear, stable, and "orderly" (that which we can readily understand, measure, and control) and ignore that which is unclear, unstable, and "disorderly" (that which is more fragmented, intractable, and difficult to control)? These preferences betray our professional identity. They reveal our professional culture's dominant values, interests, and beliefs.

Although many organizational scientists remain skeptical about whether the discipline is "truly" a science, few could doubt that science, as an ideology as much as a method (Larson, 1977), dominates the profession. To understand social systems as a scientist, is to view them as organized worlds with objective, tractable properties: stable laws, rational order, and enduring and discoverable structures (Reinharz, 1979). As social scientists, we strive to understand the objective, enduring properties of social systems in the hope of learning how better to control them (e.g., Hubbard, 1990; Keller, 1987).

Although some scientists and social scientists do focus on the "disorderly" properties of systems (e.g., Chaos Theory), much of this work attempts to locate the enduring "order" of the disorder. Most studies in organizational science, including those outside the domain of culture research, that explicitly focus on ambiguities construct ambiguity as an abnormal condition to control. For example, studies of role ambiguity tend to assume that ambiguity is a pathological condition and, therefore, concentrate on locating moderator variables that enable individuals to cope with or control this experience (e.g., Kahn, Wolfe, Quinn, Snock, & Rosenthal, 1964). Similarly, other studies, which focus on ways that organizations can strategically use or cope with ambiguity (e.g., Eisenberg, 1984; McCaskey, 1982), implicitly assume that the experience of ambiguity is somehow abnormal and should be controlled. Even those studies that speak to the benefits of ambiguity (e.g., March, 1976; Weick, 1979), tend to treat ambiguity as an abnormal condition that affects a range of individual and organizational processes, such as decision making. Questions about how to manage or control this condition sometimes surface even in these treatments.

Thus, even in its approach to ambiguities, science must maintain its fundamental quest for truth, and, at some level, its pursuit of control; simply acknowledging ambiguities may be inconsistent with the values of science. The pursuit of control also conforms well to bureaucratic interests (e.g., Calas & Smircich, 1989; Ferguson, 1984; Krieger, 1987). Indeed, Weberian rationality asserts bureaucracy as an organizational form whose order is based on removing ambiguity in the pursuit of continuity, stability, and manageability (e.g., Ferguson, 1984; Millman & Kanter, 1975).

How these deeply institutionalized values and interests shape the nature of our research questions, approaches, and theories is dramatically demonstrated in the evolution of the concept of culture within organizational theory. Initially, organizational scholars used the culture concept as a metaphor to study organizations as symbolic enterprises—as forums in which meanings are socially constructed and expressed. Culture was the code word for the subjective side of organizational life and its study represented an ontological rebellion against the dominant functionalist, or "scientific," paradigm (Barley, Meyer, & Gash, 1988). Culture researchers were also more willing to employ less traditional ("less scientific") qualitative methods and challenge the limitations of the more traditional ones (Van Maanen, 1979, 1983).

But as it became part of the vocabulary of organizational scholarship, more and more researchers began to employ culture as a variable rather than as a "root metaphor," something an "organization had" versus something "it was" (Calas & Smircich, 1987; Smircich, 1983b). Organizations that "had" certain types of cultures ostensibly could achieve desired outcomes. Thus, culture became a mechanism with which to achieve managerial effectiveness and control. Several researchers began to link various types of cultures (e.g., "strong vs. weak") to certain outcome variables (e.g., satisfaction, productivity, internal integration) (e.g., Deal & Kennedy, 1982; Wilkins & Ouchi, 1983). "Culture" became the type of construct it was initially imported to challenge: another objective and enduring property of the organization that could be readily identified, measured, and ultimately controlled. Not surprisingly, several researchers began to search for the antecedents of "strong cultures" and other properties of culture that might lead to desired outcomes (Barley et al., 1988; Staw, 1984). Popular management books on the topic (e.g., Davis, 1984; Peters & Waterman, 1982) propagated and perhaps furthered this general approach in the academic literature. In any case, after a stunningly short period, the dominant treatment of culture in both academic and popular literatures looked much like traditional organization science: another independent, dependent, or moderator variable that could further such objectives as control and productivity.[2]

This transformation—from an alternative to, to an exemplar of, functionalist managerial research—points to some important forces in and lessons for culture researchers (Calas & Smircich, 1987). Barley et al. (1988) attribute this transformation primarily to political forces favoring managerial interests, but they also acknowledge the overwhelming resilience of functionalism in our culture. The dominance of functionalism can in turn be explained by the profession's embeddedness in the institution of science. In particular, the ideology of science (in the interest of managerialism) can explain how a concept that was initially used to help appreciate the symbolic features of organizational life was transformed to a concept that promised to provide control over these features (Harding, 1986; Hubbard, 1990). In this quest for control, ambiguities must be suppressed in favor of a dominant and stable set of values, beliefs, and interpretations.

Methodological Biases Against Ambiguities

Our profession's embeddedness in science can also explain why our discipline's favored methods have been oriented toward eliminating or ignoring ambiguities. For example, survey methods, which are used occasionally to study culture, do not allow for equivocal or unclear responses. Respondents to a survey must choose a single answer and are presumed to be clear and unambivalent about their response (Reinharz, 1979).

More popular quantitative methods for the study of culture include content analysis, which often relies on data elicited through interviews (e.g., Martin, Sitkin, & Boehm, 1985) and more recently the Q-sort method (e.g., Chatman, 1989; O'Reilly, Chatman, & Caldwell, 1990), which asks respondents to select among a choice of presented values. In different ways, these methods try to locate consensus (e.g., about values), often at a very high level of abstraction. For example, studies relying on content analysis assume discrete pockets of consensus and clarity within subcultures, even if some such studies focus on the disagreements between subcultures (e.g., Martin et al., 1985). The Q-sort method makes central what has been "agreed upon" in the firm, and then tries to identify the "fit" between dominant firm values and individual (e.g., O'Reilly et al., 1990). These methods use standard reliability and validity checks to assert the significance (and meaningfulness) of their results. Further, and most importantly, the methods assume that the identified cultural properties (i.e., shared values) are stable and clear. Whether these properties are derived from the data (content analysis) or asserted by the researcher and then selected by subjects (Q-sort), they are assumed to be meaningful to the cultural members, rather than artifacts of the research environment. Naturally left out by these methods are those aspects of culture that are diffuse, unclear, volatile, and irreconcilable.

The potential for interview methodology to capture ambiguities is also limited. The dominance of science in this society helps explain why our language to express that which is unclear, diffuse, or contradictory seems so deficient (March, 1976). When ambiguity experiences do surface in interviews, respondents sometimes describe their experience in a way that eliminates or somehow clarifies them. For example, in a recent study (Meyerson, 1989), when respondents were asked to describe sources of ambiguity in their roles, they tended to clarify the roles as they described them. When they talked about a contradiction, they often did so in a way that specified the contingencies or overarching principles, and in so doing resolved the inherent contradiction. Further, as I will describe below, interviews may be most appropriate for capturing that which is socially desirable. Thus, the problems of interview methodology are exacerbated when this method is used to elicit ambiguities in organizational and occupational cultures that value clarity and consensus and devalue ambiguities.

Finally, even the method of representing cultures through more qualitative traditional ethnographies has tended to eliminate ambiguities. Studies that reflect ambiguities are often taken to be sloppy or incomplete rather than reflective of a different type of reality. They may be discounted as "interesting" but not valid (Weick, 1989). Further, ethnographies that acknowledge the ambiguities of cultural life risk the fate of being discarded as bad stories, which could be fatal in this genre. Without the full authority of science, ethnographies must tell good stories to be convincing (Clifford, 1986; Van Maanen, 1987; 1990a). Good stories have clear story lines. Thus, ambiguities which cloud a story may fundamentally undermine the authority of an ethnographic text.

Authors of classic ethnographics remove ambiguities in the process of studying and writing about cultures. "By representing the Nuer, the Trobriands, or the Balinese as whole subjects, sources of meaningful intention, the ethnographer transforms the research situation's ambiguities and diversities of meaning into an integrated portrait. But it is important to notice what has dropped out of sight" (Clifford, 1983, p. 132). The following section explores "what has dropped out of sight."

What Acknowledging Ambiguity Can Bring to Studies of Culture

In the last few years, a number of anthropologists, even those who have gained professional status on the basis of, what Clifford terms, their "scientific ethnographies" have been considering, self reflectively, what has been "left out of sight" of culture studies and what institutional biases account for these exclusions (e.g., Clifford & Marcus; 1986; Geertz, 1988b; Marcus & Fisher, 1986). This discourse has not only produced insightful critiques of traditional ethnography, it has also generated experiments in alternative genres (e.g., Crapanzano, 1986; Rosaldo, 1986). Clifford (1983) considers some of these alternative visions of culture:

> For Bakhtin, preoccupied with the representation of non-homogeneous wholes, there are no integrated cultural worlds or languages. All attempts to posit such abstract unities are constructs of monological power. A 'culture' is, concretely, an open-ended, creative dialogue of subcultures, of insiders and outsiders, of diverse factions; a "language" is the interplay and struggle of regional dialects, professional jargons, generic commonplaces, the speech of different age groups, individuals, and so forth. (pp. 136-137)

By challenging the epistemological and political authority of a once privileged dominant interpretation of culture, such critiques lend legitimacy to
multiple interpretations and multiple interests and thereby make central the
ambiguities of cultural life.

Likewise, a formulation of culture that acknowledges ambiguities will more
likely recognize and potentially legitimate a diverse chorus of voices, interests,
and perspectives that potentially exists within an organization; this perspective
thereby undermines universalistic claims of authority of a single dominant
voice. Clear, stable, and universal structures and symbols are seen as inven-
tions of management for the purpose of control; indeed, from this perspective,
the activity of culture is "plural and beyond the control of any individual"
(Clifford, 1983, p. 139).

A view that acknowledges ambiguities suggests new metaphors of culture,
such as a web (Martin & Meyerson, 1988). This image depicts culture as a
web of diverse, loosely coupled, and volatile networks of symbols and
relationships. When the importance of various issues, relationships, or voices
shift, so too would the specific image of culture (Martin & Meyerson, 1988;
Meyerson & Martin, 1987). This view, which sees culture as dynamic and
multivocal, represents a radical departure from those views that depict culture
as a mechanistic, hierarchical system of stable relationships and universal
symbols. Because of this perspective's implicit critique of the assumptions
underlying traditional conceptions of organizational cultures, it shares much
in common with feminist and other critiques of bureaucracy. As an alternative
to traditional mechanistic, univocal, and bureaucratic depictions of organizations, these scholars have also offered images, such as a web, that view
organizations as organic, multivocal, and political enterprises (Calas &
Smircich, 1989; Ferguson, 1984; Krieger, 1987; Martin, 1990d; Smircich,
1985b). Such images make central the ambiguities of organizational life and
the power processes that tend to suppress these ambiguities.

To organizational culture research, the potential contributions of an
approach that recognizes ambiguities could be comparable to those theoretical and epistemological challenges that feminist and postmodern scholars have been making in a variety of disciplines (e.g., Flax, 1990a, 1990b;
Keller, 1987). These scholars are posing important new questions to their
fields. For example, feminist historians who acknowledge the ambiguities
within historical representations are trying to uncover multiple representations and understand how one representation became legitimated as *the*
correct representation. These scholars have attempted to illuminate the
cultural and institutional processes that explain how one set of historical
representations get privileged while the multitude of other possible repre-

sentations get suppressed (Scott, 1988). Feminist scholars have waged similar critiques of the natural sciences in attempt to explain how one "way of knowing" and thus one set of interpretations has become privileged over other ways and understandings (e.g., Harding, 1986; Hubbard, 1990; Keller, 1987). As they recognize diverse ways of knowing, these scholars also make possible diverse, and sometimes irreconcilable, types of understandings of physical phenomena. By acknowledging the ambiguities of social or physical life, these self-reflective critiques demand implicitly, if not explicitly, that researchers examine the cultural and political assumptions that privilege one set of epistemologies, methods, interests, and thus understandings, while suppressing others.

Besides the theoretical, political, and epistemological insights that an ambiguity-acknowledging perspective can bring to the study of culture, it may also provide some timely practical understandings for those concerned with managing organizations. Specifically, those concerned about managing cultural diversity, innovation, highly complex technologies, and unclear technologies may benefit from insights generated by culture research that focuses on ambiguities. Some of the recent work in the field of human resources that discusses the management of culturally diverse workforces hints at the need to manage the ambiguity that inevitably results when people with diverse racial, ethnic, and societal backgrounds work together (Cox & Blake, 1990). Yet ironically, even these works tend to talk about the need to *manage* the ambiguity, rather than the need to learn how to live with it. Similarly, research on the management of innovation often points to the ambiguity and chaos inherent in the innovation process, specifically the need to leave considerable ambiguity in the role definitions of potential innovators (e.g., Nonaka & Yamanouchi, 1989; Pascale, 1990; Peters, 1987). These studies suggest that managers and innovators must somehow learn to live with ambiguity.

In addition, as Weick points out in this volume, the inherent complexity of some technologies will inevitably result in ambiguities in individuals' interpretation of events, which lead to system vulnerability. As illustrated by the Tenerife disaster, such ambiguities can be of great consequence to individuals and organizations. Finally, in Chapter 9 I described the lack of clarity inherent in the "technology" of social work. Many of the core processes, like caring, establishing relationships, and providing empathy are extremely difficult to specify. Yet for many of today's most pressing health problems, such as AIDS and old age, these more ambiguous process technologies may be every bit as appropriate as the clearer "scientific" medical technologies. Organizational and occupational cultures can have considerable impact on how individuals experience ambiguities (e.g., whether they experience ambiguity as freedom or threat, normal or abnormal) (Meyerson, 1989). Learning how and why organizational and occupational cultures legitimate and deligitimate ambiguities should therefore be of immediate practical concern to managers who want to enjoy the benefits of diversity and for those who want to encourage innovation.[3]

In sum, a perspective that acknowledges the ambiguities of cultural life can offer a variety of potential understandings. As a theoretical perspective, the potential of developing more holistic understandings of culture is compelling. As an epistemological stance, this perspective suggests that our task as researchers is to reflect the multiplicity of experiences and interpretations represented within a culture and to accept diverse "ways of knowing" and being. As a political position, this ambiguity-acknowledging perspective hopes to legitimate diversity in interpretations, beliefs, and interests and challenge forces that seek to value one set of interests, interpretations, and beliefs while suppressing others. And, as a practical interest, an understanding of how ambiguities are culturally enacted and experienced can provide helpful insight for organizations that want to live comfortably with diverse types of people without suppressing the diversity, for organizations that want to encourage innovation, for organizations that want to help individuals more effectively respond to highly complex information, and for organizations that want to allow and perhaps appreciate more "fuzzy" technologies. For these reasons, the task of trying to uncover and legitimate the ambiguities in cultures appears a compelling one. However, this task poses a number of methodological challenges.

Uncovering Ambiguities in Cultures

I have described some of the theoretical, epistemological, methodological, and political biases in the profession of organizational science that prevent us from acknowledging ambiguities in the cultures we study and have provided a number of reasons why it is worth trying to overcome these biases. Some of these biases surface in our questions about and interest in culture, our dominant theoretical approaches to culture, and our ways of knowing and writing culture. The limitations in our methods also reflect these biases.

In addition, the cultures of many of the organizations and occupations we study present their own obstacles to studying ambiguities. Many of the cultures we study, like our own, are deeply embedded in the institution of science (e.g., hospitals, research organizations, businesses) and are entrenched in the ethic of managerialism. Normatively, these cultures favor rationality, objectivity, and universality. Structurally, they are designed to produce order, predictability, and stability. Thus, whether the mechanism is normative or structural, many traditional western organizations and occupations strive to somehow eliminate, reduce, or suppress ambiguities.[4] Thus, the task of illuminating the ambiguities in cultures that tend to suppress them is a challenging one, particularly in light of the inappropriateness of our traditional methods of this task. Because of these obstacles, I will focus my discussion on methods that might illuminate ambiguities specifically in cultures that normatively suppress these experiences.

These prescriptions rely on and are limited by my experience in a study of hospital social workers (Meyerson, 1989), which is described in more detail in Chapter 9. The study took place in five hospitals. One hospital openly tolerated ambiguities; the other four did not.[5] The suggestions offered here are based primarily on my experiences in the four hospitals that disliked ambiguities. This study used several qualitative methods of data gathering and analysis, including over one year of participant observation, unstructured and structured interviews, and a structured written exercise. This diversity of methods enabled me to locate different sources of ambiguity and ultimately to compare the utility of each method for identifying various kinds of ambiguity experiences.

In general, the usefulness of various techniques for uncovering ambiguities largely depended upon whether, in Van Maanen's (1979) terms, the data were "presentational" or "operational." The former includes what informants choose to tell or show you, whereas the latter is what you, the researcher, hear or see. In a given context, presentational data tend to represent the norms about behaviors and interpretations—what one is supposed to experience—whereas operational data tend to reveal "actual" behaviors and interpretations—what one does experience.

The formality of methods that elicit presentational data, like interviews, may invoke self-consciousness, social desirability, and dominant values and norms. Thus, in contexts that hold strong norms against ambiguities, a researcher will find it difficult to uncover experiences of ambiguity simply by asking informants about their experiences. In my study, when I interviewed subjects who were in settings that devalued ambiguities about their experiences of ambiguity, they tended either to deny these experiences or to explain the ambiguities in a way that eliminated or minimized them (clarified the lack of clarity or resolved a contradiction). Yet when I observed these same subjects in informal settings, I often overheard them talking and joking about their experiences of ambiguity, including their feelings of confusion, uncertainty, and ambivalence. For this reason, it appears that methods that elicit presentational data, like interviews, may be better at capturing norms about ambiguity than capturing how people actually experience ambiguity. Methods that elicit presentational data will effectively confirm (and reify) an "agreed upon" or a normative set of interpretations and beliefs. Yet, experiences of ambiguity may be most interesting and most compelling in settings where people are least likely to admit these experiences. Indeed, what people lie about is often what is most central to them (Van Maanen, 1979).

Informal Settings

For this reason, to uncover ambiguities in settings that devalue them, researchers would benefit by relying primarily on operational data. Furthermore, observing informal settings may prove to be more revealing of ambiguities than observing formal settings of work. Formal settings, like interview methods, tend to invoke dominant norms of behavior and expression. One particularly sensitive supervisor realized that the social workers felt inhibited in the formal setting of highly structured meetings. During these meetings few of the social workers would voice their feelings and opinions, particularly if they were socially undesirable. To create a safer environment that would enable them to more freely express their reactions to ambiguities and other socially undesirable feelings, he designed periodic meetings that were intentionally less structured. These meetings had no agendas; they were "anything goes" time. As the supervisor intended, these meetings were filled with discussions about situations that made the social workers feel confused, unclear, or conflicted. Differences among the social workers surfaced freely. Although the social workers often complained that these meetings were a waste of time, attendance was excellent, and participation was fluid and chaotic.

These meetings were unusual in their capacity to elicit experiences of ambiguity. In most of the settings I studied, informal settings were much more revealing. Hallway chats, workshop breaks, and lunches frequently included conversations about work experiences that left the social workers feeling confused, unclear, or ambivalent. During these informal gatherings, it was not unusual to hear a group of social workers joking about a doctor who gave them little or no information about their treatment plans or whose treatment orientation conflicted with the social workers'. I tried to arrive at meetings early and leave late as conversations before and after meetings were more likely to reveal differences in opinion, interpretation, and intent among the social workers. These differences rarely surfaced during formal sessions.

Ambiguities were perhaps expressed most openly at parties. Parties suspend norms (Rosen, 1985), particularly when people have been drinking. People feel more free to talk about that which seems unclear, contradictory, and irreconcilable and to express their emotions regarding ambiguities.[6] Differences surface openly because people are more apt to voice opinions and interpretations that deviate from what might be normatively acceptable. At parties people openly debate and *play* "devil's advocate." In such settings, it is not unusual or normatively disruptive for people to move from one idea or opinion to another. One can even be hypocritical at parties and be perceived as provocative rather than deceitful. Groups exhibit hypocrisy as well. At one of the parties I attended, a group of social workers spent at least 30 minutes wavering between a self-aggrandizing discussion of their "professional" status and a self-pitying "bitch session" about their professional powerlessness. This discussion seemed to express ambivalence (and confusion) about their own sense of professionalism.

Symbolic Expressions

In addition to relying on conversations in informal settings, a variety of symbolic cues can express ambiguities. For example, the form of some rituals and practices sometimes revealed ambiguities. At a weekly staff meeting in one hospital I studied, social workers regularly came and went as they pleased, took telephone calls in the middle of the meeting, traded roles with other professionals, and shifted authority based on their relative experience pertinent to a particular issue or situation. The fluid participation, shifting roles, and chaotic and leaderless structure of this weekly meeting revealed a high level of ambiguity in the social work roles, amorphous boundaries between social workers and other professionals, and unclear authority relationships. The form of rituals and practices, as well as their content, can be important indicators of ambiguities.

Patterns of dress can also reveal ambiguities, particularly ambiguities that arise from irreconcilable beliefs about an issue. In Chapter 9 I described how discontinuities in an individual social worker's style of dress can reveal ambivalent beliefs about one's sense of professionalism. Incongruous types of decor and artifacts in one's office can reveal a similar type of ambiguity experience. These same kinds of symbols can offer evidence of irreconcilable differences among a number of social workers in addition to ambiguities experienced by an individual. For example, some of the social workers in one hospital regularly "dressed up" to the more powerful professionals in their settings. Like the doctors and administrators, some of these social workers regularly dressed in button-down shirts and ties. However, others "dressed down" to their patient population. One social worker regularly came to work in sandals, a painter's cap, and drawstring sweat pants. These incongruities among the social workers within the same hospital, which were not explained by status differences between the social workers, suggested ambiguity in what the collective of social workers believed about their professionalism.

Humor can also provide rich expressions of ambiguities. For example, jokes can express confusion over or discomfort with unclear or irreconcilable meanings. Cynicism can be an emotional reaction to ambiguity. Humor, and cynicism in particular, can release tension that often arises from seemingly unsolvable, irreconcilable, or simply unclear situations. Cynicism, for example, simultaneously expressed feelings of hopefulness and despair, idealism and realism. Cynicism regularly expressed the feeling that "the system helps people in a limited way; the system stinks." For my subjects, this form of humor was a highly adaptive coping response to their jobs of "helping people" in a system that often made them quite helpless to do so. Yet, despite the wide use and apparent acceptance of cynicism and humor in some group settings, many of the social workers I had interviewed denied that they themselves felt cynical. From this I inferred that many of the members actually experienced cynicism, but like the ambiguities it expressed, cynicism was considered socially undesirable, and so few were willing to admit these feelings when asked about them directly in interviews. Similarly, while jokes were next to impossible to elicit in interviews, they were openly expressed in informal settings.

Visual Data

In addition to these forms of operational data, there is at least one somewhat unconventional form of presentational data that seems to escape the limitations I described earlier. Visual data, such as collages, videos, graphs, and simple pictures may be unusually effective in revealing experiences that do not conform to a setting's normative code, including experiences of ambiguity. This form of data may be particularly revealing when the content of the representations is emotionally hot or value laden, and thus difficult to talk about (Harquail, 1990). For example, Harquail asked a sample of informants at a large university to build a collage to describe their images of racism at the university. The collages revealed a disparate and irreconcilable set of extremely heated feelings and opinions, sometimes within the same representation. In this way, visual data may be much more effective than our language at representing multiple or contradictory meanings simultaneously.

My study included a structured exercise that elicited visual portraits of the informants' experiences of ambiguity. I asked informants to plot the clarity of various work roles they had been performing at various points in time and, on a separate plot, the degree of internal ideological conflict they experienced at various points in time. (For both graphs, length of tenure in their profession marked the horizontal axis; degree of clarity marked the vertical axis on the first graph, while degree of internal conflict marked it on the second.) As the social workers plotted the degree of clarity in their various jobs, they described their feelings about and experiences in these jobs. Apparently, the act of drawing enabled them to talk more freely about their experiences. Seeing their experiences on paper seemed to enable the social workers to detach themselves and to suspend the norms about what sort of experiences they were and were not supposed to have and what they were and were not supposed to say. These graphs initially were designed to capture the relative magnitudes and frequencies of their ambiguity experiences, but the descriptions that accompanied the graphs provided rich qualitative data on what various ambiguities meant and how they manifested themselves at different points in the social workers' careers.

In addition, the shapes of their graphs seemed to represent their conceptions of their ambiguity experiences. These shapes conformed to four prototypes, representing four different interpretations. First, a flat plot over time (almost always at a low level) represented the notion that ambiguity is kept at a constant, usually low level. This depiction portrayed ambiguity as an experience that was successfully kept to a minimum. Second, a linear or curvilinear plot reflected the notion that ambiguity gets reduced over time as one learns the work. This was essentially a learning curve interpretation. Third, an episodic plot portrayed ambiguity experiences as specific episodes, peaks and valleys in their experiences. Peaks were associated with discrete instances, such as a change in management or a crisis in workload. This portrait made salient the contrast between "normal" low levels of ambiguity and "abnormal" high levels that occurred during crises. Finally, a continual change plot reflected the notion that experiences of ambiguity continually fluctuate, depending upon a number of random and uncontrollable circumstances. This type of plot depicted ambiguity experiences as a way of life; changes merely represented the normal ebbs and flows, rather than abnormal departures from a normal low level of ambiguity. These four different conceptions, which were represented through the shapes of their plots and hinted at in their accompanying descriptions, would not have been apparent to me had I relied upon only one type of data.

Discussion and Conclusion

This brief description of methods focused on situations, cues, and methods that might uncover ambiguities in cultures that dislike and tend to suppress them. I focused on these cultures because I believe that in these settings, which value clarity and consensus and devalue ambiguity and diversity, the task is most compelling, and most challenging. It is epistemologically and politically compelling insofar as these cultures recognize as legitimate only those inter-pretations and ways of knowing that conform to and confirm dominant interests, interpretations, and beliefs. In these cultures, acknowledging ambi-guities means recognizing diverse sets of interests, interpretations, and per-spectives. The task of uncovering ambiguities is most challenging because the ambiguities tend to be suppressed in formal research settings and are not easily accessible with traditional methods.

I have suggested that in settings where ambiguities are devalued, research-ers must rely on a variety of data sources and depend on methods that are unobtrusive. I have stressed the importance of observing informal chats, attending to jokes, and even listening for lies to capture ambiguities. Yet these methods, which may be most suitable for capturing ambiguities, may be precisely the methods that are in danger of being ruled out by university ethics committees. These committees often screen out unobtrusive methods, where the subject does not always know when he or she is being studied, because such methods may be viewed as an invasion of privacy. However, revealing the researcher's identity or intent could mean forfeiting some important sources of information. In this way, university ethics committees may make it even more difficult for researchers to study ambiguities and resist the pull toward conforming to dominant interests and theoretical formulations.

This is not to suggest that ethics committees do not have valid concerns in such situations; researchers who wish to uncover ambiguities will likely confront some real ethical dilemmas. Some of the richest potential sources of "data" may not be intended as data and may truly invade someone's privacy. Candice Clark (1989) argues: "People often can keep their internal states invisible until they voice them in safe arenas" (p. 145). Experiences that may be counter-normative, like ambiguity, which are not likely to be voiced in formal and less safe settings, may be most effectively accessed by simply listening in on others' informal conversations, gossip, and gripings—what

Clark terms "intensive eavesdropping." Yet such practices may represent an invasion of privacy. Thus, regardless of the presence or absence of a university ethics committee, the real question is whether a researcher's practices violate someone's privacy and whether informal and opportunistic research situations are within the boundaries of one's implicit or explicit research contract.

Most research contracts, however, are not very clear and the boundaries of what is and is not appropriate data and the issue of what settings and situations are fair game typically is not well defined, particularly for the participant observer. Ambiguities may be most openly expressed in settings and situations that are most fuzzy with respect to these boundaries. For example, I was invited to attend a party that followed a very emotional workshop. I was told, jokingly, to leave my notebook in my car so I could "relax and have fun." However, the social workers were unusually expressive at this party; emotions flowed freely and differences in beliefs surfaced easily. Should what I heard and observed at this party be included in my portrait of culture, or do I somehow purge what I learned?

While every situation may be unique and each researcher must determine the boundaries of his or her own research contract, my personal resolution to this situation may provide the reader with at least a useful point of departure. As I struggled with whether or not I should exclude the insights I gained at the party, I realized it was partly a question of whether or not I realistically *could* exclude these insights. I came to accept that what I learned at the party had shaped my understanding of the social workers' worlds, whether or not I explicitly admitted it. There was simply no way to purge this experience from my admittedly subjective understanding. However, the specific events, interactions, and expressions that I observed at the party did not have to be used as "data" in any written or oral account, even though these concrete experiences directly affected my understanding. Although the difference between what I presented explicitly as "evidence" for my claims and what I incorporated implicitly as the basis for my understandings may seem epistemologically very slim, the difference seemed ethically quite significant. To use the experiences as concrete evidence violated my research contract and potentially violated someone's privacy; to incorporate the experiences into my understandings violated neither my contract nor someone's privacy and was pragmatically unavoidable.

In addition, everyone at the party that I attended knew that I was a researcher and was vaguely familiar with my intent. They could, therefore, protect their own privacy. If they wanted to protect their privacy, they did not have me to their party or allow me to listen in on their informal conversations in other settings. Practices like "eavesdropping," however, where informants do not know of the researcher's identity or intent, do not provide "subjects" with the capacity to protect their own privacy. When researchers disclose their identity and rough intent, some of the responsibility for protecting privacy gets shifted to the subjects.

Clearly, there are ethical implications of doing research in these fuzzier situations and relying on practices, like eavesdropping, that could rightfully be considered overly surreptitious. The trick is to learn somehow about the ambiguities of everyday life in an ethical manner—without violating someone's privacy, without sneaking around, and without overstepping the implicit or explicit boundaries of one's research contract. Given that it may be most interesting and most compelling to uncover ambiguity experiences in the cultures that make it most challenging to do so, these issues are important for every researcher to resolve.

Notes

1. The author gratefully acknowledges Jane Dutton, Martha Feldman, Peter Frost, Larry Moore, Anat Rafaeli, Karl Weick, and Steven Zuckerman for their helpful comments on this chapter.

2. Several researchers have continued to research culture as an alternative paradigm for studying the symbolic features of organizational life and some have even discussed culture from a more critical perspective (e.g., Riley, 1983). This book and other recent efforts (e.g., Frost, 1988) represent campaigns to revive the original subjectivist intent—and its excitement—of the culture alternative in organizational studies.

3. Questions such as how ambiguities are culturally legitimated or delegitimated differ markedly from questions about how one should manage ambiguities. The former attempts to learn how cultures affect ambiguity experiences in the hope of freeing up reactions to ambiguity. This approach may allow individuals to experience ambiguity as a more normal, less threatening experience. The latter attempts to control the interpretations and feelings associated with ambiguities and the general ways in which ambiguities are experienced.

4. Some cultures (and individuals) are unusually tolerant of ambiguities. New and innovative organizations thrive on ambiguity (e.g., Pascale & Athos, 1982; Peters, 1987). Some have argued that ambiguity may be a condition that enables creativity and innovation (e.g., March, 1976; Martin & Meyerson, 1988; Meyerson, 1990; Weick, 1977, 1979). And some organizations, occupations, and departments have simply learned to live with ambiguity as a normal experience of work. Feldman (Chapter 10 and 1989) discusses ambiguity as a way of life at the Department of Energy and Meyerson (Chapter 9 and 1989) describes distinct settings of social work where ambiguities are "normal."

5. Chapter 9 provides cultural explanations for why one hospital and not the others tolerated ambiguities.

6. Meyerson (1990) contains a separate discussion of methods that allow researchers to access emotional reactions to ambiguities, including confusion, ambivalence, and cynicism, and Chapter 9 contains a discussion on cynicism as an expression of ambiguity.

19

Scholars, Travelers, Thieves:
On Concept, Method, and Cunning in Organizational Ethnography[1]

MICHAEL ROSEN

Sidney Wetmore Davidson III offered me a tie. Mr. Davidson, for 13 years a Morgan Guaranty Trust banker, a Yale man, now a partner in a New York City real estate firm and "Tres" for short, had been given this particular tie—sitting gift-boxed on an edge of his desk—as a present. He told me the story of the gift as I was commenting favorably on its aesthetics. I had seen it as I pulled up a chair to Tres' desk for a meeting. He told me that he had tried to return the tie earlier that day to the store it was purchased from and to exchange it for another. One fitting more his taste. But the store would not take it back. The tie had apparently been previously worn and spotted, the store attendant informed him, and was not therefore fit for exchange. The untrained eye could not easily pick up the grease mark in question, but as Tres and I turned the tie in the light of his desk lamp, there it was, a muted mark in the colors of the silk about two thirds of the way down the front.

The tie could be cleaned by a professional, of course. But regardless, its coloring and design was a bit too bold, Tres commented. And given that he could not exchange it for another, perhaps I would enjoy the tie's wear.

"A Hermes tie!" Steven Michael Coyle nearly shouted as he walked into Tres' office and noticed us holding the tie up to the light for inspection. "It's beautiful!" he said with awe.

"Would you like it?" I heard Tres ask Coyle.

"You bet," Coyle responded much as I imagined a schoolboy would to being offered an "A" for a course not yet complete. Obsequious acceptance. Or perhaps I was just jealous that the tie I had not fully wanted was now fully lost.

Coyle, also a product of WASP private education, a financial analyst in his former job and a master's in economics, was playing gratitude to the hilt. "Oh wow!" he kept up the barrage. "I've *always* wanted a *Hermes* tie! Thank you, Tres, thank you! It's beautiful."

Pieces of the Frame

The text presented here is written specifically and somewhat hurriedly for the edited volume of which it is part. I have been invited to write this text, whose mandate is to "prepare some comments on how your particular paradigm orientation . . . impacts on methodological issues or informs/translates into method" on the direct basis of the edited "Breakfast at Spiro's" (Rosen, 1985) presented in Chapter 5. A fair challenge, no doubt, but one not fully possible for me to address. For the surety behind "Breakfast at Spiro's," a work informed by a theoretic derived rather directly from British social anthropology, has faded over the years behind a barrage of post-modern uncertainties over truth, representation, rhetoric, and the fiction of ethnography.

This chapter is an amalgam of some past but a majority of more current writings. It is also an attempt toward compliance with the essence of the editors' mandate, for it highlights a world view from which I now labor: an anthropologically derived understanding of culture, social structure, and their interrelationships. This is an understanding radicalized through the looking glass of Critical Theory, that is, through Critical Theory's Marxist focus on power, interest, hegemony, and consent. The epistemology and methodology of ethnography is then briefly addressed herein. And at the end, the world view woven here is conceptually challenged with no complete attempt at reconciliation made through an exploration of post-modern notions surrounding the writing of culture. A quilted work is woven which might uncover understandings and chill securities.

Culture . . .

The reality of any social process, Berger and Luckmann (1966, p. 12) would have us understand, is constructed in the face of chaos. That is, culture is built on the edge. That which appears to be objective—the naturalness of formal organization, the structuring of hierarchies, the immutability of economic laws, nine innings to a baseball game, the stability of order—is only illusorily so, where fronts are actively maintained through management of common backstages of meaning. Reality is actively socially constructed, where the processes of this building are focused on more below.

Works in the anthropological tradition of the study of culture invariably focus (save for the most materialist efforts) on this social constructedness, on the shared transactions simultaneously constituting and shaping the meanings underlying people's lives. This assumption of social constructedness becomes both a point of departure and a focus of analysis.

The logic of social construction is linear. "Since we can perceive nothing except through the knowledge structure in which perception is embedded," Astley notes (1985, p. 498) we cannot speak of any reality other than a social reality. For the knowledge structure through which reality is interpreted and thus created is socially constructed. This knowledge structure is what anthropologists and other social constructionists construe as "cultural": a constructed document or public rhetoric (Geertz 1980, p. 102) developed over time through the shared, accumulated experiences of members of any social grouping, giving rise to such system specific ideational elements as assumptions, ideas, values, and norms. These are "envehicled meanings" (Geertz 1980, p. 135), with symbols the vehicles through which communication occurs. Symbols are here the "objects, acts, relationships, or linguistic formations that stand *ambiguously* for a multiplicity of meanings, evoke emotions, and impel men to action" (Cohen 1974, p. 23). They are thus anything that signifies an intersubjective process, and thus public (Geertz, 1980, p. 135).

Although culture emerges from action, it continuously acts back upon it as well, recreating and transforming action through the provision of meaning. To function in a setting, and to gain meaning from behavior, culture

systems are more or less internalized. At the heart of ethnography, therefore, lies the assumption that, because culture is a concept about meaning
and its construction, about ideas, values, beliefs and assumptions, it is
reasonably studied from a social constructionist, interpretivist perspective.
That is, from a perspective exploring how the shared meaning system of
the members of any particular social group is created and re-created in
relationship to the social processes of organization.

Le Monde d'Hermes

"Le Monde d'Hermes," it is called. The world of Hermes. An
experience in elegance. A retailer of consumer goods of only the
highest distinction. In both quality and price. Of goods meeting
the "high standards at the Legendary house of Hermes" (*The
World of Hermes,* 1990, p. 16). In "all of our addresses around
the world" (1990, p. 9). Twenty-five countries and hundreds of
only the most important cities.

Paris, of course, is its headquarters. And France its heart. Not
everyone's France, Hermes tells us, but Hermes' "own France,
the country that is much less the France of ideology than of
enthusiasms, . . . Leisure, . . . exhilaration, . . . sensual pleasure, the sun, grass," says its President, Jean-Louis Dumas-
Hermes (1990, p. 3).

Hermes first entered the business world in 1837 as a maker
and retailer of horse tack. And one hundred and twenty-one years
later, in 1958 and for reasons not important here, Hermes
entered the business of silk manufacture, printing and retailing.
The silk trade now particularly consists of women's scarves and
men's ties.

. . . and Structure

The "Other" (one could say *an* "Other," reining in dimensions of
analysis)—where "Other" is understood in Heidegger's sense as the "original unifying unity of what tends apart"—of culture as discussed here is
social structure.

In his classic study of the Nuer, Evans-Pritchard (1940) heightens this concept of social structure to the level of master concept, noting that:

> By social structure we mean relations between groups which have a high degree of consistency and constancy. The groups remain the same irrespective of their specific content of individuals at any particular moment, so that generation after generation of people pass through them. Men are born into them, or enter them later in life and move out of them at death; the structure endures. (p. 262)

Rosaldo (1986) likens this approach towards social structure as "a house with many rooms that people pass through over the course of their life-times: the people come and go, but the house remains the same" (p. 94). Social structure takes here an immutable and solid air. People, and perhaps their ideas, are fluid and pass with time, but their institutions are rigid and remain.

But even houses are changed to suit their occupants. Kitchens are modernized, bathrooms enlarged, rooms added as children are born or grandparents move in. That is, even rigid structure is malleable. And nowhere nearly as slowly as people imagine and the continents drift.

A more fluid approach to social structure was consequently adopted by anthropologists as new thought collided with old. Turner (1974), for example, chose to redefine social structure as "the more stable aspects of action and interrelationships" (p. 36). No longer immutable but instead "more stable," Turner opted to understand social structure as the "frame of social order that consists in a system of roles, statuses, and positions occupied by individuals through time" in any social group (Myerhoff, 1975, p. 33).

The Hermes Tie

Emanuel Gruss. Age 69. Risk arbitrageur and principal partner in Oscar Gruss and Son, Inc., member of the New York Stock Exchange:

> Ria (his wife) likes these Hermes ties more than I do. They have a certain recognition and a certain status, you see. They sell at a certain price, a high price. Wearing a Hermes tie is like a woman wearing a diamond brooch, and when people see them they associate you with a particular status. I prefer British ties, which are more masculine and manly. Hermes

ties are more flowery and easy; they go together better with the rest of your clothing. I prefer a Dunhill, for example, a British regimental tie.

Riane Gruss. Age 58. Homemaker, philanthropist and wife of Emanuel Gruss:

It's not just the status. Hermes ties are beautiful. They're made of top quality silk, the colors are beautiful, and the patterns are intricate. They are a symbol of good taste and affluence. And they show a certain conservatism. But maybe not in that order. Hermes ties have been in New York for fifteen or twenty years, and they have been a status symbol for the past ten years or so. Now they're probably a little passe. You see a lot of people now going to the Turnball and Asser ties.

Enacting Equilibrium

But the roles, statuses, and positions constituting a group's structural frame may change. And political activity came to be recognized by some, particularly within the British tradition of social anthropology, as a principal dynamic channeling such change (Gluckman, 1977). As understood herein, the condition of human life not infrequently finds people competing one against the other to enhance their own place, often within a framework defined by conflicting and/or ambiguous rules (Kuper, 1973, p. 177). Norms are not only often ambiguous, but also directly in conflict with one another.

Utilizing such ambiguity and conflict, people manipulate rules and symbols to pick a course through the maze of norms governing social life, occasionally acting to enhance their social fortune along the way. And we see simple social equilibrium only if we white-wash the playing out of social process. The more closely we look, the more we see that there is no "neat integration of groups or norms" (Kuper, 1973, p. 177).

This politically informed approach to social process represented a radical departure from anthropology's orthodoxy as traced from Durkheim (1947) and Malinowksi (1922) to Radcliffe-Brown (1922) to Evans-Pritchard (1937), from function to structure, particularly within the British school as identified above. Each in a different way, Leach (1954) and Gluckman

(1977) led this break beyond orthodoxy and its simple equilibrium models of social process towards an understanding in which competition and conflict are very real and necessarily to be accounted for.

As Gluckman (1963) understood it, there is a social equilibrium to be represented in ethnographic accounts, but it is a complex one achieved only through the balancing of oppositions in a dialectical process played out very much in the terrain of symbolic action.

Within this view, ritual becomes not merely a processual unit for re-creating social order by acting out its underlying premises—premises based on unity. Instead, Gluckman (1963) came to see ritual:

> not simply as expressing cohesion and impressing the value of society and its social sentiments on people, as in Durkheim's and Radcliffe-Brown's theories, but as exaggerating real conflicts of social rules and affirming that there was unity despite these conflicts. (p. 18)

And without going into detail for lack of space, the study of ritual forms a central place in the study of social construction. Ritual defines a segment of reality, functioning as a frame within which we define ourselves. For as Myerhoff (1977) notes, "in ritual, not only is seeing believing, doing is believing," (p. 223).

The Hermes Tie

Sidney Wetmore Davidson, III. Age 38. Partner, Park Square Associates, Inc., New York City real estate development firm:

> In certain circles the Hermes tie is a power tie. Particularly in finance, in important companies with something of a Euro touch, First Boston, Morgan Guaranty Trust, Morgan Stanley. If you go to a closing dinner for a major loan or corporate acquisition or something else important like that, ten out of ten people will be wearing a Hermes tie. At Morgan Guaranty Trust, while I was there, the people who wore Hermes ties were the ones with international experience. Domestic bankers wore them less frequently.
>
> The importance of the Hermes tie, its significance, is not a WASPy thing, because if you asked my father he wouldn't know about the meaning of Hermes.

You want to be careful about the Hermes tie you select. I could take you up to Hermes and point out the ones the Euro financiers would be wearing versus the ones someone read about Hermes and decided they should wear them. Hermes started out as a saddle shop for the nobility. I remember going to one chateau in the Loire and seeing all the saddles there, each made by Hermes. Enormously expensive.

I just think they're beautiful ties. The silk is very special, and the colors are wonderful.

A Chilean girlfriend gave me my first Hermes tie. Her entire family was educated in Europe. Specifically in England and France.

Hegemony, Commodities, and Consent

Conflict is simple to recognize standing on Normandy's Omaha Beach or watching Captain Kirk command the Enterprise in yet another pitched intergalactic missile barrage against the Klingons. Control is readily comprehended standing in the slave quarters of Washington's Mount Vernon or watching Cool Hand Luke digging holes in a Louisiana prison yard; Steve McQueen's "failure to communicate." These are instances of control through domination and of conflict over clear differences of interest.

But in our society, the society of IBM, Ford Motors, the Teenage Mutant Ninja Turtles, Ronald Reagan, and Spam, fundamental conflicts of interest are often structural and not so visible. And control is largely hegemonic, cradled essentially in the interplay of social and cultural relations defining capitalism. More specifically, control is cradled in the relations of production and consumption constituting the commodity.

It is in the nature of capitalism, Marx (1977, p. 967) notes, to constantly grow, where this expansion holds a dual nature. The capitalist market grows insofar as it includes ever new producers and consumers. Simultaneously, it grows as ever more facets of social existence are commoditized and exchanged. Herein, as capitalist production is increasingly highly developed, more products take on the nature of commodities, that is, their production and exchange is predicated on a valorization process separate from the service they ultimately perform as use-values. There nevertheless exists an "indissoluble union" (Marx 1977, p. 952) within the same commodity between this valorization process and a labor process, and it is here that control through consent becomes pervasive in advanced multinational capitalism. Market logic becomes so extensive that control of the labor process through domination becomes superfluous. There is rarely need any longer—from a functionalist perspective—to chain the galleon slaves to their oars. Instead, as members of the advanced/industrialized segment of the multinational capitalist system act out their roles as producers and/or appropriators of surplus value, and nearly always as consumers of valorized commodities, a socially common sensical and individually self-evident market logic prevails.[2] Everything is naturally bought and sold. People sell their labor, buy their entertainment, pay others to raise their children and even occasionally to bear them. And when nearly all facets of human social existence are bought and sold, that is, when nearly all participants in an economy are buyers and sellers of valorized commodities and perceive themselves naturally to be so, control is achieved through consent. The perception of naturalness in this commoditized social existence is precisely the essence of such control.

Hermes

Hermes, messenger of the gods and son of Zeus and Maia, is himself the god of scholars, travelers and thieves (Homer, 1946, 366). It is also important to note that Hermes is a trickster: "a god of cunning and tricks" (Crapanzano, 1986, p. 52). And within his craft, Hermes understood the composition of truth and representation. For when Hermes undertook the task of messenger of the gods, he promised Zeus not to lie. But he did not promise to tell the whole truth. Zeus is presumed to have understood (Crapanzano, 1986, p. 53).

On Method and Towards Epistemology

Discussion to this point has focused largely on the development of a conceptual framework for understanding sociocultural process in the administrative forms of organization characterizing multinational capitalist society. As the mandate behind this piece stipulates, however, a relationship between paradigm and method is to be forged, a natural enough forging, it turns out, given the symbiosis between culture theory and ethnography.

For an ethnographer, social process is not best captured in hypothetical deductions, convariances, and degrees of freedom. Instead, understanding social process involves getting inside the world of those generating it, constructing an interpretation of "other people's constructions of what they and their compatriots are up to" (Geertz, 1973, p. 9). Nuance and uniqueness are as important in this endeavor as is normally frequent behavior.

Ethnography itself is a method for both data collection and analysis, each irrevocably mated to the other. It is based upon achieving a conscious and systematic interpretation of the culture system operating for those the ethnographer observes to those who may eventually take in the ethnographer's end product, perhaps a film or video, a journal article, a conference presentation, or, most commonly, a book.

Interpretation is the consummate goal of ethnography because meaning is understood in the social constructionist realm to derive from interpretation, where knowledge is significant only insofar as it is meaningful (Spooner, 1983, p. 3). We accept an ethnographic explanation as meaningful if it appears plausible against our own set of explicit and implicit assumptions about social process (Douglas, 1975), if we can associate the framework and data the ethnographer proposes against the interpretation framework we have systematized throughout our lives.

In ethnograhic explanation a framework for producing meaning may be understood to derive ultimately from one or a combination of three fundamental forms. These are based in establishing: (a) the appropriateness of the reported data to human needs (functionalism); (b) the tendency of the reported data to reinforce social and cultural equilibrium (structural-functionalism); or (c) the consonance of the data with presumed meta-patterns of thought (structuralism) (Spooner, 1983, p. 3). Our current forms of ethnographic explanation may be understood to derive from one or a combination of these basic approaches.

Although an ethnographic report may—and depending on the writer frequently does—claim interpretive authority, each report is limited insofar as it derives from what is a partial perspective. Any interpretation is also only a second or third order construction. The ethnographer interprets that which he or she observes, experiences, or is told by others, recording this cultural data in field notes and consciously and unconsciously letting it settle against a tableau of meaning structures within his or her own imaginings. The resulting ethnographic interpretations are reworked as time and data accumulate and permit (Van Maanen, 1988, p. 75), mediated by experiences in and out of the field. What appears as written ethnography, therefore, is as much a product of the time and context in which it was written as of any purported truth of interpretation.

However, while the authority of an interpretation is never absolute, its value does not rest on whether an alternative explanation can account for the same data. Instead, its value rests on whether the explanation accounts for the data in a plausible manner, or whether we are able to provide our own accountings for the reported data. An ethnographic work is valid even in this latter case, because the goal of generating meaning for the cultural data of another is accomplished.

Finally, ethnographers study others to find out more about both themselves and the others (Spooner, 1983, p. 3). In so doing, they change not only their own lives, but also the lives of those studied. In the process they bring the place of epistemology, the place of the meaning of data and inquiry, to the forefront of activity. As Spooner (1983) notes, epistemological issues inform:

> how to select the data you [the ethnographer] work with, how you can logically delimit their context or universe, and see the relationship between the data and the purpose for which they were gathered, and—most important of all—their significance or what they will *mean* and how to test that meaning scientifically. (p. 3)

Hermes

Hermes, etymologically, is "he of the stone heap" (Crapanzano, 1986). And Hermes was associated with boundary stones, stones demarcating borders. The herm, a head and a phallus on a pillar, subsequently replaced the stone heap, and Hermes became a phallic god and a god of fertility. He is also the tutelary god of speech and writing, communicative tools also demarcating borders, the borders of what we know (Crapanzano, 1986, p. 52). Stones, images, and ideas piled up on the edges of our collective fields. Herms declaring the limits of what we own and where we go.[3]

But we have come to realize that, unlike the existential surety of stone heaps, truth is nearly impossible to fix and meaning equally impossible to represent. It is in this sense that the ethnographic text, Crapanzano (1986, p. 51) wants us to know, is always provisional, though the ethnographer labors to obfuscate its tentative nature. Where the whole truth cannot be found, or more rightly does not exist, the traditional ethnographer, yet fighting against the void, "assumes a final interpretation—a definitive reading" of the culture he or she has gone out to study (Crapanzano, 1986, p. 51).

This labor of fixing a definitive interpretation of an other's culture is an exercise in hermeneutics, where hermeneutics, Geertz (1983, p. 5) would have us understand, is "an attempt somehow to understand how it is we understand understandings not our own." The post-modern challenge to ethnography, on the other hand, to the interpretation and representation of an other's culture, begins with Hermes' recognition of the never whole nature of truth, its always provisional character. Confronting this challenge does not lead back to hermeneutics. It points instead towards a direction more Nietzchean: "all constructed truths are made possible by powerful 'lies' of exclusion and rhetorics." Herein, "even the best ethnographic texts—serious, true fictions—are systems, or economies, of truth" (Clifford, 1986, p. 7). And though space again prohibits fuller exploration, fashioning the ethnographic text informed by the certain uncertainties of post-modern thought is recognized ultimately as a labor of inventing, rather than representing, an other's culture (Clifford, 1986, p. 2). Ethnographic writing is thus always the writing of fiction. Fiction in its Latin sense of "something made or fashioned," and also fiction in the fully inventive sense of something made up (Clifford, 1986, p. 6). Where truth is fully partial.

The Hermes Tie

Alfred Shoenberg. Age 53. Investment banker and managing partner in Shoenberg Hieber, Inc., member of the New York Stock Exchange:

> I don't want Hermes ties with the traditional patterns, those coming from horse tack. Because that's like advertising. But Hermes has great silk. It lasts forever. And their new tie patterns are wonderful. They have gone into florals, wheat, animals. It used to be just a bunch of humdrum patterns of horse hardwear from saddles and bridles and other horse tack. But it's exceptional stuff. Bright colors. I can remember when Hermes used to have their old shop on 57th street. They've been around for a long time. They used to sell mainly just scarves and bags in New York, and their prices used to be all exceptionally high. Now they have put in some cheaper

items, spread their line, so there are more things to afford and more to draw in the customer.

Ina Shoenberg. Age 57. Horsewoman and wife of Alfred Schoenberg:

> I'll tell you the truth, Freddie (her husband) likes the patterns of Hermes ties. They are substantial ties. Their silk is not an inconsequential fabric. But if it said J.C. Penney [on the label] he wouldn't wear it.

Horsey Stuff

This chapter has briefly explored the concepts of culture, social structure, and their interrelationships from an ethnographer's social constructionist stance. The role of power and politics was then addressed in relationship to the reproduction of social process, as was the special place of ritual. The expression of power relations within our multinational capitalist society through relations of consent embedded in market logic was next briefly stated, completing a model of social process as I understand it. And completing this text, the method and epistemology of ethnography was presented and then tempered in light of the oxymoronic certainties of post-modern thought.

The Hermes Tie

Christopher Hall Bartle. Age 37. New York City real estate attorney:

> If I see someone wearing a Hermes tie, it speaks to me of a world of style and leisure, a lot of style, a lot of money, a lot of time. And Hermes ties are the best because the silk lasts for a long time. Their design used to be a bit nicer, a bit tighter. But they still use very good silk, and their designs are still very refined and even somewhat whimsical. They started off as a tack maker, and they got very good at silk. That led to the silk scarves, many of which also have a horse motif in their design. It's still sort of horsey stuff.

Notes

1. I am indebted to Peter Frost for his invitation, encouragement, and criticisms of this chapter, to Joanne Martin for challenges not yet sufficiently met, and to Larry Moore for deadlines, syntax, and spelling.

2. This discussion centers on an understanding of the production and distribution of surplus value within capitalism as presented within Marx's analytic framework. Where appropriate the reader is referred to *Capital,* (Marx, 1977, Vol. I).

3. Joanne Martin has been sufficiently kind and critical to note that the postmodern voice intoned here should be directed on itself, at a minimum to recognize and perhaps also to address what she points out to be the traditionally masculine picture portrayed herein. This picture is constituted by the unmistakably phallic nature of men's ties, Hermes the phallic god declaring what "we" own and where "we" go, the unstated common sense assumption of some speaker given voice here that essentially all participants in "high finance" are men, the fact that the only women given voice here are heard primarily as men's wives and so on. Joanne Martin is correct; the picture painted has masculine lines. I have selected the Hermes tie as a metaphor for the commodity in advanced capitalism, a particular commodity elevated to a special role by the powerful and hence fit for a discussion of hegemonic control. I have selected to discuss Hermes the god for his role as a messenger of fact and thus also irrevocably as a molder of truth. And the god Hermes is consequently an embodiment of postmodern concerns toward meaning, interpretation, and representation. But the subconscious concerns behind these selections, the silence behind the confluence of phalluses, between silk and god, should be annunciated, though speaking towards this silence would require more space than provided by the editors here and perhaps would head in a direction other than they intended. Further, the silk tie is integrally part of the male business uniform in contemporary westernized society. It is not uniformly part of the female's. This distinction and its silent assumptions also beg more consideration and space. I am accordingly available to think and write, and welcome invitations

20

Culture Is the Medium of Life

BARBARA CZARNIAWSKA-JOERGES

The cultural frame of analysis brings to organizational studies both new freedoms and new constraints. Like every other frame, it helps to reveal and focus certain phenomena by neglecting and covering others, a fact that we failed to observe enjoying the new vistas. Also, while playing on the new meadows, we took some time to notice that some of our friends disappeared, even if they promised to meet us in the place we all thought we knew. The cultural frame of reference turned out to be many frames, sometimes dramatically different from one another.

Now that the first wave of enthusiasm is over, the disappointed can start looking for a better perspective while whose who are still satisfied can lean back and look critically at what they do. The task is, however, not to detect all the flaws and arrive at the perfect perspective for organization studies, but to reflect on the one we are using as one of many—but the one we happen to cherish and find useful. For quite some time we defended it by attacking competitors. Now it is time to make use of all the constructive criticisms which have been provided and to start the process of self-reflection, to become less defensive and more creative.

This chapter is one attempt at such reflection. It is built along the following lines: two definitional kinds of concepts have been used in culture studies and form the backbone of my discussion. They are the ostensive and performative definitions of cultural phenomena. The ostensive definition, a more traditional type, forms a reference point for the bulk of literature well known to the readers. My focus is, however, on a performative definition of cultural phenomena which, I believe, needs to

285

be developed and attended to. This definitional construction is then used to frame, first, the very processes of organizing and, second, the wider phenomena in which organizing is inevitably embedded. Next, organizing is seen in a three-dimensional perspective, composed of interacting symbolic, practical and political aspects, as illustrated by examples of studies conducted within the cultural perspective. The embeddedness, or the cultural context, is then analyzed, both in relation to organizing as such and to theorizing about it. A self-reflective note on interpreting research itself as a cultural experience, closes the discussion pointing toward meta-levels of reflection.

Ostensive Versus Performative Definitions of Culture

Bruno Latour (1986) analyzed the present state of sociology and its possible developments by contrasting two definitions of society: an ostensive and a performative one. The same operation can be performed on definitions of culture, not to achieve yet another classification but to highlight the consequences of adopting any given kind of definition.

The ostensive definition of culture assumes that, *in principle,* it is possible to discover properties that are typical for a given culture and that could explain its evolution, although in practice they might be difficult to detect. The performative definition admits that it is impossible in principle to describe properties characterizing any given culture, but *in practice* (with a given purpose at hand, Schütz, 1964/1979) it is possible to do so.

Actors, be they individuals or groups, *live in the culture* as ostensively defined. Even if they are active, their actions are restricted because they are only a part of a larger pattern. If, however, culture is to be performatively defined, it is the actors who in practice *define*—both for themselves and for others—*what culture is,* what it contains, what is the whole, and what are the parts.

In searching for an ostensive definition, actors are "useful informants," but because they are simply a part of a larger pattern, they must not be relied upon too much as they never see the whole pattern themselves. "The whole pattern" in the formative definition is, however, what is perceived by the actors as the whole pattern in their action-oriented cultural lives and, therefore, there are no actors who know "less" or "more" compared to each other and to the researcher. People's knowledge is the basis for their practical action and thus is of interest to the researcher.

The search for an ostensive definition assumes that, with a proper methodology, social scientists can eventually sort out the actors' opinions, beliefs, and behaviors so as to complete the whole picture. Within the realm of the performative definitions, however, it is obvious that social scientists raise the same questions as any other actors although they might use a different rhetoric in formulating their answers. The chosen rhetoric is, further, a practical way of enforcing their understanding of what culture is about, analogous to other practical ways used by other actors (McCloskey, 1985/1986).

Thus, ostensive definitions are attempts to *explain principles,* whereas performative definitions *explore practices.* In what follows, I would plead for shifting from principle to practice in cultural studies of organizations. To paraphrase Latour once more, one could say that culture "is not the referent of an ostensive definition discovered by social scientists despite the ignorance of their informants. Rather it is performed through everyone's efforts to define it" (Latour, 1986, p. 273).

Let me begin with one performative definition of culture (naturally, there are many possible) which I find useful in approaching organizations. In the most general sense, *culture can be viewed as a bubble (of meaning) covering the world,* a bubble that we both create and live within. Its film covers everything that we turn our eye to; it is, as stated in the title, the medium of (social) life.

What about Nature, though? (The generality of the above definition calls for the use of capitals). Contrasting Nature with Culture makes sense only within what Latour (1989) calls "our Modern Constitution." The Modern Constitution asserts simultaneously the nonhuman origin of knowledge (our impressions and cognitive maps), and the complete separation between the two (in order to hear the voice of Nature, we must fight against voices which originate in our heads). In his outline of an Amodern Constitution, Latour proposes to collapse the third element (the complete separation) while preserving the first two, albeit with a changed status. Accordingly, Latour proposes to tackle Nature and Culture as consequences of a given scientific practice, prominent during the Modern Times. This means that Nature and Culture can be seen as results of interpretive practices, usually called "the scientific method" but which might be more appropriately called "an anthropological practice." To come back to my definition, then, culture covers all such interpretive practices: both those that call for the separation of the two poles and those that propose to collapse them; those that search for ostensive definitions and those that are satisfied with performative ones.

Such an all-encompassing definition allows us to establish the starting point, but in order to proceed further, more detailed exploration of this definition of framework is needed.

Organizations as Cultural Phenomena

One of the most handy performative definitions of culture is one used for many years in anthropology; *culture is a way of life* (Leach, 1982). Large and complex organizations are among the most characteristic contemporary ways of structuring our time and attention. In this they are complemented by a host of small business organizations, voluntary organizations, interest organizations, and so forth. Western countries are organized societies (Perrow, 1989). From this perspective, organizations are cultural phenomena themselves, rather than "arenas for cultural phenomena" or sites of "organizational cultures."

The original recognition of that fact came across most visibly in the wave of organizational symbolism (see especially Barry Turner, 1971, for the early examples). The symbolic meaning of organizational practices was brought to the fore with feelings of exhilaration resulting from an "aha" experience which both confirms what we already knew and gives it a meaningful form, a convincing figure emerging from a well-known ground. But the symbolic focus carried us into forgetting other figures that might possibly be made out of the same ground and, hopefully, combined into a three-dimensional picture. In my view, these three thickly interwoven dimensions are: *the symbolic, the practical, and the political* (Czarniawska-Joerges, 1990). Following are the examples of research attempting to reveal the complexity of organizations as cultural phenomena.

The Symbolic: Budget as Conversation

Budgeting was one of the first organizing processes that was taken under a symbolist magnifying glass. Conventional studies of budget processes were repeatedly bringing in confusing results. Although budgets are considered to be important control instruments, especially in public sector organizations, the observed practices reported a steady discrepancy between the budgetary statements and the subsequent activity. Also contrary to the assumption that budget processes were arenas for important decisions, empirical studies revealed that budgets usually confirmed decisions made elsewhere. A study of a Norwegian municipality led Johan P. Olsen

(1970) to interpret the budget process as a ritual. Budgeting did not serve to turn values and demands into concrete activities, but to strengthen these values and ideas related to them. Olsen saw budgeting as a ritualistic act venerating reason as the basis of organizational activity.

This observation opened a new perspective on the process of budgeting, until then seen exclusively within a directly instrumental perspective. A budget can still be seen as fulfilling many important functions, but not those that were traditionally ascribed to it. I can serve to communicate a stand in a political debate without a need to formulate an explicit stance (Czarniawska-Joerges & Jacobsson, 1989). The budget techniques can be reformed to signal that public sector organizations are following the demands of modernity (Czarniawska-Joerges & Jacobsson, 1989). In general, budgeting creates many communicative opportunities, both inside and outside organizations.

The studies of budgeting practices convincingly illustrated the usefulness of the cultural frame of reference. Capable of grasping the functional aspect of organizational action, additional possibilities for examining the existential aspects of organizational life were created. At the same time, the cultural frame of reference seemed less prone to dangers of reductionism, stressing complexity and interconnections rather than imposing a single view on any organizational process. This advantage can be clearly observed in new studies of organizational technology, together with dangers ensuing from relying too heavily on novel aspects of the phenomena as opposed to the well-known ones.

The Practical: Computers as Animals, Actors, But Also as Tools

It could be claimed that it was Braverman (1974) who visualized the computer as a political actor, rather than just a tool. But it is cultural analysis that recognized that this most characteristic piece of organizational machinery can acquire a variety of complex attributes. Depending on the emotional attitude towards the computers, they are seen as bats—or as butterflies (Joerges, 1989). For the true aficionados, however, this was not enough. Marvin Minsky (1986) declared that computers are our true children, our biological children, being, really, the progeny of dinosaurs (in an interview with a German Film-maker, Peter Weiss; "Machine Dreams," 1988). With less love but equal radicalism, the "new sociology of technology" proposes to conceive of computers as social actors. Steve Woolgar (1985), for instance, claimed that "we need to eschew approaches that are unnecessarily parasitic of participants' dichotomies, and develop a sociological approach which takes as its focus the human/mechanical language community, the community composed of 'expert machines and machine experts' " (p. 568). One can see this program as a historical reversal of its predecessor: the man-machine system. Where the former sinned by machinizing humans, the latter makes it good by humanizing machines.

Whether one likes the new sociology of technology or not, it is obvious that new machinery, especially microelectronic control technologies, plays an important role in unscaling organizational complexities. Organizational actors and researchers alike feel that they must go along with these changes, and this necessitates resymbolizations. Some of the new symbols help to create new realities; some, alas, help to reproduce the old ones. Computers are often projected as splendid male creatures, speaking friendly and patronizingly to their female users. This reinforcement of traditional gender and occupational roles is apparent in early marketing images of the machines (Joerges, 1989).

Although symbolic aspects of technology are given full attention, the political aspects are noticed, not surprisingly, somewhat less often. But truly flabbergasting is the fact that the most obvious, that is, practical aspects of computers (machines do work!), are relatively least noticed (Joerges, 1988). The cultural frame of reference should ensure that we do not neglect the practical aspect of all organizational actions, beginning with the machines.

The Political: Power as an Experiential Construct

The political aspect is sometimes perceived as imposed on organizations by conflict-minded researchers; the consensus perspective does not see any need for political interpretations of organizational life. However, people in organizations talk about power. They certainly did in several studies which I conducted in various organizations (Czarniawska-Joerges, 1988b) even though I never asked them about it. They used the concept to interpret the significance of actions—their own and other people's—which they were describing. This provided a legitimate reason to ask students of business administration in different countries for accounts of organizational events that they experienced as related to organizational power (Czarniawska-Joerges & Kranas, in press).

In ostensive definitions of organizational power, "power" is one of those organizational attributes, influencing factors, or "structures" whose existence we take for granted. Consider, for example, the famous definition of power by Berle (1967): "Power invariably fills one vacuum in human organization. As between chaos and power, the latter always prevail" (p. 37). If, however, we assume that organizations are constantly being made (the bubble of culture is constantly reproduced), that we are actually dealing with processes of "organizing" (Weick, 1969/1979), power also becomes something that is being constructed rather than located at the outset of organizational action together with other "attributes." What students related in our study were the ways organizations are being made, and "power" was one of the results which varied according to the variability found in other organizational processes. The students did not come up with a common "definition" of power, nor were we able to deduce one from what they said. The study made it perfectly clear that the students' definitions were performative ones; they built them in accordance with their experience and the accessible rhetoric. The differences in definitions reflected different ways of (organizational) life.

How to account for these variations in a more systematic fashion? In the above examples I avoided introducing the issue of context, in order to be able to concentrate on it more fully in what follows.

Cultural Context of Organizing

Still another way of conceptualizing culture in the performance mode (which I see as alternative but not competitive to the one used in the previous section) is that of *culture as a thought world* (Douglas, 1986). This way of understanding culture makes sense especially when we turn to processes and phenomena that happen beyond our perception although we speculate about them. An ostensive definition would most likely introduce concepts like "nation cultures"; however, all what we have said until now indicates that there is no way (or, rather, no use) to delimit concrete units of analysis or to establish borders between them. Yet we need a concept that will help us to extend our analysis of organizational practices into something that is bigger than themselves, but made of the same fabric, something that is an extension of those practices rather than another ontological unit that can be contracted with it (like in the dichotomy "organization versus environment"). A concept which I find useful is *a cultural context of organizing* which can be understood as an historically formed network of organizational and social processes and systems of values and beliefs (Czarniawska, 1986; Hofstede & Boddewyn, 1977). A thought world, shared by a time-and-space collective (Sellerberg, 1987)—

containing constructs conceived with the purpose of making sense of certain events—can be seen as a collection of texts in making, some of which deal with organizing whereas others do not. Undoubtedly, however, the texts on organizing influence the other texts and in turn are influenced by them. Let us have a look at how such links are formed and how they operate.

Myths, Prophecies, and Other Linking Practices

From 1978 to 1982 I conducted a study of control relationships between central headquarters and the companies in retail businesses in Poland and the United States (Czarniawska, 1985a). Later, I studied analogous relationships between central public agencies and ministries in Sweden (1985b). The study was designed along conventional lines, and except for a traditional "cross-cultural comparison," no conscious cultural perspective was adopted. The cultural frame of reference invited itself.

I asked my interlocutors at all levels a variety of questions, but never one which was nevertheless always answered: what makes organizations effective? These spontaneous utterances formed patterns, which I called the *myths of origin of organizational effectiveness* (assuming, after Cohen, 1969, that myth is a narrative of sacred quality which, by offering a dramatized version of origins of transformations, provides a socially shared explanation of important phenomena).

The myths presented remained in a strong but negative relationship to organizational practices as described by the same actors. On the other hand, they were positively related to shared cultural traditions, such as societal values, history, and other myths. The myths narrated by the U.S. general managers and Swedish general directors had roots in the official version of the history of the two countries, whereas the Polish managing directors related a myth based on an idealized version of U.S. reality.

All of these myths reflected certain important societal values, maybe those which are most challenged by everyday practices. Thanks to the fact that myths help to save important values, organizational control can follow a pattern that is demanded by various contingencies. Other symbolic acts help to mediate the discrepancy between what is believed and what is perceived (on mediatory myths, see Abravanel, 1983). Consequently, each myth has its supporting rituals, actions that symbolically confirm the contents of the myths (for example, organizational ceremonies, public speeches, and the like). Ideologies, on the other hand, interpret the present state of affairs, offer a vision of the future (alluding to a myth or a prophecy), and formulate a prescription of how to obtain it (Czarniawska-Joerges, 1988a). One should add here that prophecies are narrations of the same character as myths, but are future-oriented. Indeed, the myth of origins of organizational effectiveness as related by the Polish managers turned recently into a prophecy: as Felix Rohatyn put it, the Eastern and Central European countries tried to reshape themselves into an idealized version of U.S. reality (Rohatyn, 1990).

A variety of symbolic acts links present organizational practices to their cultural context, extending from the (commonly represented) past to the (commonly dreamed) future. Because there are many myths and prophecies available at any point in time, fashions play a selective role, indicating which myths and prophecies are "in" and which are "out," directing the traffic of ideas within and between contexts.

The Travels of Ideas

Readers who consider fashion to be too frivolous a mechanism to be included into the organizational theory discourse should ask themselves a question: How is it possible that the same or very similar ideas materialize in many organizations, often very distant in space, at the same time? A wave of decentralization reforms that reached Swedish municipalities between the years 1977-1988 touched many local governments profoundly, some perfunctorily, and others not at all (Czarniawska-Joerges, 1988a). Somewhat later, most regions in Sweden built up a new unit whose aim was to improve regional cooperation between the research and education institutions on one side and business companies on the other, but they all denied any central influence upon them and claimed that the idea came to them quite independently (Beckman, 1987).

Idea-spreading is often discussed with the help of the concept of *diffusion* (Rogers, 1962; for a recent review see Levitt & March, 1988). This chemical metaphor leaves, however, the mechanism of the phenomenon unexplored. We can possibly agree that ideas move from "more satiated" to "less satiated" contexts, but how do they travel? Even if ideas become reified in common thinking, most physical laws still do not apply. We must look for a social mechanism of spreading and *fashion* seems to be the most suitable (Czarniawska-Joerges, 1990).

One attempt to defend the concept of fashion from the taint of frivolity is to discuss it in highly idealistic terms, something like Zeitgeist. In the present context it is more natural to concentrate on its commercial aspect: fashion is a social mechanism which influences the market and distorts the demand and supply curves. It consists in a collective choice among tastes, things, ideas orientated towards finding what is typical for a given time (Blumer, 1973).

Often following fashion feels like a duty—fashion is the expression of what is *modern,* and it is a duty, especially for people in high organizational positions, to bring progress into organizations. Following fashion can be, in a company, a way of keeping up with the competition, and in public administration a way of keeping up with the times in the interest of the mandator. But other aspects must be emphasized as well. Fashion always has a function of releasing from responsibility (Sellerberg, 1987). In fact, fashion is a highly paradoxical phenomenon. Georg Simmel observed that fashion allows to conform to what is commonly accepted and at the same time to experiment with something new: to be alike *and* to be different (Simmel, 1973).

In this sense fashion stands for change, as opposed to tradition. Tarde, the classic of imitation analysis, contrasted the control of the "timeless society" (tradition) with the control of "times we live in," a fashion within a time-collective, as Sellerberg (1987) interprets it.

Not all organizational ideas, however, that are around at a given time are tried out by all organizations. Fashion has its boundaries, and time-collective is also a space-collective. How to delineate, for performative purposes, its ever shifting boundaries? A useful way might be to follow the processes of structuration of organizational fields (DiMaggio & Powell, 1983; Giddens, 1979). An increase of interactions among certain organizations, an emergence of interorganizational structures of domination and coalition, a shared information, and, finally, a development of "field consciousness"—that is, an awareness of belonging to the same thought world—indicate the time and space boundaries where a collective selects among a common repertoire of ideas.

Local Theories of Organization

It would be absurd to assume that organization researchers themselves operate free of a cultural context of any kind; rather, it is only too obvious that we, too, belong to various thought worlds. Paradigms reflect fashions in the professional time-collective, but the space-collective also leaves its mark.

An often repeated criticism challenged the imperialism of the U.S. organization theory (see for example Mrela & Kostecki, 1981), although interestingly enough, many classic works (Etzioni, 1961; March & Simon,

1958; Perrow, 1976/1986) contain a warning that the interpretations they proffer are derived from and valid for U.S. organizations. The alleged imperialism, then, is at least partly due to the willingness on the part of recipients to accept the U.S. organization theory as universal. This phenomenon can be read as a part of a general McDonaldization of the contemporary world, but also as instrumental in an attempt to universalize other local organization theories (Czarniawska & Wolff, 1987). Consequently, one can observe a Scandinavization of decision-making studies, a Europeization of cultural studies, and a Canadization of strategy-oriented research, to coin a few examples.

A postulate of full rights for local organization theories, as opposed to a search for the universal organization theory, may be read as parochialism. But nothing is further from my intentions in postulating it; indeed, there is no way to understand local practices without gaining understanding of the nonlocal, or different local practices. The universal human nature, provided it exists (or rather, can be constructed as another ostensive definition), would be of a very limited use in concrete organizations. On the other hand, knowledge of other practices and other interpretations, indeed, the awareness of other thought worlds, can only deepen the understanding of the phenomena at hand (Geertz, 1988b) and increase our solidarity both with the community we live in and communities that are alien to us (Rorty, 1989). Additionally, the exchange of local interpretations can lead to accumulation of interpretive concepts and practices, rather than accumulations of positive statements concerning organizations.

What we called "the Viking organization theory" (Czarniawska & Wolff, 1987) is a good example. The Scandinavian based organization studies extended the decision-making frame of reference to action theory. Decisions are to be understood in the light of actions and vice versa. This extension of the theoretical perspective revealed the usefulness of diversified definitions of rationality, composed in a performative mode. One can speak about decision rationality, action rationality, and the reciprocal rationality of decision and action (Brunsson, 1985). But woe to those who will treat these definitions as ostensive and try to adopt them literally in a different context. In organizations different from those that provided the ground for the Viking theory (for example, private sector rather than public sector and non-Scandinavian organizations) the action-decision ratio is differently shaped and interpreted. A definition that has a high performative value for a researcher (and in context of the mainstream career, the ostensive definitions, have, paradoxically, the highest performative value) might be of no use for a practitioner. Changing contexts should help us to understand this phenomenon and to make wise use of it.

Research as Cultural Experience

All that has been said points to the value of anthropologically inspired methods in understanding organizations (Czarniawska-Joerges, 1990). But isn't it so that anthropology's internal taboo forbids the study of one's own culture? In spite of the risk of being accused of being old-fashioned, says Leach (1985), it is his duty to remind the anthropologists about the dangers of studying the culture of one's origins: unproblematic acculturation prevents true perceptiveness.

Obviously, the culture-as-bubble notion cannot accommodate such a proscription, as it eschews the concept of borders and delineating differences. Not so the other two conceptualizations: culture-as-a-way-of-life and culture-as-a-thought-world. Shouldn't we be always studying others' ways of life and alien thought worlds, as it could not have been the fish who discovered the water? Taken literally, the warning would only apply to self-reflective studies, and enough has been said to defend the legitimacy of such studies. (See for example the collections of readings edited by Clifford & Marcus, 1986, or Woolgar, 1988.) Let us then move to what is conventionally meant by this criticism: the taking for granted of "one's own culture."

In the first place, the way of life of most organizations, with the exception of those that we belong to, is not at all the same as our way of life (Sanday, 1981). Second, it is an illusion that we can escape our thought world and immerse ourselves, naked of prejudice, into another one. The best we can do is to expand our thought world by understanding the possibility of other worlds or "subuniverses of meaning" (Berger & Luckmann, 1966). Rather than fight the battle on what is the legitimate object of study in cultural studies, I propose to focus on seeing research practice as a cultural practice, in literal and metaphorical sense.

Research activity consists of abandoning the taken-for-grantedness of organizational life in order to problematize practices of organizational actors. However, doing so, it soon becomes clear that this is not a one-way process. With the possible exception of cases where powerful self-defenses are used, problematizing what other people do provokes the reverse action: our own practices are problematized in turn. As long as we "play native" we can get acceptance in strange worlds, but not understanding of them.

("Playing native" requires a non-problematic stance towards what is happening, taking for granted of what-is.) If we want the understanding, we must ask; by posing questions, we problematize; by problematizing, we reveal ourselves as not really belonging.

All would be well if the natives came with answers as required; alas, they tend to come with questions or incomprehensible answers that challenge the original question. Our own practices become problematic; and inevitably, our identity comes into question when, rather than being taken for granted, we are challenged to recreate our identity in an unfamiliar setting. Most people do not know what organization researchers do; many of them have some images that we fail to recognize or accept, as they come from mass media, idiosyncratic encounters with other representatives of our species, or analogies from natural sciences. Cultural colonialism is one possible way of dealing with such a situation but, especially on the home grounds, it is hard to establish a basis for a superiority claim that would survive. The way out is to retreat, or to enter a dialogue on negotiated conditions.

Let me end with a literary example of such a dialogue, to be found in David Lodge's (1989) novel, *Nice Work*. The two main characters, Vic and Robyn are natives of what they believe is the same world, the contemporary British culture. Their forced encounter reveals them to each other as strangers, inhabiting worlds that never meet: that of men, industry, and conservative politics as opposed to that of women, academia, and radical politics. Their paths crossed by chance: somebody "up there" came upon an idea that the university people might benefit from observing the industrial managers at work. The protagonists' first reaction to the confrontation is an urge to colonialize: each is certain of the superiority of their own world and the inevitability of the other's falling for it. Alas, the antagonists are equally formidable and a new way must be forged. Humbly and hesitantly, they learn from and about each other, in this way learning about themselves. The novel's happy ending does not have to be seen as a testimony of what usually happens; rather, it is a sketch of an ideal that might be impossible, but still remains attractive. We live in multiple strange worlds whose colonization is quite impossible; why not accept their existence and make ourselves more familiar with them?

The cultural perspective emerges in this light as more than just a choice of an attractive research paradigm. Rather, it is a necessary step to understand the multiple realities of the postmodern world, where organizations are both the major producers and the main products of these realities.

21

Comments and Discussion

HARRISON M. TRICE

The following observations on these four chapters have tended to center around a research commonality in them, and around two prominent general themes found in them. My reactions to both make up a third aspect. Because of limitations of space, expressions of respect and admiration for these papers will be muted. But for those who read between the lines, as students of culture often do, my high regard for their "keeping the flame alive" should become evident.

On Methodology and Fiction

Although not highly explicit, among the four authors there is a tendency to shy away from quantitative methods; given the inherently fuzzy nature of culture, this is probably as it should be. At the same time, in these presentations the authors are rather vague about how their qualitative data on organizational culture would be, or has been, collected and analyzed.[1] Granted that their methods have been discussed in more detail elsewhere, the point remains that the collection, analysis, and interpretation of culturally relevant data were not prominent features either here or elsewhere. This is all too typical, and seems to be especially true of how we actually carry out analyses of our qualitative data. Although this in no way represents a lack of deep concern for rigor, it is nevertheless a feature of our work that could profitably receive more attention. This lack of systematic analysis may well reflect a well-known confession of Geertz (1973) that he had never

> gotten anywhere near the bottom of anything I have written about. Cultural analysis is intrinsically incomplete. And, worse than that, the more deeply it goes the less complete it is. (p. 29)

Thus, although the data for analysis may well be "thick descriptions" characterized by a particularism oriented toward the native's point of view, there typically is a paucity of systematically derived evidence offered from which the native's subjectivity, experience, and intentions can be assessed. Somehow, if we sleep on the data, or write fiction from it, or "let it emerge," we, ipso facto, have confidence in it and are ready to put it forward as worthy of scholarly consideration. We seem to be quite happy with our thick descriptions, giving relatively little attention to the actual mechanisms that we use to analyze the data once we get it. It is as if systematic and uniform analyses were secondary to the writing of fiction and narratives. Thus Clifford (1986) writes that ". . . ethnographic writings can be properly called fictions in the sense of something made or fashioned . . . but it is important to preserve the meaning not merely of making, but also of making up, of inventing things not actually real" (p. 6). In Rosen's chapter in this section he reaches a similar conclusion: "ethnographic writing is always the writing of fiction."

Two rather well-known research methods appear to have been largely overlooked by scholars interested in organizational cultures. Both help to reduce, but not eliminate, the fiction involved in the analysis of cultural data. Both represent a careful, self critical analysis of a researchers' own work, including scrupulously careful attention to an informant's meanings (Clifford & Marcus, 1986). Users need not claim that they embrace detached objectivity. Yet both methods delineate and outline a systematic way, with some describable precision, for actually going above data analysis.

One—the use of the Thematic Apperception Tests (TAT) and their stories—provides both an unobtrusive way to collect culturally relevant data and a scheme for actually scoring the stories in a way that allows detailed, even statistical, evidence about specific cultural themes (Bock, 1988). In the case of the TAT, it is the story-telling and fictional projections of the natives about their own culture that make up the data for analysis. Presumably this fact lessens the fictional burden of the researcher. Moreover, all four authors seem to be trying to get at the tacit, somewhat submerged, but not deeply hidden, aspects of culture. This objective clearly suggests the projective properties of the TAT. Meyerson observes that people tend to keep their internal feelings invisible until in safe settings. Projective instruments such as the TAT tap these internal states indirectly and unobtrusively and are free of the many ethical problems that come from interviewing and participative observation.

The second—the constant comparative method—seeks out in the data empirical indicators of culturally relevant concepts and repeatedly compares them in the data (often some form of field notes or research interviews) to one another, thereby confronting similarities, differences, and degrees of consistency of meaning among the indicators (Strauss, 1987; Turner, 1981). This method involves a search for persistent categories that are grounded in the data, and the ultimate formulation of a coding system and its systematic use in the search and discovery of theory about cultural phenomena within the data (Glaser & Strauss, 1967; Martin & Turner, 1986). What is to prevent cultural researchers from attaching such a methodology to the qualitative data generated in the ubiquitous use of field notes to provide more rigor and less fiction? Let us turn first to a brief sketch of the TAT as a research tool and second to the constant comparative method as an analytical technique for use with qualitative data.

Students of organizational cultures have usually found the comparison of cultures difficult. The use of the TAT, however, could make for the identification of at least a core of cultural themes on which data could be collected across organizations in the same national culture. The adaptation of the method to the workplace would require the creation of ambiguous and ill-defined pictures of human actors (probably 10 in all) in blurred work settings. Subjects would be asked to tell (project) a story about each picture as it is presented. Typically there is no time limit and each story is recorded verbatim. Each subject responds to directions regarding the broad outline of a story plot: Who are they? What is happening? What led up to it? What is the outcome? Since the pictures are vaguely familiar, and almost "anyone can tell a story," data collection is less threatening then interviews and questionnaires. Pictures would be scored on specific themes believed to be pertinent to organizational cultures, reported from other research, or emergent from pretests on pilot samples.

According to Colby (1966) TAT-like pictures and scoring procedures have been used to analyze and interpret folklore, drawings, literature, and the content of reported dreams. A cogent example is the report of Gladwin and Sarason (1953). They used modified TAT pictures among the natives of Truk, a cluster of small islands in Micronesia. Sarason interpreted the

TATs in terms of specific cultural themes, for example, inconsistency of parent-child relationships, separation anxieties, and suppression of hostile feelings. The study featured an interesting division of labor: Gladwin, an ethnographer, worked completely independent of Sarason, a psychiatrist. Gladwin gathered all the ethnographic and life-history data and administered modified TAT pictures. He then wrote a cultural analysis and description. Sarason took the TAT stories, interpreted them, and independently came up with many of the major features of Truk life that Gladwin had included in his ethnographic account.

Cultural themes that could be used in collecting TAT data in work organizations in the U.S. have been identified by numerous researchers. Sethia and Von Glinow (1985) located four types of meaning systems in work organizations: apathetic, caring, exacting, and integrative. Earlier Harrison (1972) constructed four types: power oriented, rational and orderly oriented, person oriented, and task oriented. All of these are potential cultural themes on which the TATs of members could be scored and contrasted with samples from other organizations. Presumably TATs might, at least in part, substitute for the lengthy, time-consuming fieldwork that few academics can muster. At the same time their use may be quite "etic"-directed unless care is taken initially to put them in an "emic" framework.

In Chapter 18 Meyerson suggests a readiness among researchers for unobtrusive instruments such as the TAT. She experimented with "visual data" such as collages, videos, graphs, and simple pictures. Unfortunately her analysis of some of these types of data focused on only one feature of an organization's culture—its ambiguities. TAT scoring could incorporate numerous other possible cultural themes, providing an inventory of the themes in an organization's core belief system. In the process, ambiguity could be seen in a gestalt perspective rather than in isolation, as is the case in Meyerson's graphs. For instance, the sharedness of values and beliefs could be scored in the stories along with indicators of ambiguity.

But the analysis of more commonly generated data—such as field notes from observations and participation observations—is probably a more immediate research problem for those who want to study organizational cultures than is the development of projective instruments. Field notes seem to be ubiquitous among qualitative researchers, but ". . . the processes by which these are transformed into 'analysis' . . . are still poorly covered" (Ellen, 1984, p. 3). Fortunately the nature and generation of field notes has been extensively discussed in Sanjek (1990a). This volume should do much to make the collection and use of field notes far more respectable and effective than they had been in the past. For that matter, the Sanjek book also makes it quite clear that field-workers have at times collected literally thousands of pages of field notes, often upgraded from "scratch notes." And therein lies the problem.

How can any researcher systematically analyze such a massive array of qualitative field data? Two possibilities come to mind: (1) use of the constant comparative method on a sample, or prominent part of the data, in order to precipitate out field grounded indexes (categories); and (2) the uploading of all transcribed notes on a computer and use of computer programs such as ETHNOGRAPH (Johnson & Johnson, 1990) or QUALOG (Shelly, 1988) to scan the data in terms of discovered categories. These codes (categories, indexes) are also entered into the computer files. In the case of QUALOG a file is created which records every instance that the index word is used throughout the entire body of data. When a researcher wishes to find all instances of a particular index no papers need be shuffled endlessly; the information is literally at one's finger tips. Granted there are headaches. At Cornell we have worked through some of them, and, on balance, see QUALOG as a possible way out of the quagmire (Hathaway, 1989). At the same time, it is an enormous amount of work, and rather costly.

Despite the problems and controversies these research possibilities would probably create, they nevertheless are, in this responder's judgment, in the tradition of Sanjek's (1990b) description of such qualitative classics as *Coral Gardens and Their Magic* and *Street Corner Society*. He writes as follows about them: "They are not novels, nor plays, nor journalism. They are to be evaluated by different canons. They are ethnography, and made from field notes" (p. 413).

Finally, it seems appropriate to suggest that both of these specific methods provide a rather natural bridge between quantitative and qualitative methods. Rarely have these two methodologies been combined. Siehl and Martin's (1984) qualitative/quantitative study of socialization in an organizational culture is an exception. Both the TAT and the constant comparative method can reach a quantitative point where counting and scaling can be introduced to explain rather than describe a phenomenon. The qualitative research mode can also be used as the basic materials from which hypotheses and quantitative instruments can be constructed for deductive rather than inductive data gathering.

Sharedness Versus Ambiguity

One of the most striking features of this brace of articles is the definitions of culture offered by Schein, on the one hand, and Meyerson on the other. Because cultural research becomes expressed and focused on the basis of explicit definitions of culture as a phenomenon, the sharp contrast between the two is revealing. Meyerson makes ". . . central the ambiguities in cultural life." In her chapter, she reflects the fragmentation perspective described in "Part I: Introduction-Ten Empirical Studies of Culture." For Schein, however, "it does not make sense to think of cultures of ambiguity and conflict . . . the concept of sharing or consensus is core to the definition . . ." He reflects the integration perspective described in the Introduction. At first blush it seems as if each has overlooked the other's position because of space or haste. After all, there is no reason why both of these dimensions cannot be subsumed within the same definition. But a careful second reading suggests that they both are deadly serious. Furthermore, in the final analysis, both are right and both are wrong.

But Schein seems to be more right than Meyerson for the simple reason that it seems unlikely that a culture would form when there were only ambiguities and fragmentations at its center, even though they might make up much of what actually does constitute a given occupation's or organization's culture.[2] If ambiguity and fragmentation are the essence of relationships, and if the feeble and transitory consensus that does form fluctuates constantly with these dominant forces, as the fragmentation perspective suggests, then, ipso facto, there is practically no culture to study. Quite simply, culture scarcely exists in the fragmentation perspective. It would have little, if any, capacity to grapple with ongoing collective uncertainties and runs the high risk of spinning off into gross individuation. Foregoing a static orientation, in a dynamic sense mechanisms of conflict reduction may well emerge to reduce, to some tolerable degree, the confusion and ambiguity, or relationships will dissolve further into individuated chaos. Reversed, there could readily be instances of high consensus regarding common and shared beliefs and values associated with continuity in a culture.

Meyerson, however, has a good, if, somewhat exaggerated, point to the effect that much of the popular literature, and some not so popular, rests on the mistaken assumption that organizational culture consists of shared meanings and commonalities that are quite homogeneous, monolithic, and organization-wide (Deal & Kennedy, 1982; Peters & Waterman, 1982). Ambiguous forces are a part of culture, and need to be duly incorporated into operational definitions. Moreover, she is far from alone in this view. It is also true that concepts of loose coupling (Weick, 1976) and subcultures (Trice & Morand, 1991) have been widely accepted as reflecting the ambivalences and ambiguities of organizational reality. These were preceded by less recognized, but nevertheless relevant, notions about the inherent "fuzziness" of culture (Bellman & Zadeh, 1970; Pierce, 1977). At the social-psychological level much has been made of role ambiguity as a feature of group life (Kahn, Wolf, Quinn, Snoeck, & Rosenthal, 1964).

Schein's position also seems rather exaggerated and representative of a singular focus. Paradoxes, contradictions, inconsistencies, double binds, dilemmas, ironies, and irresolutions of them abound in most modern cultures, including those of work organizations. For example the examination of paradoxes in organization life has received considerable recent attention:

> Observers are becoming more sensitive to the presence of simultaneous opposites or contradictions in effective management and organizational behavior. More and more writers recognize that paradoxes are indigenous to effective organizational functioning, and, in particular, to individuals, organizations, and industries facing a modern post-industrial environment. (Cameron & Quinn, 1988, p. 1)

And Van de Ven and Poole (1988, p. 23) advise that a very legitimate response to these ambiguities is to "learn to live with paradox." They insist that "as theorists we may feel a strain toward cognitive consistency, but that does not mean that the world is consistent."

But, like Meyerson, Schein also has a point, a good one, to the effect that there does exist in organizational cultures, as in all cultures, a center, a core set of ideological guidelines, that requires a minimal consensus and consistency. Without such an assumption there is little, if any, possibility of explaining "the amazing persistence and fixity observed in common organizational life" (Van de Ven & Poole, 1988, p. 20). In short, some organizations may be on the verge of anarchy, but even they are nevertheless "organized anarchies," not anarchies as such (Weick, 1985, p. 109). Consistency, consensus, harmony, and integration do occur even though in the midst of inconsistencies, ambiguities, conflicts, disruption, and dissolution. These two sets of forces appear to be reciprocal to one another. It is even conceivable that they somehow are essential to each other. Such a condition is the ultimate paradox in the puzzle of organizational behavior.

Czarniawska-Joerges and Rosen seem to fall between these two opposing definitions. The former writes of culture "as a bubble (of meaning) covering the world . . . it is the medium of (social) life." She insists that "organizations are cultural phenomena themselves," and implies that the word "culture" is not merely a metaphor, or an independent variable, but that organizations are cultures. At the same time, she underscores the political aspects of cultural analysis, avoiding the "consensus perspective," and thereby recognizing that conflicts and power struggles are a dynamic feature within the cultural "bubble." In this focus she joins those who note the prominence of subcultures and countercultures in organizational life (Trice & Morand, 1991).

Rosen also seems to come down between the two opposites, but does it via an examination of symbols and rituals, combined with an emphasis on their interpretation in terms of power and politics. He underscores, however, how provisional these interpretations actually are. He infers some degree of order and uneasy consensus in this mix, but also that the resulting norms are ". . . not only ambiguous, but also directly in conflict with one another." He cites both Edmund Leach and Max Gluckman, anthropologists who analyzed the interrelations between both conflict and order. Czarniawska-Joerges and Rosen seem to suggest that we need an operational definition of culture that includes both the forces of integration and ambiguity as well as an intermingling of the two.

Against this backdrop the problem facing students of organizational cultures is to realize that the rather polar viewpoints of Schein and Meyerson are each only a single focus, both relevant, but neither one the whole story. Moore (1975) succinctly puts the matter:

> There seems to be a continuous struggle between the pressures toward establishing and/or maintaining order and regularity, and the underlying circumstance that counteractivities, discontinuities, variety, and complexity make social life inherently unsuited to total ordering. . . . Order never fully takes over, nor could it. The cultural, contractual, and technical imperatives always leave gaps . . . and are themselves full of ambiguities, inconsistencies, and often contradictions. (p. 219-220)

Such a position sets the stage for the introduction of the notion of cultural centers and peripheries (Shils, 1975). Assumptions of either consensus or dissensus are not in and of themselves sufficient to encompass the way culture is shared, or the way a cluster of beliefs can form a cultural center. When, however, we examine cultural phenomena in terms of the relation between cultural centers and their peripheries, both foci come into an understandable relationship. Enough consensus about core values to generate minimal cooperation and coordination throughout the system seems to characterize the relationship between center and periphery. It is stronger in the center, but contains discernible traces even in the outer peripheries. Shils (1975, p. xii) writes: "Societies are full of conflicts . . . Those who are in conflict with each other respond to the name by which they designate their membership in their somehow encompassing society, and they recognize some identity through time and across lines of conflict."

Later, Shils (1988, p. 251) expanded on the center/periphery idea: ". . . it espouses and embodies beliefs about things thought, by itself and by other centers *and by their peripheries* (emphasis added), to be of transcendent importance, that is, 'serious.' 'Serious' things are things thought to be fundamental, that is, which affect the fate of human beings on earth, in life and in death." At the same time "no periphery is homogeneous . . . Many but not all the internal differences at the periphery are accompanied by degrees of distance from the center" (p. 256). In sum, a set of ultimate ideologies appears to consistently emerge at the center where there is considerable consensus about each one even though they may conflict among one another. These, in turn, radiate outward from the center toward the periphery in varying degrees of consensus to diverse segments of the periphery. This process tends to make for a motley and tangled skein of meanings loosely held together by a distinct center. Meyerson and Martin (1987, p. 630) have summarized this paradigm as "differentiation," that is, "complex organizations reflect broader societal cultures and contain elements of occupational, hierarchial, class, racial, ethnic, and gender based identifications. These sources of diversity often create overlapping, nested subcultures."

What Was Left Out

Two culturally relevant themes received scant attention in the four chapters. Relatively little attention was given to (1) cultural forms and (2) occupational cultures as a prominent subculture that call for attention in their own right. Although Czarniawska-Joerges gives consideration to organizational rituals and myths, there seems to be among the authors an overall and notable absence of mention or discussion of the cultural forms—symbols, language (metaphors, proverbs, jokes, gossip, songs, gestures, and jargon), narratives and stories, myths, rituals, taboos, and rites and ceremonials that function to deliver cultural messages. Confusing, conflictual, and ambivalent as these often are (Turner, 1990), they nevertheless are the major sense-making mechanisms and should play a prominent role in cultural analyses (Beyer & Trice, 1987). Rosen's incisive analysis of the rites of renewal involved in "Breakfast at Spiro's" in Chapter 5 is clearly an instance of focus on cultural forms. His emphasis in Chapter 19 on ritual and ceremony appeared, however, to be considerably less. If we view these forms as an essential part of culture it is important that we consistently incorporate them in some reasonable, perhaps limited way, in everything we do. How do they contribute to the ambiguity that Meyerson points to, or to the consensus of assumptions and core beliefs that Schein finds so pivotal? Or do they do both almost simultaneously? How can they be incorporated into cultural audits? (Wilkins, 1983a). Which ones are "key symbols" (Ortner, 1973, p. 1340), and which ones are trivial and almost meaningless? Was "Breakfast at Spiro's" a potent sense maker in Rosen's advertising agency? Is the relationship between core ideologies and forms a direct one, easily discernible, or a more subtle and indirect one, or a collage of unlikely and unexpected juxtapositions of both? One point does, despite these questions, seem clear: A relationship does exist and without it culture would not exist.

The second theme that was "left out," although mentioned, especially by Meyerson, is a consideration of occupational cultures. The absence is in no way unique to this set of authors. As a matter of fact, studies of organizational cultures in general outnumber studies of occupational cultures by a large margin. Yet occupations are probably the most distinctive subcultures in organizational life (Van Maanen & Barley, 1984). Many people derive their identity as persons and their social status from their occupations. Indeed, well established occupations have cultures just as organizations do (Trice & Beyer, 1991). As a consequence various types of acculturation emerge between organizational cultures and occupational cultures. In some instances occupational communities dominate the organization; in a second type the two cultures accommodate themselves to one another. In a third type an occupational culture comes to be assimilated into, and dominated by, the organization. Finally there are those instances in which an occupation attempts to reject both the administrative rationality of the organization and its own occupational expertise, creating an authority of democratic consensus (Sonnenstuhl & Trice, 1991).

Within this framework cultural researchers can analyze the ideologies unique to a given occupation, the cultural forms that relate to those ideologies, and how organizational and occupational cultures interrelate. Thus, in the first type, within law firms and accounting firms, management functions are performed by occupational members who bring their occupational ideology to the tasks of administration. As a result persistent

conflict seldom arises between the rank and file and the occupationa
managers as long as the occupational community remains in control of the
content of its work. In the second type, corporate physicians manage to
retain much of their occupation's culture, but nevertheless must accommodate to the production emphasis of management. In this mode a degree of
balance between health needs and profit needs emerges. Printers are ar
example of the third type. They were once considered to be the epitome of
skilled craftsmen. Their occupational culture was distinctive, making for
a community of core beliefs and cultural forms. But their culture has been
dramatically assimilated by management's persistent efforts to deskil
them. The last type has generated a distinctive ideology that imbues
both the skill dimension and the administrative. Egalitarian, democratic
ideals prevail. Thus in producer cooperatives, feminist health collectives
and free schools both occupational and organizational cultures become
melded into one collective effort to produce a new work organization ir
which everyone has a voice in formulating what tasks are to be performed
and only those decisions arrived at by group consensus carry moral
authority (Jackall & Levin, 1984).

Notes

1. *Editor's Note:* Harrison Trice is correct in his observation that these four authors did no
discuss how they collected qualitative data relevant to their presentations in this monograph. Ir
their defense, we point out that we asked them to focus on other issues of their work.

2. Meyerson studied an occupation notorious for its ambiguous and fragmented occupationa
culture (Loseke & Cahill, 1986). It comes as no surprise that it is riddled with ambiguities. Hac
she studied accountants the results might have been quite different.

IIC
Framebreaking

"When you wake up in the morning, Pooh," said Piglet at last, "What's the first thing you say to yourself?" "What's for breakfast?" Said Pooh. "What do you say, Piglet?" "I say, I wonder what's going to happen exciting today?" said Piglet. Pooh nodded thoughtfully. "It's the same thing" he said.

—BENJAMIN HOFF
(The Tao of Pooh, 1983)

Reframing Organizational Culture is being published in 1991, a time of ferment and transition in the worlds of ideas and of action. There is an impermanence and a flux to things both theoretic and concrete which needs to be acknowledged by anyone who wishes to do research on a topic such as culture. Indeed our whole purpose in writing and titling this as a book about framing and reframing as the process of inquiry about organizational culture is to acknowledge the importance to knowledge acquisition of different perspectives. Each perspective contributes, yet each limits what we take as knowledge about the phenomenon. There may be flux within organizational culture research, but to understand the meaning of this statement we need to look outside and around the whole organizational research perspective enterprise. One such context is the transition of *Culture* from a modern to a postmodern era. It is an era in which the very context of our experience is seen to be *cultural*—a made rather than received world. It is a political not a natural world. There are, therefore, no naturally dominant or authoritative voices on the meaning of life. From a postmodern perspective, even nature, as Hutcheon (1989, p. 2) observes, "doesn't grow on trees."

What this requires is an exercise in reframing at a truly fundamental level of seeing, believing, thinking, and acting. It poses exciting and upending opportunities for scholars of organizational culture. "Masquerade: Organizational Culture as Metafiction," which comprises this section, captures the flavor and the intention of a postmodern examination of organizational culture. We hope it sparks much thought, debate, and exploration among the readers of this book.

22

Masquerade:
Organizational Culture as Metafiction

ANONYMOUS AUTHORS

Milano

It is 10:00 p.m. in Milano on a June 1987 summer night. Darkness has just enveloped the city. Lights from the passing traffic create a backdrop of color in an otherwise solemn urban landscape. But it is fun to be in Milano. We had finished our session that afternoon and were now feeling the warmth of being among "old" friends—at ease to agree or disagree with us. We have met most of these friends during the past three days but, like the streets of Milano, new and old blend so well that you stop paying attention to the difference and let yourself go into the rich experience that they form together. We are milling around the inside/outside that comprises the Bar Magenta. It is fine if you want to take your beer to the sidewalk and avoid the crowd inside. The conversation forms a chain of engagements in and out and back inside. So, it doesn't really matter where you are located, you are always inside the discourse.

It seems that since the afternoon all we can talk about is *the* meaning of organization culture. We had an encounter with Debbie, Joanne, Caren, and Mary Jo[1] over the possibility of abandoning "culture" and what that would mean for organization theory. Would the demise of "culture" announce the demise of organization theory as we know it? That conversation carried over to dinnertime, continuing while we all savored the banquet that Pasquale organized for this SCOS meeting.[2] Our table also included Hope and Silvia. What a great time we were having! The mirrored space of the hotel's great room did not have anything institutional about it; the seven course dinner—each one more delicious than the previous one—was an Italian miracle in "large batch" cooking. It was good to be in this company where serious topics, ironic criticism, and plain giddiness easily mixed and nobody needed to sound "boring smart" to fully participate.

The topic continued full-fledged as we entered Bar Magenta for a nightcap. Together with Mark and Mats, we are ready to have a "serious go" at unraveling "The Meaning." The conversation gains momentum when Mats asks the proverbial rhetorical question:

> *How, then, can the rise and rapid expansion of studies of organizational culture be understood?*

Mark thinks that we must understand this situation from a historical viewpoint:

> *Novel, perhaps disturbing, as the approach of studies in organizational culture and symbolism might seem, it is not without precedent in the history of ideas. In its general aim of understanding reality, it parallels 19th-century Romanticism both as to historic origin and philosophical orientation. Both movements are grounded on the recognition that not all areas of human experience can be known through reason, that some areas are accessible only to nonrational faculties. Not all human concerns can be with hard facts; many lie with intangibles such as emotional events or the perception of time. Should these areas be left out of human inquiry because reason, that conventional spotlight, fails to illuminate them? It is out of an endeavor to somehow capture these elusive aspects that Romanticism was born, and that the symbolist perspective in organizational analysis is now evolving.*

And, of course, we are in Europe and "debate" is an illuminating style of conversation, so Mats cannot fully agree with Mark's statement and proceeds to offer an alternative explanation:

> *The extension and popularity of a theory or a school (direction of interest) depends partly on its intellectual/theoretical qualities, partly on the degree of correspondence to the needs of the dominating elite and other important groups of interest, and/or a general market for academic knowledge (that could be seen as a function or an aspect of the "Zeitgeist," the spirit of the present time).*

But Mark does not find Mats' explanation sufficient and proceeds to expand on his view:

> *The Romantic movement that swept through Europe beginning in the late 18th century and flowering in the 19th arose as the antithesis of mechanistic rationalism. The neo-classical belief in the supremacy of reason as the ultimate cognitive instrument was challenged by the Romantics, who argued that the Romantic perception of reality could actually open more doors to larger areas of experience by utilizing all human faculties. This approach made all of reality a meaningful whole, resolving apparent fractures and contradictions in phenomena in the light of imaginative vision. Reality was conceived by the Romantics as an organic body of ideas (in the Platonic sense) constituted by symbols and myths. This was directly opposed to the neo-classical mode of dissecting and quantifying reality into discrete parts. The symbolist approach, like the Romantic, originated in dissatisfaction with the exclusively analytical-quantitative approaches dominating organizational analysis until recently.*

There is no pause before Mats responds:

> *It is usual that while the representatives of a discipline or an orientation stress how development goes forward and upward, observers whose orientation is the sociology of knowledge and science are often more skeptical and claim that ideological and other societal conditions influence the theoretical content in a way that makes it difficult to speak of a clear-cut development towards "better" theories.*

Do we hear an ironic edge in this response?

While the exchange is going on we are becoming increasingly uncomfortable. Too much socialization into the U.S. culture and its low tolerance for conflict would, no doubt, account for our reaction but we are restless and unable to engage in any self-reflexivity over our feelings. (Others may say that we were tired of being spectators and were now ready for action). In any case, we think it is time to offer an explanation that could reconcile both parts, and we venture:

> *Our answer is to locate the organizational culture literature in the midst of a wide cultural/historical debate taking place in the western world: that debate is the transition from modernism to postmodernism.*

And as we repeat almost the same words presented that afternoon to a broader audience, we now hear in them our interest in preserving the intellectual historicism of Mark's views while keeping the commodification orientation of Mats'. So we continue:

Modernism refers to activities that try to present an opposition to a "dominant normativity," as a way of questioning. Why does it have to be your way and not mine? Why is your truth more truthful than mine? The problem of modernity is that at some point its opposition (its "less truthful truth") becomes rationalized as or incorporated into the dominant truth. Thus, it is unable to be in opposition anymore. We see the interpretive/social constructionist organizational culture literature as an oppositional/modernist movement in organizational theory and research, and recognize its failure to gain any major grounds in its oppositional stance.

Without denying our views, Mats offers a more cynical version:

I believe that the concept of organizational culture can be seen as an organizing principle for theorists within the field. Through modifications of the more or less traditional approaches, organizational researchers with an interest in the "software' (human, immaterial) rather than the "hardware" (technological, material) side of organizations are grouped around the concept of culture (symbols). By relating to the modern concepts, these approaches are provided with an aura of modernity, progressiveness, novelty, and increased market value. At a very concrete level there are benefits in the form of special conferences and networks as well as good opportunities for publishing in the large number of journals with special issues on "organization culture" or "symbolic management" that motivate connection with the organizational culture movement.'

Good—we think—and promptly interject:

Right now it seems that organizational culture is in the tradition. Its language (myths, stories, rites . . .) has been turned into a fad by traditional approaches in organizational theory and research, which has mummified, rationalized, and used its "soft" rhetoric to convey an image of cultural refinement—"high modernism" at its best. To the extent that "culture" has been appropriated, incorporated, into the functionalist, positivist, technical interest—made part of the "traditional organizational literature"—the organizational culture literature may be, to borrow a phrase from Habermas, "dominant but dead."

This latter comment rekindles Mark's interest in the conversation. We are citing some critical concepts but have forgotten the intellectual heritage that allows us to think this way. Mark is ready to remind us:

Romanticism, less obviously, has also had an impact on Marxism and neo-Hegelian thought and thus on the sociologists of the Frankfurt School. If Romanticism has had such substantial impact on social science, then it is more than likely to provide ideological templates for the organizational culture and symbolism perspective. Weber's ideal-typical method and his concept of social action carry the stamp of Romantic thought. Romanticism's reception by the Frankfurt School proves the critical potential of the Romantic legacy.

And suddenly we all remember that Ralph and Walt were adamant on this point when they said some time before:

The critical theory of Jurgen Habermas is a useful perspective for analysis of approaches to knowledge. When applied to organizational symbolism, his approach shows how the contributions of symbolism have led to developments in the practical interest but severe underdevelopment of the emancipatory interest. An attempt to reclaim the potential of symbolic research in the service of the technical interest and traditional powerholders is also revealed. Not only does such a critique reveal these patterns in the current literature, it points out how knowledge in pursuit of the emancipatory interest might expand the study of symbolism. Most notably, the approach leads to a focus on means of preserving divergence and avoidance of all aspects of organizational life that constrain conscious self-control. From this perspective, mainstream work in the field is at best nonemancipatory and often anti-emancipatory in its interests. As such, the field of organizational symbolism remains incomplete in its search for knowledge of organizations, and requires more stress on human autonomy and responsibility in the value choices revealed by the kinds of knowledge it pursues.

Mark is, indeed, back into the conversation. His point has been well sustained by all of us and he proceeds to say:

The critical potential of the symbolist perspective lies not only in its epistemological force but also in its love of distance, since loving the distant encourages one to compare the immediate with the distant. Accordingly, as you have argued—he says, citing one of us—if the distant interpretations of an organizational culture offered by a researcher are made available for consideration and reflection, "the analysis of the organization as a culture may serve the same purposes as that served by therapy for an individual." Moreover, loving the distant may be a first step to try to change the immediate in order to achieve the distant. Some Romantics, Byron, for example, became change agents as revolutionaries.

Too much Romanticism for Mats—it seems—as he brings us back to the reality of the present:

> *The general social context of organizations in the 1980s: Social psychologists and cultural theorists describe a broad trend toward increasingly felt needs for involvement, subjectivity, expressiveness, meaning, and social togetherness. In former historical periods strong socialization agencies, for example, the family and the church, have lost ground and the space for new socialization agencies has increased. The corporation's role in this regard then comes into focus.*

As he finishes these words we can understand why in the "neo-Romanticism" of organizational culture there is little room for revolution, Byron notwithstanding.

Thus, as we try to articulate a position that is neither Mats' nor Mark's, we recognize the presence of theirs within our own:

> *We believe it is necessary to understand the organizational culture literature against the wider cultural context of the postmodern era. Postmodernism is a response to modernism. As a response to modernism it does not try to oppose but to resist. Activities of postmodernism do not offer a better or greater truth; they only suspend judgment while uncovering/exposing the structures of better or greater truth. They do not propose a dominant view but observe and comment on the multiplicity of fragmentary views. They understand these events in/as the context of our present world, where fragmentation and multiplicity flourish in the face of any attempt at grand solutions. Postmodernist activities move within and among these ever changing fragments to make/understand the world better over and over again.*

And as our small circle gets fragmented among the clouds of cigarette smoke (some said they were traces of Puff the Magic Dragon which Durkard had brought along) and we have some photographs taken with Barry, Mats, and Yvonne, we still insist:

> *Taking a postmodern view of the organizational field permits us to "think culturally" rather than to "think of culture." The latter is the cultural framework for most of the current organizational culture literature, a basically acultural and ahistorical view of the world. The former is the cultural framework which can make all organizational literature culturally conscious.*

San Francisco

It is August 1990. We are sitting around in Peter's room at the San Francisco Hilton. Our mood is ambivalent. Some time ago we were asked to write an original piece for this book on "the researcher as culture-maker" and now we feel that there is not too much point in doing so. We have looked at other pieces in the book's working manuscript and notice that several of them are not original. Although the introduction announces that "since 1985 . . . the proliferation of research on organizational culture has continued unabated," many of the writings are selections or adaptations of pre-1985 works.

Our ambivalence could be attributed in part to a sense of being overworked and not wanting to take on one more project. Why not reproduce some of our prior writings, as others did? But on further analysis we find that some other issues also bother us. Partially it is the fact that we thought we had written our "last word" about organizational culture in Milano, and that we have moved on to "postmodern organization theorizing" since then. Who wants to write *about* organizational culture again, even if it is about the way we, researchers, "make" our literature? Partially it is the fact that we find a striking absence in the collection of works: our European colleagues who have been working hard through SCOS to strengthen the "culture/symbolism" aspects of organizational analysis. Partially, it is finding ourselves encased in a genre—that of organizational culture writings—from which we find no escape.

We have brought up these issues with Peter a few days before. Our suggestion at the time was to have a conversation in San Francisco among all of us—we and the book's editors—on the topic of "the researcher as culture-maker." If we tape and transcribe the conversation—we thought—it will be a way to do some experimental writing while preserving the topic of interest. It would also be a way to explore together some of the issues that were bothering us and, thus, expand the topic.

Unfortunately, the suggestion did not work. The logistics were difficult and we are not able to meet face to face until today, and only for a short time. Other Academy commitments haunt all of us. We leave the room with the general feeling that we are in the same place we were before except that the assignment is more open than we thought at first. For example, Meryl said "we will know what 'it' is when we see it," and Joanne encouraged us to do something like "you did for the SCOS meeting at INSEAD last year."

September 1990 arrives and we are still trying to figure out how to finish this piece. We have settled for the few paragraphs written above and are now ready to provide some analytical commentaries. We are concerned about the ways readers will interpret what we are trying to do. How might you read the above lines?

More Tales of the Field? A Very Short Story on Culture-Making—as we reflect upon the possibility that some may read the Milano/San Francisco stories for their content, we are tempted to finish the chapter right here. Hey, after all we researchers are *people* like everybody else! See, we have feelings, quarrel with each other, have our likes and dislikes, and that influences our work and what we write about . . . A useful psychologizing explanation.

Or we may provide an institutional interpretation. In this case we would be illustrating how what the researcher as culture-maker does—as part of our profession—for example, go to conferences, travel to other countries, meet interesting colleagues, talk about our work and its content, forms by itself a type of organizational story.

But as we were writing our stories we were concerned with *representing* well what was going on. As many "culture-makers" have realized, the nature of writing what is *really* going on is no simple matter. Few of us believe anymore that the issue of representation is one of "truth" versus "falsity," and most of us recognize that "writing culture" is a matter of what James calls "partial truths" as much as it is a matter of genre and the kind of "tale" we want to tell. So you might read our stories above as a story *about* making cultural stories.

For example, if we use John's classification, we may say that our stories rely, first, on a *confessional* strategy. We have personalized our authority, provided our point of view, respected our informants. But our tale is also *impressionistic,* insofar as it is a dramatic recall of a series of events where we ask the reader to relive our experiences. Whatever knowledge is to be had will appear in a fragmented fashion which requires the reader to stay with us to the end. And, of course, as we are trying to make an interesting dramatization we rely on conversations and a sense of intimacy (gossip?) to appeal to our readers. However, if we take a closer look at our commentaries in this part, the tale is, foremost, a *realist* story. Here, in this section, we are making sure that the reader will not "go home" without an analytic frame to understand "the researcher as culture-maker."

Now, up to this point we have pretended that we could tell you the story of "the researcher as culture-maker" as if it were any other organizational culture story, multiple interpretations included. After all, why should our situation be different from the ones we write about? However, different from other organizational stories, this one has particular nuances that we should explore further.

Telling our stories, like those about Milano and San Francisco, may pass as just some more organizational stories, the only difference in ours being that we—the authors—are also the actors. But what is special about that? Autobiography rather than biography? Perhaps the tale of "ultimate subjectivity," the real insider's tale? Is is more complicated than that.

Different from other organizational stories, ours are not finished before we proceed to do some analyses or interpretations. In fact, the analytical or interpretive part of our tale could be considered the core of our story because that is what the "culture" of the "culture-maker" is all about, that is, devising analytical or interpretive schemes to help the reader "know," or "writing knowledge."

Thus, as we write these lines we reflect on the irony of this tale. When we write about what others do we are writing from our authorial status, and we provide our analyses as the outsider looking in, even as we try to portray the "inner life" of the other. We *are not* them; we are just trying to know them, and to be able to tell others about them.

However, as we try to portray ourselves, the "culture-makers," in all our doings, there is no end to the story. As we try to say/tell what we do, the explanation/interpretation becomes the object of explanation/interpretation, over and over again. Like a play of mirrors, what we do is what we do is what we do is what we do . . . and so on. If we desire to put an end to the story we must rely on one of two fictions. We may rely on our "knowledgeable authority" and end up with a purely self-referential text (i.e., that's what we do because we say so) or we may rely on another text crafted by a colleague (i.e., citations that would support our points) and on the prior authority of that text. These fictions are precisely how we—culture-makers—"authorize" our portrayals of the others.

On trying to tell the "culture-maker" story the only thing we achieve, then, is calling into question the authority of all our productions. That is, with this observation what comes to the fore is that from here on it is "turtles all the way down." For the minute one tries to define the nature of one's own text, its status is up for grabs. And what becomes even more problematic is the *origin* of our assumed authority as "culture (knowledge) makers."

With this said, we don't have any other alternative than to go back and re-examine the issues which we were trying to raise when we began this piece of writing. On bringing together these many conversations various things were at stake. First, we were—and still are—bothered by the continuation of "organizational culture" as a form of organizational analysis because, as expressed by Mark, the romantic appeal of this form—including its more critical versions—maintains the humanistic tradition and its emancipatory promises intact. As such, "organizational culture" becomes a "metamyth" because it attempts to correct (through its analyses of myths, stories, symbols) the apparent deficiencies of "rational/positivist" organizational analysis without noticing that both forms share the same metaphysical bases.

The "myth of correction," and its corollary assumption of moving toward a more adequate analysis of organizational realities, depends not only on the possibility of the "progress of knowledge" but equally on the possibility of an authorial imagination—that of the researcher—which will make possible better interpretations. These assumptions are able to cover over "the turtles . . ." because they depend on an "outside" as their object. Lacking reflexivity, these assumptions make it unnecessary to call into question the authorial imagination.

Thus, "organizational culture" similar to the "rational/positivist" modalities of organizational analysis, is a modern form of "knowledge" which depends, precisely, on the possibility of what Richard calls the *productive imagination* of an author capable of going beyond what has already been said to produce an original thought and more truthful insights.

However, the minute we "culture-makers" start questioning the outcome of our productivity—the texts that we fashion and the way they are done—it is difficult to be sure about the "origin" of "our" imagination. Mats' commentaries on the "commodification" of organizational knowledge is one of the many dimensions on which we can question our "productive imagination" because it is the "knowledge market" that decides what "sells," and it is "the market" that defines what can be said and by whom, that is, authorship, originality, and productivity are defined a posteriori under conditions of power/knowledge, as Michel would have said.

But as we maintain our postmodern stance the problematics of "original knowledge" appear in still other forms. If as "insiders" we abandon the myth of "productivity" and of "original authorship" we are doing so not only because of the probabilistic nature of what appears as "knowledge" (about organizational culture or anything else) but, more critically, because of our doubts at this point of any possible "originality," whether publishable or not. "Originality" as a unique form of personal insight for better comprehension of an *original* "truth," "beauty," or "good," is a difficult myth to sustain in our current society.

Perhaps our current society is more like the multiple plays of mirrors to which we referred when meditating about our own "culture-making"—a society where there is not clear distinction between "the real" and its "image," and where images (from different kinds of screens) are our everyday realities. Where is *the original* when Andre reminds us that "image is everything"? Where is *the original* in a society where what can be said bounces from information point to information point, making the global rounds, without known author or final destination? And as we watch "the Bush/Hussein TV war" and the "line in the sand" from the comfort of our kitchen we realize, again, the irony of our times if all we can do is to continue to portray "the realities" of "organizational culture" in an "original text."

Thus, as products of our own society, our "knowledge" shares the parodic elements of that society; and as we recognize here the myths of "authorship," of "originality," and of "higher knowledge," we also recognize our privileged location among the "knowledgeable," among those who through repetition sustain the myths of "the productive imagination." In this sense then this text is very "real." Neither fact nor fiction, it has been produced as another reflection, another image, another mirror of our own culture.

And let us not forget that while this space appears to offer to us the opportunity to resist the modern myths by allowing us to talk about the problematics of postmodernism and knowledge-making, there is also the unavoidable condition of the text in which we are encased: as this text makes "us" the "authors" of an "original" when it becomes a public document, its effect—whether positive or negative—will always attain the repetition, the continued talking about "organizational culture."

But as we dance around in our masks we try to resist once again. Who are the authors of this text? Where does this text come from? The authors are all of us in the following intertext—as Roland would have it—with no privilege other than our first names in order of (dis)appearance—and all our "original texts" are just another repetition.

Intertext

Debbie, Joanne, Caren, and Mary Jo are some of our friends from the U.S. We probably became closer friends in Milano in 1987 as we discussed the possibility/impossibility of continuing the organizational culture work as it has been up to that point. Debbie's and Joanne's work for Milano has been a very strong inspiration for the general shape of this volume. Our own work, and space here, owes a lot to their friendship.

Pasquale was the organizer of the Standing Conference on Organizational Symbolism (SCOS) for 1987. He played his role as host impeccably, and that made it possible for the participants to be at ease and become close in a very short time in spite (or perhaps because) of the constant toll of church bells.

Hope and Silvia—two of our friends from Italy. Even though we met them for the first time in Milano in 1987, they were our "old friends" from the very beginning. We have shared a lot of good times since then, both socially and intellectually. They have given us courage and support as well as hospitality, which we wish to reciprocate more frequently. Many of our words are theirs.

Mark—we knew his work since 1985. It is a pity that we do not get too many papers from other countries in our USA journals because this voice from Germany, like many other non-North American voices, has a lot of interesting things to say. Our impression from reading him in the *Journal of Management* (Vol. 11, No. 2) was further reiterated when talking with him in Milano in 1987. His words reproduced here are from the *Journal of Management* article.

Mats is a Swedish friend with whom we share a lot of common interests. When we were using his critical work in our courses, before we ever met him, we were certain that his voice was close to ours. On meeting him in 1987 it was a pleasure to share the face-to-face. That was the only dimension missing from the friendship that was, no doubt, already there. His voice in this paper is reproduced from *Dragon,* the SCOS journal, (1986, No. 7).

Ralph and Walt are well known voices in our U.S. circles. We sympathize with their critical posture and their historical orientation. Walt is a closer friend and has shared with us in our more recent endeavors. They were not in Milano in 1987 but their voices, from the *Journal of Management* (Vol. 11, No. 2) were very congenial with our conversation.

Byron—6th baron (1788-1824) George Gordon Byron—English—wrote things like:

> Thou hast a voice, great Mountain, to repeal
> Large codes of fraud and woe; not understood
> By all, but which the wise, and great, and good
> Interpret, or make felt, or deeply feel.

We never met him, but for us the "organizational culture" literature is a current parody of his flight of Romantic imagination. However, having lost this memory, "organizational culture" has become post-modern pastiche: parody without humor. Mark's comments are the occasion to bring the memory back.

Burkard was the other presenter in our session in Milano. His rendition and sing-along version of "Puff the Magic Dragon" in that session created a very good backdrop for our irreverences about "organizational culture" later on. We are indebted to him for this, and have benefited from reading his work from Wuppertal since then.

Barry—as a well-known English scholar we had read his work often. It was a pleasant surprise to find out that he was our discussant in the Milano session. Since then our ties have become closer as our lives have crossed paths in person and in print many times.

Yvonne—we met this Danish friend when we met Mats. From the beginning we learned about our common interests in feminist theory, which we were beginning to pursue. Our friendship has been strengthened by our shared intellectual and everyday-life struggles, living as feminists in a nonfeminist world. Mats' voice often joins Yvonne's and we value particularly the solidarity we feel with them across the Atlantic.

We wish that we could share with you the photographs that we took that night at Bar Magenta. Don't you feel now that you should know how these people look? In the patriarchal regime of "the gaze," there is that funny situation about "the image" being "worth a thousand words."

Peter: Old friend . . . Are you inside, outside, or all around this writing?

Meryl: We hope this is 'it' . . .

Joanne: We are sorry if this one is not as *seductive* as you expected. We did not have the "heart" (left in San Francisco?) to do "a mintzberg" this time.

James: Our comments are partially inspired by his words, such as "Once cultures are no longer prefigured visually . . . it becomes possible to think of a cultural poetics that is an interplay of voices, of positioned utterances. In a discursive rather than a visual paradigm, the dominant metaphors for ethnography shift away from the observing eye and toward expressive speech (and gesture). The writer's 'voice' pervades and situates the analysis, and objective, distancing rhetoric is renounced." He continues a few pages later: "If 'culture' is not an object to be described, neither it is a unified corpus of symbols and meanings that can be definitively interpreted. Culture is contested, temporal, and emergent. Representation and explanation—both by insiders and outsiders—is implicated in this emergence. The specification of discourses I have been tracing is thus more than a matter of making carefully limited claims. It is thoroughly historicist and self-reflexive." And later he says: "It has become clear that every version of an 'other,' wherever found, is also the construction of a 'self,' and the making of ethnographic texts . . . has always included a process of 'self-fashioning.' . . . Cultural *poesis*—and politics—is the constant reconstitution of selves and others through specific exclusions, conventions, and discursive practices." Perhaps you would like to read more from him in *Writing Culture* (University of Cal. Press, 1986).

John: We invoke his work here with some ambivalence. We've appreciated the same traditions but, different from James', his intertext carefully and explicitly leaves out anything that may call into question 'authorship,' 'self-hood' and the status of his own text. These *Tales of the Field* (University of Chicago Press, 1988) are an interesting exercise of balancing on top of the first turtle as if it were the last one.

Richard: On reading him we have found another voice with which to express our concerns around "culture (knowledge) making." In a way he "corrects" our inspiration from James. His text alerts us to the current situation where print is subordinated to other representational images, and the domain(s) of the visual increasingly constitute our contemporary culture. In this world where image re-production pervades every discursive space, that is, it is how and what we talk about . . . "There is no possibility of a single founding reference. Language, as an open-ended play of signifiers, is no longer thought to refer to some 'real' meaning *external* to language (i.e., some 'transcendental signified' called truth or human subjectivity). Deprived of the concept of *origin,* the concept of imagination itself collapses. For imagination always presupposed the idea of origination: the derivation of our images from some original presence." And a few lines below: "The deconstruction of the category 'origin' is heralded by the famous *textual revolution.* The humanist concept of 'man' gives way to the anti-humanist concept of intertextual play. The autonomous subject disappears into the anonymous operations of language . . . The modern philosophy of the creative imagination—whether it be "in the form of Kant's transcendental imagination or Sartre's absurd passion—cannot, it would seem, survive this deconstructive turn." More "from" him in *The Wake of Imagination* (U. of Minnesota Press, 1988).

Michel: So much of him lives in the works we and others do that it is difficult to remember that he is not around anymore. Among the many words from him that have helped to shape the illusion of our "knowledge" are some early ones such as: "Strangely enough, man is probably no more than a rift in the order of things, or, in any case, a configuration whose outlines are determined by the new position he has so recently taken up in the field of knowledge. Whence all the chimeras of the new humanisms, all the facile solutions of an 'anthropology' understood as a universal reflection on man;" and some very late ones such as: "My problem has always been . . . the problem of the relationship between subject and truth. How does the subject enter into a certain game of truth? My first problem was . . . for example, How has the mad subject been placed in this game of truth defined by knowledge or a medical model? And it is in doing this analysis that I noticed that . . . there were practices . . . which sent me back to the problem of institutions of power . . . So it was that I was led to pose the problem of power/knowledge, which is not for me the fundamental problem but an instrument allowing the analysis . . . of the problem of relationship between subject and games of truth." As a first reading we recommend *The Order of Things* (Pantheon, 1971).

Andre: Probably the penultimate postmodern athlete salutes us from the screen while selling "image-makers" from Japan, and then enters center court as a walking billboard from Madison Avenue. But, can he play? What is his game? We still don't know the answer. After watching the matches for two weeks in a row all we are left with is a great smile and "a humble explanation;" "the best man won." Great entertainment and nice performances . . . it may as well have been a TV serial. Or was it?

Roland: Told us about intertextuality many years ago, and since then we have taken ourselves much less seriously. He is not around anymore either, but left behind some very wonderful words. Among our favorites: "We know that a text is not a line of words realizing a single 'theological' meaning (the 'message' of the Author-God) but a multi-dimensional space in which a variety of writings, none of them original, blend and clash. The text is a tissue of quotations drawn from the innumerable centers of culture . . . the writer can only imitate a gesture that is always anterior, never original. His only power is to mix writings, to counter the ones with the others, in such a way as never to rest in any one of them. Did he wish to *express himself,* he ought at least to know that the inner 'thing' he thinks to 'translate' is itself only a ready-formed dictionary, its words only explainable through other words, and so on indefinitely . . . Life never does more than imitate the book, and the book itself is only a tissue of signs, an imitation that is lost, infinitely deferred." Perhaps you would like to read *Image-Music-Text* (Fontana, 1977).

We: We are . . . but how can we tell you? We are the discourses that work through us . . . we are all these multiple discourses . . . and then some others like "If woman is truth, *she* at least knows that there is no truth, that truth has no place here and that no one has a place for truth. And she is a woman because she herself does not believe in truth itself, because she does not believe in what she is, in what she is believed to be, in what she thus is not." And in appropriating these words from Jacques we continue to "be," and so are able to move into the next intertext.

Intertext

Jacques: Oh! never mind . . . he would not like to be "the last word" anyway . . . and you, reader, can supply your own turtles.

Notes

1. Readers interested in the full names of individuals mentioned in this chapter can find them included with the names of the authors of this chapter in "About the Contributors."

2. This meeting was a conference: "The Symbolics of Corporate Artifacts" coordinated by Pasquale Gagliardi in June, 1987. It represented that year's academic event in the annual series of Conferences organized by the Board of SCOS, the Standing Committee on Organizational Symbolism.

3. After delivering a lecture on the solar system, philosopher-psychologist William James was approached by an elderly lady who claimed she had a theory superior to the one he had described. "We don't live on a ball rotating around the sun," she said, "We live on a crust of earth on the back of a giant turtle." Not wishing to demolish this absurd argument with the massive scientific evidence at his command, James decided to dissuade his opponent gently. "If your theory is correct, madam, what does this turtle stand on?" "You are a very clever man, Mr. James, and that is a good question, but I can answer that. The first turtle stands on the back of a second, far larger turtle." "But what does this second turtle stand on?" James asked patiently. The old lady crowed triumphantly. "It's no use, Mr. James—it's turtles all the way down" (cited by Bernard Nietschmann [1974] as the epigraph for his article "When the Turtle Collapses, the World Ends." *Natural History, 83*(6), 34-42).

In Nietschmann's article the epigraph has no citation, and we have heard the same anecdote with different actors (e.g., a colonial officer in India and a native), thus its folkloric "origin." We should mention, however, that the epigraph in Nietschmann's article has a particular function. It precedes a contemporary ethnography on Miskito Indians in Nicaragua whose traditional system, based on fishing green turtles, maintained a perfect ecological/economic balance. "Development" brought the collapse of the system, and destroyed the society's welfare, when turtle fishing became a trade/industrial concern.

IID
Context and Choices in Organizational Research

This world was everywhere the same until name and shape began: then one could say: "He has made such a name and such a shape." Even today everything is different by name and shape.

—P. FREUND
(*Myths of Creation*, 1965, p. 5, from the Hindu
Brihadaranyaka-Upanishad).

In this section, we have chosen to focus on the influences on an act of organizational research that stem from prior conditions, implicit choices, and other characteristics associated with the particular researcher and research context. These influences apply whether a researcher is studying organizational culture or other organizational phenomena. There are several reasons for taking this approach. First, explicit methodological choice points have been well discussed elsewhere. Second, it seems appropriate to turn the mirror of culture research on ourselves. What do we mean by this?

In one sense, the study of organizational culture can be thought of as an effort to describe the context in which organizational members work. For instance, results of a culture study in an organization may encompass descriptions of core values, assumptions, symbols, subgroups and their traditions, and the common (i.e., ordinary and shared) experience of working there. These represent some aspects of the context in which people in organizations work. In addition, we have become aware of other influences that might best be labeled historical. Learnings from political perspectives have made us aware of the need to consider constituencies that are variously powerful, represented, and overlooked in a setting. Recent adaptations of postmodern and feminist perspectives on organizational inquiry have opened our eyes to the need to consider actor characteristics such as gender and ethnicity as part of the influential context.

Most importantly, we have come to realize that such features of work contexts and their members influence the organizational members' ways of viewing and doing their work. Similarly, organizational researchers work in organizational and occupational settings. We can expect our present and historical contexts to influence the ways we view and do our work. We will argue that tracing the influence of traditional methodological choices tells only part of the story, that we must become aware of broader contextual influences on the process and outcomes of organizational research. In making this argument, we view the researcher as an occupationally and historically situated actor. Analysis of the chapters in Part II reveals three relevant themes associated with the context of research. In terms of organizational research they can be discussed as (a) a professional occupation, (b) a value-based enterprise, and (c) a personal activity. In this section, we will describe and illustrate each of these three themes, and use them to draw together learnings from Part II.

Organizational Research as a Professional Occupation

Of late, it has been our habit to talk about paradigms as approaches to cultural research. However, if we view organizational research as a cultural activity, we are likely to focus on professional traditions and to think of paradigms as basic assumptions associated with particular traditions. Along these lines, organizational researchers are considered members of a profession.

A profession is an occupation based on specialized knowledge, in which there are formal training programs run by members of the profession, associations that define membership and offer self-regulatory mechanisms, and a code of ethics (Blankenship, 1977, pp. 4-6; Wilensky, 1964, pp. 137-158).

In the organizational sciences, we have doctoral programs developed and run by faculty which train neophyte researchers in acceptable research practices. The Academy of Management (AoM) and other professional associations convene national and local meetings at which we exchange and discuss our research, instantiate a marketplace of jobs for new members and members in transition, and socialize. The AoM administers three major journals distributed to all members, and thus serves as gatekeeper to a major research outlet. These and other publishing outlets are governed by members of the profession; another instance of self-regulation. The AoM commissioned the development of a code of ethics to which organizational researchers are asked to subscribe. Progress in one's career is evaluated by peers and senior colleagues outside of one's own institutions, as well as by colleagues inside.

The doing of organizational research is influenced, in part, by these professional aspects of the field. In the past, we have tended to treat the act of research as one of choice and free will; here, we wish to highlight aspects of research as displays of cultural tradition. For instance, the training one receives shapes where one looks for problems, as well as how one looks at them; what one overlooks; to whom and where one turns for assistance, funding, and access to research sites; what one considers to be high and low quality work. In essence, focus and anti-focus, the included and excluded, the foreground and background—in terms of conceptual, empirical, practical issues—are shaped by the socialization and training one experiences as one becomes a member of the profession. As a seasoned researcher designs and conducts a study, most of the time, much of what that individual does comes out of the template of his or her professional tradition. The chapters in Part II demonstrate several such traditions.

Among the writings in Part II, three chapters deal with the dominant professional tradition of culture research among organizational scientists, and two suggest less mainstream organizational research traditions. In chapter 13 Bryman describes it, in chapters 18 and 20, respectively, and Meyerson and Czarniawska-Joerges critique it. Schein and Jones in chapters 17 and 12 represent other professional traditions and their associated paradigms that may be brought to bear in understanding organizational culture.

We begin with Bryman's commentary on *Street Corner Society*. In chapter 13, he outlines characteristics of good qualitative research in the Chicago school tradition of participant observation. The practices include seeing through the eyes of natives, providing contextual understanding, being concerned with process, and having the research emerge in response to the process of inquiry, that is, remaining flexible. Good participant observation requires spending significant time in the field, providing conceptual and theoretical focus, and using natives' categories to describe their world. In this genre, the researcher attends to local practices as they are linked to underlying values. What we have here is the description of the practices of the Chicago school as a particular professional tradition, a cultural community, if you will.

In a timely critique of this mainstream tradition in Chapter 18, "On Acknowledging and Uncovering Ambiguities in Cultures," Meyerson demonstrates how ambiguity is excluded from culture studies "as an artifact of our community's values and beliefs." She articulates as a goal of inquiry to pick up diffuse, unclear, volatile, irreconcilable aspects of culture (p. 255). Her focus is on local practices. She finds them revealed in "operational data," which she contrasts with official or "presentational data" (p. 265). Her research practices, though perhaps little different from those Bryman advocates, are guided by a different goal.

In another critique, Czarniawska-Joerges sets Bryman's mainstream paradigm in context as a product of U.S. social science. In Chapter 20 "Culture Is the Medium of Life," she raises our awareness of different paradigms and professional traditions among European organizational culture researchers. In this way, professional traditions can be seen as cultural practices. And, like Meyerson, she is concerned to distinguish group's practices from its principles. Her aim is to focus on practices attending to "performative" rather than "ostensive" definitions.

Czarniawska-Joerges also calls attention to potential effects of doing such research on researchers. She notes that it is important to keep the insiders world problematic in order to gain understanding; going native cuts short the aim. In maintaining the problematic status of another's world, she observes that the researcher's own practices become problematic.

In Chapter 17, "What Is Culture?" Schein brings to bear a different professional tradition for appreciating organizational culture—the clinical method. Through serving in a consultant role, Schein relates how an outsider can help insiders become aware of their own values, assumptions and artifacts. It is a model that makes explicit the epistemological challenge in culture research—that is, we are after what is for the most part taken-for-granted. At the extreme, the clinical method can be contrasted with participant observation in two ways: the clinical method captures more reflection and less action by insiders, and the product represents greater participation by insiders in the interpretive process.

Finally, Michael Owen Jones describes another paradigm and professional tradition for examining workplace culture—that of the folklorist. In Chapter 12, "On Fieldwork, Symbols, and Folklore in the Writings of William Foote Whyte," he shows how a researcher's pursuit of a "people's traditional, symbolic forms and processes" can help reveal what they take for granted and find most difficult to discuss. As he contrasts the traditional, symbolic practices of machinists in Northern factory with those of workers in a Southern hosiery mill, Jones instructs the reader about systematic research on a group's folklore. In theory, a folklorist's approach contrast significantly with the clinical method Schein describes. Whereas Schein' clinician provokes interactions with insiders, Jones' folklorist collect behavioral remains and observes without participation. In practice, this approach has some overlap with the participant observation tradition; in both, a group's behavioral "droppings," so to speak, are captured.

In reviewing papers in Part II, we see demonstrations of various paradigms or research traditions, each with a particular focus and objective, epistemological foundation, and set of data collection methods. In turn, each research tradition is nurtured through a professional tradition, or culture, if you will. Each tradition entails training in the accepted practices and the acceptable exceptions—what we agree to not notice (e.g., ambiguity).

For discussion purposes, we have drawn the traditions as fairly distinct. However, not only do traditions flow together, but as members and participants we switch and realign ourselves among allied ones, and in conducting research, we piece together fragments from several even contradictory research traditions. If the reader sees himself in several, that too mirrors the kind of ambiguity inherent in culture, whether in the situations we observe or attendant to the cultural milieux in which we participate as professionals.

Researchers are well advised to recognize the subtle influences of their professional affiliations and backgrounds, lest they fall prey to *the fallacy of present choice*. The design of a piece of research is not a matter of making "present choices" among methodological alternatives; neither choice nor present action tells the whole story. Much of the design one "chooses," one does not choose directly. Rather the choice occurs by drift rather than deliberate action, as one affiliates with and is socialized into one's professional track. In this sense, choice is the wrong word to describe how a researcher comes to pursue a particular methodology and epistemology in a specific study. Further, such preferences or leanings have emerged long before the study at hand is being designed. If, as we are warranting, the design of new research studies is a function of past influences, it behooves us to become aware of past influences we bring to current inquiries, to avoid the fallacy of present choice. We do not mean to suggest that one cannot broaden or alter one's professional affiliation, only to note that doing so is unusual and takes deliberate action. Rosen's contribution discussed below demonstrates the power of shifting one's lens or, at a minimum, observing oneself viewing through a particular lens.

Organizational Research as Value-Based Enterprise

Beyond the general value characteristics of a professional tradition, values underlie organizational research in at least two critical respects: in the world of the observed and in the actions of the observer. In situations observed, whether for research or other purposes, we may expect that the set of interests of some particular party is dominant, whether the parties to the situation are aware of it or not (and often some or all are not). Others' interests are subservient; the dominance or power of one group or individual commands the consent of others. For the most part, relationships of dominance and subservience, command and consent, are fairly stable. These relationships and the status or power of each party are fundamental to the worldview of each; they are not simply a part of that worldview. A critical epistemology would have us recognize and reflect these dynamics in any organizational inquiry. As reviewed below, Rosen's analysis in Chapter 19, "Scholars, Travelers, Thieves: On Concept, Method, and Cunning in Organizational Ethnography," of the Hermes tie incident is most instructive on this point.

Second, any organizational researcher represents a particular set of interests in the observed situation, whether the researcher is aware of it or not. The act of "looking" itself is always positioned, as Jermier's discussion in Chapter 15 reveals. In this second sense, then, organizational inquiry is not value-free. Let us look at these two points in more detail.

Through the vignette of passing on the unreturnable Hermes tie, Rosen exemplifies each of the three themes of this section: organizational research as professional occupation, as value-based enterprise, and as personal activity. As British social anthropologist, Rosen generates an ethnographic record in which the observed culture is represented. Then as post-modernist, Rosen demonstrates that the ethnographic text is more invention than representation—it is created by the ethnographer and is thus fictional. Finally, as critical theorist, Rosen highlights the network of "power, interest, hegemony, and consent" among parties to the "Hermes tie" interactions. He reveals for us a political underbelly of organizational interactions. The point for Rosen is that cultural observation is incomplete without an account of this political subtext, of the role of values in the world of the observed.

The second issue—the role of values in the actions of the observed—is addressed by Jermier in Chapter 15, "Critical Epistemology and the Study of Organizational Culture: Reflections on William F. Whyte's *Street Corner Society*." He begins by tracing epistemological influences on Whyte as researcher. Jermier describes the pressures of positivism Whyte experienced at Harvard and the detachment emphasized in the Chicago school during the time Whyte was there as a research associate writing the appendix to *Street Corner Society*. Despite these pressures, notes Jermier, Whyte ". . . practiced fieldwork and wrote ethnography in a subtle subjectivist style ahead of his time." (p. 227) Jermier then spells out the stance of a researcher pursuing a critical epistemology. "Social research has emancipatory potential . . . it must define [within its domain of analysis] primary causes of domination and oppression . . ." (p. 230). "[R]esearcher subjectivity and partisanship are essential to overcoming technocratic domination and orienting the human sciences toward serving the interests of oppressed and disadvantaged groups" (p. 228). This perspective makes it clear that in organizational research, the observer inevitably supports a particular set of interests; we are never "value-free."

We do not wish to set apart such value issues. Rather, we wish to suggest that a critical or value-based perspective should inform work across paradigms. Consider what it would entail to produce critical ethnography, critical clinical inquiry, critical folklorist accounts. In each, we would take up the call, both to reflect in our accounts the power relationships in settings we observe and to observe the power dynamics we reflect in the studies we conduct. In this way we might avoid the *fallacy of interest-free research*. That is, "free inquiry is never free. It's just not glaringly obvious who is manipulating it" (Burke, 1989).

Organizational Research as Personal Activity: Agency in Research

In Chapter 22, "Masquerade: Organizational Culture as Metafiction," the un-named authors relate their process in inquiry, not as afterword, but as primary text. The authors of this piece requested not to be named as a symbol of the meaning of their postmodern message: the concept of the individual actor as not being an independent creator of events and reports. Authorship becomes deemphasized in the presentation of a message. The authors of this piece create a rich narrative out of the volley of views, quotes, questions, and reflections that have occurred in the context of friendship, play, professional performance, and international visits. They convey how purposeful and casual conversations and readings contributed to the emergence of ideas. They enact a postmodern text, the essence of which is recognition of the many voices. Above all, they demonstrate the derivative and collective nature of the constructions. As postmodernists, they reveal that "realities" are socially constructed, multiple interpretations are the rule, and interpretation is affected by the identity and position of all parties to the inquiry. The authors of this piece render the researcher as culture-maker.

In a similar vein, Riley conveys the way in which organizational culture research represents a researcher's narrative about the narrative in the setting studied. In Chapter 14, "Cornerville as Narration," she urges us to not privilege a particular voice, "because we as researchers are in but a certain stage of a conversation . . ." (p. 219). The centrality of time and place are clear from her critique. "[T]heoretical constructions, methodological guidelines, and personal imperatives are seen as results of historical accident, as turns the conversation has taken." (p. 219).

We saw in the earlier discussion of value issues that a researcher is always "positioned," that is, always represents one or another particular set of interests (e.g., the interests of management, of clerical personnel). Similarly, a researcher and a specific study are always "positioned" vis-à-vis the personal characteristics of the researcher (e.g., gender, age, ethnicity) and the history of the inquiry, or the personal characteristics of the study, if you will (e.g., its context in time and place, the stream of interactions contributing to it). A research narrative voiced by a middle-aged white man will differ from a narrative voiced by a young black woman. A research narrative prepared in the intellectual climate of the United States today will differ from one prepared in Eastern Europe a few years ago. Awareness of such information is needed by both the reader and the researcher. Without knowledge of such characteristics, a reader cannot easily appreciate the context of the narrative produced and will have difficulty interpreting statements about the setting studied. Without awareness of such characteristics and their influence in positioning the study, the researcher is likely to succumb to an *objectivist fallacy* and to forget that the act of observation affects what is observed.

In summary, we have tried to demonstrate that a person conducting organizational research—on workplace culture or any other phenomenon—brings to the study a particular professional background with paradigmatic preferences for subjects of inquiry and assumptions about them and a network of ideas, colleagues, and relative influence. Design of a research study is not strictly a matter of present choice. The researcher also represents a particular value stance, a window on a facet of the phenomenon under study. All interests or perspectives are not represented in a single study of the phenomenon or group in which it is examined; no study is interest-free. Our final point has been in a postmodern tradition. The researcher's creation is ultimately positioned on the personal characteristics of its creator and the unique configuration of interactions that situate the work in its time and place.

PART III

AN EPILOGUE AND A CLOSING

I. December 5, 1945

VI. December 26, 1945

III. December 18, 1945

VII. December 28, 1945

IV. December 22, 1945

IX. January 5, 1946

V. December 24, 1945

XI. January 17, 1946

Picasso, "Bull" Copyright © 1991 ARS, N.Y./Spadem

IIIA
Looking Back

At eighteen, I thought that the theory presented in our astronomy class was the "truth" and that my friend's belief, the Biblical one, was mere fantasy. It should have given me pause, however, that the theory propounded in college was not the one I had learned in high school, only three or four years earlier. My high school teacher had told us about the Laplace nebular hypothesis to account for the origin of the earth and the solar system; whereas now, in college, I was being given the Chamberlin-Moulton plantesimal hypothesis. . . . If the Laplace hypothesis was no longer scientifically sound, in what respect was it different from a "myth"?

—P. FREUND
(Myths of Creation, 1965, p. 3)

We started this book in the spirit of rekindling the flame of organizational culture. In fact, we have found that the flame is very much alive and that there is not one flame but many. No matter where or when one marks the beginnings of the contemporary resurgence of interest in organizational culture, today it is a field of vigor and variety. Just over a decade ago, in just a few years a number of symposia, conferences, and writings appeared that brought considerable attention to the field, (e.g., Davis, 1984; Deal & Kennedy, 1982; Frost et al., 1985; Kilmann, Saxton, & Serpa, 1985; Pettigrew, 1979; Pondy et al., 1983; Sathe, 1985; Schein, 1983). Since then there has been a steady flow of culture-related writing of surprising size, scope, and diversity. Any examination of this body of work quickly shows that the multiple layers of meaning that constitute organizational culture may be unpacked in many different ways with many different consequences, and that tremendous difficulty surrounds the identification of shared meanings. Hence this book, promoting an awareness of how rich the concept of organizational culture is and the different ways in which it may be conceived and studied.

Organizational culture researchers, like the researchers of other organizational phenomena, are faced with and act upon a series of choices, each of which impacts the others. To date, these choices have not been very well articulated or perhaps not even recognized. We have addressed the issue of choice in a number of ways. As shown in Part I, there are choices in *perspective*. Culture researchers begin with and tend to work within one of three fundamental perspectives which Martin and Meyerson (1988) identified as integration, differentiation, and fragmentation. What prompts the choice of a perspective? In Part II, Section D, we discussed the shaping of such choices in terms of the socialization of professionals in a field. There are, of course, other major influences on a researcher's perspective. (For example, Stablein [1988] attributed an important role to a researcher's preference for the scientific, humanistic, managerial, and critical ideologies.) The central point of focusing on perspectives as we have done is to remind ourselves that our theoretical perspectives (as well as our ideologies) shape the research that we ultimately undertake in important ways. Part I of this book described and illustrated this point through empirical exemplars of each of the three theoretical perspectives.

Cultural researchers also make choices regarding the *design* and *methods* of the inquiry and in Part II of the book we examined, through the voices of several scholars, including our own, the way researchers think about this kind of choice. Although theoretical and conceptual perspectives can and do influence choices of design and method, there is reciprocity involved in the process, because what follows from the implementation of design and method can and often does influence what the researcher comes to see as the theoretical meaning of his or her work. The world of cultural research is full of surprises!

Moreover, as noted earlier, in the case of some individuals currently in the field, the same researcher can use different theoretical perspectives for addressing different questions about research. However, in some cases, the shift in perspective may reflect changes in the scholar's own beliefs and understandings about the nature of organizational culture. We identified the work of Rosen in Chapters 5 and 13 as a prime example of this kind of shift in perspective.

What becomes clear, as one examines the interactions among theoretical perspectives and design and method in this way, is that for some researchers shifts between perspectives on organizational culture may be a practical matter. For example, the researcher may choose an integration perspective on culture as suitable to investigate and interpret one set of questions and a fragmentation perspective as more appropriate for a different investigation and/or interpretation. This researcher buys into the assumptions and the world view of the integration perspective and is shaped and conditioned by that particular interpretive frame while that particular study is the focus of his or her attention. But he or she buys into a different set of assumptions and the world view of the fragmentation perspective for a second, different study. In this example, the researcher's ideology would seem to incorporate different perspectives on the meaning of organizational culture. For other researchers, this is not necessarily so. At one point in time and until or unless an *ideological* shift impacts on these individuals, what they as researchers take as perspective on organizational culture is quite stable. Within our framework, these researchers identify with the tenets of one of the integration, differentiation, or fragmentation perspectives and pursue knowledge about organizational culture within that perspective for an extended period of time.

The field benefits from both single and multiple frame approaches to organizational culture research. For those who come into organizational culture research in the future, we advocate broad and flexible thinking in order to provide a rich array of ideas and information about a phenomenon that, in our view, can never be wholly understood by one frame, through a single design, or by using one research technique. The reality at present, we believe, is that, for the most part, investigators working within one perspective tend to overlook information about meanings that investigators of alternative perspectives will readily see.

Stated thusly, one might conclude that cultural inquiry should attempt a meta-theoretical integration of all three perspectives. We, with Martin and Meyerson, argue that the beliefs and assumptions of each perspective are fundamentally incompatible and cross-perspective theoretical integration would very likely destroy the integrity of each; it would destroy their power and political reasons for being as well. An alternative inquiry strategy might be to adopt a single perspective and simply ignore the others. This strategy too is overly simplistic because each perspective in some ways complements the others. It is perhaps just too soon to advocate either perspective autonomy or unification. At a minimum, cultural investigators should begin by reading the work done in perspectives other than their own. They might also, collaboratively or alone, consider studying single cultural contexts using all three perspectives sequentially so that the integrity of each perspective is preserved, yet the complementary benefits of a multiple-perspective approach are made available. Eventually, projects that embrace more than one of these perspectives may be suggestive of how we might transcend present theoretical viewpoints. Until such time, however, we do need to be alert to the duality of meaning creation—on the one hand, the meanings of organizational culture can only be considered as real by those members who share frameworks for inputting meaning, and, on the other hand, the meanings of organizational culture are identified and understood by those inquirers who share a similar perspective on what meanings are and do.

At the present time, organizational culture research may be characterized as exhibiting both diversity and growth. We refer not only to the number of publications, although these have substantially increased in recent years, but also to the number of ways organizational culture is conceived, studied, and related to other organizational factors. Culture research has moved from simply listing manifest elements (e.g., stories, rituals, and language) to describing complex constellations of several levels of meaning, (e.g., manifest elements, patterns of belief and associated values, and fundamental assumptions). Culture research likewise has moved from asking simple, direct questions of what informants think is their culture to using a variety of qualitative and quantitative methods more and more used in conjunction and triangulation. Culture research is moving from a focus on one organization's culture to studies that compare cultures and begin to relate culture to many other aspects of organizational theory (e.g., change, effectiveness, structure, strategy, etc.) and to a variety of organizational behaviors. It was not so long ago when we heard the question: "Is organizational culture a fad?" We then heard the question: "What does knowing the culture really add to our understanding of organizational patterning, dynamics, or development?" With the diversity and growth of alternative conceptions and methodologies, and the number of theoretical and pragmatic linkages to culture, new questions have arisen. This book, for example, has begun to address such questions as: "In what ways are culture studies similar and dissimilar, and what do they assume, ignore and emphasize?" and "How is organizational culture investigated, and what are the uniquenesses, strengths, and weaknesses of these methodologies?"

IIIB
Looking Inward

The coeditors of this book, like other contributors to the observers of the arena of organizational culture, each travel a somewhat different journey. Our life experiences, our education and training, our professional affiliations, our reasons for being attracted to organizational culture, the ways we go about our culture, work, and so forth are in many ways unique. Our individual paths have at times joined and at other times separated. As coeditors we joined together in this book in our intention to heighten the awareness of cultural researchers about the choices currently available in perspectives and methodologies. Instead of concluding this book with one collective voice (implying unanimity of view), we have elected to speak as individuals—hopefully, thereby illustrating both the origins as well as the consequences of the many choices we have made and will be making.

Five personal statements follow, each generally guided by three questions:

- Who am I and/or how did I come to where I currently am as a cultural researcher?
- What are my reactions to what has been presented in this book?
- Where might I go from here?

23

Mirror Talk:
Self-Framing Experiences Along the Culture Trail

PETER J. FROST

I was born in South Africa, where I spent most of the first three decades of my life. In the late 1950s I earned an undergraduate honors degree in chemistry, but after spending almost a year working at various laboring jobs in the United Kingdom and touring both there and in Europe, I came to realize that I was more interested in a career dealing with people than with exclusively technical concerns. I returned to South Africa, started over in personnel management, and spent eight years working my way up a career ladder while pursuing part-time studies in psychology, which culminated in a master's degree. I then went with my wife, Nola, and our two small children to the United States and completed my doctoral degree at the University of Minnesota, where I benefited from having Tom Mahoney as my mentor. I returned to South Africa and worked for 18 months as a personnel consultant in a large conglomerate of organizations in the consumer service sector. In late 1974 I immigrated to Canada and in January 1975 commenced an academic career at the University of British Columbia (UBC), where I am at present.

In 1979, after I had gained tenure and a promotion to associate professor, I searched for new projects that would be quite open-ended and extensive. My work to that point had largely focused on empirical studies,

---

AUTHOR'S NOTE: This statement draws from a lengthier reflective piece: "Creating Scholarship and Journeying through Academia: Reflections and Interpretations from the Field" by Peter J. Frost, 1989, published in the *Journal of Applied Behavioral Science, 25*(4), 399-418.

with the exception of an edited anthology of stories about life in organizations, *Organizational Reality: Reports from the Firing Line* (Frost, Mitchell, & Nord, 1985). I had tried consciously to keep the institutional hoops of tenure and promotion from determining which topics and research I addressed during the early phase of my life as an academic. At this time I was even more determined to avoid what I perceived to be a common trap in academia in North America: doing research primarily to have something published to put on one's vita or to move up another rung on the academic ladder.

I'd like to talk about two adventures in the realm of culture and symbolism in the late 1970s and early 1980s that are relevant to this reflection. The first adventure led to the publishing in 1983 of *Organizational Symbolism,* which I coedited with the late Lou Pondy, Gareth Morgan, and Tom Dandridge. This book originated in a conference on the topic which was held at Lou Pondy's home in Champaign, Illinois, in 1979. That year I had become somewhat intrigued with the concepts of symbolism and of culture and had read the article by Tom Peters (1978) on the management of organizational symbols and the writings of Geertz (1973) and a few others on the subject of culture. At the time I was also reviewing a provocative manuscript for *Administrative Science Quarterly* on metaphors and organizational analysis, which had been sent to me by Lou Pondy in his role as associate editor of that journal. I had met Pondy briefly and knew of his reputation as a creative and energetic scholar. I received a letter Pondy sent to several people in the field announcing an informal conference on symbolism and inviting those interested to attend. A formal presentation of papers would take place, and a wide discussion of ideas beyond such papers by those attending would be encouraged. The attendance would be limited by the size of the venue.

Although I had no work in progress in this arena, nor any relevant credentials, I was powerfully drawn to attend the conference. Indeed, this attraction was so strong that I can only describe it as irresistible. I simply *had* to attend this event! This may seem a rather dramatic statement, but it reflects the way I felt at the time. As the conference approached, another part of me said I ought not to go. After all, I had no paper to contribute, was not an expert on the subject, and dreaded making the rather long and tiring journey to attend a conference where I would likely not know anybody. I recall expressing these conflicting thoughts and feelings at the time to my wife. The urge to attend ultimately won out easily. Although I had been working on other projects, I put them aside quickly, picked up the pace of my reading in this area, drew funds from a small research budget, and booked my flight to Champaign, Illinois.

One of the first persons I met at Lou Pondy's home was Gareth Morgan. He came in the front door carrying his backpack and looking much like a hiker who had finished a long day on the road. As we became acquainted and talked about our research interests, I realized that he was the author of the metaphor manuscript I had just finished reviewing during the flight from Vancouver. (The paper was subsequently published in *Administrative Science Quarterly* [Morgan 1980], and in my view is a rich and influential work in this field.) Our meeting at this conference was the start of a friendship and a productive association that resulted in our collaborative efforts on the *Organizational Symbolism* book.

The conference itself was enjoyable socially, but until the closing session I considered it an intellectual disappointment. I could not get on track with the material as a whole, finding it still too unformed and unfocused. I recall wondering to myself why I had bothered to come, why I had experienced such a compulsion to attend. I simply could not understand what the ideas contributed to organizational analysis or to anything else of interest to me.

Only at the very end of the conference, when Dick Daft and Lou Pondy offered summarizing and closing thoughts, did the "light go on" for me. Then I began to appreciate the material and see how it could be organized to give it a voice. I sensed that much of the work being reported at the conference would be too unorthodox for acceptance in the major journals of our field. Furthermore, even with strong editing and committed authorship, some of the work would still be too long to be included in journals, which inevitably put a premium on space. I recall thinking as well that this early body of work should be kept together, for it had a cumulative effect that would best be realized if the material were given an appropriate organizing framework, and if it were strongly edited and reported in a single book. Furthermore, I conjectured that these ideas would likely reach the audience of scholars in the field more quickly if they were presented in book form, rather than submitted through the typically lengthy formal process of manuscript review for journals. (This assumption was later disproved, in ways I found rather painful.)

Interestingly, while watching this process, Gareth Morgan quite independently came to much the same set of conclusions. At the end of the conference we discovered and discussed our common opinions and perceptions. We approached Lou Pondy with the suggestion that Gareth and I take some of the responsibility of editing a work such as we envisioned, along with Lou and Tom Dandridge. Because Lou was slated to visit my university (UBC) later that summer for a month or so as a visiting scholar, and Gareth (then visiting Pennsylvania State University) wanted to explore Canada and the United States and could include in his trip a visit to UBC, we tentatively agreed to pursue the idea of editing a book based on the conference. Tom Dandridge was invited to join us in Vancouver. We intended to develop a framework, write some of the material for the book, edit the work of others, and, as audiotapes of parts of the conference became available, to examine them as potential contents for the book.

Tom Dandridge was unable to join us in Vancouver, but Gareth Morgan and I worked intensively on the introductory chapter and a second empirical piece for the book based on the audiotapes of Dick Daft's closing statements. When Lou arrived we finished the introduction and the framework for the book.

By the end of that summer we were excited and pleased about having the framework tentatively established and were happy with the progress we had made in working on the manuscripts of authors who supported our efforts. We believed they felt as enthusiastic as we did about the worth of the project and were ready for the publishers of the world. My successful experience with Goodyear Publishers and *Organizational Reality* (Frost, Mitchell, & Nord, 1985) led me to expect the book to be quickly accepted by publishers and readers alike.

This was not the case. Three years later, the symbolism manuscript was finally accepted as a monograph in the JAI series managed by Sam Bacharach (we have always grateful to him for taking the risk with us). Ironically, once we had a contract with JAI, we received several inquiries from publishers interested in signing us up for this work.

My second relevant adventure along the way to the development of the present book, began with a conversation with Craig Lundberg and Joanne Martin at the opening social hour of the Western Academy of Management meetings in Santa Barbara, California, in March 1983. The precise details of that conversation are vague now, but the gist of it was that Craig said that he and Joanne felt it was important to have a conference on organizational culture soon to harness the excitement and energy being generated in the field by the topic. They thought it would be useful to build on the momentum of an earlier March 1983 Conference on Folklore and Myth hosted by Michael Jones of UCLA and his associates. I indicated with enthusiasm that I thought this was a very appropriate idea and volunteered to help coordinate such an effort, offering UBC as a venue. I had no prior intention to do this or to involve UBC as a site, but it seemed a natural thing to do. I knew Larry Moore at UBC had a strong interest in the topic. I was aware of the valuable experience in conference running that the Organizational Behavior (OB) group in our Faculty of Commerce had gained when Craig Pinder and Larry Moore hosted the Middle Range Theory Conference at UBC in 1978. I was confident that if others in the group accepted the relevance and importance of the project, I would get full cooperation and support from them. Larry Moore and Meryl Louis subsequently joined Craig Lundberg, Joanne Martin, and me as coordinators of the conference. On April 1, 1984, the Organization Culture Conference commenced in the magnificent Museum of Anthropology of UBC. Two years later, in 1985, a book based largely on the conference material, edited by the five of us, was published by Sage.

The conference itself was successful and turbulent. We tried to create a culture for the participants, to put symbols and rituals into the content, to inject emotion and feeling tone into the event, an academic conference, a gathering that often is primarily an intellectual exercise. These interventions worked to a degree. Many, although not all participants reported positively on the conference at its completion. With the passage of time, most of those who recall it and have talked with us say they experienced the conference as innovative and provocative. During the conference itself, however, there frequently were expressions of anger, dissatisfaction, and confusion. It was not always clear to everyone what was going on in the conference process or why. Some participants disagreed with the direction of the conference, some took offense at parts of the emotionally loaded cultural events—the story-telling about the pain and suffering of Laotians fleeing the Vietnam War, the folksongs that criticized not only the oppression of workers by the bosses in earlier eras but also the alienation of modern day workers and the role managers play in contributing to this malaise.

Signs intended by us as one kind of symbol were interpreted as another and challenged by some participants or silently derided by others. We introduced to the conference a beautifully carved Pacific North Coast Indian Talking Stick. In that culture it is a symbol of wisdom conferred on the person who holds it and addresses the community. Our Talking Stick was passed from one academic session Chair to the next during the conference. Its intended purpose in our Conference was to give each Chair the power and wisdom to conduct a good session. Our motives were partly serious, partly playful. We wanted also some way to ease the Chairs' time-keeping task across the speakers in their sessions. By the second day of the Conference, some participants saw it as a symbol exclusively of control. Eventually, with some anger, they tried to wrest it, even to steal it from the Chairs and the organizers of the Conference. (As the Talking Stick was on loan from the Faculty of Commerce and worth a considerable sum of money, this was a source of anxiety to the conference coordinators.)

At the closing session of the conference one group presented to the participants and the coordinators an alternative Talking Stick—one they had made out of an old umbrella and assorted items which symbolized to them and to many in the audience important, amusing or notable moments and controversies of the conference. It was a parody of the carved Talking Stick.

After the conference, there was discussion among the coordinators and attending members from the European group SCOS (Standing Committee on Organizational Symbolism) about purchasing the official Talking Stick and taking it to Lund, Sweden for use in the first international SCOS Conference on Organizational Culture later that year. In the end, SCOS decided to create its own Talking Stick—which endured, not without its own controversy, across some subsequent years of SCOS Conferences.

I learned only years later, from some of the insiders, that among the female participants at the conference there was a running joke not shared with the men about the maleness of the Talking Stick symbol. It was seen with amusement as a phallic symbol waved around by male Chairs as evidence of control and power. There were doubtless other participants who do not even recall the Talking Stick or for whom it was a sign without symbolic meaning or impact.

I believe there were times of shared positive experience during the conference, including moments during the opening ceremonies in the Museum of Anthropology and during the closing session. I believe also that the tensions, confusions, strong emotions, debates, conflicts, and exhilarations of the event were consistent with the experiences of a culture, albeit a temporary one. In the end, people made sense of their experience of the conference and moved on. Some of what we as coordinators intended worked out, some did not. Our sense making of the event inevitably has been a more intense process than it was for most other participants as we had so much more vested in the conference. What I have found fascinating and personally educative about reflecting back on it is how the mapping and interpreting of this conference is an ongoing, unfolding process.

I am aware that I have left out some details consciously and will have unconsciously suppressed others. I have cast the description of the conference in the context of a culture and, as that unfolded, as an exemplar of several perspectives of culture presented in this book. I could have positioned it in terms of the content of the presentations or as an event that played a part, to greater or lesser extent, in the careers of each of the coordinators, or as a datum in the history of the emergence or re-emergence of culture in the field of organizational studies. Different entry points and assumptions would likely create a different shape and focus for the story.

Given that one wishes to revisit the experience of an event later in time and is open to alternative experiences and interpretations of that event by others who were "there," then the richness and complexity of what we construct as reality becomes evident and instructive. Not only has my understanding of the Organizational Culture Conference as an event changed (I see more facets now and have asked more and different questions than I would have seven years ago), but I am aware that there are still other interpretations of its meaning in the minds of those others which will intersect with mine in places and diverge significantly in others. All such interpretations have legitimacy, some will be more influential than others. Each of the interpretations will tell us something about the event, some will be more durable than others.

Five years after the conference on April 1, 1989, the five of us met in Vancouver for a weekend to discuss the possibility of a new project on organizational culture. This book is the result of that meeting.

What these experiences and others like them have taught me about myself are that I tend to initiate and persist with projects that I genuinely enjoy and am excited about. There is a strong element of passion in my research pursuits and a fairly high degree of intuitive feel and awareness goes into deciding what will excite my interests and in clarifying what I sense to be important projects to be examined in the field. In addition, I like projects that are collaborative, that involve not only my own writing and research, but involve also interchanges with others that harness their ideas and work in developing knowledge, which inevitably improve my own. There has also been a great deal of serendipity and much collegial support along the way. I have many times been fortunate enough to be in the right place with the right people at the right time.

Writing and editing this book with my colleagues and friends has given me other concepts, language and lenses on my work and the way I do work. I seem to be drawn to situations that are ambiguous and open-ended at the beginning. I enter processes often with a gut feel that there is something going on of interest and perhaps of importance but not with any clarity about what questions to ask or what the product might look like. Both the *Organizational Symbolism* book and the Organizational Culture Conference started that way. Immersion in the process, particularly when I do it collaboratively, seems to produce insights and frames that serve to shape the substance of the project. When that collaborative immersion works well, I experience it as a "flow" process described as a state in which

> there is no split between the self and the environment, the stimulus and the response, the past and the present. Action and awareness are merged. There are no dualisms. The self disappears. (Quinn, 1988, p. 13)

It may also be an example of what it feels like to have a peak experience (Maslow, 1970).

I think that in the small group settings of research collaboration this approximates the harmony condition talked about in the integrative culture perspective in this book. At some point in the process, the egos of those involved in the process vanish, and the participants do not compete with each other for time and space. Sometimes this may happen because important assumptions and values of the individuals involved coalesce and become shared, so a culture as Schein and others describe it emerges. At other times a condition seems to be created whereby each person feels and trusts that he or she can enter the process in an authentic and unique way and be heard and accepted *whatever* their core values and assumptions. The latter condition would reflect harmony without the necessity of postulating a shared culture. Whatever the dynamic, it is a fragile process that requires careful attention and nurturing by all the participants. It exists in a context such that this flow occurs intermittently rather than all the time.

When I have a hard look at what work I do *and* how I do it, given the three major perspectives of this book I note the following. Much of my writing in recent years could be categorized into the integrative (e.g., Egri & Frost, 1991; Frost & Egri, 1990) and the differentiated (Frost, 1987; Frost & Egri, 1991; Stablein & Frost, 1991) cultural perspectives. These are not works directly on organizational culture but they have to do with leadership and power which in my view are intrinsically linked with culture. The way I approach my work is to live with ambiguity for a considerable period of time. My other simultaneously preferred mode of operation is collaborative, rather than competitive (Kilmann & Thomas, 1977). I wouldn't say I am insensitive to conflicting world views and approaches to research. My inclination, however, is to search for overlaps and to find ways to enhance the quality and create that synergistic flow I mentioned earlier. Sometimes it works out that way, sometimes the gulfs widen. I am less comfortable living with conflict and strong differences of opinion than I am with consensus. I find this intriguing given my strong intellectual interest in organizational power and politics. That is, I enjoy working with a topic that posits conflict as an inevitable and perhaps even core component of organizational life, but prefer the personal experience of harmony and consensus.

Where will I go next and how has this book influenced the directions I take? I have always been interested in frameworks that encourage the recognition and expression of diverse perspectives on organizational phenomena. I have also enjoyed projects that are intended to demystify what we do as organizational researchers. Working on this book, initially using Joanne Martin and Debra Meyerson's three perspectives on culture and then harnessing images of other contributors to the book has reinforced those tendencies in me. What has become more clearly focused for me is the playfulness, the flexibility, and the power that comes from working with these various perspectives and images in the book.

One major segment of my work in the next several years will be in the arena of the environment and the organizational issues that need to be enacted, clarified, and applied to this arena. One useful place to start into the process of understanding environmental problems as organizational researchers might well be to accept as working hypotheses that experiences, elements and systems of harmony, conflict and ambiguity all contribute to the environmental problems we encounter and to their solutions. Furthermore, we might start by assuming that what is figure and what is ground among harmony, conflict, and ambiguity will be in part a function of who the researcher is and in part what is experienced within the arena created for study.

What might happen when we work these images of harmony, conflict, and ambiguity in various figure-ground configurations given an awareness that we are doing this with our own enacted map of environmental concerns? We just might prevent the usual stampede of researchers up blind alleys of "single minded" attacks on the problem once environment becomes a "hot" topic as is distinctly possible in the next decade. We might avoid mistaking as harmonic and unproblematic the "environmentally responsive" measures of organizations to environmental problems which are not and are instead a cover for "business as usual." We might be more alert for cues that identify where there is genuine conflict of values and opinion among various organizational shareholders about which way to deal with environmental problems. We might become more attuned to the possibility of absences of real boundaries around some environmental issues and gain an understanding for what the ambiguities are and how they might be engaged. We also might become more aware how much of what we see and define as reasons for and solutions to the environmental issues is created by our fundamental frames for erecting the world and how much this is focused by cultural programming (Douglas & Wildavsky, 1982).

A caveat is in order, one that emerges from the messages in this book, as I receive them. What I have said above begins to sound very much like a new system for organizational research, a "3-Dimensional Model of Environmental Analysis," with the images and the framework borrowed from Martin and Meyerson (1988) and then reified, coded, documented and the practices programmed and prescribed. There might even by a symposium on this new system at the Academy of Management Annual Meetings some year. If these things were to happen it would be an unfortunate mistake, for we would have lost the meaning of what ideas and the development and use of knowledge is all about. It is not about permanence and progress. It is about inventing some understandings at a point in time and then a spiral of discourse around and beyond that invention.

What I have learned from this project is the value of staying in touch with the process one has both created for oneself and is experiencing, of working with images as heuristics rather than definers of reality, of being on the lookout for fresher images than the ones one started with, of recognizing the idiosyncrasy of some of the ways we combine things to make a story—that probably works for some people and not for others. I am alerted also to the continual emergence of understanding that comes from keeping the process alive and vital. So while I probably will become involved in Environmental Studies, I might use the images of this book and I might not. I might begin with them and end up with others. What I will retain is the memory of the collaborative experiment it has been. It started almost a decade ago and still endures. Now that's something quite permanent in an impermanent world. But, of course, we are all different people now—and so is the field. We and what we do are, after all, always "works in process!"

24

A Personal Journey:
From Integration to Differentiation
to Fragmentation to Feminism

JOANNE MARTIN

In 1978 I was a new Assistant Professor and Alan Wilkins was a Ph.D. student who wanted one more reader for his dissertation committee. I protested, "But I don't know anything about organizational culture or qualitative methods. I'm a quantitative, experimental social psychologist. I study inequality and distributive injustice. I'm not even sure what an organizational culture is."

Alan was gently persistent. He brought me anthropological articles to read and, as soon as I finished one, he replaced it with another. I noticed that whenever I got a few minutes to read, I would choose the papers Alan brought, instead of the injustice research I was "supposed" to be reading. Eventually I had to admit that my behavior was saying something about my preferences; I agreed to be a reader on Alan's thesis (Wilkins, 1979). Soon thereafter, I started doing culture (as well as justice) research. Alan was the first in a long line of Ph.D. students who became my teachers.

In my first attempts to do this new kind of research, I (like many others) approached culture from an Integration perspective. Drawing on the work of organizational scholars such as Schein (1985b) and Clark (1972), I defined culture in terms of values shared on an organization-wide basis. I included in my data only those cultural manifestations that were consistent with each other and that generated (apparently) organization-wide consensus. I saw culture as a potential source of organizational commitment, and perhaps productivity (e.g., Martin, 1982; Martin, Feldman, Hatch, & Sitkin, 1983; Martin & Powers, 1983a; Siehl & Martin, 1984). Unquestioningly, in spite of my leftist political commitments, I had absorbed the managerial viewpoint and functionalist concerns that are characteristic of most organizational behavior research in the U.S. I was also methodologically conservative, trying wherever possible to use my quantitative training to study culture.

At that time, as now, qualitative researchers dominated the study of culture. Some of them were decidedly not pleased with my attempts to introduce quantitative ways of "measuring culture." Qualitative methods, they said, gave far greater depth of insight and were less likely to thoughtlessly mimic the perspectives and desires of top managers, rather than the viewpoints of a full range of cultural members. In addition, some of these scholars disagreed with the assumptions of the Integration perspective. They argued, in terms that I have come to label the Differentiation perspective, that: cultural manifestations are often inconsistent; consensus is most likely to emerge within subcultural boundaries; cultures often evolve in directions contrary to the desires of top management; conflicts of interest between groups (and classes) of employees are inevitable; and a functionalist approach to the study of culture is misguided (e.g., Christensen & Kreiner, 1984; Gregory, 1983; Jermier, 1985; Louis, 1985; Smircich, 1983b; Turner, 1986; Van Maanen & Barley, 1984).

Prompted by these readings and by student-teachers such as Michael Boehm, Mary Jo Hatch, Caren Siehl, and Sim Sitkin, I slowly began to attend to the evidence of subcultural differentiation in my own data and my growing discomfort with the discrepancy between my political commitments and the managerial and functionalist assumptions implicit in my culture (but not my injustice) research. Tentatively, and with great misgivings, I started to mix qualitative and quantitative methods (Martin, 1990a; Siehl & Martin, 1988). Eventually I tried purely qualitative approaches, (although I have not yet dared to do an ethnography). I began to publish, with these students as co-authors, studies challenging the Integration perspective. Some of these papers questioned the existence of links between culture and financial performance (e.g., Siehl & Martin, 1990); others documented the scarcity of organization-wide consensus and the prevalence of inconsistency and subcultural differentiation (Martin & Siehl, 1983; Martin, Sitkin, & Boehm, 1985). I was just beginning to feel comfortable with studying culture from a Differentiation perspective when "disaster" (in the form of postmodernism) struck.

It was my own fault. For 10 years I had participated in an interdisciplinary faculty seminar on postmodern feminist theory. Initially, my reasons
for joining the seminar were personal. For years I was the only woman on
the business school faculty and this seminar was the only way I had to meet
other women faculty in the university. They were warm, friendly, and very
smart. Because most of them worked in the humanities, they usually
focused their powerful feminist critiques on literature and philosophical
treatises. This focus (and the distaste of some seminar members for the
wonders of statistics and the scientific method) made it easy for me to
regard this seminar as my intellectual "dessert"—fascinating, but irrelevant to my "real work."

Then, one day, a top executive, well known for his humanitarian concern
for employee well-being, gave a speech at the business school. He detailed
with pride all the things his corporation was doing to "help" women
employees. The more he talked, the more convinced I became that something was wrong. I obtained a transcript of his speech and studied it
carefully, but I couldn't find much overt sexism. I was sure it was there—
somehow "between the lines" of what he said. The next day I tried again,
this time using a postmodern analytic strategy (deconstruction). Suddenly,
I could read the silences "between the lines" and see layer after layer of
unstated, sexist assumptions (Martin, 1990b).

If I could deconstruct an executive's speech, then I could and did
deconstruct some of the classics of organizational theory (Martin, in press;
Martin, 1990c). Postmodern analytic strategies gave me a way of unveiling
the hidden uncertainties implicit in the "edges" of empirically based claims
to know the truth. With trepidation, I also used postmodern strategies to
explore the hidden biases in my own writing. After reading more broadly
(particularly the work of Calas & Smircich, 1989b; Derrida, 1976; Flax,
1990b; Jaggar, 1983; and Spivak, 1988), I began to see how postmodern
feminist theory could provide a way of reading the silences that permeate
the cultural research I (and others) have done.

This critique made me see that Integration and Differentiation studies
of culture define culture as that which is clear, banishing the ambiguities,
so characteristic of organizational life, to some domain that was supposedly "not culture." With Debra Meyerson (and drawing on the work of such
researchers as Feldman, 1989; March, 1978; and Weick, 1979) I tried to
articulate a third perspective on culture (Martin & Meyerson, 1988; Meyerson & Martin, 1987). This Fragmentation viewpoint incorporates an understanding of ambiguities into culture. This perspective acknowledges the
uncontrollable uncertainties that provide the texture of contemporary life.

It reveals the discontinuities that characterize interactions across time and across people and creates a need for experimenting with new ways of writing about culture. Drawing on feminist theory, the Fragmentation perspective can attend to the counterpoints provided by the silenced voices of women and minorities in a way that acknowledges the complexities of multiple and fragmented selves. In short, for me, the Fragmentation viewpoint recreates the intellectual excitement, the sense of being on the frontiers of new insight, that I first had when Alan Wilkins brought me those papers to read so many years ago.

Before I jump headlong into a postmodern, feminist abyss, I wanted to write a book that would pull together much of the cultural research I (and others) had done in the last decade. I have just finished the manuscript (Martin, in press). In it, I try to work within all three perspectives (Integration, Differentiation, and Fragmentation), sequentially, without creating pressures toward theoretical assimilation that would erode the strength and ideological integrity of any one of these viewpoints. This single-authored book and the coedited volume you are now reading feel, for me, like a period after a decade-long sentence.

Next, I will merge my longstanding interests in injustice and culture by joining those who are trying to develop a feminist approach to organizational theory and research (e.g., Calas & Smirich, 1989a; Ferguson, 1984; Kolb & Bartunek, in press; Mumby & Putnam, 1990). I know this new focus for my work will not be welcomed by some, but the culture research was also perceived as a risky endeavor when I and others began to work in this arena in the early 1980s. I see feminist scholarship as a way of bringing my personal life and my research into greater congruence. For years I have worked in an academic field and in a business school dominated—in subtle as well as obvious ways—by white men. I suspect I am already deep into my first ethnographic feminist study. I might call it "Living on the Edge: Woman in a Man's World."

25

Musings on Self, Culture, and Inquiry

CRAIG C. LUNDBERG

Throughout my whole adult life I've been an oxymoron—a diligent dilettante, simultaneously attracted and dismayed by a host of seemingly opposite endeavors and positions. Industrious and cosmopolitan to a fault, I have shuttled, intellectually, emotionally and physically, back and forth, back and forth, rationalizing one focus, one stance today over yesterday's—and doing it all over again tomorrow about another focus and stance. My meta-rationalization for this promotes a self-image of me as a continual learner, which so far seems true. Regardless of my excuse/explanation, alternating back and forth is what I do. Teaching and scholarship, work and leisure, science and art, emotionally passionate and rationally cool, serious and silly, cowboy and professor, ad infinitum. I've shuttled among alternatives and opposites so long that it almost seems normal at times. Sometimes I even carry it off with a semblance of style. Regardless, it is who I am and I come to it through much practice.

After a youth of horses and mountains and books and sports and hospitals and friends and family, college was the ultimate smorgasbord. I took and loved one or a few courses in *everything*—from poetry to physics, from music to metaphysics, from art to anthropology, from engineering to ethics—and had a job, played three sports, joined a fraternity and clubs, got married, hunted and fished, traveled, and binged on foreign films, ski racing, Chinese food, intense debates, Russian short stories, and so on—on life. After graduation there was "the job" (with its long hours, savvy associates, focused work, and the intrigue of business) and "the wife and child" (forcing questions on me I'd never considered). My life narrowed in those years and I eventually confronted basic, disturbing personal questions for the first time: How competent, ethical, caring, and ambitious was I? What did I really want to do, know, be? My initial responses of course waffled. So, like so many young people in business who need time to redirect or find themselves, I entered an MBA program. Seduced early by clean, clear decision-making models, I was later rescued by an even greater infatuation with organizational behavior's forerunner, human relations. Luckily, too, there was the model/mentor for half of my subsequent professional life, the business professor (John W. Hennessey, Jr.) who exemplified what can be accomplished, personally and organizationally, with high energy and quality relationships. So, inspired to emulate him and his career, I took my young family eastward to the Ivy Leagues to acquire the ticket needed for a position in higher education.

For some of us, once in a while there occurs a congruence of persons, place, and activity that promote real growth. Cornell was that for me. The work load staggered. Ideas and facts were the only currency allowed. Everyone seemed smarter and more experienced and somehow more sophisticated than I was. The pace was swift (book-a-week seminars were badges of honor), and the standards were high (course grades in two digits!). There were also enabling people, a great library, and so many fascinating questions to consider. It was there that my other primary professional model/mentor (W. F. Whyte) demonstrated what sustained, disciplined inquiry could discover and patiently helped me find my own voice.

The faculty I admired most all did field studies (e.g., W. F. Whyte, 1943, 1948, 1955; Leighton, 1945; Burling, Lentz, & Wilson, 1956). L. J. Henderson's (1938) dictum that the investigator have an "intimate, habitual, familiarity with things" became both credo and marching orders for graduate work. So I embraced "learning from the field" (Whyte & Whyte, 1984) and became a "clinician" (Schein, 1987) using "qualitative" methodologies (Van Maanen, Dobbs, & Faulkner, 1982). The hours, days, weeks, months of observation and interviewing piled up. Any conceptualization attempted had to be oh, so carefully grounded. Elsewhere, however, the applied social sciences of the late 1950s and early 1960s were becoming analytically sophisticated, emphasizing theory and theory testing. Tightly designed surveys and experiments with their attendant quantification were on the ascendance. It became increasingly difficult not to join up. It was Elliott Jaques' *The Changing Culture of a Factory* (1952) that provided me with a model for working. Jaques explained the formal system, for example, management policies and practices and business and work procedures, as a consequence of the interaction of social structure (roles and role relationships), culture (the customary way of doing things), and personality (the total psychological make-up of the individual). This approach continues to make sense to me, with its themes of everything always in a context, emergent phenomena beyond designed-in intentions, meaning the consequence of a configuration of persons, relationships, places and things, and some type and level of always ubiquitous change.

Over the years, my work, given my initial training, personal proclivities, and the fact that I have always been associated with business schools, cycled between exposing the dysfunctionality of managerial practices, illuminating the human complexities of sociotechnical systems, questioning faddish inquiry approaches, and inductively conceptualizing organizational changes. I now see that working primarily with managers over the years has prompted me to alternate between being their critic and adopting their elitism and ideology. This "friendly rascal" stance toward managers seems to especially permeate my writings on organizational culture.

When organizational culture emerged nearly a decade ago as a "popular" topic (e.g., Deal & Kennedy, 1982; Davis, 1984) it was like coming home. After all, I was a combination cultural-applied anthropologist, an industrial sociologist by training with a strong W. F. Whyte/F. J. Roethlisberger-like human relations background. From the outset, expressing an interest in organizational culture has brought about new colleagues and deliciously intense conversations. Culture legitimated for me many of my intellectual biases, shed light on many other familiar but unsatisfyingly explained phenomena and topics, and gave me a perceived expertise in the eyes of my students and associates. I willingly entered into the early debates such as, "can organizational culture be managed?" Not surprisingly, however, I kept changing my mind. At that time I was (as I am now) concerned with organizational change and development, alternating between making sense out of interventional reality (e.g., Lundberg, 1980) and possibility (e.g., Lundberg, 1984). This focus brought me initially to culture work by considering the feasibility of cultural interventions (Lundberg, 1985). That work, as unsatisfyingly rationalistic as it now appears, was a key steppingstone for me, for in it I saw for the first time organizations as learning systems (developed later in Lundberg, 1989a). It also prompted me to clarify what I believed organizational culture to be. Since then I have utilized what I term a "levels of meaning" approach (similar to others, especially Dyer, 1984; Ott, 1989; Schein, 1985b). This framework, although applicable to both umbrella organizations and their sub-units, does tend to induce a static "integrationist" perspective. I have alternated these conceptual efforts, again not surprisingly, with inventing very pragmatic tools, for example, a culture-surfacing technique (Lundberg, 1990) and suggesting roles for culture practitioners (Lundberg, 1989a).

In the spring of 1983, while walking on the beach at Santa Monica with Joanne Martin, I voiced the belief that to make strides in understanding organizational culture we needed to build a library of comparative cases, and that this in turn required some agreement among culture researchers on key constructs. Of course I did not then appreciate the variety of researcher opinions about what are core organizational assumptions, and did not appreciate the stylistic conventions and literary forms that inform and shape our writing about culture (Moerman, 1988; Van Maanen, 1988). Much of this appreciation began in April 1984 at the conference on organizational culture and the meaning of work life in the workplace (reported in Frost et al., 1985). With the outpouring of writing that has occurred since then I slowly have come to just a few firm convictions about culture. Much as I would like the ease of thinking that a typology of cultural types provides, all that I have seen are grossly oversimplified and dangerously misleading (e.g., Sethia & Von Glinow, 1985). Similarly, I have come to distrust all linear accounts of cultural movement (e.g., Turnstall, 1983) because they can be too easily taken as prescriptions and too often appear to be rationalizations. On the other hand, I have grown to prefer writing on culture in which there is information that lets me decipher the author's point of view. Rich descriptions (Geertz, 1983) also are always preferred, especially if the mundane aspects of organizational life are included along with the dramatic. Let me also confess that I have come to see that the crucial shared understandings in organizations are less about what and why and more about member and organizational hows—social recipes, scripts, rules, and meta rules (Winch, 1958). My early integrationist leanings have softened. On the one hand, I still devote a lot of my energy, albeit idealistically, to facilitating the congruence of persons and social systems. On the other hand, I find myself vigorously promoting variety (after Weick, 1979) both within and among organizations. You may conclude, as I have, that much of the work portrayed in Part I of this book attracts me, but that I am uncomfortable with the implicit sanctioning of methods that obfuscate the semantic rules linking facts and phenomena.

In what am I likely to invest my energy in the future? The possible agenda for any culture scholar or researcher is enormous. Temptations abound. Informed by this book and what I have been up to of late, I would predict some opposites at least for a while, that is, n̨ ɔnmanagerial settings, nonbusiness organizations, more work with **ambiguit̨** ɔ and fragmentation perspectives, less clinical work, and so forth. Perhaps. I can, however, begin to create a prescriptive self-agenda of foci that I believe need work and for which I might have talent. My initial agenda includes: to carefully explore how the perspectives utilized in this book relate to what we know of paradigms and paradigm types; to better understand how organizational culture impacts human attention, especially as culture constrains and/or assists in the perception and appreciation of anomalies by organization members; to investigate culture change in ways that elucidate its tempos and rhythms and to better understand features of organizations that either interrupt or accelerate culture change; to acquire some insight into both the genre and the concrete forms of organizational rules for what is or is not appropriate cultural behavior; to untangle in my mind the consequences of viewing organizational culture as a means, end, or milieu; to continue to use metaphors as a way of helping organizational members think about their culture but to clarify how metaphors actually transmit cultural meanings; to learn how to facilitate organizational members' development of their own "local theory" (Elden, 1982) of their culture, and, similarly, to learn how I might begin to portray organizational culture more dynamically as in a contingency map. This agenda already seems both just a start and overwhelming. I feel the pull of each of these foci for work and, not surprisingly, also feel the pull of all those that I did not mention.

Working on this book has really felt good to me. Some of this feeling of course stems from how we worked, the magical discovery, creativity, synthesis, and consensus we coeditors have experienced. My good feelings also may be attributed to what we have attempted—to raise awareness and choices about paradigmatic and epistemological alternatives and to show both the excitement and potential of culture research. Work on organizational culture, nicely exemplified by the contributors to this book, seems to me to exemplify a lot of what is right in the behavioral sciences today. Understanding an organization's culture is puzzle work, not problem solving. It takes tenacious attention to concrete phenomena, interpretive honesty, and a pluralistic conceptual sensitivity. Culture researchers seemingly are more excited by possibilities than seeking comfort in someone else's "one best way." All of this not only seems right but feels good.

26

Reflections on an Interpretive Way of Life

MERYL REIS LOUIS

My story is not unlike those of my colleagues. It is punctuated by a series of events and interactions, experiences that catalyzed my interests and orientation.

My story begins when at 20 I left UCLA with bachelor's and master's degrees in management in hand. In 1968, I went to work for Arthur Andersen and Company (AA&Co.) as a member of the management consulting division of the Los Angeles office, the first woman hired into this unit. At that time, AA&Co. and other big eight accounting firms devoted substantial resources to training and socializing new members of their professional staffs. One could expect to spend about seven weeks in training during the first year and five weeks a year thereafter. The usual format was a week-long off-site session at which administrative, technical, and general professional material was conveyed to groups of 50 to 70 new employees from offices around the country. As this was a period of great expansion for AA&Co., I was afforded a participant observer's catbird seat for better than five years. I went from a startled to a reflective participant, and then rotated through a variety of insider/observer roles associated with the firm's professional socialization activities. In parallel with my growing sense of what the firm was doing, I found myself tracing the process of learning the ropes from the point of view of those of us going through it. I experienced and witnessed the entry of new members as well as moves through the hierarchy. It surprised me that the substantial efforts and resources the firm devoted to smoothing the process did not prevent an upending experience that was nearly inevitable among new members and occurred often among people in new roles. I left AA&Co. with vivid images of the inadequacy of the firm's well-intentioned, well-funded entry and socialization practices. It seemed to me that they were based on too little appreciation of the normal experience of a person in transition. I returned to UCLA with a sense of the need to locate or develop a description of what individuals experience as they enter unfamiliar organizational settings.

As I began my doctoral work in 1974, three interrelated questions crystallized from my AA&Co. experience.

1. What is the experience of being in transition, of changing one's work role? Are there features that are common across different types of work role transitions?
2. How do newcomers cope with such experiences? Through what processes do individuals make sense of their transition experiences?
3. With what do newcomers cope as they enter and adapt in unfamiliar organizational settings? What else besides the formal task do newcomers master during the journey from outsider to insider?

This third question lead me directly into workplace culture. In essence, my interest in workplace culture and my approach to studying it were born simultaneously. I followed individuals on their journeys from outsider to insider as they variously violated, deciphered, challenged, accepted, shaped, and took for granted shared understandings of the locale.

Underlying each of the three questions is a facet of my orientation to inquiry. I seek to capture the actor's point of view, in this case the newcomer—my orientation is interpretive. I am most interested in how one makes and finds meaning in a situation—my orientation is cognitive. I seek out aspects of a situation that go beyond the objective and/or prescribed features—my orientation is cultural. The three questions serve me as a triangle of inquiry. Deeper understandings of actors' transitions fuels my pursuit of cognitive processes; examining newcomers' coping sheds light on workplace culture which, in turn, enriches my awareness of newcomers' tasks (cf. Louis, 1980; Louis, 1990). In addition, each question has led me into other pursuits, most of which fold back onto the original questions. For instance, it turns out that surprise is a key feature of the experience of transition. I have found it useful to consider when else such surprise occurs at work and whether the processes of coping with surprise during organizational entry are applicable in other situations (cf. Louis & Sutton, 1991).

In addition to my AA&Co. years, a second shaping experience occurred before my present incarnation as an academic. For four years, I served as a volunteer paraprofessional counselor at a community mental health center. This entailed working with individual clients and co-facilitating a weekly women's group. In addition to the counseling sessions, we attended weekly "supervision" sessions at which a licensed professional reviewed selected cases of the four to six counselors present. Although this experience influenced me in several ways, the structure of the supervisions was particularly relevant to my way of being as a researcher. Every few months, we rotated to a different supervisor. Among the most notable supervisors I had were a 40-year-old male Freudian psychoanalyst (whose license plate was Freud), a 70-year-old Viennese-trained female Freudian analyst, a Jungian analyst, a Gestalt psychologist, and more than one street-wise psychiatric social worker. Through these sessions, we came to see the world, that is, our clients' worlds, through the eyes of first one then another of these varied lenses. In addition, my co-facilitator, Rosemary, and I debriefed over coffee after each group session for three years—conversations that invariably highlighted alternative interpretations of exchanges in the group or accounts of a member's encounters elsewhere. My counseling experiences, especially the supervisions and debriefing the group sessions, fully dislodged any faith I had placed in an objective reality. At the same time, I had been a witness to the powerful consequences of one's interpretation of the situation on one's thoughts, feelings, and actions. I had convincing evidence that one's "definition of the situation is real in its consequences." In my view, I have come by my interactionist position honestly.

Since becoming an academic, several experiences have marked my journey and the continuing development of my perspective. As a newly minted Ph.D., I joined the organizational behavior group at Illinois. At the end of that year, in spring 1979, Lou Pondy hosted a two-day seminar at his house to which he had invited social and organizational scientists of every stripe to discuss the then avant-garde notion of organizational symbolism. Having conversations with anthropologists and linguists gave the gathering a 1960s radical feel for me. We circulated papers and gave one another feedback. Out of this process my notions of "Organizations as Culture-Bearing Milieux" emerged along with my initial exploration of an intersubjective realm. (As Peter has related, we completed our papers in 1979, but had to wait until 1983 to see them in print.) I grappled further with the gap inherent in thinking based on a subjective/objective dimension, and the need to better articulate the meaning and implications of the intersubjective as I reviewed Burrell and Morgan's (1979) *Sociological Paradigms and Organizational Analysis* for *ASQ* (Louis, 1983b).

A year or so after Pondy's conference, I attended my first "Alta" conference; this was definitely a radical gathering. The brainchild of Mike Pacanowsky and Linda Putnam, Alta was a gathering of about 25 communications scholars with interests in interpretive approaches to organizational phenomena; at the 1980 Alta conference, Linda Smircich, Karl Weick, Roger Evered, and I from the organizational sciences joined the communications folks. The sessions stimulated many ideas, but one event was particularly provocative. Results of a study were presented in which the researchers had interpreted the actors' behaviors and had attributed intentions and motives to them; the researchers had not talked with the actors to get their views on why they had done things—their behavior was taken as sufficient evidence—nor had they asked the actors to review or confirm the researchers' attributions. The attributions were presented as findings. I couldn't figure out what I was missing. How could they think that they "knew" when they had never asked? It seemed either extreme hubris on their part or extreme naiveté on mine. Looking back, I'm pretty sure it was some of each as well as my misunderstanding of their report. In any case, the moment of my disbelief led me to describe an array of strategies for handling interpretation in research and to examine assumptions and implications of each approach (Louis, 1981). This concern with interpretation as an act of research has remained an abiding interest throughout my academic life (cf. Bartunek & Louis, in progress; Evered & Louis, 1981).

Another important influence came during my days at the Naval Postgraduate School between 1980 and 1982. I had a close look at the experiences of career military officers. Their transition situations complemented what I had seen at AA&Co. and among the panel of MBA graduates I had been following since 1977. I learned that even when transitions were made within the same organization, when one could forecast one's transition far in advance, and when one had available a range of informal information sources, the features of contrast and surprise still were ubiquitous. I also learned that, although the transition represented a move from one position to another within the same division or organizational community (e.g., shipdriving or naval aviation), specific locales are characterized by differences in basic shared understandings the mastery of which represents a central transition task. The dramatic evidence that discussion of *an* organizational culture was insufficient led me to argue for a view that a set of overlapping and nested subcultures may be found in a single organization ("Culture: Yes; Organization: No"; Louis, 1983c). Since about 1981, I have articulated a differentiation perspective.

My story concludes with the theme of collaboration. This is in truth where it began—working with supervisors and Rosemary Morris at the counseling center to explore alternative interpretations of events in our group and accounts of clients' experiences. In 1984, I joined Peter, Larry, Joanne, and Craig in organizing the culture conference at UBC. Peter has related the history of the conference and the book we prepared from it.

Looking back over my experiences I can see the shape of my basic orientation as well as the experiences through which it/I have been shaped. My approach to organizational inquiry is decidedly interpretive, inter-actionist, cognitive, and cultural. Importantly, this is also my approach to living. It is clear to me that I am an instrument of my inquiry; and the inquiry is inseparable from who I am.

But what of the future? No doubt I will continue to bring to bear this orientation in understanding the experiences of actors in organizational settings. And I will continue to seek out collaborations through which to do so. At this writing, Jean Bartunek and I are preparing a paper on the use of insider-outsider teams in organizational research. Our focus is on the act of interpreting text and field observations during the research process. Our intention is to describe alternative configurations for collaborative and iterative interpretation across researcher/organizational participant bound-aries using three case examples. We will trace effects of insider/outsider collaborations on the understandings gained and the behaviors of organi-zational participants.

Looking toward the more distant future, Lee Sproull and I are beginning to shape a program of research to study various facets of the experience of participating in electronic groups. Among the issues we are likely to pursue are the instantiation of shared meanings—the creation and transmission of culture, if you will—when text is the sole medium of communication and the role of electronic groups in facilitating entry and transition of new employees. I wonder what the status and structure of the project will be when this book appears in print. Longer term, I wonder too what experi-ences I will have had during my 1992 sabbatical travels, what events and interactions will have influenced this interpretive way of life.

27

Inside Aunt Virginia's Kitchen

LARRY F. MOORE

Of all the rooms in her house, my Aunt Virginia's kitchen is the most creative room. It is also the most continuously active room. There is the imperative of having to prepare tasty and wholesome meals for hungry mouths which, no matter how elegant or plentiful the fare, can be counted on to be just as hungry in a few hours' time. All the kitchen utensils and ingredients, including spices, are conveniently located and the recipes are kept in a handy file or stored in books on a shelf next to the stove in easy reach.

My aunt is an active person who has a wide network of friends with whom she shares recipes. Now, these recipes are only a starting point for my aunt and her cronies. Although ingredients, amounts, mixing sequences, and baking times are quite carefully specified on most recipes, Aunt Virginia has no hesitation in modifying or violating the recipe if she senses that something isn't quite right, if she thinks an improvement can be made, or if she doesn't happen to have a certain ingredient and can't borrow it. Here experienced "feel" almost always results in a better quality dish, although once in awhile something doesn't "turn out" and every now and again something gets burned. Some marvelous culinary delights have come out of Aunt Virgina's kitchen.

When I reflect carefully on what makes Aunt Virginia's kitchen such an exciting and effective place, I can identify the following 11 characteristics:

1. A focus on action
2. A receptiveness to wide-ranging ideas

3. An experimental frame of mind (outcome orientation dominates method orientation)
4. A longing to increase one's competence
5. An adequate stock of tools and ingredients, conveniently available
6. A network of supportive but critical colleagues
7. A willingness to seek and heed the wisdom of others
8. An understanding that no single approach is inherently best
9. An easy tolerance of error and failure (trying again is to be encouraged and is a necessity)
10. A pragmatic approach (modification in mid-process is O.K.)
11. A willingness to act on hunches or intuition

Taken together, these 11 features also seem to me to constitute the ideal groundwork of inquiry for organizational researchers. If present, they foster a keen desire to be active and venturesome; they legitimize the existence of multiple perspectives—both theoretical and methodological, and they advocate the development of a strong basis of support through a network of encouraging colleagues and a stock of effective investigative techniques.

In my 25 years as a student of organizational life, many of my colleagues have been troubled that the features above are seldom experienced in academic settings where organizational research programs are housed. In fact, the obverse of these features is more typical. My own research experience has underscored this same unease. Rather than speak to all these features individually, I wish to share three major concerns that seem to cut across them.

The first is an unrecognized parochialism in outlook (Cummings, 1990; Mahoney, 1985). Most organizational scholars have been trained in the foundation disciplines of psychology or sociology (rarely both) and have been steeped in the investigative methods of one of those disciplines. As a result, the theories we seek to verify and the methods we use for research are usually very narrowly grounded and reflect what Agar (1986) calls the "received view": the approach to research that focuses on the "systematic test of explicit hypotheses." It is quite easy to drift into a mode of vertical thinking (deBono, 1988) without realizing this limitation.

When I began a collaborative research project with a cultural and social anthropologist, Brenda Beck, a few years ago (Beck & Moore, 1985), our early meetings together centered on the project's objective, design, and methods of data collection and analysis. The project sought to define and understand some areas of the organizational culture and managerial style in Canada's banking industry. I entered our interactions from a background of industrial/organizational psychology; my doctoral dissertation was a controlled learning experiment and my post-doctoral empirical research was largely based on questionnaire surveys where specific hypotheses or questions were tested with instruments of known or determined reliability and validity. My mind set was, of course, very deductive, that is, I was oriented toward grounding my investigation on well-established theory, developing logical hypotheses extending the theory, testing those specific hypotheses using well-known or specially-designed instruments, and then adding my findings to the generalized fund of knowledge on which further theory could be developed.

In stark contrast, Brenda had been trained in the inductive research approach of an anthropologist; her doctoral dissertation involved living for several years in a rural village in southern India in order to analyze the local culture and a Tamil folk epic (Beck, 1982). To my surprise, Brenda was very reticent toward the notion of trying to select any one theory for testing. Her preference was to enter the setting for awhile—as a participant-observer—to try to understand the banking culture better before trying to dimensionalize or categorize anything. For her, trying to theorize about and dimensionalize a culture too soon would almost guarantee that we would overlook or underemphasize much really important information. Furthermore, she viewed the use of paper/pencil questionnaires as "merely scratching the surface" of what she thought of as culture. Brenda argued for an inductive approach: intensely study the specific elements in a setting, then allow the general patterns to emerge (see Bruyn, 1967). In the end, after many hours of teaching each other about the pros and cons of our various research preferences and our own research strengths and weaknesses, we compromised quite a bit and innovated even more in developing a research design to which we could both become strongly committed. In retrospect, this experience caused me to surface and confront my rather narrow perspective on doing research. I had to begin to think laterally and holistically.

A second concern I have, and one that is shared by many others, is that there is a lot of scholarly intolerance out there (Blackburn, 1990). We espouse eclecticism yet, in many instances, we do not encourage it. Roberts, Hulin, and Rousseau (1978) pointed out that rather rigid boundaries are in place which define for the organizational science disciplines acceptable theories, variables for study, and research methods. These boundaries are historically grounded and slow to change. In my experience, it is much harder to secure funding for pioneering research that crosses disciplinary boundaries. It is also harder to find journal editors who are willing to publish research nontraditional to their fields or even to tolerate citations that stray too far from the usual (Blackburn, 1990). Although most graduate schools have some provision for interdisciplinary studies at the Ph.D. level, the student who opts for such a program is likely to encounter firsthand the turf-defending maneuvers of his or her committee members as they stoutly advocate their discipline's pet courses, theories, methodology, and so on. The student, in effect, can become a pawn in an interdisciplinary chess game with a resultant loss of intellectual synergy. If we are to broaden the scope of our investigation of organizational phenomena, we must intensify our search for ways to encourage scholars to bridge the disciplinary boundaries (Amabile, 1988; Mahoney, 1985; Rousseau, 1985).

The third troublesome area is the political power system in which most organizational scholars find themselves enmeshed. During the three decades subsequent to the publication of the Gordon and Howell (1959) and Pierson reports (1959) North America's business schools have attempted to infuse their curricula and research with quantitative rigor. In so doing, a generalized bias toward teaching, research, and publication containing linear logic and mathematical sophistication has become entrenched. Because the disciplines of economics and mathematics underlie the majority of the functional areas of business—accounting, management information systems, operations research, finance, and marketing—senior faculty members with a logical positivist approach and a quantitative bias tend to dominate promotion and tenure committees. The organizational scholar, in order to get over the twin institutional hurdles of promotion and tenure within an agonizingly short time constraint, often must channel his or her efforts. Too often, the result is reflected in limited, fragmented studies on not very relevant questions as well as a bias toward static, as opposed to newly emerging, dynamic issues.

In short, research must be done quickly and must demonstrate quantitative elegance. On the firing line, these power/political imperatives mean that the junior organizational scholar is rewarded for sticking close to noncontroversial (previously explored) research areas and for using numerically coded data which are gathered cross-sectionally and can be subjected to rigorous and mathematically interesting manipulation. Departing very far from extant theory, conducting longitudinal research, and undertaking qualitative and non-numerical analysis with one or only a few cases are therefore strongly discouraged. At the very time in his or her career that the young organizational scientist's creative intellectual powers are peaking, the institutionalized system of rewards and punishments acts to channel and suppress.

In my view, an important goal for scholars of organizational behavior in general and of organizational culture in particular is to legitimate in the minds of our colleagues in other functional areas (e.g., finance, etc.) the types of research questions that we are asking and the investigative methods we employ. First, we have to perform high quality research on important issues using the theories and methods we are convinced are most appropriate (Van de Ven, 1989), then we must courageously and eloquently "toot our own horns." Intellectual freedom, it seems, must be earned and then defended.

Finally, I share a concern that too much research in the field of organizational behavior has been method driven rather than context driven (Lawler & Assoc., 1985).

> It seems that the field of organizational studies has developed in a backward manner—worrying about individual pieces of a very restricted puzzle before knowing (or caring) whether the context (the major determining factor) can be understood and managed. (Kilmann, 1985, p. 155)

Over the past quarter century, the vast majority of organizational scientists have been trained in psychology departments or in business schools by professors with psychology backgrounds. It is not surprising that the bulk of the empirical research in organizational behavior has been based on questionnaire survey methods using psychological constructs. Critics view our resesarch as fragmented, incremental, limited theoretically and empirically by its ahistorical and aprocessual character, and in general not as informative or helpful as it could be (Pettigrew, 1985). Mitroff (1985), for example, suggests that "we have neither in-depth, inside 'street' knowledge of the organizations we study . . . nor very good formal theories of organizations that explain much beyond the obvious" (p. 35).

Clearly, if we are to advance our understanding of organizational life, we must draw much closer to the context or substance of what we are studying; we must use multiple lenses; and we must exercise a considerable amount of intuition and flexibility. As Mahoney (1985) pointed out:

> Much of the value to our own discipline can be learned only through study of other disciplines and the potential for benefiting a larger body of scholarship is greater if the organization sciences are viewed within the context of many disciplines of scholarship. (p. 33)

Goodman (1985) stressed that:

> There are different types of knowledge, some pertinent to theory building, some pertinent to practice, some pertinent to both. For each of these types of knowledge, there are different methods of intellectual inquiry and different ways of "knowing" that either the knowledge generated or the application of the methods of inquiry is appropriate. The task is to examine the fit among the type of knowledge, the methods of inquiry and the ways of knowing. (p. 342)

As Aunt Virginia would say, "Sometimes you have to go beyond the recipe and improvise a little." For me, that notion pretty well captures what this book encourages me to do in my own research programs. (Hopefully, the proof will be in the pudding.) Overall, for me, the book seems somewhat like a spice rack containing bottles full of pungent ingredients. Obviously, the rack cannot contain all possible spices (as a trip to any spice shop would quickly reveal), but one usually finds some exciting and alluring stuff there, fostering a desire to add judicious amounts to the next stew. Most spices in concentrated form are very potent: there is significant risk that the cook may get the blend wrong. But the best cooks take this risk anticipating a few failures, but also some spectacular and serendipitous results.

For a cook, preparing a meal involves both content and process. A tangible outcome is produced, but the cook gains experience and "feel." For me, there is a strong parallel between coediting this book and preparing a meal. Both the content and the process have affected and stimulated my thinking in ways I am now aware of and in other ways yet to surface. Here are two examples, the first having to do with content and the second with process.

Part I delineates a theoretical framework that can contain and contrast how researchers have studied organizational culture. These perspectives are identified and care is taken not to favor any one perspective or to combine or assimilate them. This approach enhances categorical clarity, but, for me, masks the important notion that, from a personal growth or maturation standpoint, organizational culture researchers may move from a beginning stage (in both intellectual development and technical competence) where the issues of dominant concern are integrative in nature to a stage where issues of differentiation are paramount, and perhaps eventually to a stage where research issues having to do with uncertainty and ambiguity reign supreme. It is apparent to me that a progression pattern is evident across the three perspectives. That is, differentiation has to be based on and contain more than one integrated perspective (or view or position). Likewise, ambiguity or fragmentation has to contain elements of integration, differentiation, gaps and uncertainty (it is a much more complex perspective). For a given researcher, it could be argued that a full appreciation of ambiguity can only occur after he or she has experienced and has become frustrated with the incompleteness of the other two perspectives. Is there a maturity continuum (or maybe a spiral) for doing culture research? If so, where are each of us now? I think I have been vacillating between perspectives one and two (my research with Beck demanded perspective two cognition), but this book is making me more sensitive to the need to pay more attention to the gaps, the hidden, the unsaid and, so forth (all perspective three concerns). Does this notion generalize to researchers in the natural and physical sciences? Does a movement across the three perspectives characterize the way social scientists could/should develop or be trained? Why does truncation occur (if it does)? Could the maturity progression be shortcutted or speeded up? How?

The second example of how the book has or is affecting me concerns the creative process of editing. The five coeditors have met on two occasions and have exchanged much correspondence and many copies of manuscript across several continents both with one another and with the contributors to this volume. These occasions and interchanges have indeed been spicy. Intellectually, I have been tickled, burned, tantalized, and soothed, but never satiated. Together, we drew on our diverse experiences and knowledge, designed, redesigned, discovered some gaps, identified those best qualified to fill them, and worked toward an incomplete but forming vision. Permeating the process was something we all worked very hard at—a spirit of openness, playfulness, and curiosity. None of us has been bound by institutional imperatives (although there have been time constraints). In short, none of the three concerns I mentioned above has impeded our progress on this book. The process I believe we experienced has left me feeling good about research and about myself as a researcher. I have learned and I want to keep on learning more about organizational culture, and I expect my understanding to grow and change. Most of all, I'm glad to see this book added to the menu. I hope it tickles a few other palates. For me, it's time to return to the kitchen. There are a few other organizational culture dishes I'm experimenting with. If I get stuck I can always ask Aunt Virginia for a few more tips.

IIIC
Looking Beyond

As we come to the close of this book, we sincerely hope that it has posed several challenges for all of us. Among the major challenges we hope this book has offered are:

- The challenge of discovering which perspective your own thinking about organizational culture most likely resembles.
- The challenge of appreciating perspectives previously unknown or ignored.
- The challenge of understanding how you might have come to your current preference for a perspective.
- The challenge of deciphering your beliefs about ontology and epistomology.
- The challenge of clarifying your research orientations and methodological preferences.
- The challenge in confronting your ideological allegiance and its consequences.
- The challenge of initiating and conducting explorations that excite and interest you.
- The challenge in finding an appropriate voice for sharing your thoughts and findings about organizational culture.

As coeditors, we are acutely conscious that this book really has no ending in the conventional sense. The study of organizational cultures is both ongoing and evolving. As our personal statements above have noted, each of us sees much useful and interesting work to be done. We come to the close of this book therefore with an invitation and a wish for you. We invite you to join us in going forward in the collective journey of studying organizational culture—but along a path framed by more awareness and more conscious choices. And we wish you well on your journey. The next frames are yours.

References

Abrahams, R. D. (1968a). Introductory remarks to a rhetorical theory of folklore. *Journal of American Folklore, 81,* 143-158.

Abrahams, R. D. (1968b). A rhetoric of everyday life: Traditional conversational genres. *Southern Folklore Quarterly, 32,* 44-59.

Abravanel, H. (1983). "Mediatory myths in the service of organizational ideology." In L. R. Pondy, P. J. Frost, G. Morgan, & T. Dandridge (Eds.), *Organizational symbolism.* Greenwich, CT: JAI Press.

Adler, P., & Adler, P. (1987a). The past and future of ethnography. *Journal of Contemporary Ethnography, 16,* 4-24.

Adler, P., & Adler, P. (1987b). *Membership roles in field research.* Newbury Park, CA: Sage.

Adler, P., Adler, P., & Fontana, A. (1987). Everyday life in sociology. *Annual Review of Sociology, 13,* 217-235.

Adorno, T. W., Popper, K. R., Dahrendorf, R., Habermas, J., Albert, H., & Pilot, H. (1976). *The positivist dispute in German sociology.* New York: Harper & Row.

Agar, M. H. (1986). *Speaking of ethnography.* Beverly Hills, CA: Sage.

Alexander, J. C., & Giesen, B. (1987). From reduction to linkage: The long view of the micromacro debate. In J. C. Alexander, B. Giesen, R. Munch, & N. J. Smelser (Eds.), *The micro-macro link* (pp. 1-42). Berkeley, CA: University of California Press.

Allen, B., & Montell, L. (1981). *From memory to history.* Nashville, TN: American Association for State and Local History.

Allnutt, M. (1982). Human factors: Basic principles. In R. Hurst & L. R. Hurst (Eds.), *Pilot error,* (2nd ed., pp. 1-22). New York: Jason Aronson.

Alvesson, M. (1987a). *Organization theory and technocratic consciousness.* New York: Walter de Gruyter.

Alvesson, M. (1987b). Organizations, culture, and ideology. *International Studies of Management and Organization, 17,* 4-18.

Amabile, T. M. (1988). A model of creativity and innovations in organizations. In B. Staw & L. Cummings (Eds.). *Research in organizational behavior* (Vol. 10). Greenwich, CT: JAI Press.

Arora, S. L. (1988). "No tickee, no shirtee": Proverbial speech and leadership in academe. In M. O. Jones, M. D. Moore, & R. C. Snyder (Eds.), *Inside organizations: Understanding the human dimension* (pp. 179-189). Newbury Park, CA: Sage.

Astley, W. G. (1985). Administrative science as socially constructed truth. *Administrative Science Quarterly, 20*(4), 497-513.

Baritz, L. (1960). *The servants of power.* Westport, CT: Greenwood.

Barley, S. R. (1983a). Codes of the dead: The semiotics of funeral work. *Urban Life, 12,* 3-31.

Barley, S. R. (1983b). Semiotics and the study of occupational and organizational culture. *Administrative Science Quarterly, 28,* 393-413.

Barley, S. R., Meyer, G. W., & Gash, D. C. (1988). Cultures of culture: Academics, practitioners, and the pragmatics of normative control. *Administrative Science Quarterly, 33,* 24-60.

Barnard, C. I. (1938). *The functions of the executive*. Cambridge, MA: Harvard University Press.

Baron, S. W. (1989). Resistance and its consequences: The street culture of punks. *Youth and Society, 21*, 207-237.

Barthol, R. P., & Ku, N. D. (1959). Regression under stress to first learned behavior. *Journal of Abnormal and Social Psychology, 59*, 134-136.

Bartunek, J. M., & Moch, M. K. (1987). First order, second order, and third order change and organization development interventions: A cognitive approach. *Journal of Applied Behavioral Science, 23*, 483-500.

Baumann, R. (1986). *Story, performance, and event*. Cambridge, UK: Cambridge University Press.

Beck, B. E. F. (1982). *The three twins: The telling of a South Indian folk epic*. Bloomington: Indiana University Press.

Beck, B. E. F., & Moore, L. F. (1985). Linking the host culture to organizational variables. In P. J. Frost, L. F. Moore, M. R. Louis, C. C. Lundberg, & J. Martin (Eds.), *Organizational culture*. Beverly Hills, CA: Sage.

Becker, H. S. (1982). Culture: A sociological view. *Yale Review, 71*, 513-527.

Beckman, B. (1987). *Att bilda FOU-organ*. ERU-raport 51, Stockholm, Sweden.

Bedian, A. G., & Armenakis, A. A. (1981). A path-analytic study of the consequences of role conflict and ambiguity. *Academy of Management Journal, 24*, 417-424.

Bell, C., & Newby, H. (1977). Introduction: The rise of methodological pluralism. In C. Bell & H. Newby (Eds.), *Doing sociological research*. London: Allen & Unwin.

Bellman, R. E., & Zadeh, L. A. (1970). Decision-making in a fuzzy environment. *Management Science, 17*(4), B144-B164.

Berle, A. (1967). *Power*. New York: Harcourt, Brace and World.

Berger, P., & Luckmann, T. (1966). *The social construction of reality*. Harmondsworth, Middlesex: Penguin.

Berger, P. L., & Pullberg, S. (1966). Reification and the sociological critique of consciousnesss. *New Left Review, 35*, 56-71.

Bernstein, R. (1983). *Beyond objectivism and relativism: Science, hermenutics, and praxis*. Oxford, UK: Oxford University Press.

Bernstein, R. J. (1976). *The restructuring of social and political theory*. New York: Harcourt Brace Jovanovich.

Beyer, J., & Trice, H. (1987, Spring). How an organization's rites reveal its culture. *Organizational Dynamics*, pp. 5-24.

Birnbaum, S. (1988). *Steve Birnbaum brings you the best of Disneyland*. Los Angeles, CA: Hearst Publications Magazines.

Blackburn, R. (1972). The new capitalism. In R. Blackburn (Ed.), *Ideology in social science* (pp. 56-71). Glasgow, Scotland: Collins.

Blackburn, R. S. (1990). Organizational behavior: Whom do we talk to and who talks to us? *Journal of Management. 16*(2), 279-305.

Blandenship, R. L. (1977). *Colleagues in organizations: The social construction of professional work*. New York: John Wiley.

Blumer, H. (1973). Fashion: From class differentiation to collective selection. In G. Wills & D. Midgley (Eds.), *Fashion marketing*. London: Allen & Unwin.

Boas, F. (1948). *Race, language and culture*. New York: Macmillan.

Bock, P. K. (1988). *Rethinking psychological anthropology*. New York: W. H. Freeman.

Bottomore, T. (1984). *The Frankfurt school*. New York: Tavistock.

Brandes, S. H. (1975). Family misfortune stories in American folklore. *Journal of the Folklore Institute, 12*, 5-17.

Braverman, H. (1974). *Labor and monopoly capital: The degradation of work in the twentieth century.* New York: Monthly Review Press.

Bregman, N. J., & McAllister, H. A. (1982). Motivation and skin temperature biofeedback: Yerkes-Dodson revisited. *Psychophysiology, 19,* 282-285.

Bronner, S. J. (1984). Folklore in the bureaucracy. In F. Richmond & K. Nazar (Eds.), *Tools for management: A symposium from the Pennsylvania Evaluation Network.* Harrisburg, PA: PEN Publications.

Brunsson, N. (1985). *The irrational organization.* London: John Wiley.

Brunvand, J. H. (1978). *The study of American folklore: An introduction* (2nd ed.). New York: W. W. Norton.

Bruyn, S. T. (1967). The new empiricists: Participant observer and phenomenologist. *Sociology and Social Research, 51*(3), 317-322.

Bryman, A. (1988a). *Quantity and quality in social research.* London: Unwin Hyman.

Bryman, A. (1988b). Introduction: "Inside accounts" and social resesarch in organizations. In A. Bryman (Ed.), *Quantity and quality in social research.* London: Unwin Hyman.

Bryman, A. (1989). *Research methods and organization studies.* London: Unwin Hyman.

Burawoy, M. (1985). *The politics of production.* London: Verso.

Burke, J. (1989, October 1). *Goodbye Descartes! Information and change* [A public lecture]. Vancouver, B. C., Canada.

Burling, T., E. M. Lentz, & R. N. Wilson (1956). *The give and take in hospitals.* New York: G. P. Putnam's Sons.

Burrell, G., & Morgan, G. (1979). *Sociological paradigms and organisational analysis.* London: Heinemann.

Burton, F. (1978). *The politics of legitimacy: Struggles in a Belfast community.* London: Routledge & Kegan Paul.

Business Week (1980, October 27). Corporate culture: The hard-to-change values that spell success or failure, pp. 146-80.

Calinescu, M. (1987). *Five faces of modernity.* Durham, NC: Duke University Press.

Calas, M. B., & Smircich, L. (1987, June). *Post-culture: Is the organizational culture literature dominant but dead?* Paper presented at the International Conference on Organizational Symbolism and Corporate Culture, Milan, Italy.

Calas, M. B., & Smircich, L. (1989a). *Rewriting gender into organizational theorizing: Directions from feminist perspectives.* Paper presented at the International Conference on Re-thinking Organization: New Directions in Organizational Research and Analysis. University of Lancaster, England.

Calas, M. B., & Smircich, L. (1989b, August). *Using the "F" word: Feminist theories and the social consequences of organizational research.* Paper presented at the annual meetings of the Academy of Management, Washington, DC.

Cameron, K., & Quinn, R. E. (1988). Organizational paradox and transformation. In K. Cameron & R. E. Quin (Eds.), *Paradox and transformation: Toward a theory of change in organizations and management.* Cambridge, MA: Ballinger.

Chandler, A. P. (1977). *The visible hand.* Cambridge, MA: Harvard University Press.

Chapple, E. D., & Coon, C. S. (1942). *Principles of anthropology.* New York: H. Holt.

Chatman, J. A. (1989). Improving organizational research: A model of person-organization fit. *Academy of Management Review, 14,* 333-349.

Christensen, S., & Kreiner, K. (1984). *On the origin of organizational cultures.* Paper prepared for the first International Conference on Organizational Symbolism and Corporate Culture, Lund, Sweden.

Clark, B. (1972). The organizational saga in higher education. *Administrative Science Quarterly, 17,* 178-184.

Clark, C. (1989). Studying sympathy: Methodological confessions. In D. D. Franks & E. D. McCarthy (Eds.), *The sociology of emotions: Original essays and research papers* (pp. 137-152). Greenwich, CT: JAI Press.

Clifford, J. (1983). On ethnographic authority. *Representations, 1,* 118-146.

Clifford, J. (1986). Introduction: Partial truths. In J. Clifford & G. E. Marcus (Eds.), *Writing culture: The poetics and the politics of ethnography* (pp. 1-26). Berkeley: University of California Press.

Clifford, J., & Marcus, G. E. (1986). *Writing culture: The poetics and the politics of ethnography.* Berkeley: University of California Press.

Cohen, A. (1974). *Two-dimensional man.* Berkeley: University of California Press.

Cohen, M. D., & March, J. G. (1986). *Leadership and ambiguity: The American college president* (2nd ed.). Boston, MA: Harvard Business School Press.

Colby, B. N. (1966). The analysis of cultural content and the patterning of narrative concerns in text. *American Anthropologist, 68,* 374-388.

Collins, C. (1978). *Twenty-four to the dozen: Folklore in a hosiery mill.* Unpublished doctoral dissertation, Indiana University, Bloomington, IN.

Conklin, H. C. (1955). Hununoo color categories. *Southwestern Journal of Anthropology, 11,* 339-344.

Cooper, R., & Burrell, G. (1988). Modernism, postmodernism and organizational analysis: An introduction. *Organization Studies, 9*(1), 91-112.

Coser, L. A. (1980). *The pleasures of sociology.* New York: New American Library.

Cox, T., Jr., & Blake, S. (1990). *Managing cultural diversity: Implications for organizational competitiveness.* Unpublished manuscript, University of Michigan, Ann Arbor, MI.

Crapanzano, V. (1986). Hermes' dilemma: The masking of subversion in ethnographic descriptions. In J. Clifford & G. E. Marcus (Eds.), *Writing culture: The poetics and the politics of ethnography* (pp. 51-76). Berkeley: University of California Press.

Cummings, L. L. (1990). Management education drifts into the 21st century. *The Executive, 4*(3), 66-67.

Czarniawska, B. (1985a). *Controlling top management in large organizations.* Aldershot, Sweden: Gower.

Czarniawska, B. (1985b). The ugly sister: On the relationships between the private and the public sectors in Sweden. *Scandinavian Journal of Management Studies, 2*(2), 93-103.

Czarniawska, B. (1986). The management of meaning in Polish crisis. *Journal of Management Studies, 23*(3), 313-331.

Czarniawska-Joerges, B. (1988a). *Ideological control in non-ideological organizations.* New York: Praeger.

Czarniawska-Joerges, B. (1988b). Power as an experimental concept. *Scandinavian Journal of Management, 4*(1/2), 31-44.

Czarniawska-Joerges, B. (1990). *Toward an anthropology of organizations.* Unpublished manuscript, Lund, Sweden: Lund University.

Czarniawska-Joerges, B., & Jacobsson, B. (1989). Budget in a cold climate. *Accounting, Organizations and Society, 14*(1/2), 29-39.

Czarniawska-Joerges, B., & Joerges, B. (1990, February). Organizational change as materialization of ideas. *The study of democracy and power in Sweden* (Report No. 37). Lund, Sweden: Lund University.

Czarniawska-Joerges, B., & Kranas, G. (in press). Power in the eyes of the innocent. *Scandinavian Journal of Management.*

Czarniawska, B., & Wolff, R. (1987). How we decide and how we act—On the assumptions of Viking Organization Theory. In R. Wolff (Ed.), *Organizing for industrial development.* Berlin: de Gruyter.

D'Antonio, W. V. (1984). A classic revisited—Closing the circle? *American Sociological Review, 13,* 14-37.

Dandridge, T. C. (1976). *Symbols at work: The types and functions of symbols in selected organizations.* Unpublished doctoral dissertation, Graduate School of Management, UCLA, Los Angeles, CA.

Dandridge, T. C., Mitroff, I. & Joyce, W. F. (1980). Organizational symbolism: A topic to expand organizational analysis. *Academy of Management Review, 5,* 77-82.

Davis, M. S. (1971). That's interesting! Towards a phenomenology of sociology and a sociology of phenomenology. *Philosophy of the Social Sciences, 1,* 309-344.

Davis, M. S. (1986). That's classic! The phenomenology and rhetoric of social theories. *Philosophy of the Social Sciences, 16,* 285-302.

Davis, S. M. (1984). *Managing corporate culture.* Cambridge, MA: Ballinger.

de Bono, E. (1988). *New think.* New York: Basic Books.

Deal, T. E., & Kennedy, A. A. (1982). *Corporate cultures: The rites and rituals of corporate life.* Reading, MA: Addison-Wesley.

Dégh, L. (1972). Folk narrative. In R. M. Dorsen (Ed.), *Folklore and folklife: An introduction* (pp. 53-83). Chicago, IL: University of Chicago Press.

Derrida, J. (1976). *Speech and phenomenon.* Evanston, IL: Northwestern University Press.

DiMaggio, P. J., & Powell, W. W. (1983). The iron cage revisited: Institutional isomorphism and collective rationality in organizational fields. *American Sociological Review, 48,* 147-160.

Disney Official Publications. (1982). *Your role in the show.* [Training Manual].

Disney Official Publications. (1985). *Disneyland: The first thirty years.*

Disney Official Publications. (1986). *The Disney approach to management.*

Dorson, R. M. (1972). *Folklore and folklife: An introduction.* Chicago, IL: University of Chicago Press.

Dorson, R. M. (1973). The folklore of economic occupations. In *America in legend* (pp. 127-250). New York: Pantheon Books.

Dorson, R. M. (1981). *Land of the millrats.* Cambridge, MA: Harvard University Press.

Dorson, R. M. (1983). *Handbook of American folklore.* Bloomington, IN: Indiana University Press.

Douglas, M. (1975). *Implicit meanings.* London: Routledge & Kegan Paul.

Douglas, M. (1985). Loose ends and complex arguments. *Contemporary Sociology, 14*(2), 171-173.

Douglas, M. (1986). *How institutions think.* Syracuse, NY: Syracuse University Press.

Douglas, M., & Wildavsky, A. (1982). *Risk and culture: An essay on the selection of technical and environmental dangers.* Berkeley: University of California Press.

Drexler, J. A., & Lawler, E. E. (1977). A union management cooperative project to improve the quality of work life. *Journal of Applied Behavioral Science, 13,* 373-387.

Dundes, A. (1965). *The study of folklore.* Englewood Cliffs, NJ: Prentice-Hall.

Durkheim, E. (1847). *The division of labour in society.* (Trans. G. Simpson). Glencoe, IL: Free Press.

Dyer, W. G., Jr. (1986). *Culture change in family firms.* San Francisco, CA: Jossey-Bass.

Dyer, W. G., Jr. (1984). *Cultural evolution in organizations: The case of a family owned firm.* Unpublished doctoral dissertation, Sloan School of Management, MIT.

Eco, U. (1976). *A theory of semiotics.* Bloomington, IN: University of Indiana Press.

Edwards, R. (1979). *Contested terrain.* New York: Basic Books.

Egri, C. P., & Frost, P. J. (1991). Shamanism and change: Bringing back the magic in organizational transformation. In R. W. Woodman & W. A. Pasmore (Eds.), *Research in organizational change and development.* Greenwich, CT: JAI Press.

Ehrenreich, J. H. (1985). *The altruistic imagination*. Chicago: University of Chicago Press.

Eisenberg, E. M. (1984). Ambiguity as strategy in organizational communication. *Communication Monographs, 51*, 227-242.

Elden, M. (1982). Democratization and participative research in developing local theory. *Journal of Occupational Behavior, 4*(1), 21-33.

Eliot, T. S. (1982). *Old possum's book of practical cats*. Orlando, FL: Harcourt Brace Jovanovich.

Ellen, R. F. (1984). Introduction. In R. F. Ellen (Ed.), *Ethnographic research: A guide to general conduct*. San Diego, CA: Academic Press.

Emerson, R. M. (1987). Four ways to improve the craft of fieldwork. *Journal of Contemporary Ethnography, 16*, 69-89.

Etzioni, A. (1961). *A comparative analysis of complex organizations*. New York: Free Press of Glencoe.

Evans-Pritchard, E. E. (1937). *Witchcraft, oracles and magic among the Azande of the Anglo-Egyptian Sudan*. Oxford, UK: Clarendon Press.

Evans-Pritchard, E. E. (1940). *The Nuer*. Oxford, UK: Oxford University Press.

Evered, R., & Louis, M. R. (1981). Alternative perspectives in the organizational sciences: Inquiry from the inside and inquiry from the outside. *Academy of Management Review, 6*(3), 385-395.

Feldman, M. S. (1985). Producing policy papers. *Advances in Information Processing in Organizations, 2*, 161-205.

Feldman, M. S. (1989). *Order without design: Information processing and policy making*. Palo Alto, CA: Stanford University Press.

Feldman, M. S., & March, J. G. (1981). Information in organizations as signal and symbol. *Administrative Science Quarterly, 26*, 171-186.

Feldman, S. (1986). Management in context: An essay on the relevance of culture to the understanding of organizational change. *Journal of Management Studies, 23*, 587-607.

Ferguson, K. E. (1984). *The feminist case against bureaucracy*. Philadelphia, PA: Temple University Press.

Fisher, W. R. (1987). *Human communication as narration: Toward a philosophy of reason, value, and action*. Columbia: University of South Carolina Press.

Flax, J. (1990a). Postmodernism and gender relations in feminist theory. In L. J. Nicholson (Ed.), *Feminism/Postmodernism* (pp. 39-62). New York: Routledge, Chapman, & Hall.

Flax, J. (1990b). *Thinking fragments: Psychoanalysis, feminism, and postmodernism in the contemporary west*. Berkeley: University of California Press.

Foucault, M. (1971). *The order of things. An archeology of the human sciences*. New York: Pantheon Books.

Frake, C. G. (1961). The diagnosis of disease among Subanum of Mindanao. *American Anthropologist, 63*, 113-132.

Frake, C. G. (1964). Notes of queries in ethnography. *American Anthropologist, 66*, 132-145.

Freidson, E. (1970). *The profession of medicine*. New York: Dodds & Mead.

Freidson, E. (1986). *Professional powers*. Chicago: University of Chicago Press.

Freund, P. (1965). *Myths of creation*. New York: Washington Square Press.

Frost, P. J. (1987). Power, politics, and influence. In F. Jablin, L. Putnam, K. Roberts, & L. Porter (Eds.), *Handbook of organizational communication* (pp. 503-548). Newbury Park, CA: Sage.

Frost, P. J. (1988, August). *Rekindling the flame: Researching the meaning still embedded in the culture construct*. Symposium presented at the Annual Meetings of the Academy of Management, Anaheim, CA.

Frost, P. J. (1989). Creating scholarship and journeying through academia: Reflections and interpretations from the field. *Journal of Applied Behavioral Science, 25*(4), 399-418.

Frost, P. J., & Egri, C. (1990). Appreciating executive action. In S. Suresh Srivastva, D. Cooperrider, & Associates (Eds.), *The power of positive thought and action in organizations* (pp. 284-322). San Francisco, CA: Jossey-Bass.

Frost, P. J., & Egri, C. P. (1991). The political process of innovation. In L. L. Cummings & B. Staw (Eds.), *Research in organizational behavior* (Vol. 13). Greenwich, CT: JAI Press.

Frost, P. J., Moore, L. F., Louis, M. R., Lundberg, C. C., & Martin, J. (1985). *Organizational culture.* Beverly Hills, CA: Sage.

Frost, P. J., Mitchell, V. F., & Nord, W. R. (1985). *Organizational reality: Reports from the firing line,* (3rd ed.) Glenview, IL: Scott, Foresman.

Fulk, J., & Mani, S. (1985). Distortion of communication in hierarchical relationships. In M. McLaughlin (Ed.), *Communication Yearbook* (Vol. 9, pp. 483-510). Beverly Hills, CA: Sage.

Gardenier, J. S. (1981). Ship navigational failure detection and diagnosis. In J. Rasmussen & W. B. Rouse (Eds.), *Human detection and diagnosis of system failures* (pp. 49-74). New York: Plenum.

Geckman, B. (1987). *Att Bilda FOU-organ.* Stockholm: ERU-raport 51.

Geertz, C. (1973). *The interpretation of cultures.* New York: Basic Books.

Geertz, C. (1980). *Negra.* Princeton, NJ: Princeton University Press.

Geertz, C. (1983). *Local knowledge: Further essays in interpretive anthropology.* New York: Basic Books.

Geertz, C. (1988a). Being there, writing here. *Harper's, 276*(1654), 32-38.

Geertz, C. (1988b). *Works and lives: The anthropologist as author.* Stanford: California University Press.

George, A. L. (1986). The impact of crisis-induced stress on decision making. In F. Solomon & R. Q. Marston (Eds.), *The medical implications of nuclear war* (pp. 529-552). Washington, DC: National Academy of Sciences Press.

Georges, R. A. (1969). Toward an understanding of storytelling events. *Journal of American Folklore, 82,* 313-328.

Georges, R. A. (1985). Folklore. In D. Lance (Ed.), *Sound archives: A guide to their establishment and development* (pp. 134-144). Milton Keynes, England: International Association of Sound Archives.

Georges, R. A., & Jones, M. O. (1980). *People studying people: The human element in fieldwork.* Berkeley: University of California Press.

Gherardi, S., & Turner, B. (1987). *Real men don't collect soft data.* Trento, Italy: University of Trento, Quaderno 13.

Giddens, A. (1979). *Central problems in social theory: Action, structure, and contradiction in social analysis.* Berkeley: University of California Press.

Giddens, A. (1990, January 22). Lecture at the Notion of Knowing Conference, University of Southern California.

Gilligan, C. (1982). *In a different voice.* Cambridge, MA: Harvard University Press.

Gladwin, B., & Sarason, S. B. (1953). *Truk: Man in paradise.* Chicago: University of Chicago Press.

Glaser, B., & Strauss, A. L. (1967). *The discovery of grounded theory: Strategies of qualitative research.* Chicago, IL: Aldine.

Gleick, J. (1987). *Chaos.* New York: Viking Press.

Gluckman, M. (1963). *Order and rebellion in tribal Africa.* Oxford, UK: Cohen & West.

Gluckman, M. (1977). *Politics, law and ritual in tribal Africa.* Oxford, UK: Basil Blackwell.

Goffman, E. (1961). *Encounters.* Indianapolis, IN: Bobbs-Merrill.

Goodenough, W. H. (1956). Componential analysis and the study of meaning. *Language, 32*, 195-216.

Goodman, P. S. (1985). Critical issues in doing research that contributes to theory and practice. In E. E. Lawler III & Assoc. (Eds.), *Doing research that is useful for theory and practice*. San Francisco, CA: Jossey-Bass.

Goody, J. (1982). *Cooking, cuisine, and class*. New York: Cambridge University Press.

Gordon, G. G. (1985). The relationship of corporate culture to industry sector and corporate performance. In R. H. Kilmann, M. J. Saxton, & R. Serpa (Eds.), *Gaining control of the corporate culture*. San Francisco, CA: Jossey-Bass.

Gray, B., Bougon, M.G. & Donnellon, A., (1985). Organizations as constructions and deconstructions of meaning. *Journal of Management, 11*, 83-95.

Gregory, K. L. (1983). Native-view paradigms: Multiple cultures and culture conflicts in organizations. *Administrative Science Quarterly, 28*, 359-376.

Habenstein, R. W. (1962). Conflicting organization patterns in funeral directing. *Human Organizations, 21*, 126-132.

Habermas, J. (1971). *Knowledge and human interests*. Boston, MA: Beacon Press.

Hackman, J. R. (1987). The design of work teams. In J. W. Lorsch (Ed.), *Handbook of organizational behavior* (pp. 315-342). Englewood Cliffs, NJ: Prentice-Hall.

Hage, J. (1980). *Theories of organizations*. New York: John Wiley.

Hall, D. T. (1972). A model of coping with role conflict: The role behavior of college educated women. *Administrative Science Quarterly, 17*, 471-486.

Harding, S., (1986). *The science question in feminism*. Ithaca, NY: Cornell University Press.

Harquail, C. V. (1990). *Interpretive frames for value laden issues: Images of racism at the University of Michigan*. Unpublished monograph, University of Michigan, Ann Arbor, MI.

Harris, S. G., & Sutton, R. I. (1986). Functions of parting ceremonies in dying organizations. *Academy of Management Journal, 19*, 5-30.

Harrison, R. (1972). Understanding your organization's character. *Harvard Business Review, 50*(May-June), 119-128.

Harvey, D. (1989). *The condition of postmodernity*. Oxford, UK: Basil Blackwell.

Harvey, O. J. (1953). An experimental approach to the study of status relations in informal groups. *American Sociological Review, 18*(4), 357-367.

Hathaway, B. (1989). *Computer assisted qualitative analysis* (Working Paper No. 4). Employee Assistance Education and Research Project, School of Industrial and Labor Relations, Cornell University, Ithaca, NY.

Hayashi, K. (1985). Hazard analysis in chemical complexes in Japan—especially those caused by human errors. *Economics, 28*, 835-841.

Held, D. (1980). *Introduction to critical theory*. Berkeley: University of California Press.

Henderson, L. J. (1938). *Introductory lectures in concrete sociology*. Unpublished manuscript, Harvard University, Cambridge, MA.

Hickey, J. V., Thompson, W. E., and Foster, D. L. (1988). Becoming the Easter Bunny: Socialization into a fantasy role. *Journal of Contemporary Ethnography, 17*, 67-95.

Hirokawa, R. Y., Gouran, D. S., & Martz, A. E. (1988). Understanding the sources of faulty group decision making: A lesson from the Challenger disaster. *Small Group Behavior, 19*(41), 1-433.

Hoff, B. (1983). *The Tao of Pooh*. New York: Penguin Books.

Hofstede, G. (1980). *Culture's consequences*. Beverly Hills, CA: Sage.

Hofstede, G., & Boddewyn, J. J. (1977). Introduction: Power in organizations. *International Studies of Management and Organization, 7*, 3-7.

Hofstede, G., & Bond, M. H. (1988). The Confucious connection: From cultural roots to economic growth. *Organizational Dynamics, 16*(4), 4-21.

Holroyd, K. A., & Lazarus, R. S. (1982). Stress, coping, and somatic adaptation. In L. Goldberger & S. Breznitz (Eds.), *Handbook of stress* (pp. 21-35). New York: Free Press.

Homans, G. C. (1950). *The human group.* New York: Harcourt, Brace.

Homer (1946). *The odyssey.* London: Penguin Classics.

Horkheimer, M. (1972a). Traditional and critical theory. In M. Horkheimer (Ed.), *Critical theory: Selected essays* [1937] (pp. 188-243). New York: Seabury.

Horkheimer, M. (1972b). The social function of philosophy. In M. Horkheimer (Ed.), *Critical theory: Selected essays* [1939] (pp. 253-272). New York: Seabury.

House, R. J. (1971). A path-goal theory of leadership effectiveness. *Administrative Science Quarterly, 16,* 321-338.

Hubbard, R. (1990, August). In a science restructured along feminist lines, would the laws of gravity no longer hold? Paper presented at *Revisioning knowledge and the curriculum: Feminist perspectives,* East Lansing, MI.

Huntington, J. (1981). *Social work and general medical practice.* London: Allen & Unwin.

Hurst, R. (1982). Portents and challenges. In R. Hurst & L. R. Hurst (Eds.), *Pilot error* (2nd ed., pp. 164-177). New York: Jason Aronson.

Hutcheon, L. (1989). *The politics of postmodernism.* London: Routledge.

Jackall, R., & Levin, H. M. (1984). *Worker cooperatives in America.* Berkeley: University of California Press.

Jagger, A. M. (1983). *Feminist politics and human nature.* Totowa, NJ: Rowman & Allanheld.

Jaques, E. (1952). *The changing culture of a factory.* New York: Dryden Press.

Jermier, J. M. (1981). Infusion of critical social theory into organizational analysis. In D. Dunkerly & G. Salaman (Eds.), *International yearbook of organizational studies* (pp. 195-211). London: Routledge & Kegan Paul.

Jermier, J. M. (1985). "When the sleeper wakes": A short story extending themes in radical organization theory. *Journal of Management, 11,* 67-80.

Jermier, J. M. (1988). Sabotage at work: The rational view. *Research in the Sociology of Organizations, 6,* 101-134.

Jermier, J. M., & Nord, W. (1991). Critical theory for practitioners: Towards a critical epistemology. In M. Alvesson & H. Willmott (Eds.), *Critical theory and organizational science.* London: Sage.

Jermier, J. M., Slocum, J. W., Jr., Fry, L. W., & Gaines, J. (in press). Organizational subcultures in a soft bureaucracy: Resistance behind the myth and facade of an official culture. *Organizational Science, 2.*

Joerges, B. (1988). Technology in everyday life: Conceptual queries. *Journal of the Theory of Social Behavior. 18*(2), 219-237.

Joerges, B. (1989). Romancing the machine—Reflections on the social scientific construction of computer reality. *International Studies of Management and Organization, 19*(4), 24-50.

Johnson, A., & Johnson, O. R. (1990). Quality into quantity: On the measurement potential of ethnographic fieldnotes. In R. Sanjek (Ed.), *Fieldnotes: The making of anthropology.* Ithaca, NY: Cornell University Press.

Jones, M. O. (1981). A feeling for form . . . as illustrated by people at work. In C. Lindahl & N. Burlakoff, *Folklore on two continents: Essays in honor of Linda Degh* (pp. 260-269). Bloomington, IN: Trickster Press. Reprinted in M. O. Jones (Ed.), *Exploring folk art: Twenty years on craft, work, and aesthetics* (pp. 119-131). Ann Arbor, MI: UMI Press.

Jones, M. O. (1984). Works of art, art as work, and the arts of working: Implications for the study of organizational life. *Western Folklore, 43,* 172-179.

Jones, M. O. (1985a). Is ethics the issue? In P. J. Frost, L. F. Moore, M. R. Louis, C. C. Lundberg, & J. Martin (Eds.), *Organizational culture* (pp. 235-252). Beverly Hills, CA: Sage.

Jones, M. O. (1985b). The material culture of corporate life. *Material culture, 17*(2-3), 95-105. Reprinted in M. O. Jones (Ed.), *Exploring folk art: Twenty years on craft, work, and aesthetics* (pp. 177-185). Ann Arbor, MI: UMI Press.

Jones, M. O. (1985c). On folklorists studying organizations: A reply to Robert S. McCarl. *American Folklore Society Newsletter, 14*(April), 5-6, 8.

Jones, M. O. (1987a). Aesthetics at work: Art and ambience in an organization. In M. O. Jones (Ed.), *Exploring folk art: Twenty years on craft, work, and aesthetics* (pp. 133-157). Ann Arbor, MI: UMI Press.

Jones, M. O. (1987b). *Exploring folk art: Twenty years on craft, work, and aesthetics.* Ann Arbor, MI: UMI Press.

Jones, M. O. (1987c). Making work art and art work: The aesthetic impulse in organizations and education. In D. Blandy & K. Congdon (Eds.), *Art in a democracy.* New York: Teachers College Press.

Jones, M. O. (1987d). Preaching what we practice: Pedagogical techniques regarding the analysis of objects in organizations. In M. O. Jones (Ed.), *Exploring folk art: Twenty years on craft, work, and aesthetics* (pp. 187-195). Ann Arbor, MI: UMI Press.

Jones, M. O. (1988a). *How does folklore fit in?* Paper presented at the Annual Meetings of the Academy of Management, Anaheim, CA: August.

Jones, M. O. (1988b). Informal organization and the functions of folklore in the writings of Chester I. Barnard, CEO of the New Jersey Bell Telephone Company. *New Jersey Folklife, 13,* 10-16.

Jones, M. O. (1988c). In search of meaning: Using qualitative methods in research and application. In M. O. Jones, M. D. Moore, & R. C. Snyder (Eds.), *Inside organizations: Understanding the human dimension* (pp. 31-47). Newbury Park, CA: Sage.

Jones, M. O. (1989). Self-reflections in organizations: An outsider remarks on looking at culture and lore from the inside. *The Journal of Social Theory in Art Education, 9*(April), 117-126.

Jones, M. O. (1990a). A folklore approach to emotions in work. *American Behavioral Scientist, 33,* 278-286.

Jones, M. O. (1990b). Emotions in work: A folklore approach. *American Behavioral Scientist, 33,* 3.

Jones, M. O., Moore, M. D., & Snyder, R. C. (1988), *Inside organizations: Understanding the human dimension* (pp. 31-47). Newbury Park, CA: Sage.

Kahn, R. L., Wolfe, D. M., Quinn, R. P., Snoek, J. D., and Rosenthal, R. A. (1964). *Organizational stress: Studies in role conflict and ambiguity.* New York: John Wiley.

Kaplan, A. (1984). Philosophy of science in anthropology. *Annual Review of Anthropology, 13,* 25-40.

Kay, P. (1969). Comments on Colby. In S. A. Tyler (Ed.), *Cognitive anthropology* (pp. 78-90). New York: Holt, Rinehart & Winston.

Keller, E. F. (1987). The gender/science system: Or, is sex to gender as nature is to science? *Hypatia, 2*(3), 33-44.

Kerenyi, C. (1951). *The gods of the Greeks.* London: Thames and Hutcheon.

Kilmann, R. H. (1984). *Beyond the quick fix.* San Francisco, CA: Jossey-Bass.

Kilmann, R. H. (1985) Doing research that makes a difference. In E. E. Lawler III and Assoc. (Eds.), *Doing research that is useful for theory and practice.* San Francisco, CA: Jossey-Bass.

Kilmann, R. H., Saxton, M. J., Serpa, R., & Assoc. (1985). *Gaining control of the corporate culture.* San Francisco: Jossey-Bass.

Kilmann, R. H., & Thomas, K. W. (1977). Developing a forced choice measure of conflict-handling behavior: The Mode Instrument. *Educational and Psychological Measurement, 37*, 309-325.

King, M. J. (1981). Disneyland and Walt Disney World: Traditional values in futuristic form. *Journal of Popular Culture, 15*, 116-140.

Knights, D., Willmott, H. C. (1987). Organizational culture as management strategy: A critique and illustration from the financial services industry. *International Studies of Management and Organization, 17*, 40-63.

Kolb, D. M., & Bartunek, J. M. (Eds.). (in press). *Behind the scenes: Disputing in the crevices.* Newbury Park, CA: Sage.

Kontash, M. (1987). *No kidding.* Toronto: McClelland & Stewart.

Krieger, S. (1987). *Organization theory: Implications of recent feminist research.* Paper presented at the School of Business Administration, University of California, Berkeley.

Kuper, A. (1973). *Anthropology and anthropologists: The modern British school.* New York: Pica Press.

Larson, M. S. (1977). *The rise of professionalism: A sociological analysis.* Berkeley: University of California Press.

Latour, B. (1986). The powers of association. In J. Law (Ed.), *Power, action, and belief. A new sociology of knowledge?* London: Routledge & Kegan Paul.

Latour, B. (1989, October). *One more turn after the social turn . . . Dialetics revisited.* Paper presented at the symposium at Reilly, France.

Lawler, E. E., III, & Associates. (1985). *Doing research that is useful for theory and practice.* San Francisco, CA: Jossey-Bass.

Leach, E. R. (1954). *Political systems of Highland Burma.* London: Bell.

Leach, E. (1982). *Social anthropology.* Oxford, UK: Oxford University Press.

Leach, E. (1985, November 29). Observers who are part of the system. *The Times Higher Education Supplement.*

Leighton, A. H. (1945). *The governing of men.* Princeton, NJ: Princeton University Press.

Levitt, B., & March, J. G. (1988). Organizational learning. *Annual Review of Sociology, 14*, 319-340.

Lodge, D. (1989). *Nice work.* London: Penguin Books.

Loseke, D., & Cahill, S. E. (1986). Actors in search of a character: Student workers' quest for professional identity. *Symbolic Interaction, 9*, 245-258.

Louis, M. R. (1980). Surprise and sense making: What newcomers experience in entering unfamiliar organizational settings. *Administrative Science Quarterly, 25*(2), 226-251.

Louis, M. R. (1981). A cultural perspective on organizations: The need for and consequences of viewing organizations as culture-bearing milieux. *Human Systems Management, 2*(4), 246-258.

Louis, M. R. (1983a). Organizations as culture bearing milieux. In L. R. Pondy, P. J. Frost, G. Morgan, & T. Dandridge (Eds.), *Organizational symbolism,* Greenwich, CT: JAI Press.

Louis, M. R. (1983b). Review of *Sociological Paradigms and Organizational Analysis,* G. Burrell and G. Morgan. *Administrative Science Quarterly, 28*(1), 153-156.

Louis, M. R. (1983c, August). Culture: yes; organization: no. Paper presented at the meetings of the Academy of Management, Dallas, TX.

Louis, M. R. (1985). Sourcing workplace cultures: Why, when, and how? In R. H. Kilmann & Assoc. (Eds.), *Managing corporate culture.* San Francisco, CA: Jossey-Bass.

Louis, M. R. (1990). Newcomers as lay ethnographers: Acculturation durign organizational socialization. In B. Schneider (Ed.), *Organizational climate and culture.* San Francisco: CA: Jossey-Bass.

Louis, M. R., & Sutton, R. I. (1991). Shifting cognitive gears: From habits of mind to active thinking. *Human Relations, 44*(1), 55-76.

Lounsbury, F. C. (1956). A semantic analysis of Pawnee kinship usage. *Language, 32,* 158-194.

Lounsbury, F. C. (1969). The structural analysis of kinship semantics. In S. Tyler (Ed.), *Cognitive anthropology* (pp. 193-211). New York: Holt, Rinehart & Winston.

Lowe, R., & McGrath, J. E. (1971). Stress, arousal, and performance: Some findings calling for a new theory. (Project report, AF1 161-67, AFOSR, 1971). University of Illinois, Champaign-Urbana.

Lundberg, C. C. (1980). On organizational development interventions: A general systems cybernetic perspective. In T. Cummings (Ed.), *Systems theory for organization development.* New York: John Wiley.

Lundberg, C. C. (1984). Strategies for organizational transitioning. In J. R. Kimberly & R. E. Quinn (Eds.), *Managing organizational transitions.* Homewood, IL: Richard D. Irwin.

Lundberg, C. C. (1985). On the feasibility of cultural intervention in organizations. In P. J. Frost, L. F. Moore, M. R. Louis, C. C. Lundberg, & J. Martin (Eds.), *Organizational culture.* Beverly Hills, CA: Sage.

Lundberg, C. C. (1989a). On organizational learning: Implications and opportunities for organizational development. In R. W. Woodman & W. A. Pasmore (Eds.), *Research in organizational change and development* (Vol. 3). Greenwich, CT: JAI Press.

Lundberg, C. C. (1989b). Working with culture. *Journal of Organizational Change Management, 1*(2), 6-14.

Lundberg, C. C. (1990). Surfacing organizational culture. *Journal of Managerial Psychology, 5*(4), 19-26.

Lyotard, J. F. (1984). *The postmodern condition: A report on knowledge* (G. Bennington & B. Massumi, trans.). Minneapolis: University of Minnesota Press.

Mahoney, T. A. (1985). Journal publishing and the organization sciences: An analysis of exchanges. In L. Cummings & P. J. Frost (Eds.), *Publishing in the organizational sciences,* Homewood, IL: Richard D. Irwin.

Malinowski, B. (1922). *Argonauts of the Western Pacific.* London: Routledge & Kegan Paul.

March, J. G. (1976). The technology of foolishness. In J. G. March & J. P. Olsen (Eds.), *Ambiguity and choice in organizations* (pp. 60-81). Bergen, Norway: Universitesforlaget.

March, J. G. (1978). Bounded rationality, ambiguity, and the engineering of choice. *Bell Journal of Economics, 9,* 587-608.

March, J. G., & Olsen, J. P. (1976). *Ambiguity and choice in organizations.* Bergen, Norway: Universitesforlaget.

March, J. G., & Simon, H. (1958). *Organizations.* New York: John Wiley.

Marcus, G. E., & Fischer, M. M. J. (1986). *Anthropology as cultural critique.* Chicago, IL: University of Chicago Press.

Martin, J. (1982). Stories and scripts in organizational settings. In A. H. Hastorf & A. M. Isen (Eds.), *Cognitive social psychology.* New York: Elsevier-North Holland.

Martin, J. (1990a). Breaking up the mono-method monopolies in organizational research. In J. Hassard & D. Pym (Eds.), *The theory and philosophy of organization: Critical issues and new perspectives.* London: Routledge & Kegan Paul.

Martin, J. (1990b). Deconstructing organizational taboos: The suppression of gender conflict in organizations. *Organizational Science, 1,* 339-359.

Martin, J. (1990c). *Reading silences: The hidden dynamics of racial politics in a garbage can analysis of desegregation decision making.* Manuscript under review.

Martin, J. (1990d). Re-reading Weber: Searching for feminist alternatives to bureaucracy. In L. Smircich (Ed.), *[Re]visions of organizational and management theory: The general construction of Max Weber, Herbert Simon, and Douglas McGregor.* Symposium conducted at the annual meeting of the Academy of Management, San Francisco, CA.

Martin, J. (in press). Re-reading Weber: A feminist analysis. In Freeman, E. (Ed.), *Ruffin Series in business ethics.* Oxford, UK: Oxford University Press.

Martin, J. (in press). *Harmony, conflict, and ambiguity in organizational culture* (tentative title). New York: Oxford University Press.

Martin, J., Feldman, M., Hatch, M. J., & Sitkin, S. B. (1983). The uniqueness paradox in organizational stories. *Administrative Science Quarterly, 28,* 438-453.

Martin, J., & Meyerson, D. (1988). Organizational culture and the denial, channeling, and acknowledgement of ambiguity. In L. R. Pondy, R. J. Boland, Jr., & H. Thomas (Eds.), *Managing ambiguity and change.* New York: John Wiley.

Martin, J., & Powers, M. E. (1983a). Organizational stories: More vivid and persuasive than quantitative data. In B. Staw (Ed.), *Psychological foundations of organizational behavior* (2nd ed.). Glenview, IL: Scott, Foresman.

Martin, J., & Powers, M. E. (1983b). Truth or corporate propaganda: The value of a good war story. In L. R. Pondy, P. J. Frost, G. Morgan, & T. Dandridge (Eds.), *Organizational symbolism* (pp. 93-107). Greenwich, CT: JAI Press.

Martin, J., & Siehl, C. (1983). Organizational culture and counter-culture: An uneasy symbiosis. *Organizational Dynamics, 12,* 52-64.

Martin, J., Sitkin, S. B., & Boehm, M. (1985). Founders and the elusiveness of a cultural legacy. In P. J. Frost, L. F. Moore, M. R. Louis, C. C. Lundberg, & J. Martin (Eds.), *Organizational culture* (pp. 99-124). Beverly Hills, CA: Sage.

Martin, P. Y., & Turner, B. A. (1986). Grounded theory and organizational research. *Journal of Applied Behavioral Science, 22*(2), 141-157.

Marx, K. (1977). *Capital* (Vol. 1). (B. Fowkes, trans.). New York: Vintage Books.

Maslow, A. (1970). *Toward motivation and personality* (2nd ed.). New York: Harper & Row.

McCaskey, M. B. (1982). *The executive challenge: Managing ambiguity and change.* Marshfield, MA: Pitman.

McCloskey, D. (1986). *The rhetoric of economics.* [1985]. Brighton, Sussex: Harvester.

McDonald, P. (1988). The Los Angeles Olympic Organizing Committee: Developing organizational culture in the short run. In M. O. Jones, M. D. Moore, & R. C. Snyder (Eds.), *Inside organizations: Understanding the human dimension.* Newbury Park, CA: Sage.

McGrath, J. E. (1976). Stress and behavior in organizations. In M. D. Dunnette (Ed.), *Handbook in industrial and organizational psychology* (pp. 1251-1285). Chicago: Rand McNally.

Mekeel, S. (1943). Comparative notes on the "social role of the settlement house" as contrasted with that of the United States Indian Service. *Applied Anthropology, 3,* 1, 5-8.

Merton, R. (1976). *Sociological ambivalence and other essays.* London: Macmillan.

Metzger, D., & Williams, G. (1958). *Collected papers of Charles Sanders Pierce.* Cambridge, MA: Harvard University Press.

Meyer, A. (in press). Visual data in organizational research. *Organizational Science.*

Metzger, D., & Williams, G. (1963). A formal ethnographic analysis of Tenajapa Ladino weddings. *American Anthropologist, 65,* 1076-1101.

Meyerson, D. (1989). *The social construction of ambiguity and burnout: A study of hospital social workers.* Unpublished doctoral dissertation, Stanford University, Palo Alto, CA.

Meyerson, D. (1990). Uncovering socially undesirable emotions: Experiences of ambiguity in organizations. *American Behavioral Scientist, 33*(3), 296-307.

Meyerson, D., & Martin, J. (1987). Cultural change: An integration of three different views. *Journal of Management Studies, 24,* 623-647.

Miles, M. B. (1979). Qualitative data as an attractive nuisance: The problem of analysis. *Administrative Science Quarterly, 24,* 590-601.

Miles, M. B., & Huberman, A. M. (1984). *Qualitative data analysis.* Beverly Hills, CA: Sage.

Millman, M., & Kanter, R. M. (1975). Another voice: "Feminist perspectives on social life and social science." In S. Harding (Ed.), *Feminism and methodology* (pp. 29-36). Blooming-ton, IN: Indiana University Press.

Minsky, M. (1986). *The society of mind.* New York: Simon & Schuster.

Mintzberg, H. (1979). An emergent strategy of direct research. *Administrative Science Quarterly, 24,* 582-589.

Mishler, E. G. (1979). Meaning in context: Is there any other kind? *Harvard Educational Review, 49,* 1-19.

Mitroff, I. I. (1985). Why our old pictures of the world do not work anymore. In E. E. Lawler III & Assoc. (Eds.), *Doing research that is useful for theory and practice.* San Francisco, CA: Jossey-Bass.

Moch, M. K., & Bartunek, J. (1990). *Creating alternative realities at work: The quality of work life experiment at Foodcom.* New York: Harper Business.

Moch, M. K., & Fields, W. C. (1985). Developing a content analysis of language use for facilitating understanding in organizations. In S. Mitchell & S. Bachrach (Eds.), *Perspectives in organizational sociology: Theory and research* (Vol. 5, pp. 81-126). Greenwich, CT: JAI Press.

Moch, M. K., & Huff, A. S. (1983). Power enactment through language and ritual. *Journal of Business Research, 11,* 293-316.

Moerman, M. (1988). *Talking culture: Ethnography and conversation analysis.* Philadelphia: University of Pennsylvania Press.

Moore, S. F. (1975). Epilog: Uncertainties in situations, indeterminacies in culture. In S. F. Moore & B. G. Myerhoff (Eds.), *Symbols and politics in communal ideology.* Ithaca, NY: Cornell University Press.

Morgan, G. (1980). Paradigms, metaphors, and puzzle solving in organizational theory. *Administrative Science Quarterly, 25,* 605-622.

Morgan, G. (1986). *Images of organizations.* Beverly Hills, CA: Sage.

Morgan, G., Frost, P. J., & Pondy, L. R. (1983). Organizational symbolism. In L. R. Pondy, P. J. Frost, G. Morgan, & T. Dandridge (Eds.), *Organizational symbolism* (pp. 3-35). Greenwich, CT: JAI Press.

Mosley, L. (1983). *Disney's world.* New York: Stein and Day.

Mowday, R. T., & Steers, R. M. (1979). *Research in organizations: Issues and controversies.* Santa Monica, CA: Goodyear.

Mrela, K., & Kostecki, M. J. (1981). Social sciences usurped: Reflections on the Americanization of sociology. In K. Mrela & M. Kostecki (Eds.), *Barriers and perspectives.* Warszawa, Poland: PAN.

Mumby, D. (1987). The political functions of narrative in organizations. *Communication Monographs, 54,* 438-453.

Mumby, D., & Putnam, L. L. (1990). *Bounded rationality as an organizational construct: A feminist critique.* Paper presented at the annual meeting of the Academy of Management, San Francisco, CA.

Munch, R. & Smelser, N. J. (1987). Relating the micro and macro. In J. C. Alexander, B. Giesen, R. Munch, & N. J. Smelser (Eds.), *The micro-macro link* (pp. 356-387). Berkeley: University of California.

Myerhoff, B. (1975). Organization and ecstasy: Deliberate and accidental communities among Huichol Indians and American youths. In S. Moore & B. G. Myerhoff (Eds.), *Symbol and politics in communal ideology* (pp. 33-67). Ithaca, NY: Cornell University Press.

Myerhoff, B. (1975). We don't wrap herring in a printed page: Fustion, fictions and continuity in secular ritual. In S. Moore & B. G. Myerhoff (Eds.), *Secular ritual* (pp. 199-226). Assen, The Netherlands: Van Gorcum and Company.

National Journal (1979, March 17). Bad reviews for Schlesinger's longest running energy show. pp. 424-428.

National Journal (1980, October 4). The engery department at three—Still trying to establish itself. pp. 1644-1649.

New York Times (1979a, June 14). Why Carter wants Schlesinger to stay. P. D1.

New York Times (1979b, July 16). Wide criticism is aimed at energy department. P. 16.

Newsweek (1979, July 23). To lift a nation's spirit. Pp. 20-26.

Nicholson, L. J. (1990). *Feminism/postmodernism.* New York: Routledge, Chapman, & Hall.

Nickerson, B. E. (1976). *Industrial lore: A study of an urban factory.* Unpublished doctoral dissertation, Folklore Institute, Indiana University, Bloomington, IN.

Nickerson, B. E. (1990). Antagonism at work: Them and us, a widget world view. *American Behavioral Scientist, 33,* 308-317.

Nonaka, I., & Yamanouchi, T. (1989). Managing innovation as a self-renewing process. *Journal of Business Venturing, 4,* 299-315.

O'Reilly, C., Chatman, J. A., & Caldwell, D. F. (1990, August). *People, jobs, and organizational culture: A q-sort approach to assessing fit.* Paper presented at the meetings of the Academy of Management, San Francisco, CA.

Olsen, J. P. (1970). Local budgeting: Decision making or a ritual act? *Scandinavian Political Studies,* 85-118.

Oring, E. (Ed.), (1986). *Folk groups and folklore genres: An introduction.* Logan: Utah State University Press.

Oring, E. (1989). *Folk groups and folklore genres: A reader.* Logan: Utah State University Press.

Ortner, S. B. (1973). On key symbols. *American Anthropologist, 75,* 1338-1346.

Ott, J. S. (1989). *The organizational culture perspective.* Chicago: Dorsey Press.

Pascale, R. T. (1990). *Managing on the edge.* New York: Simon & Schuster.

Pascale, R. T., & Athos, A. G. (1981). *The art of Japanese management.* New York: Warner Books.

Peirce, C. (1958). *Collected papers of Charles Sanders Pierce.* Cambridge, MA: Harvard University Press.

Perrow, C. (1981). Normal accident at Three Mile Island. *Society, 18*(5), 17-26.

Perrow, C. (1984). *Normal accidents.* New York: Basic Books.

Perrow, C. (1986). *Complex organizations. A critical essay* [1976]. New York: Random House.

Perrow, C. (1989). *A society of organizations.* Work in progress.

Peters, T. J. (1978, Autumn). Symbols, patterns, and settings: An optimistic case for getting things done. *Organizational Dynamics.*

Peters, T. J. (1987). *Thriving on chaos: Handbook for a management revolution.* New York: Knopf.

Peters, T. J., & Waterman, R. H. (1982). *In search of excellence.* New York: Harper & Row.

Pettigrew, A. M. (1979). On studying organizational cultures. *Administrative Science Quarterly, 24,* 570-581.

Pettigrew, A. M. (1985). Contextualist research: A natural way to link theory and practice. In E. E. Lawler III & Assoc. (Eds.), *Doing research that is useful for theory and practice.* San Francisco, CA: Jossey-Bass.

Pierce, J. E. (1977). Culture: A collection of fuzzy sets. *Human Organizations, 36*(2), 197-199.

Pine, V. (1975). *Caretaker of the dead: The American funeral director.* New York: Irving.

Pondy, L. R., Frost, P. J., Morgan, G., & Dandridge, T. (1983). *Organizational symbolism.* Greenwich, CT: JAI Press.

Quinn, R. E. (1988). *Beyond rational management: Mastering the paradoxes and competing demands of high performance.* San Francisco, CA: Jossey-Bass.

Radcliffe-Brown, A. R. (1922). *The Andaman Islanders.* Cambridge, UK: Cambridge University Press.

Reinharz, S. (1979). *On becoming a social scientist.* San Francisco, CA: Jossey-Bass.

Riley, P. (1983). A structurationist account of political cultures. *Administrative Science Quarterly, 28,* 414-437.

Riley, P., Hollihan, T., & Freadhoff, K. (in press). Scientific argument in organization: Power and advocacy in a late modern environment. In F. van Eemeren, R. Grootendorst, J. A. Blair, & C. Willard (Eds.), *Proceedings of Second ISSA International Conference on Argumentation.* Dordrecht, The Netherlands: Forris Publications.

Rizzo, J. R., House, R. J., & Lirzman, S. I. (1970). Role conflict and ambiguity in organizations. *Administrative Science Quarterly, 15,* 150-163.

Roberts, K., Hulin, C., & Rousseau, D. (1978). *Developing interdisciplinary science of organizations.* San Francisco, CA: Jossey-Bass.

Robinson, J. A. (1981). Personal narratives reconsidered. *Journal of American Folklore, 94,* 58-85.

Rogers, E. (1962). *Diffusion of innovations.* New York: The Free Press of Glencoe.

Rohatyn, F. (1990). Becoming what they think we are. *New York Review of Books, 37*(6).

Rohlen, T. (1974). *For harmony and strength: Japanese white-collar organization in anthropological perspectives.* Berkeley: University of California Press.

Rorty, R. (1979). *Philosophy and the mirror of nature.* Princeton, Princeton University Press.

Rorty, R. (1989). *Contingency, irony and solidarity.* Cambridge, UK: Cambridge University Press.

Rosaldo, R. (1986). From the door of his tent: The fieldworkers and the inquisitor. In J. Clifford & G. E. Marcus (Eds.), *Writing culture: The poetics and the politics of ethnography* (pp. 77-97). Berkeley: University of California Press.

Rose, M. (1975). *Industrial behavior.* London: Allen Lane.

Rosen, M. (1984). *Power and culture in bureaucracy: A study of bureaucracy as a control mechanism in monopoly capitalism.* Unpublished Dissertation, University of Pennsylvania, Philadelphia.

Rosen, M. (1985). Breakfast at Spiro's: dramaturgy and dominance. *Journal of Management, 11*(2), 31-48.

Rosen, M. (1986). Some notes from the field: On ethnography and organizational science. *Dragon, 6,* 57-67.

Ross, B. (1988). Transcript of speech of Hurrah Club executives.

Rousseau, D. M. (1985). Issues of level in organizational research: Multi-level and Cross-level Perspectives. In B. Staw & L. Cummings (Eds.), *Research in organizational behavior* (Vol. 7). Greenwich, CT: JAI Press.

Runcie, J. (1988). "Deviant behavior": Achieving autonomy in a machine-pace environment. In M. O. Jones, M. D. Moore, & R. C. Snyder (Eds.), *Inside organizations: Understanding the human dimension* (pp. 129-140). Newbury Park, CA: Sage.

Rushdie, S. (1990). Is nothing sacred? *Granta: A Paperback Magazine of New Writing, 31,* 98-125.

Sackmann, S. (1989). The role of metaphors in organization transformation. *Human Relations, 42,* 463-485.

Said, E. W. (1989). Representing the colonized: Anthropology's interlocutors. *Critical Inquiry, 15,* 205-225.

Sanday, P. R. (1979). The ethnographic paradigm(s). *Administrative Science Quarterly, 24*(4), 527-538.

Sanday, P. R. (1981). *Female power and male dominance: On the origins of sexual inequality.* Cambridge, UK: Cambridge University Press.

Sanjek, R. (1990a). *Fieldnotes: The making of anthropology.* Ithaca, NY: Cornell University Press.

Sanjek, R. (1990b). On ethnographic validity. In R. Sanjek (Ed.), *Fieldnotes: The making of anthropology.* Ithaca, NY: Cornell University Press.

Santino, J. (1978). The outlaw emotions: Workers' narratives from three contemporary occupations. Unpublished doctoral dissertation, Department of Folklore and Folklife, University of Pennsylvania, Philadelphia.

Santino, J. (1983). Miles of smiles, years of struggle: The negotiation of black occupational identity through personal experience narrative. *Journal of American Folklore, 96,* 393-412.

Santino, J. (1986). A servant or a man, a hostess or a women: A study of expressive culture in two transportation occupations. *Journal of American Folklore, 99,* 304-319.

Santino, J. (1990). The outlaw emotions: Narrative expressions on the rules and roles of occupational identity. *American Behavioral Scientist, 33,* 318-329.

Sathe, V. (1985). *Culture and related corporate realities.* Homewood, IL: Richard D. Irwin.

Saussure, F. (1966). *Course in general linguistics* (C. Baily et al. Eds. & Trans). New York: McGraw-Hill.

Schall, M. S. (1983). A communication-rules approach to organizational culture. *Administrative Science Quarterly, 28,* 557-581.

Schein, E. H. (1981). Does Japanese management have a message for American managers? *Sloan Management Review, 23,* 55-68.

Schein, E. H. (1983). The role of the founder in creating organizational culture. *Organizational Dynamics, 12,* 13-28.

Schein, E. H. (1985a). *Organizational culture and leadership.* San Francisco: CA: Jossey-Bass.

Schein, E. H. (1985b). Organizational culture: Skill, defense mechanism, or addiction? In F. R. Brush & J. B. Overmier (Eds.), *Affect, conditioning, and cognition.* Hillsdale, NJ: Lawrence Erlbaum.

Schein, E. H. (1987). *The clinical perspective in fieldwork.* Newbury Park, CA: Sage.

Schein, E. H. (1990). Organizational culture. *American Psychologist, 45*(2), 109-119.

Schickel, R. (1985). *The Disney version* (rev. ed.). New York: Simon & Schuster. (Original work published 1968.)

Schön, D. (1971). *Beyond the stable state.* New York: Random House.

Schütz, A. (1979). *Collected papers I. The problem of social reality.* The Habue, The Netherlands: Martinus Nijhoff. (Original work published 1964.)

Schwartz, P., & Lever, J. (1976). Fear and loathing at a college mixer. *Urban Life, 4,* 413-432.

Schwartzman, H. B. (1983). Stories at work: Play in an organizational context. In E. M. Bruner (Ed.), *Text, play and story: The construction and reconstruction of self and society.* Proceedings of the American Ethnological Society.

Scott, J. (1988). *Gender and the politics of history.* New York: Columbia University Press.

Sehlinger, B. (1987). *The unofficial guide to Disneyland.* New York: Prentice-Hall.

Sellerberg, A-M. (1987). *Avstånd och attraktion. Om modets växlingar.* Stockholm: Carlssons.

Sethia, N. K., & Van Glinow, M. A. (1985). Arriving at four cultures by managing the award system. In R. H. Kilmann, M. J. Saxton, & R. Serpa (Eds.), *Gaining control of the corporate culture.* San Francisco, CA: Jossey-Bass.

Shelley, A. L. (1988, August). *Analytic strategies and computer assistance as tools of qualitative researchers.* Paper presented at the annual meeting of the American Sociological Association, Atlanta, GA.

Sherif, M. (1953). *Groups in harmony and tension.* New York: Harper & Row.

Shils, E. (1975). *Center and periphery: Essays in macrosociology.* Chicago, IL: University of Chicago Press.

Shils, E. (1988). Center and periphery: An idea and its career, 1935-1987. In L. Greenfield & M. Martin (Eds.), *Center and periphery: An idea and its career.* Chicago, IL: University of Chicago Press.

Shrivastava, P. (1987). *Bhopal: Anatomy of a crisis.* Cambridge, MA: Ballinger.

Siehl, C., & Martin, J. (1984). The role of symbolic management: How can managers effectively transmit organizational culture? In J. C. Hunt, D. Hosking, C. Schriesheim, & R. Stewart (Eds.), *Leaders and managers: International perspectives on managerial behavior and leadership.* New York: Pergamon.

Siehl, C., & Martin, J. (1988). Measuring organizational culture: Mixing qualitative and quantitative methods. In M. O. Jones, M. D. Moore, & R. C. Snyder (Eds.), *Inside organizations: Understanding the human dimension* (pp. 79-103). Newbury Park, CA: Sage.

Siehl, C., & Martin, J. (1990). Organizational culture: A key to financial performance? In B. Schneider (Ed.), *Organizational climate and culture* (Frontiers of Industrial and Organizational Psychology). San Francisco, CA: Jossey-Bass.

Simmel, G. (1973). Fashion. In G. Wills & D. Midgley (Eds.), *Fashion marketing.* London: Allen & Unwin.

Smircich, L. (1983a). Concepts of culture and organizational analysis. *Administrative Science Quarterly, 28,* 339-358.

Smircich, L. (1983b). Organizations as shared meaning. In L. R. Pondy, P. J. Frost, G. Morgan, & T. Dandridge (Eds.), *Organizational symbolism.* Greenwich, CT: JAI Press.

Smircich, L. (1985a). Is the concept of culture a paradigm for understanding organizations and ourselves? In P. J. Frost, L. F. Moore, M. R. Louis, C. C. Lundberg, & J. Martin (Eds.), *Organizational culture* (pp. 55-72). Beverly Hills, CA: Sage.

Smircich, L. (1985b, August). *Toward a women centered organization theory.* Paper presented at the meetings of the Academy of Management, San Diego, CA.

Smircich, L., & Calas, M. (1987). Organizational Culture: A critical assessment. In F. Jablin, L. Putnam, K. Roberts, & L. Porter (Eds.), *Handbook of organizational communication* (pp. 228-263). Newbury Park, CA: Sage.

Smircich, L., & Morgan, G. (1983). Leadership: The management of meaning. *The Journal of Applied Behavioral Science, 18,* 257-273.

Smith, P. B. (1973). *Groups within organizations.* New York: Harper & Row.

Smith, R. C., & Eisenberg, E. M. (1987). Conflict at Disneyland: A root metaphor analysis. *Communication Monographs, 54,* 367-380.

Sonnenstuhl, W. J., & Trice, H. M. (1991). Linking organizational and occupational theory through the concept of culture. In *Research in the Sociology of Organizations,* Greenwich, CT: JAI Press.

Spivak, G. C. (1988). *In other worlds: Essays in cultural politics.* New York: Routledge.

Spooner, B. (1983, December 20). Anthropologists and the people they study, and the significance of anthropology for non-anthropologists. Unpublished lecture notes, University of Pennsylvania, Philadelphia, PA.

Spradley, J. P. (1979). *The ethnographic interview.* New York: Holt, Rinehart & Winston.

Spradley, J. P. (1980). *Participant observation.* New York: Holt, Rinehart & Winston.

Sproull, L. S., & Sproull, R. F. (1982). Managing and analyzing behavioral records: Explorations in nonnumeric data analysis. *Human Organization, 41*(4), 283-290.

Sproull, L. S., Weiner, S., & Wolf, D. (1978). *Organizing an anarchy.* Chicago, IL: The University of Chicago Press.

Stablein, R. E. (1988, November). *Structure of debate in organizational studies*. Paper presented at the annual conference of Australian Management Educators, Perth, Australia.

Stablein, R., & Frost, P. J. (in press). *Doing exemplary empirical research in the organizational sciences*. Newbury Park, CA: Sage.

Stahl, S. K. D. (1975). *The personal narrative as a folklore genre*. Unpublished doctoral dissertation, Indiana University, Bloomington.

Stahl, S. K. D. (1977). The personal narrative as folklore. *Journal of the Folklore Institute, 14*, 9-30.

Stahl, S. K. D. (1985). A literary folkloristic methodology for the study of meaning in personal narrative. *Journal of Folklore Research, 22*, 45-69.

Stahl, S. K. D. (1989). *Literary folkloristics and the personal narrative*. Bloomington: Indiana University Press.

Stanley, D. H. (1979). The personal narrative and the personal novel: Folklore as frame and structure for literature. *Southern Folklore Quarterly, 43*, 107-120.

Starr, P. (1982). *The social transformation of American medicine*. New York: Basic Books.

Staw, B. M. (1984). Organizational Behavior: A review and reformulation of the field's outcome variables. *Annual Review of Psychology, 35*, 627-666.

Staw, B. M., Sandelands, L. E., & Dutton, J. E. (1981). Threat-rigidity effects in organizational behavior: A multilevel analysis. *Administrative Science Quarterly, 26*, 501-524.

Stewart, P. (1989). The folklorist as academic administrator. In C. Camp (Ed.), *Time and temperature: A centennial publication of the American Folklore Society* (p. 18). Washington, DC: The American Folklore Society.

Stimpson, C. (1990, August). Mind changes. Paper presented at *Revisioning knowledge and the curriculum: Feminist perspectives*. East Lansing, MI.

Stohl, C., & Redding, W. C. (1987). Messages and message exchange processes. In F. Jablin, L. Putnam, K. Roberts, & L. Porter (Eds.), *Handbook of organizational communication* (pp. 451-502). Newbury Park, CA: Sage.

Strauss, A. L. (1987). *Qualitative analysis for social scientists*. New York: Cambridge University Press.

Swidler, A. (1986). Culture in action; Symbols and strategies. *American Sociological Review, 51*, 273-286.

The World of Hermes 1990. (1990). No. 18. (Private Corporate Catalogue).

Time (1979, July 23). Carter at the crossroads, pp. 20-26, 29.

Toelken, B. (1979). *The dynamics of folklore*. Boston: Houghton Mifflin.

Tommerup, P. (1990). Stories about an inspiring leader's "rapture" and the symbolics of employee fulfillment. *American Behavioral Scientist, 33*, 374-385.

Trice, H. M. (1987). Review of *Organizational Culture*. P. J. Frost, L. F. Moore, M. R. Louis, C. C. Lundberg, & J. Martin (Eds.). *Administrative Science Quarterly, 32*, 617-620.

Trice, H., & Beyer, J. (1984). Studying organizational cultures through rites and ceremonials. *Academy of Management Review, 9*, 653-669.

Trice, H., & Beyer, J. (1991). *The cultures of work organizations*. Englewood Cliffs, NJ: Prentice-Hall.

Trice, H., & Morand, D. (1991). Cultural diversity: Subcultures and countercultures in work organizations. In G. Miller (Ed.), *Organizational sociology*, Greenwich, CT: JAI Press.

Trice, H. M., Belasco, J., & Alutto, J. A. (1969). The role of ceremonials in organizational behavior. *Industrial and Labor Relations Review, 23*, 40-51.

Turner, B. A. (1971). *Exploring the industrial subculture*. London: Macmillan.

Turner, B. A. (1981). Some practical aspects of qualitative data analysis: One way of organizing the cognitive processes associated with the generation of grounded theory. *Quality and Quantity, 15*, 225-247.

Turner, B. A. (1986). Sociological aspects of organizational symbolism. *Organizational Studies, 7*, 101-115.

Turner, B. A. (1990). Introduction. In B. A. Turner (Ed.), *Organizational symbolism* (pp. 1-11). New York: Walter de Gruyter.

Turner, V. (1974). *Dramas, fields, and metaphors.* Ithaca, NY: Cornell University Press.

Turnstall, W. B. (1983). Culture transition at AT&T. *Sloan Management Review, 25*(1), 1-12.

Tyler, S. (1969). *Cognitive anthropology.* New York: Holt, Rinehart & Winston.

Van de Ven, A. (1989). Nothing is quite so practical as a good theory. *Academy of Management Review, 14*(4), 486-489.

Van de Ven, A., & Poole, M. S. (1988). Paradoxical requirements for a theory of change. In K. S. Cameron & R. S. Quinn (Eds.), *Paradox and transformation: Toward a theory of change in organization and management.* Cambridge, MA: Ballinger Publishing.

Van Maanen, J. (1976). Breaking-in: Socialization to work. In R. Dubin (Ed.), *Handbook of work, organization, and society* (pp. 67-130). Chicago, IL: Rand McNally.

Van Maanen, J. (1977). Experiencing organization. In J. Van Maanen (Ed.), *Organizational careers* (pp. 15-45). New York: John Wiley.

Van Maanen, J. (1979). The fact of fiction in organizational ethnography. *Administrative Science Quarterly, 24,* 539-611.

Van Maanen, J. (1983). *Qualitative methodology.* Beverly Hills, CA: Sage.

Van Maanen, J. (1988). *Tales of the field: On writing ethnography.* Chicago: University of Chicago Press.

Van Maanen, J. (1990a). *Trade secrets: On writing ethnography.* Unpublished paper, Sloan School of Management, M.I.T., Boston, MA.

Van Maanen, J. (1990b). *Trade secrets.* Colloquium presentation, University of South Florida, College of Business.

Van Maanen, J., & Barley, S. R. (1984). Occupational communities: Culture and control in organizations. In B. M. Staw & L. L. Cummings (Eds.). *Research in organizational behavior* (Vol. 6, pp. 287-366). Greenwich, CT: JAI Press.

Van Maanen, J., & Barley, S. R. (1985). Cultural organization: Fragments of a theory. In P. J. Frost, L. F. Moore, M. R. Louis, C. C. Lundberg, & J. Martin (Eds.), *Organizational culture.* Beverly Hills, CA: Sage.

Van Maanen, J., Dabbs, J. M., & Faulkner, R. R. (1982). *Varieties of qualitative research.* Beverly Hills, CA: Sage.

Van Maanen, J., & Kunda, G. (1989). Real feelings: Emotional expressions and organization culture. In B. Staw & L. L. Cummings (Eds.), *Research in organization behavior* (Vol. 11, pp. 43-103). Greenwich, CT: JAI Press.

Van Maanen, J., & Schein, E. H. (1979). Toward a theory of organizational socialization. In B. Staw & L. L. Cummings (Eds.), *Research in organization behavior* (Vol. 1, pp. 209-269). Greenwich, CT: JAI Press.

Wallace, S. A. (1986). *The culture of an organization: A case study.* Unpublished doctoral dissertation, Marquette University, Milwaukee, WI.

Waller, W. (1937). The rating and dating complex. *American Sociological Review, 2,* 727-734.

Weick, K. (1976). Educational organizations as loosely coupled systems. *Administrative Science Quarterly, 21,* 1-19.

Weick, K. (1979). *The social psychology of organizing.* Reading, MA: Addison-Wesley.

Weick, K. (1985). Sources of order in underorganized systems: Themes in recent organizational theory. In Y. S. Lincoln (Ed.), *Organizational theory and inquiry: The paradigm revolution.* Beverly Hills, CA: Sage.

Weick, K. (1990). The vulnerable system: An analysis of the Tenerife air disaster. *Journal of Management, 16*(3), 571-593.

Weick, K. E. (1977). Re-punctuating the problem. In P. S. Goodman & J. M. Pennings (Eds.), *New perspectives on organizational effectiveness* (pp. 193-225). San Francisco, CA: Jossey-Bass.

Weick, K. E. (1989). Theory construction as disciplined imagination. *Academy of Management Review, 14*, 516-531.

Wells, P. A. (1988). The paradox of functional dysfunction in a Girl Scout camp: Implications of cultural diversity for achieving organizational goals. In M. O. Jones, M. D. Moore, & R. C. Snyder (Eds.), *Inside organizations: Understanding the human dimension* (pp. 109-117). Newbury Park, CA: Sage.

Werner, O., & Schepfle, G. M. (1987). *Systematic fieldwork: Foundations of ethnography and interviewing* (Vol. 1). Newbury Park, CA: Sage.

Westney, D. E. (1987). *Imitation and innovation*. Cambridge, MA: Harvard University Press.

Whyte, W. F. (1941). The social role of the settlement house. *Applied Anthropology, 1,* 1.

Whyte, W. F. (1943a). A challenge to political scientists. *American Political Science Review, 37,* 692-697.

Whyte, W. F. (1943b). A slum sex code. *American Journal of Sociology, 49*(1), 24-31.

Whyte, W. F. (1943c). Social organization in the slums. *American Sociological Review, 8*(1), 34-39.

Whyte, W. F. (1943d). *Street corner society*. Chicago, IL: University of Chicago Press.

Whyte, W. F. (1944). Vocational education in industry: A case study. *Applied Anthropology, 3*(4), 1-6.

Whyte, W. F. (1945). *Industry and society*. New York: McGraw-Hill.

Whyte, W. F. (1948). Incentives for productivity: The Bundy Tubing Company case. *Applied Anthropology, 7*(2), 1-16.

Whyte, W. F. (1948). *Human relations in the restaurant industry*. New York: McGraw-Hill.

Whyte, W. F. (1949a). Semantics and Industrial Relations, *Human Organization, 8*(2), 4-10.

Whyte, W. F. (1949b). Patterns of interaction in union-management relations. *Human Organization, 8*(4), 13-19.

Whyte, W. F. (1951). *Pattern for industrial peace*. New York: Harper & Bros.

Whyte, W. F. (1953). Interviewing for organizational research. *Human Organization, 12*(2), 15-22.

Whyte, W. F. (1955). *Street corner society* (2nd ed.). Chicago, IL: University of Chicago Press.

Whyte, W. F. (1959). An integration approach to the theory of organization. In M. Haire (Ed.), *Modern organization theory* (pp. 155-183). New York: John Wiley.

Whyte, W. F. (1961). *Men at work*. Homewood, IL: Dorsey Press and Richard D. Irwin.

Whyte, W. F. (1964). On street corner society. In E. Burgess & D. Bogue (Eds.), *Contributions to urban sociology*. Chicago, IL: University of Chicago Press.

Whyte, W. F. (1969). *Organizational behavior: Theory and application*. Homewood, IL: Richard D. Irwin and Dorsey Press.

Whyte, W. F. (1976). Theory, methods, and strategy in organizational behavior research. *Cornell Journal of Social Relations, 2,* 47-51.

Whyte, W. F. (1978). Organizational behavior research—Where do we go from here? In E. M. Eddy & W. Partridge (Eds.), *Applied anthropology in America* (pp. 129-143). New York: Columbia University Press.

Whyte, W. F. (1981). *Street corner society* (3rd ed.). Chicago, IL: University of Chicago Press.

Whyte, W. F. (1987). From human relations to organizational behavior: Reflections on the changing scene. *Industrial and Labor Relations Review, 40,* 487-500.

Whyte, W. F., & Alberti, G. (1976). *Power, politics, and progress: Social change in rural Peru*. New York: Elsevier.

Whyte, W. F., Dalton, M., Roy, D., & Sayles, L. (1955). *Money and motivation.* New York: Harper & Bros.

Whyte, W. F., & Gardner, B. B. (1945). The man in the middle: Position and problems of the foreman. [Special issue, Committee on human relations in industry, The University of Chicago.] *Applied Anthropology, 4*(2).

Whyte, W. F., Hamilton, E. L., & Wiley, M. (1964). *Action research for management: A case report on research and action in industry.* Homewood, IL: Richard D. Irwin.

Whyte, W. F., & Whyte, K. K. (1984). *Learning from the field: A guide from experience.* Beverly Hills, CA: Sage.

Whyte, W. F., & Whyte, K. K. (1988). *Making Mondragon: The growth and dynamics of the worker cooperative complex.* Ithaca, NY: ILR Press.

Wilensky, H. L. (1964). The professionalization of everyone? *American Journal of Sociology, 70*, 137-158.

Wilkins, A. (1979). *Organizational stories as an expression of management philosophy.* Unpublished doctoral dissertation, Stanford University, Palo Alto, CA.

Wilkins, A. (1984). The creation of company cultures: The role of stories and human resource systems. *Human Resource Management, 23*, 41-60.

Wilkins, A. L. (1983a). The culture audit: A tool for understanding organizations. *Organizational dynamics, 12*(3), 24-28.

Wilkins, A. L. (1983b). Organizational stories as symbols which control the organization. In P. J. Frost, L. F. Moore, M. R. Louis, C. C. Lundberg, & J. Martin (Eds.), *Organizational culture* (pp. 81-91). Beverly Hills, CA: Sage.

Wilkins, A. L., & Ouchi, W. G. (1983). Efficient cultures: Exploring the relationship between culture and organizational performances. *Administrative Science Quarterly, 28*, 468-481.

Willis, P. (1981). The main reality. Unpublished paper, Centre for Contemporary Cultural Studies, University of Birmingham, UK.

Wilson, W. A. (1988). Dealing with organizational stress: Lessons from the folklore of Mormon missionaries. In M. O. Jones, M. D. Moore, & R. C. Snyder (Eds.), *Inside organizations: Understanding the human dimension* (pp. 271-279). Newbury Park, CA: Sage.

Winch, P. (1958). *The idea of a social science.* London: Routledge & Kegan Paul.

Woolgar, S. (1985). Why not sociology of machines? The case of sociology and artificial intelligence. *Sociology, 19*, 557-572.

Woolgar, S. (Ed.), (1988). *Knowledge and reflexivity. New frontiers in the sociology of knowledge.* Beverly Hills, CA: Sage.

Wright, E. O. (1984). A general framework for the analysis of class structure. *Politics and Society, 13*, 383-423.

Wuthnow, R., Hunter, J. D., Bergeson, A., & Kurzweil, E. (1984). *Cultural analysis.* London: Routledge & Kegan Paul.

Young, E. (1986). Where the daffodils blow: Elements of communal imagery in a northern suburb. In A. P. Cohen (Ed.), *Symbolizing boundaries: Identity and diversity in British cultures.* London: Manchester University Press.

Young, E. (1989). On Naming the Rose: Interests and multiple meanings elements of organizational change. *Organizational Studies, 10*(2), 187-206.

Young, I. M. (1990). The ideal of community and the politics of difference. In L. J. Nicholson (Ed.), *Feminism/postmodernism* (pp. 281-299). New York: Routledge, Chapman, & Hall.

Zeleny, M. (1986). The law of requisite variety: Is it applicable to human systems? *Human Systems Management, 6*, 269-271.

About the Contributors

Stephen R. Barley is Associate Professor of Organizational Behavior at Cornell University's School of Industrial and Labor Relations. He received his doctorate in organizational studies from the Massachusetts Institute of Technology in 1984. His research has focused on the implications of microelectronic technologies for the social organization of work, the commercialization of biotechnology in the United States, and organizational culture. His papers have appeared in *Administrative Science Quarterly, Organizational Science,* and a number of other journals and edited books. Along with Pamela Tolbert, Barley recently edited a special volume of *Research in the Sociology of Organizations* on professions and organizations.

Jean M. Bartunek is Professor of Organizational Studies in the Carroll School of Management at Boston College. Her current research focuses on processes of empowerment in organizations and on the intersection of organizational conflict and change.

Alan Bryman is Reader in Social Research in the Department of Social Sciences, Loughborough University, England. His main areas of interest lie in the fields of research methodology and leadership. He is the author of a number of books, including *Quantity and Quality in Social Research* (1988) and *Research Methods and Organizational Studies* (1989).

Marta B. Calas is Professor at the College of Business Administration, University of Massachusetts. She sometimes writes, along with Linda Smircich, about organizational culture as metafiction, and uses everybody's signifiers for those purposes. This time the words, voices, and images of some of the authors and editors of this monograph were used, as well as those of Andre Aggassiz, Mats Alversson, Roland Barthes, Yvonne Billing, Hope Botit, Lord Byron, James Clifford, Jacques Derrida, Mark Ebers, Michel Foucault, Pasquale Gagliardi, Silvia Gherardi, Mary Jo Hatch, Richard Kearney, Burkard Sievers, Ralph Stablein, Barry Turner, and Walter Nord.

Barbara Czarniawska-Joerges is Professor of Business Administration at Lund University, Sweden. Her research focuses on control processes in complex organizations. She has published widely in the area of business administration in Polish, her native language, as well as in Swedish and English.

Martha S. Feldman is an Associate Professor of Political Science and Public Policy at the University of Michigan, Ann Arbor. Her research interests involve how people construct their social reality and how they act in a social context. Her particular focus has been on organizational decision making and how various forms of information and communication are involved in that process. She is currently studying organizational routines as a form of intelligence that is organizational rather than individual. Her publications include *Order Without Design: Information Production and Policy Making* (1989), *Reconstructing Reality in the Courtroom* (co-authored with W. Lance Bennett) and *Information in Organizations as Signal and Symbol* (co-authored with James G. March).

Peter J. Frost is Associate Dean of the Faculty of Commerce and Business Administration and holds the Edgar F. Kaiser Jr. Chair in Organizational Behavior at the University of British Columbia. His research interests are in the areas of organizational culture, politics, and innovation, and more recently in the area of environmentalism. He has published, with others, books on organizational symbolism and culture. He is completing, with Ralph Stablein, a monograph on doing exemplary research in the organizational sciences to be published by Sage.

John M. Jermier is Professor of Organizational Behavior in the College of Business, University of South Florida. Much of his work has focused on the development of a critical science of organizations with a particular interest in research philosophy and methodology.

Michael Owen Jones is Professor of History and Folklore and Director of the Folklore and Mythology Center at UCLA. His research focuses on traditional, symbolic behavior in organizational settings. He studies narrating, ritual, the use of metaphors, and other folklore as aesthetic forms, expressions of values and concerns, coping strategies, and sources of support. His research goals include applying insights to improving the design, development, and administration of organizations.

Meryl Reis Louis is Associate Professor of Organizational Behavior at Boston University's School of Management. Her research interests have centered on cognitive processes in work settings, career transitions, and workplace cultures. For the past 12 years, she has been studying "life after MBA school" with a panel of graduates from four major MBA programs.

Craig C. Lundberg is the Blanchard Professor of Human Resource Management, School of Hotel Administration, Cornell University. A Fellow of the Academy of Management and currently editor of *Consultation,* he continues to be fascinated with organizational change, inquiry systems, and service organizations as well as organizational culture.

Joanne Martin is Professor of Organizational Behavior in the Graduate School of Business, and (by courtesy) in the Sociology Department at Stanford University. She has published extensively in two fields of interest: economic injustice and organizational culture. More recently, she has begun to examine the dynamics of sexism and racism in organizational theory.

Peggy McDonald is a Brand Manager at the Clorox Company in Oakland, California. She received her MBA degree from UCLA in 1984, specializing in marketing and organizational strategy. Prior to her experience at the Los Angeles Olympic Organizing Committee, she worked as a graphic designer and program coordinator in arts administration and public management.

Debra E. Meyerson is Assistant Professor of Organizational Behavior and Human Resources at University of Michigan's School of Business. She received her doctorate in organizational behavior from Stanford University. Her current research focuses on ambiguity and culture, including projects that focus on the relationship between (a) institutional and occupational beliefs about ambiguity and discretion, (b) group tolerance for ambiguity and the process of product innovation and creativity, and (c) organizational beliefs about ambiguity and tolerance for diversity. She has also written articles on the expression and meaning of ambiguities in organizations and recently on the social construction of ethics in organizations.

Michael K. Moch is Professor of Management in the Graduate School of Business Administration at Michigan State University. He currently is studying how managers continuously interpret and re-interpret choice situations as a function of external cues and information about previous performance. He recently published a book with Jean Bartunek, *Creating Alternative*

Realities at Work (1990), which addresses the problem of dynamic decision making from a Quality of Work Life perspective.

Larry F. Moore is Associate Professor of Organizational Behavior at the University of British Columbia. His research interests have included the attitudes and motivation of professionals, managers, and volunteers and human resource planning and administration. Currently, he is investigating aspects of the organizational culture in Canada's banking industry, particularly as it pertains to management style and gender treatment. He is also examining university/business subculture relations and how they impact on the transfer of technology.

Patricia Riley is Associate Professor of Organizational Communication in the Department of Communication Arts and Sciences at the University of Southern California in Los Angeles. Her research investigates the political activities and institutions that perpetuate and transform organizational cultures, with a particular focus on organizational strategy.

Michael Rosen is a New York City real estate developer, property owner, and construction contractor who occasionally impersonates a social theoretician and semi-professional academic. Previous to his current work, Michael Rosen was a full-time and thoroughly professional academic and social theoretician occasionally impersonating a stockbroker, ad-man, illicit drug world voyeur, and finally, for the money and glory, a real estate industry mogul. His current academic work—written for free—spins in the chaotic interstices of symbolic social constructivism, critical theory, and postmodernism.

Edgar H. Schein is Professor of Management in the MIT Sloan School of Management. His research has focused on organizations, career development, organizational culture, and process consultation.

Linda Smircich is Professor at the College of Business Administration, University of Massachusetts. She sometimes writes, along with Marta B. Calas, about organizational culture as metafiction, and uses everybody's signifiers for those purposes. This time the words, voices, and images of some of the authors and editors of this monograph were used, as well as those of Andre Aggassiz, Mats Alversson, Roland Barthes, Yvonne Billing, Hope Botit, Lord Byron, James Clifford, Jacques Derrida, Mark Ebers, Michel

Foucault, Pasquale Gagliardi, Silvia Gherardi, Mary Jo Hatch, Richard Kearney, Burkard Sievers, Ralph Stablein, Barry Turner, and Walter Nord.

Harrison M. Trice is Professor in the Department of Organizational Behavior, School of Industrial and Labor Relations, at Cornell University. His writings on organizational culture date back to the late 1960s and early 1970s. Currently, he has pulled together much of his scholarly writings into two books, one on organizational cultures and one on occupational cultures.

John Van Maanen is the Erwin Schell Professor of Organization Studies in the Sloan School of Management, M.I.T. He has published a number of books and articles in the general area of occupational sociology. Cultural descriptions figure prominently in his studies of the work worlds of patrol officers on city streets in the United States, police detectives and their guv'nors in London, fishermen in the northeastern Atlantic, and, currently, ride operators at Disneyland. His most recent book is about narratives and is titled *Tales of the Field* (1988).

Karl E. Weick is the Rensis Likert Collegiate Professor of Organizational Behavior and Psychology at the University of Michigan, and is also a former editor of *Administrative Science Quarterly*. Weick studies such topics as how people make sense of confusing events, the effects of stress on thinking and imagination, the consequences of indeterminancy in social systems, and high reliability organizations.

William Foote Whyte has been president of the Industrial Relations Research Association, the American Sociological Association, and the Society for Applied Anthropology. *Street Corner Society* is his best-known book. Recent books include *Making Mondragón: The Growth and Dynamics of the Worker Cooperative Complex* and *Social Theory for Action: How Individuals and Organizations Learn to Change* (in press). He is now Professor Emeritus and Research Director of Programs for Employment and Workplace Systems in Cornell University's School of Industrial and Labor Relations. He has a doctorate in sociology from the University of Chicago.

Ed Young holds a doctorate in social anthropology from the University of Manchester, where he is a Fellow in Human Resource Management in the Health Services Management Unit. He runs the general management training scheme for young managers who join the British Health Service.